THE
Madness
OF
MARY
LINCOLN

*Mary Lincoln. Courtesy Sangamon Valley Collection
at Lincoln Library, Springfield, Illinois.*

THE
Madness
OF
MARY
LINCOLN

JASON
EMERSON

SOUTHERN ILLINOIS
UNIVERSITY
PRESS

CARBONDALE

09   08   07   4   3   2

Library of Congress Cataloging-in-Publication Data
Emerson, Jason, 1975–
The madness of Mary Lincoln / Jason Emerson.
p. cm.
Includes bibliographical references and index.
ISBN-13: 978-0-8093-2771-3 (cloth : alk. paper)
ISBN-10: 0-8093-2771-6 (cloth : alk. paper)
1. Lincoln, Mary Todd, 1818–1882—Mental health. 2. Presidents' spouses—
United States—Biography. 3. Lincoln, Abraham, 1809–1865—Family.
4. Insanity—United States—Case studies. I. Title.
E457.25.L55E46 2007
973.7092—dc22
[B]   2007003343

In Memory of Mary Lou Livingstone
(March 20, 1925–January 8, 2006)
A most wonderful lady full of love and encouragement,
who always believed in me.
I wish she could have lived to see this book.
She would have loved it.

Contents

Illustrations

Acknowledgments

AN AUTHOR RARELY COMPLETES any literary endeavor alone, especially not a book of history. First and foremost, I will be forever grateful to the children of Frederic N. Towers: Frederic C. Towers, Judy Reemtsma, and Dorcy Burns. They gave me complete access to the contents of their father's Lincoln trunk, allowing me to be the first historian to write about Mary Lincoln's "lost insanity letters." They didn't have to do that, but they did, and they gave me great support as well, especially Judy, who provided me with a place to stay on my first trip to New York City. Thank you. Also to James Gordon, relative of Myra Bradwell, who likewise gave me unfettered access to the papers of Myra Pritchard in his private collection, without which the true fate of the lost insanity letters would be only partially known.

I never could have made this book as complete as it is without the assistance of Dr. James S. Brust, chair of the department of psychiatry and medical director of the psychiatric unit at San Pedro Peninsula Hospital, San Pedro, California, and coauthor of *Where Custer Fell: Photographs of the Little Bighorn Battlefield Then and Now.* Dr. Brust helped me understand so many facets of psychiatry in general and as pertain to Mary Lincoln's case in particular that I can never repay him. He read my entire manuscript and helped me realize just how complex Mary's mental illness was and how it evolved throughout her lifetime. Dr. Brust also was a great general copyeditor and saved me from many embarrassing mistakes. Dr. Eugene Taylor, Harvard Medical School Lecturer on Psychiatry, senior psychologist at Massachusetts General Hospital, and author of *Shadow Culture: Psychology and Spirituality in America*, helped me understand Spiritualism, the link between Spiritualism and insanity as perceived in the nineteenth century, and addiction versus psychological dependence. Dr. Dennis Nissim-Sabat, professor of psychology, University of Mary Washington, in Fredericksburg, Virginia, helped me understand certain aspects of the history of psychiatry.

More indispensable aid came from my friend Tai Gerhart Edwards, a wonderful historian and my first, best (nonprofessional) editor, whom I met in the history graduate program at George Mason University. Her comments on my manuscript were frustratingly cogent and reliable and made the book ten times better than it would have been without her help.

As all historians know, not many people during your research are as critically important as the librarians and archivists at the many repositories you must visit. I received gracious aid from: Kim Bauer, Bryon Andreasen, Jennifer Ericson, and Cheryl Schnirring at the Abraham Lincoln Presidential Library, Springfield, Illinois; Brian Knight, Seth Bongartz, and the entire staff at Hildene, the Lincoln Family Home, in Manchester, Vermont; Cindy Van Horn and Carolyn Texley at The Lincoln Museum, in Fort Wayne, Indiana; Debbie Vaughan at the Chicago History Museum; Jane Westenfeld at the Pelletier Library, Allegheny College, in Meadville, Pennsylvania; Elizabeth B. Dunn at the Rare Book, Manuscript, and Special Collections Library, Duke University; the staff at the Rappahannock Regional Library, in Fredericksburg, Virginia, for all their help with my numerous Inter-Library Loan requests; and the staff at the University of Mary Washington, Simpson Library—the best university library I have ever used, without which I could not have accomplished as much research as I did.

Numerous distinguished Lincoln scholars also gave me support and encouragement along the journey toward my first book, and I am indeed grateful to them. I can only hope to live up to the standards they have individually and collectively set in the world of Lincoln scholarship: Catherine Clinton, who encouraged me to write this book; Wayne Temple, who gave me great help finding the Illinois lunacy statutes and is simply the most knowledgeable Lincoln scholar I have ever met; Jane L. Friedman, biographer of Myra Bradwell, who helped me on my road to discovery; and the outstanding historians Michael Burlingame, Harold Holzer, Frank J. Williams, Steven L. Carson, John Y. Simon, Michael W. Kauffman, Norbert Hirschhorn, and Rodney Ross.

Thanks also to Richard Snow, editor of *American Heritage* magazine, for accepting my article about Mary's lost letters, which introduced their discovery to the public, and to Claire Lui, *American Heritage* research assistant, an indefatigable fact-checker.

Thanks to my friends and family: Paul Lewis and the Fredericksburg Athenaeum for their support and for indulging me in my series of lectures on Abraham, Mary, and Robert Lincoln; Aby and Blake Bethem, of Bistro Bethem in Fredericksburg, wonderful bosses who listened to my constant Lincoln babble and gave me the freedom I needed for writing and research; Cathleen "Cat" Mancuso at the Lincoln Home National Historic Site, in Springfield, Illinois, for hiring me way back in 1994 and beginning me on my wonderful journey into Lincoln lore; my aunt

Emmy Gronberg and cousin Michelle Gronberg, for allowing me to stay with them on research trips.

Finally, I never would have discovered the lost insanity letters, or written this book, without the unconditional love and support of my two girls. My wonderful wife, Kathleen, goes to work every day and gives me the freedom to stay home and write and travel for research when necessary. She's a little tired of hearing about Mary and Robert Lincoln, I know, but she understands my passion for historical research and writing. And my daughter, Olivia, the sweetest little girl in the world, lets daddy do lots of writing (and takes nice long naps), even though she wants to play. I love you girls. Thank you.

THE
Madness
OF
MARY
LINCOLN

Introduction

NEARLY EVERY DISCUSSION OF THE LIFE of Mary Todd Lincoln, wife of Abraham Lincoln, culminates in the question, "Was she really crazy?" From there, the discussion inevitably moves toward a juxtaposition of the two theories of her insanity case: (1) she was mentally ill, and her loving son, Robert, committed her to a sanitarium in 1875 because he felt it was his duty, difficult as it was, to keep her safe from herself as well as from others; or, (2) she was the sane victim of a male chauvinist society that sought to shut away her embarrassment to the Lincoln legacy, while the cold-blooded and rapacious Robert was politically and monetarily motivated to incarcerate her against her will. But how does one decide which theory is correct and based on what evidence?

This is one of the more intriguing historical debates within the world of Lincoln scholarship. It concerns not simply the question of Mary Lincoln's sanity versus insanity or the fact or fiction behind her words and actions but also the possible impact her personality and disorder may have had on Abraham Lincoln, the reason her oldest son had her committed and whether it was maliciously or altruistically motivated, the impact of medications and Spiritualism on people and their physicians during the late nineteenth century, and the diagnosis and treatment of mental illness during the same period in American history. These questions have been debated for decades.

Many of the issues were seemingly put to rest in 1986 with the publication of Mark E. Neely and R. Gerald McMurtry's book *The Insanity File: The Case of Mary Todd Lincoln*, which was intended to be the complete documentation of the insanity episode. It was based on Robert Lincoln's personal documentary record of the entire affair, which he tied with a pink ribbon and labeled "MTL Insanity File."[1] Illinois State Historian James T. Hickey discovered the file in Robert Lincoln's bedroom closet at his Vermont home in 1975.[2] Neely and McMurtry's book, however, only led to deeper entrenchment for advocates of both sides of the insanity debate.

Now, a new examination and interpretation of the insanity case is possible. New documentation has been found and previous documentation freshly reconsidered that make it necessary to examine the events surrounding Mary Lincoln's insanity case once again. In early 2005, while in the midst of research on Robert Lincoln, I discovered the so-called lost insanity letters of Mary Lincoln. The story of my discovery is detailed in chapter 10. These letters detail the long and intimate correspondence between Mary Lincoln and Myra and James Bradwell, Mary's legal advisers and the people most responsible for securing her release from the sanitarium. The letters were known to have existed but never found. It was assumed Robert Lincoln destroyed them, not only because they proved so elusive, but also because he had previously admitted attempting to destroy all of his mother's correspondence from the insanity period.

Many historians tried and failed to find the letters, which only added to their mythos. W. A. Evans wrote in 1932, "It is to be regretted that we have nothing of the Bradwell correspondence except the tradition."[3] Ruth Painter Randall, author of the seminal 1953 book *Mary Lincoln: Biography of a Marriage*, dismissed the lost letters in one sentence: "Her letters to the Bradwells have vanished."[4] The compilers of Mary's life and letters, Justin and Linda Turner, wrote in 1972, "None of Mrs. Lincoln's letters to the Bradwells remains, and there is reason to believe Robert had theirs destroyed, so damning were they to him."[5] Ida Tarbell, a biographer of Abraham Lincoln, learned of the Lincoln–Bradwell letters during an interview with James Bradwell but never mentioned them in her writings.[6] The administrators of the Abraham Lincoln Presidential Library and Museum found the mystery of the lost letters so intriguing they included mention of them in the museum's 2005 "Ghosts of the Library" presentation.

When I tracked them down, the letters had been stored, unknown for forty years, in an attic, in a steamer trunk previously owned by Frederic N. Towers, Robert Todd Lincoln's attorney. The trunk contained hundreds of documents, mostly from the early twentieth century, neatly arranged and indexed, concerning the business and family affairs of Robert Lincoln and his family. Within this mass of materials lay also the lost insanity documents. There were twenty, previously unseen and unpublished letters written by Mary Lincoln in the trunk, complemented by five other unpublished letters from various authors regarding the insanity case (see appendix 1). Included as well was the entire documentary record of how and why the letters had been acquired from a granddaughter of the Bradwells by Robert Lincoln's widow, Mary Harlan Lincoln. The story of Mary Harlan Lincoln's acquisition and eventual suppression of the letters, as well as their subsequent preservation, is discussed in chapter 10. That story is based not only on the materials in the Towers Lincoln trunk but also on the personal papers of the Bradwell family, still privately owned by a relative, and other previously unknown materials found in several public archives.

The lost letters offer numerous new insights into Mary's mental and physical condition before, during, and after the 1875 insanity episode; on the actions she took to secure her freedom from the sanitarium; on the opinions of her family and friends of her incarceration; on her friendship with and dependence on the family of Myra Bradwell; on the estrangement between Mary and her son Robert as a result of the insanity episode; and on her life in Europe after her release from the sanitarium.

Prior to the finding of these letters, only eleven letters written by Mary Lincoln were known to exist for the period 1874–75. This cache adds eight more letters for this time period but also includes letters from 1872–73 and 1876–78. This is important because, as the compilers of Mary's collected letters wrote, "Letters written by Mary Lincoln in the period between 1871 and 1876 today are the rarest of items," while nearly all extant letters from 1877 until her death in 1882 were merely about financial matters.[7]

Also found in the steamer trunk was Mary Lincoln's "lost" will, drawn up by James Bradwell in 1873, which was known to have once existed but was assumed destroyed and has never been viewed before or published in any form. Finally, the trunk contained a 111-page unpublished manuscript about the insanity case based on the letters, titled "The Dark Days of Abraham Lincoln's Widow, as Revealed by Her Own Letters," written in the late 1920s by Myra and James Bradwell's granddaughter. The existence of this manuscript played a key role in the disappearance of the lost letters from history.

This new examination of the insanity case also incorporates recently discovered letters pertaining to the event acquired by the Illinois State Historical Library in 1999. Those letters, written to Mary Lincoln's physician Dr. Willis Danforth and her friend Prof. David Swing, revealed that she was more engaged with people than had been previously assumed, fueled a theory that she had a chemical dependence on chloral hydrate, and offered insight into her psychotic delusions. The letters were published in the *Journal of Illinois History* in 2003 but have never been given a wider audience nor incorporated into a book-length examination of the insanity case.

This newly discovered material fills enormous gaps in the insanity story. There currently are two books in print that offer detailed examinations of the case: Neely and McMurtry's *Insanity File*, published in 1986, and *Mary Todd Lincoln: A Biography*, by Jean H. Baker, published in 1987.

Both books were based upon Robert Todd Lincoln's personal Insanity File, which documented the case but had, up until that time, never been seen or published. Interestingly, while both books used the same source, they offered radically different interpretations and antithetical conclusions, as outlined above. The authors of neither of these books had access to the seven letters about the insanity event donated to the Illinois State Historical Society in 1999, nor did they have access to the twenty-five letters I discovered and the story of their suppression.

Added to the new evidence included in this book are various contemporary newspaper articles, journal articles, and book excerpts written since 1987, which also shed new light on the insanity event. Some of the most interesting and pertinent articles include psychiatric diagnoses of Mary Lincoln written by experts who examined the historical records, as well as physiological examinations of Mary Lincoln that consider how her physical health may have contributed to her mental health, or perhaps even created misinterpretations of her symptoms. These analyses have been ignored in the historiography.

A necessary addition, also, to this fresh interpretation of the insanity case is a long overdue reconsideration of Robert Lincoln's motivations in taking the commitment action. Robert Lincoln has been a much misunderstood and largely ignored person in the Lincoln field, and the insanity case cannot be fully comprehended without attempting to understand the depths to which Robert and the rest of his family were pained and humiliated by this episode. A fresh look at the life and papers of Robert T. Lincoln show that he was not a fiend, nor an apathetic aristocrat, but a dutiful son whose actions were taken to best protect his mother from her own demons. I have been studying Robert Lincoln's life for the past four years and have found numerous letters, documents, and newspaper articles previously unknown and unpublished that further illuminate his life and motivations and add great depth to the insanity debate.

Robert's letters show that he suppressed the insanity case not only because it embarrassed him but also because he had no love for or trust in journalists and historians, whom he considered inveterate liars and hacks. He feared what would be written about his mother if her words in these letters—words that he deemed morally illicit due to her mental state when she wrote them—were ever made public. Robert's extreme Victorian sense of family privacy, as well as his sense of manly duty to preserve and protect the memory and legacy of Abraham Lincoln, could not allow such misinterpretation to occur.

Some people may question the propriety of publishing these long lost letters. After all, the known history, as well as the concomitant documentation found with these items, proves beyond a doubt that Robert Lincoln did not want this material published. To continue their suppression, however, would be to fail to clarify the ongoing misinterpretation of an incomplete story. Robert Lincoln's preservation of the insanity case documentary record only could have been intended for the elucidation of posterity. As his personal Insanity File already has been viewed and utilized in previous works, I think he would want this newly uncovered evidence added to the story. One of the many reasons that the insanity case has been so misunderstood is the paucity of primary materials related to it, and more specifically, the lack of any understanding of the main protagonist in the episode: Robert T. Lincoln.

Lastly, the majority of historical examinations fail to study the insanity case within the context of Mary's life and instead view it in a vacuum. The signs of her mental illness began long before her 1875 commitment—even before Abraham Lincoln's assassination on April 14, 1865, which Mary's contemporaries generally considered her breaking point. Looking at Mary's early life, one can discern early manifestations of Manic-Depressive Illness (now called Bipolar Disorder), with symptoms of depression, delusions (of persecution, poverty, and various somatic ailments), hallucinations, inflated self-esteem, decreased or interrupted sleep, mood swings, and extravagant spending (monomania). These early manifestations later developed into full-blown Manic-Depressive episodes, with the above symptoms, usually magnified, as well as threats of physical violence against others and attempts at suicide. This multiplicity of psychotic episodes show that she did not suffer simply from one "insanity episode" that led to her commitment in 1875—which is the general understanding—but rather she suffered numerous episodes throughout her life that led to the inevitable denouement.

To finally pull all of this primary and secondary material together into a coherent whole for the first time allows a clearer picture of Mary Lincoln's insanity case, its causes, events, and ramifications. It allows a better understanding of Robert Lincoln, which in turn clarifies the history of the insanity episode and more fully illuminates Mary Lincoln. It chases away the shadows of innuendo, conjecture, and bias that have long shrouded the general perception of Mary's post-assassination life and permits us to see her, not as a pathetic, ranting lunatic with wild eyes and unkempt hair, but as a sympathetic figure sitting alone in a darkened room, whose intellect and emotions were overwhelmed by mental illness and whose life was so tragically marred by pain and loss.

I   *Much like an April Day*

ON WEDNESDAY APRIL 12, 1865, President Abraham Lincoln wrote a playful yet tender note to his wife notifying her that he would join her daily carriage ride on Friday, the fourteenth. It was a pleasant spring day, and the Lincolns, who rode alone at the president's request, discussed their plans for life after his presidency. They would travel across America to visit California, then to Europe, and Lincoln particularly wanted to visit Jerusalem.[1] They considered whether to return to their house in Springfield, Illinois, or live in Chicago upon Lincoln's retirement from the White House.[2] "During the drive he was so gay," Mary said, "that I said to him, laughingly, 'Dear Husband, you almost startle me by your great cheerfulness,' he replied, 'and well I may feel so, Mary, I consider *this* day, the war, has come to a close."[3] The Lincolns continued the blissful closeness of their afternoon carriage ride at Ford's Theatre that night, watching a performance of *Our American Cousin* in the company of Clara Harris and Major Henry R. Rathbone.[4] Mary was supremely happy, and she smiled and leaned onto her husband several times.[5] "What will Miss Harris think of my hanging on to you so?" she whispered contentedly to her husband. "She won't think anything of it," the president replied. When John Wilkes Booth fired the fatal shot into Lincoln's brain during act 3, scene 2, Mary Lincoln was holding her husband's hand.[6]

"The president is shot!" she shrieked as Booth leaped to the stage from the twelve-foot-high box and cried, "*Sic semper tyrannis!*"[7] As soldiers, civilians, and physicians crowded into the presidential box, Mary Lincoln pleaded with Dr. Charles Leale, "Oh, Doctor, do what you can for my dear husband, do what you can for him."[8] Lincoln's body was carried across Tenth Street to the Petersen house, while the stunned First Lady followed. Twenty-one year-old Captain Robert Lincoln, just returned from the surrender at Appomattox Courthouse and visiting with his friend John Hay in the White House, was sent for, and he arrived at the Petersen house not long after.[9] While Secretary of War Edwin M. Stanton directed the machinations of the government manhunt from a side room of the Petersen house, Mary Lincoln was alternating between weeping at her husband's side and wailing in the front parlor. "Why didn't he shoot me?" she shrieked when she saw one acquaintance. "Why didn't he shoot me?"[10] Clara Harris, covered in her fiancé's blood from his arm wound caused by Booth's dagger, tried to comfort the First Lady, but every time she approached, Mary would look on her with horror and scream, "Oh! My husband's blood, my dear husband's blood!"[11] Robert comforted his mother during this period and at times stood vigil in the death room, seeking his own comfort from Senator Charles Sumner.[12] When Lincoln finally breathed his last at 7:22 A.M. on April 15, Mary Lincoln's grief was inconsolable.

Robert escorted his mother back to the White House, where they reunited with the youngest Lincoln boy, Tad, who had been at the National Theater that night watching a children's play. "Returning to Mrs. Lincoln's room, I found her in a new paroxysm of grief," Mary's seamstress, Elizabeth Keckly, later wrote.[13] "Robert was bending over his mother with tender affection, and little Tad was couched at the foot of the bed, with a world of agony in his young face."[14] Keckly was with the Lincolns in the White House during those dark post-assassination days. She watched as the First Family became adjusted to their new reality, especially the relationship and reactions of Robert and Mary. "Robert was very tender to his mother in the days of her sorrow. He suffered deeply, as his haggard face indicated, but he was ever manly and collected when in the presence of his mother."[15] President Andrew Johnson allowed Mary Lincoln much latitude in her bereavement as to when she would move out of the White House. She did not vacate the house until more than one month after the assassination. On May 22, 1865, Mary and her boys left to begin a new life in Chicago.[16]

In the audacity of John Wilkes Booth's act and the aftermath of Reconstruction, Americans often overlook the very deep impact that Lincoln's assassination had on his immediate family. Not only did it leave eleven-year-old Tad without a father and twenty-one-year-old Robert as head of the family but it also left Mary Lincoln a shattered widow. Many family friends, contemporaries, and subsequent historians attribute the breaking point of Mary Lincoln's tenuous mental state to that "very dreadful night," as Robert later called it. Robert considered his mother's derangement the direct result of it.[17] Mary Lincoln herself wrote only seven months after the assassination, "When I reflect, as I am always doing, upon the overwhelming loss, of that, *most* idolized boy [her son Willie in 1862], and the crushing blow, that deprived me, of my *all in all* of this life [Abraham], I wonder that I retain my reason & live."[18] Yet upon a deeper look into Mary Lincoln's life, it becomes evident that her peculiarities and peccadilloes began long before that fateful Good Friday in 1865.

The deathbed of Abraham Lincoln. Library of Congress, LC-USZ262-7443.

The courtship of Abraham Lincoln and Mary Todd was incongruous, to say the least. The rich and aristocratic Todd family of Lexington, Kentucky, did not consider the uncouth, backwoods Lincoln a suitable match for the cultured and educated Mary. Yet Mary and Abraham had much in common. They both loved poetry and literature, both believed in Whig political principles and idolized Henry Clay (whom Mary knew personally), both loved children, and both suffered the death of their mother at an early age.[19] For Mary Todd, this was the first great loss of her life, and one that was compounded by her father's remarriage to a woman who resented Robert Todd's first brood of children.[20] By October 1839, twenty-year-old Mary was so weary of living and clashing with her stepmother that she sought escape in Springfield, Illinois, in the home of her sister, Elizabeth Edwards.[21]

Mary immediately became one of the belles of the town, enchanting all the eligible young men. "The sunshine in her heart was reflected in her face," said her sister-in-law.[22] Even her most vociferous critic, William Herndon, conceded that she was a stunning woman, full of charm, culture, and grace.[23] She had a high intelligence, a quick wit, and a noticeable beauty. "She is the very creature of excitement," one young lawyer wrote in 1840, while Mary's brother-in-law, Ninian Edwards, said of her, "She could make a bishop forget his prayers."[24]

Mary soon led the young men of the town on "a merry dance," counting among her suitors a grandson of Patrick Henry, future U.S. Senators Stephen A. Douglas, Edward D. Baker, James Shields, and Lyman Trumbull and, of course, Abraham Lincoln. "Mary was quick, gay and in the social world somewhat brilliant," her sister, Elizabeth Edwards, stated years later. "She loved show and power, and was the most ambitious woman I ever knew. She used to contend when a girl, to her friends in Kentucky, that she was destined to marry a President."[25] Mary's sister was witness to the courting of Mary Todd and Abraham Lincoln, much of which occurred at the Edwardses' home. "Mary invariably led the conversation. Mr. Lincoln would sit at her side and listen. He scarcely said a word, but gazed on her as if irresistibly drawn towards her by some superior and unseen power."[26]

Abraham and Mary were wed—despite one broken engagement and an eighteen-month hiatus in their relationship—in November 1842.[27] Lincoln had inscribed on the inside of Mary's wedding band the phrase "Love is Eternal," and the marriage was, by most accounts, based on a foundation of love. "My wife is as handsome as when she was a girl, and I, a poor nobody then, fell in love with her; and what is more, I have never fallen out," Lincoln is reported to have said during the White House years.[28] General Daniel Sickles, who knew the Lincolns on a personal level during the Civil War, stated he had "never seen a more devoted couple;" while abolitionist Jane Grey Swisshelm noted their devotion in the way that Mary "completely merged herself in her husband."[29]

Letters between Abraham and Mary that testify to their feelings are rare today. The most well known is an exchange of letters during 1848 when Lincoln was a member of Congress and lived in Washington, while Mary and their two sons, Robert and Edward, lived with the Todd family in Lexington, Kentucky. "In this troublesome world, we are never quite satisfied," Lincoln wrote. "When you were here, I thought you hindered me some in attending to business but now, having nothing but business—no vanity—it has grown exceedingly tasteless to me. I hate to sit down and direct accounts, and I hate to stay in this old room by myself."[30] Part of Mary's response stated, "How much I wish, instead of writing, we were together this evening, I feel very sad away from you."[31]

Of course, the Lincoln marriage was not perfect, and both Abraham and Mary had their faults. Mary Lincoln was intelligent, witty, vivacious, and cultured, but she also was spoiled, petulant, selfish, nervous, and excitable. This duality of personality can be traced all the way back to her childhood.[32] Mary's cousin once wrote that, as a child, Mary was "very highly strung . . . having an emotional temperament much like an April day, sunning all over with laughter one moment, the next crying as though her heart would break."[33] During the Springfield years, it was familiarly stated that Mary was "always either in the garret or the cellar."[34] In the White House, presidential secretary William O. Stoddard wrote, "It was not easy, at first, to understand why a lady who could be one day so kindly, so considerate, so generous, so thoughtful and so hopeful, could, upon another day, appear so unreasonable, so irritable, so despondent, so even niggardly, and so prone to see the dark, the wrong side of men and women and events."[35] This emotionalism dominated Mary, shaped her personality, and formed the background for her later hysteria and self-indulgence following the deaths of her husband and children, according to one psychologist and biographer. "No other [trait] was more potent in changing [her personality] from the grade termed 'abnormal' to that termed 'pathologic,' and in changing her mentality from balanced to unbalanced."[36]

One of Mary's most memorable traits was her "unusually high temper . . . that invariably got the better of her" and made her many enemies.[37] When offended or antagonized, "her agreeable qualities instantly disappeared beneath a wave of stinging satire or sarcastic bitterness."[38] John Hay and John Nicolay, President Lincoln's White House secretaries, dubbed Mary the "Hellcat"; Herndon later called her a "she-wolf" and "the female wildcat of the age" and stated that her irascible nature caused Lincoln a lifetime of trouble and unhappiness.[39] Yet her temper was mercurial, and she nearly always was regretful when her anger passed. In fact, Mary suffered from severe migraine headaches her entire adult life, which may have had some impact on her temper as well.[40]

James Gourley, a Springfield neighbor, said the Lincolns had their ups and downs, like all families, but got along as well as anyone. "Lincoln yielded to his wife—in fact, almost any other man, had he known the woman as I did, would have done the same thing."[41] Lincoln sometimes would ignore his wife's hysterics, Gourley stated, and frequently he would laugh at her.[42] If Mary did not calm down, Lincoln would simply pick up one of the children and leave the house. Gourley's reminiscences are in accord with others from the White House years. Mary's seamstress, Elizabeth Keckly, wrote in 1868 that Lincoln "was a kind and indulgent husband, and when he saw faults in his wife he excused them as he would excuse the impulsive acts of a child."[43] Most accounts of their married years in Springfield, collected after Lincoln's death in 1865, coincide with the statements that Mary was mercurial and often difficult, while Lincoln was often detached, yet ever patient.

Abraham Lincoln, however, was not a model husband. He was away from home riding the Eighth Judicial Circuit for six to eight months a year, leaving Mary alone with the children.[44] This terrified Mary, as she was constantly in dire fear of house fires and burglars, and either she or her husband often arranged for a neighbor boy to sleep in the house with her as protection.[45] As Lincoln's political career ascended, he also spent time away to give political speeches and attend campaign rallies. For Mary, who was not only lonely but also afraid of being by herself in the house (and was especially terrified of thunder and lightning storms), such travel was not ideal. Mary resented Lincoln's time on the judicial circuit because he was the only lawyer who stayed away from home the entire circuit. Also, because he was the senior partner in the law firm of Lincoln and Herndon, Mary felt Lincoln should have stayed in Springfield and sent Herndon out to traverse the state each term. In fact, Mary once told a neighbor that if Lincoln stayed home as he should, she could have loved him better.[46]

But even when Lincoln was home, he still was a difficult husband for Mary. Lincoln was busy and often distracted by politics and work; he eschewed normal social graces, such as wearing appropriate attire both in and out of the house; he often said inappropriate things in public.[47] Lincoln also was disrespectful to Mary as a homemaker. Lincoln often arrived late, or not at all, for dinner; he would bring friends home for dinner with him without notifying Mary; he was indifferent to food and never complimented her on her cooking. As Joshua Wolf Shenk characterized their relationship in his acclaimed study of Lincoln's melancholy, "the Lincolns' marriage had barrels of difficulties, exacerbated by her volatility and his withdrawal."[48]

Abraham Lincoln's psychological influence on his wife cannot be ignored. His love and patience were the perfect anodynes for her volatile temper and erratic emotionalism. When once teased about his wife's tantrums, Lincoln replied, "If you knew how little harm it does me, and how much good it does her, you wouldn't wonder that I am meek."[49] Lincoln was not weak in this regard, simply indulgent and patient, even parental. As Michael Burlingame has shown, Lincoln assumed the role of "father surrogate" to Mary, someone to indulge, love, and protect her.[50] In fact, Mary's White House seamstress stated that nothing pleased Mary quite so much as when Lincoln referred to her as his "child wife."[51] This was the essence of Lincoln's influence on Mary: he played multiple roles in her life, satisfying multiple needs. "He was . . . from my eighteenth year—Always—lover—husband—father & *all all to me*—Truly my all," she wrote in 1869.[52] Lincoln was the buffer between her and the rest of society that she sorely needed, and the absence of his restraining influence after 1865 would have dire consequences.

Still, times were good during the early years of the Lincoln marriage. Two sons were born—Robert in 1843 and Edward (Eddie) in 1846—Lincoln had served one term in Congress, and his law practice was flourishing. But the next great tragedy of Mary's life, rather a succession of tragedies, occurred in 1849–50. Mary's father, Robert S. Todd, died in July 1849. Her emotions, while recovering from that loss, were then put under strain when the Lincolns' four year-old son, Eddie, became ill in December. In January 1850, Mary's maternal grandmother, Elizabeth Parker, to whom Mary went for solace during the years after her mother's death, died. Then just a few short weeks later, in February 1850, Eddie died after a fifty-two day struggle with what is now diagnosed as tuberculosis.[53] Mary was so distraught that she shut herself in her room for days and refused to eat or sleep, forcing Lincoln to plead, "Mary, you must eat, for we must live."[54] Lincoln himself suffered a profound grief at Eddie's death but "resolved to keep his feelings under a firm sway."[55]

Mary was shattered by such loss in so short a period, but she recovered, aided by the support she received. She had Abraham and seven-year-old Robert to comfort her and became pregnant with another child just one month later. Mary also had family and friends in Springfield with whom to commiserate. In time, two more boys were born into the Lincoln family—Willie and Tad—and Abraham Lincoln's political prominence grew.[56] Despite this success causing Lincoln to be absent more frequently, Mary was extremely proud of her husband and just as ambitious. She reveled in his growing notoriety.

Once Lincoln attained the presidency, Mary felt she had arrived at her true and entitled destiny. Yet the great stress and consternation of the White House years, one could argue, only pushed her mind closer to the edge of what was later called insanity. From the time of her husband's election, Mary was in constant fear of his assassination and therefore of her own loss.[57] She constantly asked about better protection for his life, although he always rebuffed her suggestions.

Washington society disliked Mary Lincoln. They openly scoffed at her Western uncouthness and simultaneously resented her sense of regal entitlement and haughty air, which led her on huge spending sprees and lavish partying in the midst of war.[58] Mary also was disparaged for her "inordinate greed, coupled with an utter lack of sense of propriety," which manifested itself in her easy willingness to accept gifts for her influence with the president and in her susceptibility to the most obvious flattery.[59] One psychiatrist called this Mary's "narcissistic lavishness," about which he succinctly explained, "She thrived on adulation, required attention, reveled in adornment, and was sensitive to snubs."[60] Northerners considered her a rebel, since she was from Kentucky; Southerners considered her a traitor; and she was therefore derided by the presses of both sections of the country.

A major turning point for Mary's emotional and mental states came with the next loss in her life, the death of twelve-year-old Willie in February 1862. Of all the Lincoln boys, Willie was the most like his father—precocious, honest, kind, and thoughtful—and today is considered the favorite son of both parents. Willie was "an amiable good hearted boy," who "had more judgment and foresight than any boy of his age that I have ever known," wrote Horatio Nelson Taft, father of Tad and Willie's daily playmates.[61] "He was so bravely and beautifully himself," eulogized family friend and editor N. P. Willis. "A wild flower, transplanted from the prairie to the hothouse, he retained his prairie habits, unalterably pure and simple, till he died."[62] Both the Lincolns felt this loss grievously, but for Mary, who always was an extremely emotional woman, her sorrow at Willie's death was incapacitating. She stayed confined to her room for weeks, prompting Robert Lincoln to request Mary's older sister, Elizabeth Edwards, to come stay at the White House.[63] When she left two months later, the president arranged for a nurse.[64] Mary could not look at anything connected with Willie. She removed all his clothes and possessions and never again invited Willie and Tad's daily playmates, Bud and Holly Taft, to the White House.[65]

Benjamin French, the commissioner of public buildings, wrote in his diary that Mary "was terribly affected by her loss, and almost refused to be comforted."[66] Elizabeth Keckly, Mary's seamstress, wrote, "Mrs. Lincoln's grief was inconsolable. In one of her paroxysms of grief the President kindly bent over his wife, took her by the arm, and gently led her to a window. With a stately, solemn gesture, he pointed to the lunatic asylum. 'Mother, do you see that large white building on the hill yonder? Try and control your grief, or it will drive you mad, and we may have to send you there.'"[67]

Mary's few mentions of Willie in extant letters she wrote over the ensuing year reveal she created an apotheosis for her son, calling him "too precious for this earth" and their "idolised" and "sainted" boy.[68] Her letters also attest to the weakness of her emotional state, for in May 1862 she stated how she was "so completely unnerved, that I can scarcely command myself to write."[69] In July she wrote, "the anguish of the thought [that Willie is gone] oftentimes, for days overcomes me."[70] By the first anniversary of Willie's death, Mary still was crushed, showing what psychiatrists call an "exaggerated grief reaction" in her hypersensitive and sustained response to her son's death. "Only those, who have passed through such bereavements, can realize, how the heart bleeds at the return, of these anniversaries," she wrote.[71] This last statement is interesting, since it was on the tenth anniversary of Lincoln's assassination that Mary had her most dramatic break with sanity.

It is important to note that Keckly's reminiscence is not the only reported instance of Abraham Lincoln commenting on his wife's mental state. William Herndon, Lincoln's law partner, stated in 1882 that "Mr. Lincoln held his wife partly insane for years, and this shows his toleration of her nature—his great forbearance of her outlandish acts, otherwise not understood by the great world."[72] William P. Wood, superintendent of the Old Capitol Prison, said in 1887 that Lincoln confided in him during the war that his wife's caprices, "I am satisfied, are the result of partial insanity."[73]

These two statements may be true but are troublesome, since there is no corroboration, and they were written seventeen and twenty-two years after Lincoln's death, respectively. Herndon called Lincoln "The most shut-mouthed man I ever knew" and made mention of "Lincoln's reticence, secretiveness, his somewhat unsocial nature, his somewhat retired disposition."[74] Mary said that Lincoln "was *not*, a demonstrative man," even with her: "When he felt most deeply, he expressed, the least."[75] To think Lincoln would comment on something as intensely private as his wife's "insanity" to a mere acquaintance such as Wood is, therefore, doubtful; and to trust any statement of Herndon about Mary, whom he avowedly despised, is problematic. Keckly's story, however, published in 1868, long before Mary's 1875 insanity trial, is well known and generally accepted. It produces an interesting historical irony that for all the opprobrium toward Robert for committing his mother to a sanitarium, it was in fact Abraham Lincoln who was the first recorded family member to suggest that Mary might need hospitalization.

Lincoln, however, was the reason Mary retained her sanity after Willie's death in 1862. Besides his calming influence, and despite all her physical and emotional pain during those first two years in the White House, she knew she must be strong for the overwhelming burdens her husband had to bear as president of a divided nation. Mary told her sister that after Willie's death, she felt she had "fallen into a deep pit of gloom and despair without a ray of light anywhere. If I had not felt the spur of necessity urging me to cheer Mr. Lincoln, whose grief was as great as my own, I could never have smiled again."[76] In early 1865, Robert marveled at what a "brave front" his mother put on, even though they all knew she was suffering. "Most women would be in bed groaning, but not mother! She just straightens herself up a little more and says, 'It is better to laugh than

Lincoln and his family. Library of Congress, LC-USZ262-134039.

be sighing.' Tad would go all to pieces if she reversed the words of that opera, and so would my father."[77] Robert's statement was made about his mother's physical, rather than emotional, health, but it serves as an interesting juxtaposition to the personal self-pitying of her letters.

The suffering Robert alluded to came from Mary's July 2, 1863, carriage accident, during which, while riding into Washington from the Soldier's Home, the driver's seat of the presidential carriage became detached, throwing the driver to the ground. The frightened horses began a frantic run along the Rock Creek Road, near the Mount Pleasant Hospital, and Mary leaped from the carriage to save herself.[78] The news reports of the incident stated that Mary was stunned, bruised, and battered, but no bones were broken, and her injuries, which were immediately attended to by surgeons from the nearby hospital, did not appear serious. She did suffer a bleeding wound on the back of her head caused by a sharp stone, which doctors at the nearby hospital quickly stitched up.[79] The president telegraphed Robert at Cambridge not to worry, "Your mother very slightly hurt by her fall."[80]

Mary took to her bed, and Lincoln sent for Rebecca Pomroy, the nurse who cared for Mary and Tad after Willie's death, to attend her.[81] Unfortunately, as was common during the Civil War era, Mary's seemingly benign wound became infected. It was three weeks before she was up and about, and her recovery seems to have been incomplete. Mary had suffered severe migraine headaches her entire adult life, and now she had them with greater frequency after the accident. Robert Lincoln later told his aunt that his mother never fully recovered from her head injury, which implied, but did not explicitly state, that it had an impact on her mental health as well.

Besides the physical aspect of the injury, there also was an emotional one. Mary's nurse wrote in her diary the accident was really an assassination attempt on the president, with the driver's seat having been sabotaged.[82] This undoubtedly deepened Mary's existing fear for her husband's life. On a family level, the president spent little time with his injured wife, as he was busy coordinating and monitoring the ongoing battle of Gettysburg. Robert also did not come immediately to see his mother and even ignored his father's telegrams about it.[83] These circumstances must have furthered Mary's sense of loss of connection with her own family, for with Willie dead, Robert away at college, and Abraham busy with the war, Mary had only Tad to give her undivided attention.

Mary's intense grief over Willie's death, coupled with the effects of her head injury, did not cause her to go mad but did bring her nearer the breaking point. Emily Todd Helm, Mary's half sister, noticed in 1863 that Mary was nervous, excitable, and wrought up and that she seemed in constant fear of more sorrows being added to her life.[84] "I believe if anything should happen to you or Robert or Tad it would kill her," Emily told the president.[85] Emily also recorded in her diary a most disturbing and now-famous event in which Mary came into her room at night, smiling and with eyes full of tears, to tell her that Willie visited her at night to comfort her sorrow:

> "He lives Emily," she said with a thrill in her voice I can never forget. "He comes to me every night, and stands at the foot of my bed with the same sweet, adorable smile he always had; he does not always come alone; little Eddie is sometimes with him and twice he has come with our brother Alec, he tells me he loves his Uncle Alec and is with him most of the time.[86] You cannot dream of the comfort this gives me. When I thought of my little son in immensity, alone, without his mother to direct him, no one to hold his little hand in loving guidance, it nearly broke my heart." Sister Mary's eyes were wide and shining and I had the feeling of awe as if I were in the presence of the supernatural. It *is* unnatural and abnormal, it frightens me.[87]

These visions could have been mere dreams, products of Mary's unconscious mind, or, what sounds more likely, hallucinations. If the latter, they were Mary's first truly psychotic symptoms. In either case, they show Mary exhibiting complex defenses to help ease the burden of her overwhelming loss.[88] Indeed, in later years, at the end of her life, Mary would sleep only on one side of her bed, saving the other side as "the president's place."[89] And again, in 1880, even though she had cut Robert from her life, still she reveled in newspaper speculations of her oldest son for president, a momentary reprieve of the loss of her son and her own loss of social position, which would be reaffirmed by her offspring.[90] "I never in my life saw a more peculiarly constituted woman. Search the world over, and you will not find her counterpart," Mary's White House seamstress declared.[91]

Mary's fear, often and unfortunately, went beyond personal family matters and into the public domain. She so deeply feared the loss of another son's life that for the duration of the war she refused to let Robert join the army, causing her son's resentment and her husband's embarrassment. "We have lost one son, and his loss is as much as I can bear, without being called upon to make another sacrifice," Mary would say, while Lincoln argued that many mothers had lost all their children, and Mary should not be so selfish.[92] Publicly, Mary admitted that it was her fault Robert was in college and not in the army, maintaining that "an educated man can serve his country with more intelligent purpose than an ignoramus."[93] Lincoln acquiesced to his wife's anxiety until nearly the end of the war, after Robert had graduated from Harvard.[94]

Mary also was a jealous woman and feared the loss of her husband to politics, politicians, friends, and other women. Thurlow Weed said Mary "had a singular prejudice against anyone who seemed to have any influence with her husband."[95] She distrusted Secretary of State William Seward, once chastising her husband, "It makes me mad to see you sit still and let that hypocrite, Seward, twine you around his finger as if you were a skein of thread."[96] She (like other cabinet members) also resented his monopoly on Lincoln's time. By the fall of 1862, Lincoln and Seward were together every day.[97]

One of Mary's most famous episodes of jealousy (and temper) occurred during a visit to army headquarters at City Point, Virginia, in March 1865. Twice, while inspecting troops at the front, President Lincoln's entourage included a general's wife. The first time, Mary was not present but heard that Mrs. Charles Griffin was. "Do you mean to say that she saw the President alone? Do you know that I never allow the President to see any woman alone?" Mary exclaimed. She decided to go on the second trip, but the ambulance in which she and Julia Grant (wife of General U. S. Grant) rode became mired in the mud. The president, who was riding ahead, went out to inspect the troops accompanied by his generals, as well as by Major General Edward O. C. Ord's young and beautiful wife. Mary was furious. "What does that woman mean by riding by the side of the President and ahead of me? Does she suppose that *he* wants *her* by the side of *him*?" At the front, Mary unleashed such a verbal harangue on Mrs. Ord that the younger woman broke down in tears. She also unleashed her venom on Mrs. Grant and, later, on her husband at a military staff dinner.[98] Mrs. Grant, however, while admitting Mary's annoyance at Mrs. Ord, disputed the story as hyperbole in her memoirs, and Generals William Tecumseh Sherman and Horace Porter, both present during the incident, made no mention of any such harangue in theirs.[99]

By 1864, both Abraham and Mary were worried about the prospects of Lincoln's reelection to the presidency. Also, there were Robert's continual requests to join the army, which terrified Mary. "The souls of President and Mrs. Lincoln at the pinnacle of their ambition were filled with weariness," wrote one historian.[100] But by November, Sherman had captured Atlanta and began his march to the sea, Sheridan had cleared the Shenandoah Valley, Grant had Lee under siege at Petersburg, and Lincoln was overwhelmingly reelected. As the military victories accumulated, both the president and Mary grew happier. On April 9, Lee surrendered. The next day, rejoicing in victory, Mary wrote, "If the close of that terrible war, has left some of our hearthstones, *very, very* desolate, God, has been ever kind & merciful, in the midst of our heavy afflictions as nations, & as individuals."[101] Just five days later, Mary would be blaming that same God for his unjust afflictions.

2 *A Most Painful Time of Anxiety*

FOR FIVE WEEKS AFTER THE ASSASSINATION, Mary Lincoln stayed confined to her bedroom, allowing only the closest family and friends to visit. "I do not have the least desire to live," she wrote to her friend Madame Berghmans in her last letter from the White House. "Only my extreme agony of mind, has prevented my receiving yourself & other friends. God alone knows the agony of this crushed heart."[1] She later characterized her final six weeks at the White House as "a bed of illness & many days & nights of almost positive derangement."[2] When Mary and her sons finally vacated the White House on May 22, 1865, her celebrity had dwindled so far that few people knew or cared. The major and local newspapers made only the briefest mention of her health and her planned departure from Washington.[3]

Few people are known to have said good-bye to Mary when she left. Benjamin French, the commissioner of public buildings who worked with Mary on refurbishing both the White House and the Soldier's Home, wrote in his diary that he felt "really very sad, although she has given me a world of trouble. I think the sudden and awful death of the President, somewhat unhinged her mind, for, at times she has exhibited all the symptoms of madness. She is a most singular woman, and it is well for the nation that she is no longer in the White House. It is not proper that I should write down, *even here*, all I know!"[4] Mary's seamstress, Elizabeth Keckly, who accompanied Mary to Chicago, later wrote that, unlike the day thousands of people came to watch President Lincoln's body leave the White House, Mary's departure unfolded "with scarcely a friend to tell her good-by." The silence as Mary descended the public stairway of the White House, entered the carriage, and rode to the train depot, Keckly remembered, "was almost painful."[5]

It was a long, somber, depressing fifty-four-hour journey from Washington to Chicago. Mary sat in a daze, barely speaking; "no one could get near enough to her grief to comfort her," William Crook later said.[6] Upon their arrival, no group of citizenry was waiting to welcome them. Instead, the Lincoln family quietly took rooms at the Tremont House,

Chicago's largest and most popular hotel. This was a trying time for the Lincolns and inaugurated a new era in relations between Mary and her oldest son. At age twenty-one, Robert was now the head of the family, and in accepting that duty, he altered the entire direction of his life.

Robert had not been allowed by his parents to join the Union army until early 1865; instead, he spent the war years first as an undergraduate at Harvard University and then at Harvard Law School.[7] How long Robert intended to stay in the army after the war ended is unknown, but it is known that his chosen profession was the law. In the 1860s, the path to practicing law was either through study at an accredited law school or by apprenticing in a law office. Robert's postwar plans are unknown, but it can be logically surmised that he either planned to return to Harvard or to apprentice at a law firm in Washington.[8] Instead, he resigned his army commission and moved with his family to Chicago, thereby eschewing Harvard and leaving behind not only the Eastern friends and life he so enjoyed but also Mary Harlan, the girl he was courting.[9]

As altruistic or pathetic as Robert's sudden life change may seem today, to him, within the contemporary culture, it simply was something he had to do. It was his Duty, and Duty—capitalized and moralized—is exactly what he considered it to be. Robert was, from his time at Harvard until his death, the quintessential Victorian-era gentleman, who believed in and felicitously followed the manly tenets of duty and honor. These Victorian sensibilities prove to be the root of Robert's motivations in his mother's insanity case and go a long way toward explaining why he took the later actions he felt necessary.

The Victorian era in American history is one filled with those intangible masculine principles of duty and honor. "Duty was a crucial word for manhood. . . . Every social relationship was organized as a conjunction of roles (father–son, husband–wife, etc.) and each role was governed by a set of duties owed to others," according to social historian E. Anthony Rotundo. "Social obligation often required a man to act against his own will. To carry out such obligations, man had to learn submission to his superiors, fate, even to duty itself." Victorian people were judged on their contribution to society and fulfillment of duty, and there was a close link between manhood and social usefulness.[10] While Rotundo examined New Englanders—Robert was from the Midwest—Robert's formative years were, in fact, spent in New England: one year at Phillips Exeter Academy in New Hampshire (1859–60) and four years at Harvard (1860–64). One observer noted the Eastern influence on Robert in early 1861. "The effect of a residence within the improving influences of genteel, well dressed and well behaved Boston is plainly noticeable in his outward appearance, the comparative elegance of which presents a striking contrast to the loose, careless, awkward rigging of his Presidential father."[11]

One of the most famous stories about Robert's sense of duty—pejorative as it is—stems from the visit of the well-known dwarf Charles S. Stratton, known as "General Tom Thumb," to the White House in February 1863. Mary was delighted to host the diminutive circus entertainer and his new bride. Robert thought it ridiculous, refused to attend, and said to his mother, "My notions of duty, perhaps, are somewhat different from yours."[12] In 1876, Robert allowed himself to be appointed the town supervisor of South Chicago out of a sense of duty to his community, even though he had no desire for public office. Also, as an adult, Robert donated thousands of dollars every year for philanthropy and sat on the boards of numerous charities, public utilities, and private companies, another example of his Victorian sentiments.[13]

"The ideal man, then, was pleasant, mild-mannered, and devoted to the good of the community," Rotundo concluded. "He performed his duties faithfully, governed his passions rationally, submitted to his fate and to his place in society, and treated his dependents with firm but affectionate wisdom."[14] This description of the pious, dutiful, restrained man fits Robert Lincoln well, and, in that way, he was no different than any other Victorian gentleman. As will be shown, that notion of duty imbued Robert's correspondence his entire life, but especially during the insanity period. As the sole surviving male Lincoln, he felt it his duty to be his mother's guardian.

But duty most often does not come without self-interest, regret, or even resentment. After one week at the Tremont House, Mary decided the expense was too great, so the Lincolns moved to Hyde Park, a summer resort seven miles south of Chicago.[15] Unlike the Tremont House, Hyde Park was not first class; it had small rooms and plain furnishings. Robert spent the first day there arranging his room, unpacking his books, and conversing with Elizabeth Keckly, who accompanied the family to Chicago. Upon her remark that the new accommodations were "delightful," Robert retorted, "Since you do not have to stay here, you can safely say as much about the charming situation as you please. I presume that I must put up with it, as mother's pleasure must be consulted before my own. But candidly, I would almost as soon be dead as be compelled to remain three months in this dreary house."[16] Elizabeth Keckly then walked across the hall to find Mrs. Lincoln, as she had been the previous five weeks, sobbing on her bed.

Robert felt it keenly when his father died and the burden was then placed on him to care for his mother and younger brother Tad, but, in accordance with the rules of Gilded Age masculinity, he kept his emotional pain to himself. "Poor Robert, has borne his sorrows, manfully, yet with a broken heart," his mother wrote to a friend only three months after the assassination.[17] By June 1865, Robert had resumed his legal studies through reading law in the offices of Scammon, McCagg and Fuller in downtown Chicago and taking law courses at the "old" University of Chicago.[18] Robert felt it his duty to be diligent in learning law and therefore quickly be able to provide for himself and his family. When he declined a trip with his friend Edgar Welles to Havana in late 1865, Mary "almost marveled" that Robert refused such an offer. "In consideration, of our recent afflictions, pressing so heavily upon us, Robert, thinks it best, for the present, to be quiet, and attend to his studies."[19] Upon Edgar's return, Mary reiterated, "it is quite a trial to me, when I reflect, on the pleasure, *such a trip*, would have afforded my poor sad boy, Robert. He was conscientious, in what he considered his duty, to remain at home, for the present."[20]

Mary, on the other hand, displayed her sorrow publicly, even garishly. She always was a great mourner, but, as happened after the death of Willie in 1862, even her family and friends eventually felt she was overindulging herself. For months after the assassination, Mary saw no visitors. She could not stand the sight of old friends—it would bring back too many memories—and she felt new acquaintances could never understand her grief. She kept her youngest son, Tad, with her at all times. She wore black clothing every day for the rest of her life, even to Robert's 1868 wedding. Her despair, self-pity, and religious doubt stayed with her until her death.[21] Mary told her sister-in-law that her life during the weeks and months after the assassination was "a perfect blank," and "time seemed blotted out." "I must have been living all these weeks in a state of unconsciousness, for I remember nothing, and the awakening is terrible."[22]

Besides sorrow, Mary's post-assassination days were consumed with her great mania for money: her indefatigable need to spend it, and her paranoid belief that she had none. "The simple truth, which I cannot tell anyone not personally interested, is that my mother is on one subject not mentally responsible," Robert wrote in 1867.[23] Yet Mary's money mania—mania to possess it and to spend it on material goods—began long before the assassination. Lincoln neighbor James Gourley told of how Mary added a second floor onto the Lincoln home in Springfield while her husband was away and without his consent, causing him to scold her for running him into debt.[24] Elizabeth Keckly called Mary "penny wise and pound foolish."[25]

Mary's sister, Elizabeth Edwards, who was intimately involved in the 1875 insanity episode, told Robert that Mary had a habit of reckless spending, stating "it has always been a prominent trait in her character, to accumulate a large amount of clothing."[26] Artist Francis B. Carpenter, who lived in the White House for six months while he painted a portrait of the first reading of the Emancipation Proclamation, said Mary "was extravagantly fond of dress, and had more gowns than opportunities to wear them."[27] In fact, Mary left the White House with fifty-five boxes of possessions, mostly old clothes—a quirk Robert did not understand and said he did not want to understand.[28] "I wish to heaven the car would take fire in which you place these boxes for transportation to Chicago, and burn all of your old plunder up," he said impetuously as she packed.[29]

Once Mary arrived in Washington in 1861, she had money and spent it. The White House was so shabby and run-down that she was granted a $20,000 congressional appropriation to refurbish it. She overspent the appropriation by $7,000, causing her husband to exclaim that he would never sign a bill to cover the extra expense. "It would stink in the nostrils of the American people to have it said that the President of the United States had approved a bill overrunning an appropriation of $20,000 for *flub dubs* for this damned old house, when the soldiers cannot have blankets," Lincoln reportedly said.[30] Historian Ruth Painter Randall deftly examined the pressure Mary was under to prove her worth as the First Lady of America through her social and domestic intercourse and achievements, noting that "as her strain and feeling of insecurity in the White House increased, [Mary] demanded more and more material things. Perhaps acquiring things served as a palliative. The urge to buy had become pathologic."[31] Mary's materialism was so pronounced (and denounced) that in May 1865, upon her departure from the White House, she was accused of stealing White House property, a charge she adamantly denied.[32]

Besides money troubles, Mary also gained a haughtier and more aristocratic air to her, causing both family and friends to dislike her. Horatio Nelson Taft, an examiner for the U.S. Patent Office and father of Willie and Tad's closest playmates, twice wrote in his diary about the frequency with which one saw Mary Lincoln seated in her carriage outside a merchant's store while the clerk brought goods out for her inspection. "Here is the carriage of Mrs. Lincoln before a dry goods Store, her footman has gone into the Store. The Clerk is just going out to the carriage (where Mrs. L is waiting) with some pieces of goods for her to choose from. I should rather think that she would have a better chance at the goods if she was to go into the Store but then she *might* get jostled and gazed at and that too would be doing just as the common people do."[33]

Mary even managed to alienate her closest and oldest friend, Mercy (Levering) Conkling, who wrote to her son in 1863, "I have just written a letter to Mrs. Lincoln. Only think of me writing to her *royal highness*."[34] Mary's sister, Ann Todd Smith, likened her sister's attitude to "Queen Victoria's Court."[35] Commissioner of Public Buildings Benjamin French called Mary Lincoln "The Queen," "The American Queen," and "'The Republican Queen' who plagues me half to death with wants with which it is impossible to comply"; and he once wrote to his brother, "The President is the very soul of honesty, honor, & openness of heart. Mrs. Lincoln is—Mrs. Lincoln, & nobody else, & like no other human being I ever saw. She is not easy to get along with."[36]

Immediately upon the death of Abraham Lincoln—and therefore the loss of Mary's social position, government appropriations, and her husband's presidential income—Mary expected, and actively lobbied through friends, Congress to compensate her loss. She earnestly solicited four years of presidential salary, but received just one year's worth—$25,000—which, after deductions, totaled about $22,000.[37] Congress granted even that grudgingly after the press disclosed that President Lincoln's estate was estimated to total $75,000.[38] Public subscriptions for the relief of Mary and the boys also fell flat due to popular notions of her supposed wealth, as well as the supposed thievery scandal of her last days in the White House.[39]

The Lincoln estate, however, was not only split into thirds between Mary and the boys but also was composed mostly of property and bonds, of which only the interest was paid to the beneficiaries. Mary and Robert each received about $1,500 per year, and Tad, as a minor, received only enough to pay for his expenses. With high prices and high inflation, this meager income forced the Lincolns to live in simple style in hotels and boarding houses, a predicament Mary Lincoln freely and frequently lamented in her letters.

Mary was not only humiliated by having to board but also angry that "roving Generals have elegant mansions, showered upon them, and the American people—leave the family of the Martyred President, to struggle as best they can!"[40] Mary still owned the Lincolns' house at the corner of Eighth and Jackson Streets in Springfield, Illinois, but refused to live there because of the painful memories it would bring back and the mental aggravation it would cause.[41] Mary did actually use most of her $22,000 to—rather impulsively—purchase a home at 375 West Washington Street in Chicago, although she was forced to vacate and rent it out after only one year once she realized the cost of maintaining a home was too much for her income.[42]

Mary also was plagued by debts she had contracted without her husband's knowledge while in the White House. Once Lincoln's estate estimate was published, creditors came calling. It is unknown exactly how much Mary owed for purchases of clothing and jewelry, but estimates range from $10,000 to $70,000.[43] Supposedly, just one of Mary's debts was $27,000 owed to A. T. Stewart's fabulous Marble Dry Goods Palace in New York City.[44] Mary at first tried to hide these debts from U.S. Supreme Court Associate Justice David Davis, the estate executor, and from her son Robert, but they soon discovered the truth. "All this is very mysterious to me," Robert wrote; in fact, Robert's congressional informant told him that the knowledge of Mary's debts had a "deleterious influence" on the House committee that decided the amount to give her.[45] Yet, to her credit, Mary liquidated the debt herself by returning many of the goods she had purchased on credit and paying off the rest.[46]

Besides the emotional pain and financial stress of life after the assassination, Mary also suffered a psychological strain. In 1865, as today, the curiosity of the press was unrelenting. They watched and reported on everything connected with the Lincoln family. "Anything, *we do* is seized on—an especial way, of 'being cared for, by the American people,'" Mary wrote in July 1865.[47] But a major blow occurred in November 1866 when William H. Herndon, Abraham Lincoln's former law partner, gave his now-famous lecture, "A. Lincoln—Miss Ann Rutledge, New Salem—Pioneering, and the poem called 'Immortality'—or 'Oh, Why Should the Spirit of Mortal Be Proud,'" in which he declared that Lincoln had never loved his wife, since Ann Rutledge was his one true love. Herndon also was preparing his next lecture in which he would declare Lincoln to be an atheist. Both of these he planned to include in his Lincoln biography.

Herndon's statements, buttressed by his position as Lincoln's professional partner for seventeen years, were widely accepted as fact. His statements humiliated and enraged Mary Lincoln. They threatened her with the intangible losses of identity, legacy, respect, and legitimacy. By saying Lincoln never loved her, Herndon robbed Mary not only of her legitimate connection to her husband (as martyr wife, heir to salary and pension, and ex-First Lady) but also of her last and final solace, namely, that she would be loved, happy, and carefree had Lincoln lived. As Mary wrote in December 1865, "The comfort of my early life, always, before my marriage & ever afterwards, that my husband, always told me & his actions all proved, that he had never thought or cared for anyone but myself . . . is some solace to me in my misery."[48]

Robert, head of the family and ever protective of his mother, also was angered. "Mr. Wm. H. Herndon is making an ass of himself in his lectures," Robert wrote when he found out. "I am getting seriously annoyed at his way of doing things."[49] He wrote to Herndon—twice—and asked that he carefully consider the contents of his lectures and his book so as not to "cause pain" to the Lincoln family. "Beyond this, I do not wish, nor have I any right, to go. Your opinion may not agree with mine but that is not my affair."[50] When Robert discovered that Herndon intended to examine Mary as deeply as Abraham in his biography of the war president, Robert wrote Herndon again, this time with a bit more fervor:

> I *infer* from your letter, but I hope it is not so, that it is your purpose to make some considerable mention of my mother in your work. I say I hope it is not so, because in the first place it would not be pleasant for her or for any woman, to be made public property of in that way. With a man it is very different, for he lives out in the world and is used to being talked of. One of the unpleasant consequences of political success is that however little it may have to do with that success, his whole private life is exposed to the public gaze. That is part of the price he pays. But I see no reason why his wife and children should be included—especially while they are alive. I think no sensible man would live in a glass house and I think he ought not to be compelled to do so against his will. I feel very keenly on the subject, for the annoyance I am subjected to sometimes is nearly intolerable. I hope you will consider this matter carefully, my dear Mr. Herndon, for once done there is no undoing.[51]

This letter offers some important insights into Robert Lincoln's central character, revealing his masculine, Victorian attitude as head of the family and protector of his mother and also his views on the proper social spheres for men and women. Perhaps most important, it emphasizes Robert's severe (and lifelong) aversion to public scrutiny and publicity—further evidence of his Victorian sense of dignity and family privacy. This letter also offers insight into Robert's motivations for his mother's 1875 trial. For a man as reticent as Robert Lincoln to take the very public act of declaring his mother insane in open court, his anxiety and belief in its necessity must have been dire indeed.

Perhaps the seminal turning point in Robert Lincoln's thinking about his mother, and another stepping-stone to the insanity trial, was what has become known as the Old Clothes Scandal of 1867. Mary Lincoln, believing herself destitute, abandoned, and without recourse, tried to sell some of her old White House gowns and jewelry in New York City under a pseudonym. Yet, not only did she seek to sell them, but she wrote letters to some of the men to whom her husband had given public offices and asked/urged them to purchase some of her articles to help relieve the want of their dead benefactor's widow. When these people refused, Mary's solicitors forwarded the letters to the press. Mary Lincoln's true identity was eventually found out, hardly anything was sold, but the sale and "bribe" attempts became a sort of carnival sideshow and were thoroughly derided in the newspapers as an embarrassment to the memory of the Great Emancipator.[52]

Of course, with Robert's aversion to publicity, especially as he was attempting to build a solid legal reputation and business in Chicago at that time, this incident caused quite a row within the family. "R came up last evening like a maniac, and almost threatening his life, looking like death, because the letters of the [*New York*] *World* were published in yesterday's paper. I could not refrain from weeping when I saw him so miserable." And yet, Mary still could not see what was so wrong about what she had done or why she should have to endure "a round of newspaper abuse . . . Because I dared venture to relieve a few of my wants."[53]

Further insight into Mary's mental health can be gleaned from a letter Robert wrote to his future wife, Mary Harlan, at the time of the scandal, which laid out with valuable prescience the situation he had to endure regarding his mother:

> I suppose you have seen some of the papers so there is no need of detailing what I was told they were full of. I did not read them. The simple truth, which I cannot tell anyone not personally interested, is that my mother is on one subject not mentally responsible. I have supposed this for some time from various indications and now have no doubt of it. I have taken the advice of one or two of my friends in whom I trust most and they tell me I can do nothing. It is terribly irksome to sit still under all that has happened and say nothing, but it has to be done. The greatest misery of all is the fear of what may happen in the future. This is, of course, not to be foreseen and is what troubles me most. I have no doubt that a great many good and amiable people wonder why I do not take charge of her affairs and keep them straight but it is very hard to deal with one who is sane on all subjects but one. You could hardly believe it possible, but my mother protests to me that she is in actual want and nothing I can do or say will convince her to the contrary. Do you see that I am likely to have a good deal of trouble in the future, do what I can to prevent it.[54]

This letter not only reflects Robert's fear over the future effects of his mother's money mania but also shows that he tried, at first, to let it alone. David Davis had a much simpler reaction to Mary's antics: "The selling

Mrs. Lincoln's Wardrobe on Exhibition in New York.—Sketched by Stanley Fox.

Contemporary sketch of the Old Clothes Scandal. Library of Congress, LC-USZ62-132451.

of her clothes was an act of insanity," he wrote. "On my remonstrance to her, she plead that she had to do so as she was in danger of becoming a pauper. She really had the insane delusion that poverty stared her in the face."[55] From a psychiatric standpoint, Mary's fear of poverty would in fact qualify as a delusion—a strongly held but erroneous idea that she could not be swayed from.

The press and the public considered the Old Clothes Scandal further proof that Mary was insane, a belief that had been floating about for some time.[56] Some even saw Mary's failed attempt at selling her jewelry and clothing as rooted in her inability—during and after her husband's life—to inspire either respect or confidence and felt that "had she borne herself becomingly, the suggestion of a Lincoln fund, by voluntary contributions, would have been promptly responded to."[57] Not only was it embarrassing and indiscreet—what one editorialist called "an ignoble spectacle . . . a spectacle to vulgarize a whole nation"[58]—but poorly timed. Merely one month later, David Davis finalized settlement of Abraham Lincoln's estate. Through Davis's deft management, $27,000 was added to its value, placing the final estate at slightly more than $110,000, of which Mary, Robert, and Tad each received nearly $37,000. This still was not enough for Mary to live as she wanted or as she felt she deserved, but it certainly augmented the public's negative reaction to her embarrassing behavior. In 1868, the day after Robert's wedding, Mary and Tad sailed for Europe, ostensibly for Mary's poor health, but more likely to escape the public scrutiny. She had lost her position, social standing, influence, money, husband, and, to some extent, her son Robert, who was now a married man.

While in Europe, Mary claimed she was charged excessive prices due to her identity.[59] By December 1868, she decided it would be proper for Congress to grant her a pension, considering that her husband, as commander-in-chief, died in service to the government and that she had insufficient money to live "in a style becoming to the widow of the Chief Magistrate of a great nation."[60] This was more problematic than receiving part of her husband's salary. First of all, it was unprecedented. No civilian, let alone the widow of a fallen president, had ever received a pension. But perhaps more damaging was Mary's reputation among Washington society: the people whom she had so often wronged during the war years now had power over her, and they did not hesitate to oppose her whims, most of them doing so vocally and vociferously. As Senator Simon Cameron from Pennsylvania said, "A great deal of opposition to this bill arises from prejudice—political prejudice and social prejudice, got up in this city . . . the ladies, and even the gentlemen, the gossips of the town, did all they could to make a bad reputation for Mrs. Lincoln."[61]

Senators generally opposed the pension bill because they thought it a bad precedent and believed Mary had plenty of money from her husband's estate.[62] Yet, for some, it was more personal. The report of the Committee on Pensions, led by the bill's strongest opponent, Senator George F. Edmunds of Vermont, somewhat cryptically remarked, "There are some other facts bearing upon this subject which it is probably not needful to refer to, but which are generally known, and evidence in respect to part of which is in the possession of the committee."[63] Former Illinois governor Richard Yates, who voted against the pension bill, more explicitly said, "Amid all the perils of life, amidst its devastation, amid good and evil report, a woman should be true to her husband."[64] Even her supporters did so out of respect for Abraham, rather than Mary, Lincoln. Mrs. Lincoln "may be indiscreet" and "may have forfeited a measure" of public respect, but "she is the widow of Lincoln," one New York senator remarked during debate.[65]

Mary's opponents dragged out the debate over her pension, causing the fight to last eighteen months. Her intense belief that she could not live without a pension, and her shame and outrage over its opposition, consumed Mary, fed her rapaciousness, and contributed to her irrational mental state. "I am passing a most painful time of anxiety," she wrote in December 1869, after execrating numerous senators and assessing her chances of a favorable vote despite the "dark army" of people opposed to her.[66] As with the presidential salary issue in 1865, Mary obsessively wrote dozens of letters to numerous people inquiring, raging, begging, and lamenting her struggle for a pension. Finally, after much delay and the indefatigable support of Senator Charles Sumner, Congress granted her a $3,000 annual pension, which was signed by President Grant on July 14, 1870.[67]

In Europe, Mary received the royal treatment she felt she deserved in America, being received by the most important and influential people on the Continent. While there, Mary became a grandmother with the birth of Robert's first child, Mary "Mamie" Lincoln, named after her paternal grandmother. Tad meanwhile studied in Germany and grew into a fine, intelligent young man. Yet, when Tad was not studying, his mother kept him with her at every moment. He was, as she later stated, "my inseparable companion," without whom "the world is complete darkness."[68] Tad's post-assassination life has never fully been examined and would be a most interesting study.[69] It is likely he was terribly lonely and incredibly stifled by his mother's fear-filled, unrelenting grip. Finally, Tad was so homesick that he convinced his mother to return to America and live with Robert in Chicago.[70] Mary was terrified of a steamship journey across the Atlantic, afraid that Tad would catch a fatal illness: "Each breath I drew would be a prayer for his safety, which only those who have been as deeply bereaved as myself could fully understand."[71]

Unfortunately for Mary, her fear proved correct. On the trip home in May 1871, Tad contracted a cold. His condition slowly worsened to the point where his lungs were so filled with fluid he had to sleep sitting up. After more than one month of constant attention and devotion by Mary and Robert, Tad, age seventeen, died from pleurisy, on July 15, 1871.[72] Tad's estate of approximately $37,000 was divided equally between his mother and older brother.[73]

Robert was so distraught over Tad's death that he took a month-long holiday to the West, at his doctor's direction.[74] For Mary, it was yet another despicable blow against her, beating her down when she had finally begun to recover from the traumatic loss of her husband. It once again confirmed her statement that "Ill luck presided at my birth—certainly within the last few years it has been a *faithful attendant*."[75] At the age of fifty-two, Mary had now lost to untimely deaths both her parents, three brothers and one brother-in-law during the Civil War, three sons, and a husband, and she had alienated nearly all of her remaining family and friends.[76] Tad had been her last devoted bastion of support. Her sole surviving son, Robert, had a wife and child of his own, as well as a law practice demanding his attention. While he was not lost to Mary, he could not give her the attention she needed and demanded. He tried to be a support for her, but in trying to do his filial duty, he nearly lost his own family. The solution left Mary feeling practically alone.

3 No Right to Remain upon Earth

THE FOUR YEARS FROM TAD'S DEATH in July 1871 to the insanity trial in May 1875 were the darkest, most pitiable period in Mary Lincoln's life. It was filled with overwhelming grief, loss, and incessant tears. Mary became a homeless wanderer, roaming North America, looking for physical healing at health spas and resorts, seeking sympathy from family and friends, but never finding or accepting relief or solace or peace. During this time, she clung tenaciously to her last remaining son, Robert, and to her friends Sally Orne and Myra Bradwell. She also delved deeper into Spiritualism and séances, still seeking comfort from people who claimed to bridge the living and spiritual worlds.

It was during this time that Mary's physical and emotional health deteriorated to the point that calling her simply "eccentric" was no longer viable. "From that time [of Tad's death], Mrs. Lincoln, in the judgment of her most intimate friends, was never entirely responsible for her conduct. She was peculiar and eccentric, and had various hallucinations," Isaac N. Arnold, a family friend and the lawyer who represented Mary at the 1875 insanity trial, later wrote.[1] Mary's personal nurse stated the widow suffered from "periods of mild insanity" and "had strange delusions" in the years between 1871 and 1875. She thought gas was the invention of the devil and often would use nothing but candles for lighting; at other times, she would draw the shades and sit in the darkened room.[2]

Mary's reaction to Tad's death was not outrageous, however, and was, in fact, considering her previous reactions to family deaths, much better than Robert expected, at first.[3] This may be why he felt it safe to leave her alone at his house in Chicago while he went to the Rocky Mountains for one month of doctor-recommended respite at the same time that his wife was in Iowa tending to her sick mother. Mary felt this solitude deeply and wrote about her loneliness in her letters.[4] Whether Robert was being kind, selfish, or apathetic with this leave-taking is unknown and undocumented, although Mary's letters from the period show no animosity toward him. In fact, Mary's tone suggests that she understood and sympathized with Robert's need for a retreat.

Problems, however, occurred once the entire family was back under one roof. Ever since Robert's marriage to Mary Harlan in 1868, Mary Todd Lincoln had been effusive in her praise and generosity toward the younger Lincolns. She gave them clothing, jewelry, artwork, furniture, and loans of money. Her letters are solidly and surely paeans to the goodness and nobleness of her son and daughter-in-law. "I am particularly blessed in my children" and "my lovely young daughter-in-law, who is just as dear to me, as if she were my own child," Mary wrote in December 1869.[5] In 1868, Mary paid Robert the highest possible compliment she could utter by comparing him to his father, whom Mary lauded to apotheosis. "Robert grows every day, more and more like his father, & is a very beautiful character"; and in May 1871, she called Robert "all that is noble and good," while her daughter-in-law's "warm heart has always been mine."[6] These are just two examples of the several letters in which Mary professes an abiding love and pride in her eldest son and his wife.[7]

Mary's best and favorite way to show affection—springing from her own mania for acquiring material goods—was to shower her children with gifts. Letters from Mary Lincoln to Mary Harlan repeatedly tell the younger woman to take or use anything in her mother-in-law's house or storage. "*Anything* and *everything* is yours. . . . It will be such a relief to me to know that articles can be used and enjoyed by you," she wrote in March 1869, and "never purchase *any thing* you can find there" (referring to her house at 375 West Washington Street), she wrote six months later.[8] Besides giving the younger Lincolns her own possessions, Mary also bought them numerous items of clothing, furniture, and silverware while she traveled Europe. Mary also was generous with her money. When Tad died, she gave Robert half of his brother's estate, even though she only had to give him one-third; likewise, she loaned Robert money for speculative ventures and gave, or promised to give, him money from the sale of her house and after receiving her pension.[9] The Robert Lincolns accepted Mary's gifts sometimes willingly and sometimes grudgingly. Robert once even wrote they were "frightened" by the ostentation of some baby clothes Mary had sent, to which his mother resentfully replied that it was "not too much, for people in *our station* of life."[10]

All the gifts and letters from Mary in this period show that she and Robert were on extremely good terms. The younger Lincolns welcomed Mary into their home and into their hearts, and there was no animosity or indifference in their feelings. "I often hear from Robert and Mary," Mary wrote from France in 1868, "the latter writes me often calling me 'Dear Mother—' and says she is so happy. Wonders whether I am not almost ready to return to them."[11] Once Mary and Tad did return to America in early 1871, Mary stated, "We have received so much affection here. . . . Robert . . . and his lovely little wife will not hear of our removal."[12] The younger Lincolns repeatedly tried to draw Mary out of her cocoon of self-pity and sadness to help her enjoy life.

Before and during Tad's illness, Mary Lincoln was often a guest at the younger Lincolns' home, so it was only natural that, in the midst of her grief over Tad's death, and because she had no home of her own, she should stay with her son and his family. Tad's death, however, unhinged her and made her such a difficult houseguest that Robert had to "break up housekeeping"—a Victorian-era euphemism meaning his wife took the children and left until he got rid of his mother.[13] After Mary Harlan Lincoln's return home, the elder Mary became angry at her "for some trifle," Robert explained, "and they have never met since but when my wife has sent our children to see her, she has driven my servants out of the room by her insulting remarks concerning her mistress & this in the presence of my little girl."[14] This created yet more losses for Mary Todd Lincoln, a self-created loss of the daughter she never had, less access to her granddaughter, and a tension in the family for Robert's affections.

No records exist of how or when Mary left Robert's home, but by summer 1872, Mary was visiting health resorts in Wisconsin and later in Canada.[15] Mary's poor physical health was always one of her most conspicuous traits, particularly the migraines she suffered her entire life. Her physical deterioration after the death of a loved one or during an adverse time (such as her pension battle) does make one wonder, however, exactly how closely tied her physical condition was to her mental condition.[16] Her precarious health declined after the assassination, improved somewhat in the late 1860s when she was in Europe, and then deteriorated even more after Tad's death. Mary's letters between 1865 and 1875 are replete with references to severe indispositions, such as weak nerves, migraines, chills, boils, joint pains, incontinence, swelling, insomnia, melancholia, and fatigue. While there is no doubt she suffered from physical ailments, she seems to have been something of a hypochondriac and to have used her illness to garner attention and sympathy, even to create her own martyrdom to parallel that of her husband, perhaps in an attempt to continue, at some level, her association with him.[17]

One of Mary's most historically contentious attributes, besides her mental state, was her belief in Spiritualism. Spiritualism was the belief in the continuity of life into the afterlife; that the dead could communicate with the living through someone acting as a medium, with the communication often consisting of rapping and knocking sounds, table tipping, automatic speech, and automatic writing.[18] Spiritualists often consisted of the grieved and the gullible, seeking connections to lost loved ones.[19] Spiritualism began near Rochester, New York, in 1848 when the Fox sisters claimed they first heard and then later were able to "decode" the rapping sounds made by spirits. Spiritualism burgeoned during the Civil War, when there was so much death and loss, and by the 1890s, the movement claimed eleven million followers.[20] The movement was more often than not derided in the press as either a scam by con artists or a practice of insane people, and its reputation took a hit when the Fox sisters admitted in 1888 that their work was a hoax.[21]

Mary Lincoln began her attachment to Spiritualism in 1862, hoping to connect with her beloved son Willie.[22] She visited Spiritualists in George-town and invited them to the White House.[23] While President Lincoln did attend a few of these séances, he was not a Spiritualist; explanations for his attendance include simple curiosity, a desire to protect his gullible wife, and the enjoyment of an amusing distraction from his cares.[24] After the assassination, Mary continued visiting mediums, and then again after Tad's death. In Boston, she visited spiritual photographer William H. Mumler, recently acquitted of fraud, where she had the now-famous photograph taken showing President Lincoln's ghost behind her with hands on her shoulders.[25] She is said to have visited Moravia, New York, where she saw "twenty-two different spirit faces—among the rest, that of her son Tad."[26] Her visit to the health spa at Waukesha, Wisconsin, in 1872 also was used to visit area Spiritualists, as was a visit to St. Charles and Batavia, Illinois (site of Bellevue Sanitarium).[27]

Mary Lincoln took Spiritualist teachings and blended them with her faith in a Christian afterlife to create her own belief system. As she told Charles Sumner in July 1865, "My belief, is so assured, that Death, is only a blessed transition, to the 'pure in heart,' that a very slight veil separates us, from the 'loved & lost' and to me, there is comfort, in the thought, that though unseen by us, they are very near."[28] Four years later Mary wrote, "I am not EITHER a Spiritualist—but I sincerely believe—our loved ones, who have only, 'gone before' are permitted to watch over those who were dearer to them than life" and that she knew her husband watched over her. "I should have lost my reason long ere this—if I had entertained *other* views, than I do, on this subject."[29]

During the 1870s, Spiritualism had both adherents and opponents, although the popular mind, as evidenced in the press, seemed to regard it negatively. Many people considered Spiritualists to be deluded or in-sane, and, in fact, not long before Mary Lincoln's insanity trial, the Supreme Court of Maine tried a case in which the judges considered

William H. Mumler "spirit" photograph of Mary Todd Lincoln, circa 1870–1875. Courtesy of the College of Psychic Studies.

whether Spiritualism was, in the legal sense, an insane delusion.[30] Robert Lincoln and David Davis, with their rational legal and scientific minds, appeared to believe Spiritualism a scam, a ruse by shysters to rob Mary of her money.[31] They certainly would have agreed, as one newspaper story stated, "Given a credulous old woman, sixty thousand gold sovereigns, and a favored medium, and the result [of thievery] is a certainty."[32] President Lincoln may have allowed séances in the White House, but when female Spiritualists came to the White House after his assassination to pour "into [Mary's] ears pretended messages from her dead husband," Robert Lincoln was less forgiving than his father and ordered them out of the Executive Mansion.[33] There is evidence that Robert and Davis, as well as many other people, later thought Mary's belief in Spiritualism contributed to her mental illness.[34]

During this time of wandering, Mary kept in touch with Robert, whom she had no obvious animosity toward, despite the break with his wife, and who, in 1873, had his second child, Abraham Lincoln II, nicknamed "Jack" by the family. Robert was by this time so concerned about his mother's health and solitary lifestyle that he hired a nurse to stay with her as assistant and companion.[35] Mary also turned more to her friends Sally Orne, Eliza Slataper, Rhoda White, and David and Elizabeth Swing. Orne, in particular, was Mary's closest friend, whom she once called "in her kindness and sympathy . . . an angel of light to me."[36] These friends were loyal when the rest of the country seemingly had turned its back on her. Mary desperately needed and eagerly, even pathetically, sought their commiseration and sympathy. Her letters to them are full of catharsis. They were surrogates for the buffer between Mary and society that Abraham Lincoln had once been. The two people who superceded nearly all others, however, and became so integral to the later insanity period—in fact, to Mary's entire life—were Myra and James Bradwell. Of this couple, Mary once allegedly stated, "When all others, among them my husband's supposed friends, failed me in the most bitter hours of my life, these loyal hearts, Myra and James Bradwell, came to my assistance and rescued me under great difficulty from confinement in an insane asylum."[37]

James B. Bradwell was a Chicago attorney who had served two terms as a Cook County judge and was, in 1875, a member of the state legislature. Mary Lincoln once characterized him as "a just, good man & a lover of *truth*."[38] His wife, Myra Colby Bradwell, was an abolitionist, feminist, woman-suffragist, and founder and editor of the *Chicago Legal News*. She had passed the Illinois bar exam with high honors in 1869 but had been denied a license to practice law by the Illinois bar because she was a married woman. Both the Illinois Supreme Court and the U.S. Supreme Court upheld the denial.[39]

Exactly when Mary Lincoln met the Bradwells is unknown. Some historians claim the earliest known contact was around 1867, when the families became Chicago neighbors and James Bradwell examined the lease of Mary's house, although other historians begin the relationship around 1872, when James Bradwell drew Mary's will.[40] The newly discovered Lincoln–Bradwell correspondence and the unpublished manuscript of the Bradwell's granddaughter, Myra Helmer Pritchard, however, offer new facts about the length and depth of the friendship.[41] Mary Lincoln's house at 375 West Washington Street in Chicago, which she purchased in 1866, was "near her friends," the Bradwells, Pritchard wrote, intimating a previous association. Pritchard further stated that after the crushing blow of Tad's death in July 1871, Mary "spent evening after evening" at the Bradwell home, "being tenderly comforted" by Myra Bradwell, deepening their friendship.[42]

Further evidence uncovered in the Pritchard family papers offers an even earlier date for the friendship. Eleanor Gridley, a longtime friend of the Bradwells and later biographer of Abraham Lincoln, stated in a signed affidavit that the Bradwells had a "long and intimate acquaintance with Abraham Lincoln and his wife, Mary Todd Lincoln, both before and after he became President of the United States," and that the Bradwells often would tell her the details of that acquaintance.[43] Gridley made a similar public statement a few years later, claiming Abraham and Mary Lincoln "often visited the Bradwell home, and they, in turn, were frequent visitors of the Lincolns."[44] There is no corroboration for Gridley's statement, however, and, in fact, nowhere else is a friendship between the Bradwells and Abraham Lincoln ever mentioned in writings about either family.[45]

The earliest known letter between Mary and the Bradwells—found in Robert's Insanity File—is one to James Bradwell from October 1872. The letter seemingly, but not explicitly, provided instructions for Mary's will.[46] The earliest existing letter from Mary Lincoln to Myra Bradwell, found among the newly discovered Lincoln–Bradwell correspondence and dated November 1, 1872, is a short note wondering at Myra Bradwell's neglect of her friend and requesting "one of our old fashioned chats together."[47] By January 1873, Mary's health prevented her from a planned visit to Mrs. Bradwell, but she hoped to see her soon. "You cannot begin to know what a treat it is for me to hear you converse and be near you," Mary wrote.[48]

By July 1873, Mary, with James Bradwell as her legal adviser, had finalized her last will and testament, which divided her estate between Robert and his children.[49] (This will, which was never probated and has never before been seen by anyone outside the Bradwell family, is discussed in chapter 9.) Mary's creation of a will in 1873, when she was age fifty-four, may have stemmed from a desire not to die intestate, as had her husband, yet her belief in Spiritualism cannot be overlooked here.

Newly uncovered evidence shows that Mary, guided by "contact" with the spirit world, believed she would die in early September 1874 and was preparing for that death.[50] In January 1874, she wrote to James Bradwell to amend her will, stating, "I feel that I cannot rest, until it is done—My time now growing very short, *entre nous*, for leaving."[51] Then, in August 1874, she wrote to her son Robert with instructions for her funeral and burial, "Being fully impressed with the idea, that my stay on Earth, is growing very short."[52] This delusional belief in a fixed date of death seems likely to have been the result of psychiatric illness; either her illness created these thoughts, which she then attributed to the Spiritualist experience, or her illness made her more susceptible to the visions of a Spiritualist communicator.

After losing nearly everyone she loved, having alienated not only her sisters but now too her daughter-in-law, and with her health seemingly failing, Mary Lincoln's troubles began to manifest more profoundly. By 1873, she began to receive fairly constant medical care from Dr. Willis Danforth, one of Chicago's leading physicians, for fever and nervous derangement of the head.[53] It is known from Mary's letters and Danforth's trial testimony that Mary's symptoms included the continuing physical complaints of severe headaches, joint and muscle pains, incontinence, swelling, and insomnia; and her mental symptoms worsened to a general debility of the nervous system, anxiety, melancholia, hallucinations, and persecution complexes.

Specifically, as to her hallucinations, Mary told Danforth that an Indian spirit was removing and replacing her scalp, removing the bones from her face, and pulling wires out of her eyes; that someone was taking steel springs from her head and would not let her rest. She said her husband's spirit told her she was going to die "in a few days." She heard raps on the table conveying the time of her death and would sit and ask questions and repeat the supposed answer the table would give. When Danforth expressed doubt about what answers the table could give, she performed a final test by putting the question in a goblet on the table. The goblet was found to be cracked, a circumstance she regarded as corroboration of the table raps. Danforth said these symptoms "were indications of mental disturbance."[54]

Mary's medical treatment at this time is not entirely clear. Typical treatments for her physical symptoms included soaking in the regenerative waters of health spas, bed rest and quiet, and paregoric; typical treatments for her mental symptoms included chloral hydrate, bromide of potassium, opium, and cannabis, or various combinations of these.[55] Little is known about what specific medications she took, either with or without a prescription. It is known that she used chloral hydrate and laudanum.[56] One of Mary's newly discovered letters stated her doctor gave her "sugar pellets and harmless draughts."[57] In another recently uncovered letter, Mary asks Danforth for "4 more powders," after she "took the 5 you left" the previous night.[58] The letter does not specify the substance of the powders, but Illinois state historian Thomas F. Schwartz has surmised it was chloral hydrate, a popular Gilded Age sedative used to treat insomnia, nervousness, and tension, since Mary complained of "excessive wakefulness."[59]

Schwartz called this letter the first written proof of Mary's possible chemical dependence, which has been theorized for years but never proven.[60] There is a difference between physical dependence and psychological dependence on medications, however, and the known facts strongly suggest Mary had no physical addiction to chloral hydrate or any other drug.[61] Danforth, being a homeopathic physician, most likely would not have used medications at full strength, since the basic principle of homeopathy was extreme dilution of medication, which was believed to increase therapeutic potency.[62]

Investigation into the historical uses and effects of chloral hydrate not only disputes the addiction theory but also the contention that her use of chloral created her March insanity episode.[63] Chloral hydrate was first synthesized in 1832, but began its popularity in American asylums in the late 1860s to early 1870s. The first major study of the effects and therapeutic use of the drug was published in 1871 by Dr. J. B. Andrews, assistant physician at the New York State Lunatic Asylum. Andrews found that chloral was one of the best remedies available for certain nervous afflictions, such as mania, melancholia, dementia, paresis, and epilepsy; and, unlike opium and cannabis, it was not addictive.[64] Typical doses ranged anywhere from 15 to 60 grains per day, sometimes twice per day.[65] Chloral generally produced "profound sleep" and "allayed excitement."

Andrews reported the advantages of chloral being that it produced natural sleep from which one easily could be aroused, it was easily tolerated by the stomach and bowels, it did not injure the appetite or produce headaches, and it did not lose power by repetition. Ill effects of the drug included nausea, vomiting, and a burning sensation in the stomach if not diluted. Later studies upheld Andrews's findings.[66] Mary Lincoln's ingestion of five grains of chloral (if, in fact, it was chloral) in one night is not suggestive of dependence or addiction. Likewise, during her entire stay at Bellevue Sanitarium, she was never diagnosed or treated for severe withdrawal symptoms.[67] As for her having a psychological addiction to her medications, there is no evidence for or against such a theory.

In the midst of Mary's worsening mental state in December 1873 came the reemergence of William Herndon and his spectacular assertions about the private life of Abraham Lincoln. Whereas Herndon claimed in his 1871 lectures that Lincoln never loved his wife, in 1873 he claimed, citing his own interview with Mary Lincoln, that his former law partner had been an atheist.[68] Such an assertion mortified and enraged both Mary and Robert Lincoln, not just because it was a lie but also because disbelief in God was anathema to society's religious standards of the time.[69] One of Mary's biographers, Jean Baker, made the salient point that not only was it a low blow to Lincoln's legacy but also cut to the core of Mary's deeply held Spiritualist belief that Lincoln watched over her from the afterlife. If Lincoln did not believe in Heaven, as Herndon stated, then his spirit could not be protecting Mary, and if he was not there, then Mary was alone and without comfort.[70]

Mary's response to Herndon was first to deny the interview ever occurred, then to admit it, but call Herndon a liar.[71] Herndon slyly refused to condemn Mary but used her own words against her.[72] Coming on the heels of so much other tragedy and loss for Mary, Herndon's attack was incredibly damaging to her both personally and publicly. Herndon's friend William Jayne wrote in admiration, "In this affair with the 'First Lady of the Land' you did not like a clodhopper call her a d——d old liar . . . but like a courtly gentleman and lawyer you say that the good poor woman crushed beneath a mountain of woe, with her bruised heart and failing memory, she is not altogether a competent & trustworthy witness." Jayne continued, "I have heard no two opinions about this denial—every one I have heard speak of it pities the woman for again obtruding herself before the public."[73] Chauncey F. Black, who was the ghostwriter for Ward H. Lamon's *Life of Abraham Lincoln* (written from Herndon's Lincoln materials), similarly believed Herndon's response to be "in good tone and temper," and that "The old lady shows a great deal of temerity in obtruding herself into this controversy."[74]

Mary's losses continued upon the death of her friend Senator Charles Sumner in early 1874. Sumner had been a reliable friend to Mary during the war and after, and he, sometimes alone, championed her pension fight in the Congress. "I have lost my dearest & best friend," she wrote upon hearing of his death. "Since my ties to this world are so rapidly being severed . . . I sometimes feel, as if I had *no* right to remain upon earth."[75]

Interestingly, a previously unknown letter from Mary Lincoln to Myra Bradwell, dated February 20, 1875, shows no indication of any mental troubles. Mary was by this time traveling south with her nurse to spend the winter in Jacksonville, Florida. The letter's five hundred words rationally discuss her travels, her health, and the weather. "I am now looking down upon a yard with its roses, white lilacs and other flowers. (Although it is raining and we have had a good deal of rain in its soft, dreamy, light fashion,) since the middle of January, I remained too much out, on my balcony, took a severe cold, had much inward and outward fever for three weeks and one day when it was raging at its height I told my nurse to pack up a small trunk and valise and we would leave town," Mary began.[76] Of course, Robert Lincoln always said that his mother could appear at times perfectly normal and at other times completely irrational, but with that letter came the onset of Mary's self-proclaimed "season of sadness": the anniversaries of her sons Willie's and Eddie's February deaths and her husband's April murder.[77] While Abraham Lincoln was assassinated on Good Friday, which fell on April 14 in 1865, in 1875 Good Friday was on March 26.

No historical evidence is known to exist to explain Mary's feelings or movements between that February letter and early March. But by March 12, Mary suddenly became convinced that Robert was deathly ill, and she would not be persuaded otherwise. She sent a telegram to Robert's law partner inquiring after her son's health, stating she would start for Chicago immediately; ninety minutes later, she sent a second telegram: "My dearly beloved son Robert T. Lincoln rouse yourself and live for my sake all I have is yours from this hour. I am praying every moment for your life to be spared to your mother."[78] Robert telegraphed the station manager to discretely inquire "if Mrs. Abraham Lincoln now at Jacksonville is in any trouble mentally or otherwise." The manager responded that Mary appeared "nervous and somewhat excited," and that her nurse "thinks [she] should be at home as soon as possible."[79] Meanwhile Mary telegraphed Robert again, "Start for Chicago this evening hope you are better today you will have money on my arrival."[80] Upon hearing of his mother's anxiety, her nervousness, and her illogical actions, and seeing once again her mania about money and possessions—even to the point of trying to bribe him to live through his supposed illness—Robert knew what was happening; it was the culmination he had feared and predicted for eight years.

4 *Of Unsound Mind*

WHEN MARY ARRIVED IN CHICAGO, she "seemed startled" that a perfectly healthy Robert met her at the station.[1] He asked her to come stay at his house, but she declined since she and Robert's wife still were estranged. Instead, they went to the Grand Pacific Hotel to secure her a room and to have supper. After Mary told Robert that a man had poisoned her coffee on the train ride north, Robert decided to take a room for himself as well. He slept at the hotel, in a room next to Mary's, every night for more than two weeks.[2]

Mary slept well the first night, but most every night thereafter she was restless and would knock on Robert's door, often because she was afraid of being alone. Twice in one night, she knocked on his door and eventually asked to sleep in his room. Robert gave her the bed, and he slept on the lounge. After that, Robert called Dr. Ralph N. Isham, his personal physician, to attend his mother. Around April 1, Mary became increasingly paranoid and agitated. That morning, she tried to go downstairs in the elevator half-dressed. Robert called the elevator back and sought to induce Mary to return to her room, an interference she regarded as "impertinent." When she refused to leave the elevator, Robert, with the help of a hotel employee, "gently forced her out," to which she screamed, "You are going to murder me!" Back in her room, Mary said that the "wandering Jew" who had taken her pocketbook on the train in March would return it at three o'clock.[3] She also sat near the wall and for an hour professed to be repeating what this man was telling her through the wall.

During the afternoon, Mary approached the hotel manager, Samuel Turner, and said "something was wrong with the house," that she "heard strange sounds" in her room and was afraid to be alone. She told him the city was on fire on the South Side and then made him take her to every room with a "7" in its number in search of a Mr. Shoemaker.[4] Turner took her back upstairs and said he would return in fifteen minutes. Five minutes later, she was back downstairs, repeating her fears and saying that a strange man in the corridor was "going to molest her." She asked to stay in some other female boarder's room to be safe. Turner left her in the room of a Mrs. Dodge until she returned from dinner, but shortly thereafter he was summoned to the room where Mary's "appearance was wild and her fears were repeated." Turner concluded she was "deranged" and did not consider it safe to leave her alone. That night, Mary knocked on Robert's hotel room door so many times that he told her he would leave the hotel if she persisted.

Other hotel employees also witnessed Mary's bizarre behavior during the month of April. The hotel housekeeper, Mrs. Allen, who spent two nights in Mary's room, reported that Mary was "excited, agitated, restless and nervous" and that the widow said a small window in her room "boded ill" and "disturbed her."[5] Mrs. Allen also saw Mary "mix several kinds of medicine together." Hotel employee Maggie Gavin, who took care of Mary's room and slept with the widow in her room for four weeks, witnessed similar events. She said Mary was anxious about her son and extremely restless at night and often would pace the floor or go to Robert's room out of fear. Gavin said Mary would "complain frequently that people were speaking to her through the wall" or the floor and would call Gavin's attention to the voices. Mary also would point to nearby chimney smoke and say that the city was burning down.

Robert also experienced his mother's fear of fire, about which the physicians later would warn him. He said that since the Great Fire of Chicago in 1871, his mother had kept her trunks and property in the Fidelity Safe Deposit Company's building. In late April, however, Mary became convinced that all Chicago was going to be burned, except Robert's house, and declared that she intended to send her trunks to Milwaukee. Robert suggested that if his house were to be spared, then it would be the best storage place. Mary sent eleven trunks to Milwaukee at the end of April, however, although she told the United States Express Company agent she was going to summer in Wisconsin. The agent said he thought "her manner was very strange."

Other strange incidents at this time included one in which Mary, "carelessly dressed and excited," asked second waiter John FitzHenry to call the tallest man in the dining room to her, only to exclaim, "I am afraid, I am afraid!" Cashier Charles Dodge corroborated this story and said Mary told him a stranger had been in her room and she was afraid he would molest her.[6]

Mary's materialist mania was a keystone of the trial and was, in fact, one of Robert's major pieces of evidence of her insanity—the fact that she wasted her money (money she perpetually complained of not having) on items that she never used nor wore. Five Chicago merchants testified as to Mary's large and "reckless" purchases during the more than ten weeks between her arrival in March and the day of the hearing in mid-May. She bought $600 worth (forty pairs) of lace curtains, three watches costing $450, $700 worth of jewelry, $200 worth of soaps and perfumes, and a whole piece of silk.[7] Robert thought them all useless, since she had no home to decorate and never wore anything but black clothing without jewelry, so he returned most of the items.[8] Hotel employees Mrs. Allen and Maggie Gavin both saw Mary's closet bulging with unopened packages. Mary's mania for hoarding was also evidenced by Robert's discovery of numerous carpetbags filled with nothing but carpet-covered footstools.[9]

Dr. Willis Danforth, who had treated Mary in 1873–74, visited her around May 12, at which time she repeated to him what she had told Robert: that she was poisoned on the train ride from Florida to Chicago. Danforth examined her and found no evidence of her ingesting any poison.

Robert Lincoln may have been anxious about his mother's behavior, but having been concerned about her irrationalities since his father's assassination, he was not unprepared for it. The day of his mother's arrival in Chicago, Robert wrote to his cousin, Lizzie Grimsley Brown, who was one of only two family members with whom Mary still communicated. He informed her of the situation and sounded her out about possibly coming to Chicago to stay with Mary. Robert wrote that he had "anticipated trouble," although he was hopeful that it would "blow over," as his mother's past episodes had.[10] "I will hold myself in readiness to answer your summons promptly," Brown replied. "I can imagine your fears & sympathize with you."[11]

Unfortunately, the trouble did not blow over, and Mary's condition deteriorated. By early May, Robert "was so distressed in mind that I did not dare to trust to or act upon my own judgment," he later recalled.[12] He called in Dr. Isham and Dr. Danforth to examine his mother and, presumably, to diagnose her. He also consulted Dr. Richard J. Patterson, proprietor of Bellevue Place Sanitarium in Batavia, Illinois, and one of the region's leading mental health experts, on April 10.[13] He consulted U.S. Supreme Court Justice David Davis, who had been Abraham Lincoln's friend, colleague, presidential campaign manager, and executor of Lincoln's estate, and whom Robert considered a "second father."[14] He also consulted John Todd Stuart, who was mayor of Springfield, Illinois, Abraham Lincoln's first law partner, and Mary Lincoln's cousin. Stuart was, along with Lizzie Brown, the other family member with whom Mary Lincoln still communicated.[15]

At the suggestion of Judge Davis, Robert consulted Chicago attorney Leonard Swett, one of the premier trial lawyers of the Midwest and also a close friend, colleague, and confidant of Abraham Lincoln. "He has more resources than most men, indeed I know no one who has more," Davis wrote to Robert.[16] The addition of Swett into Robert's confidence had a major impact on later events concerning Mary Lincoln, but also in Robert's life.[17] Davis, Stuart, and Swett each had known Mary Lincoln for more than twenty years and had spoken and visited with her both before and after the assassination. Mary Lincoln once wrote to a friend that she hoped Robert "may be so fortunate, as to become well acquainted with the friends, whom his father, loved so much."[18] This hope came to fruition in early 1875, and Robert did nothing without consulting these advisers. As he later explained, "Whatever was done then was done not upon my own judgment alone nor by myself done but upon the most thorough consultation with and [illegible] consideration of the persons who I felt were nearest my father, to [my mother] and to me and to whom under the distressing circumstances I could and ought to trust for counsel and assistance."[19]

Robert, Davis, and Stuart then had "a protracted consultation" about Mary's condition and what should be done.[20] All agreed that the widow was insane, had become a danger to herself, and needed personal restraint and medical care. Stuart not only expressed that he had "no doubt" that Mary was insane but added that "Cousin Lizzie Brown" and "all [Mary's] relatives" in Springfield had the same opinion.[21]

Robert's concerns were multifaceted. Of course, he, Davis, and Stuart considered her sick and in need of medical treatment. Most importantly, however, they feared for Mary's personal safety. Her erratic actions and distracted mind made her susceptible to injury or death for any number of reasons at any time. Specifically, they knew she carried $57,000 in bonds and cash in her pockets, and they worried about her being injured or murdered by someone attempting to steal it. They also feared the loss of Mary's money and property to con men, or what were then called "sharpers." Robert and Davis knew that Mary consulted frequently with Spiritualists, whom they considered nothing but thieves preying on the gullible. For Mary's protection, Robert hired the Pinkerton National Detective Agency, whose "sole duty" was to have a man watch his mother as a sort of guardian "when she went out on the street."[22]

It has been suggested that the motivations of Robert Lincoln, David Davis, and Leonard Swett (for some reason historians have excluded John Todd Stuart) were injudicious at best; cruel, calculated, and ignominious at worst; that Robert sought his mother's commitment in order to steal her money and possessions—or at least to prevent her from giving away or selling her money and possessions and thereby preserve his future in-

Robert T. Lincoln, circa 1875. Library of Congress, LC-BH826-1900.

heritance—and that all three men were so embarrassed by her behavior that they wanted to get rid of her.[23] One theory even accused Davis and Swett of manipulating Robert into committing his mother in order to embarrass him sufficiently to destroy his political future and advance their own.[24] Such views ignore not only the evidence and the clear concern expressed in all the correspondence but also the sociohistorical context of the time.

Robert Lincoln was, as discussed in chapter 2, a product of his generation, a thoroughly Victorian gentleman who deeply revered and felicitously followed the manly tenets of duty and honor. Often the obligations of duty required a man to act against his own will. For Robert, as head of the Lincoln family, it was his duty to care for and protect his mother. The constant refrain in his letters during the entire year of the insanity episode was that all his actions were part of his duty to his mother. As he wrote to his aunt, "Rightly or wrongly I consider that I alone must assume the entire and absolute charge of her unfortunate situation and I must deal with it as my condition allows me to do. I am alone held responsible & I cannot help it. . . . I have done my duty as I best know and Providence must take care of the rest."[25] Davis also encouraged Robert's submission to duty, as when he counseled in November 1875, "You cannot escape responsibility if you wanted to, and it would be esteemed by the world bad conduct if you should try. The trouble is on you & would not let you alone even (to suppose an impossible case) you were willing & should."[26]

This opinion of "bad conduct" by society was another weight on Robert's mind. It was his duty to care for his family, and to ignore his mother's vagaries would be to fail to do his duty, which would make him appear less than the manly ideal in the eyes of his peers. By 1875, *masculinity* had entered the social lexicon and begun to represent the way men sought to describe and explain their social roles. Between 1865 and 1890, according to one social historian, "men approached all the issues that men face—physical, educational, domestic and social issues—with a new sense of having to present themselves as manly, and a clear sense of how unmanly they would be considered if they did not measure up."[27] One newspaper later opined on Robert's actions, "There was reason to apprehend that in [Mary Lincoln's] restless, troubled state of mind she might have received personal injury, and at last, when longer delay would really be cruelty and neglect of duty, her son was compelled to the painful proceeding."[28] This belief in manly duty was ubiquitous. Both David Davis and Leonard Swett believed it was their duty, as friends of Abraham Lincoln, to help Robert and Mary through their time of difficulty.[29] Isaac

Arnold, a friend of Abraham Lincoln's and the man who defended Mary during her trial, also considered it his duty to Lincoln and to the law to act on Mary's behalf in court, even though he considered her insane.[30]

So it was with this mind-set then that Robert sought advice from his father's—and mother's—most trusted friends and then from seven of the most distinguished physicians in Illinois. On Sunday, May 16, at the office of B. F. Ayer, one of the most prominent members of the Chicago bar, who would represent Robert at the insanity trial, a meeting was held to determine the state of Mary Lincoln's mental health.[31] Present were Robert, Swett, Ayer, and six physicians: Ralph N. Isham, Hosmer Allen Johnson, Charles Gilman Smith, Robert J. Patterson, Nathan Smith Davis, and James Stewart Jewell.[32]

Dr. Ralph N. Isham was Robert's personal physician. Born in Herkimer County, New York, in 1831, he learned medicine through apprenticeship and interning. He moved to Chicago in 1855 and four years later helped found the Chicago Medical College (which later became the Medical School of Northwestern University). During the Civil War, he was the surgeon in charge of the Marine Medical Hospital in Chicago. After the war, he became first surgeon of the Cook County Hospital and the Passavant Memorial Hospital. He also was the consulting surgeon on the staff of the Presbyterian Hospital. Isham accomplished these many responsibilities while conducting his own office practice.[33]

Dr. Hosmer Allen Johnson and Dr. Charles Gilman Smith had both helped treat Tad Lincoln during his final illness in 1871. Mary once characterized them as "two excellent physicians."[34] Johnson was a graduate of Chicago's Rush Medical College and later professor of medical jurisprudence.[35] Smith first attended Harvard Medical School and then the University of Pennsylvania, from which he graduated. In 1853, he moved to Chicago, where he practiced family medicine; and during the Civil War, he was one of six physicians in charge of the prisoners at Camp Douglas, Illinois. In 1868, Smith went abroad to study medicine in the hospitals of France, Germany, and England. On his return to Chicago, he lectured at the Women's Medical College and was a consulting physician at the Women's and Children's Hospital and at the Presbyterian Hospital.[36]

Dr. Robert J. Patterson was one of the Midwest's leading mental health experts. He had been medical superintendent of both the Indiana and Iowa State Hospitals for the Insane, as well as a professor of medical jurisprudence at Chicago Medical College. In 1875, he was proprietor and superintendent of Bellevue Place Sanitarium in Batavia, Illinois.[37]

Dr. Nathan Smith Davis is known as the "Father of the American Medical Association," which he founded in 1847 at age thirty, and served as its president in 1864–65. He received his medical training at the Medical College of Western New York and was awarded his degree in January 1837, just a few days past his twentieth birthday. In 1844, Davis was elected to serve in the New York Medical Society, where he worked to improve medical education and licensure. In 1849, he accepted a professorship in physiology and pathology at Rush Medical College in Chicago. He was a founder of the Chicago Medical College (along with Ralph N. Isham), the Chicago Academy of Sciences, and the Washingtonian Home for the Reformation of Inebriates. Davis was an expert on the nervous system, the lungs, and the connection between alcoholism and insanity. During his career, he published numerous papers in medical journals and served as editor of the *Chicago Medical Examiner*, the *Northwestern Journal*, and the *Journal of the American Medical Association*.[38]

Dr. James Stewart Jewell was one of the country's foremost experts on mental and nervous diseases. He studied at both Rush Medical College and the Chicago Medical College, graduating from the latter in 1860, where he was a professor of anatomy from 1864 to 1869, after which time he went abroad to study medicine in Europe. On his return to America in 1870, Jewell lectured on general pathology at Chicago Medical College. At the time of Mary Lincoln's insanity trial, Jewell was a professor and the chair of the Department of Nervous and Mental Diseases at Chicago Medical College, was regarded by his peers as an authority on these particular diseases, and confined his practice exclusively to them. He also was a cofounder of the *Quarterly Journal of Nervous and Mental Diseases* in 1874.[39]

Of the six physicians consulted, three had previously met or attended to Mary Lincoln—Isham on Mary's arrival in Chicago, Johnson and Smith during Tad's illness. Dr. Willis Danforth, Mary's previous physician, did not attend the meeting but did testify at the trial in agreement with the conclusion of the other six. Robert's advisers, David Davis and John Todd Stuart, did not attend the meeting of medical minds but were informed of the discussions afterward.[40]

The discussions of that meeting were not transcribed, but typical examinations of the insane during this period provided for physicians to begin by questioning the patient's last physician or physicians, in this case, Dr. Isham and Dr. Danforth. Dr. Johnson and Dr. Smith also would have offered any knowledge they had of Mary's health from their contacts with her during Tad's illness. Typical questions for the family during insanity consultations, what today are called "mental status exams," in 1875 involved the patient's age, general habits and temperament, bodily health, any irregularity in menstruation or onset of menopause, family history, the most recent delusions, the duration of delusions, and the most frequent topics of conversation.[41] One typical tenet for diagnosis was to determine the degree to which the patient had departed from her normal condition, and not how widely she differed from other individuals or from a fixed standard.[42] It is known that Mary's intense fear of fire was discussed, and the doctors told Robert that a person with such a delusion might suddenly jump out of a window, believing the building to be in flames. "They were pronounced and earnest that the time had come when her personal safety had to be assured," Robert later wrote.[43]

The unanimous consensus and urgings of the physicians that Mary needed treatment should not be taken lightly. As one treatise on the subject stated, it was the physician's duty not to be bullied by the family into diagnosing insanity, but to diagnose only the patient's true condition. If insanity was the diagnosis, it was the physician's duty to inform the family of the need for commitment, even if the family did not want to believe it:

> It will be your duty to tell them that each day's postponement, by so much, lessens the probabilities of recovery; that insanity, under timely and efficient treatment, is commonly recovered from; that in nine cases out of ten the patient will not know where he is, appreciate his surroundings, or recognize the fact that his comrades are lunatics—at any rate restraint and discipline applied in an asylum will be less irksome to him than if he is called to endure them in his own home. You must impress these points upon them firmly and forcibly, and make them fully understand the great responsibility that will rest upon them, if, through their unwillingness to follow your advice, the patient passes, for want of prompt and energetic treatment, into a condition of permanent mental alienation.[44]

Robert later explained separately to two people—his mother's closest friend, Sally Orne, and his own closest friend, John Hay—that the council of physicians told him every delay in his mother's treatment was making him "morally responsible for some very probable tragedy, which might occur at any moment."[45]

The next day after the meeting, Robert wrote letters, at Swett's suggestion, to each physician, asking "their written opinion as to [Mary's] real condition, irrespective of the degree of evidence we might be able to obtain in regard to it," and also to Davis and to Stuart, inquiring "as to a proper course of action, provided the physicians were willing, in writing, to pronounce her insane."[46] That phrase "irrespective of the degree of evidence" makes it clear that Swett wanted the doctors' honest opinions, not simply what would play well for a jury. Unfortunately for posterity, the six physicians offered no detailed diagnoses, but simply replied with identical one-page responses: Yes, Mary Lincoln was insane, and yes, she was a fit person to be confined to an asylum.[47] Only Dr. Davis elaborated on his opinion with the statement that "the character of her insanity is such that she may, at times, appear perfectly sane in ordinary conversation; and yet she is constantly subject to such mental hallucinations as to render her entirely unsafe if left to herself."[48] This statement was consistent with the contemporary medical notion that some patients' delusions were undetectable in normal conversation or everyday living until the subject of the delusion was broached.[49]

While Robert's advisers agreed that commitment was the only way to keep his mother safe, Mary's family was less certain. Both John Todd Stuart and Elizabeth Grimsley Brown were convinced of Mary's insanity and the need for a conservator to control her money and property, but hesitated at the prospect of "personal restraint" in an asylum.[50] Stuart asked whether Mary would "consent to remain in some private hospital" if a conservator were appointed.[51] David Davis did not think so. "The appointment of a conservator, without the confinement, will not answer the purpose. It might do with persons of different temperament from Mrs. Lincoln, but with her it would not do at all. Like you I have been satisfied for years that her unsoundness of mind affords the proper explanation for all the vagaries she has developed."[52] Davis advised that if all the physicians affirmed in writing their opinions on Mary's condition, and if Swett and Ayer, as attorneys, were satisfied they had enough evidence to make a case, then proceedings should begin immediately. He wrote to Swett:

I am aware that an unfavorable verdict would be disastrous in the extreme, but this must be risked, if after maturely considering the subject your fixed opinion is that you ought to proceed. I do not see how Robert can get along at all, unless he has the authority to subject his mother to treatment. . . . You and I were devoted friends of her husband, and in this crisis it is our duty to give to Robert the support which he so much needs. And I doubt not that he will receive the support from his relatives in Springfield. I know that he has the support of Mr. Stuart. I do not see the propriety of waiting until the commission of some act which [would] arrest public attention. It may be that medical attention, in a retreat for insane persons, would operate favorably upon her. This chance should not be lost. After all the whole case turns on the sufficiency of the evidence to procure a favorable verdict. If you are satisfied on this point, believing as I do that Mrs. Lincoln is insane and should be placed under treatment, I see no other course than judicial action. Of course this is painful to us all and especially so to Robert, but like all other painful duties, it must be met and discharged. Thoughtful and right minded men will approve and under the circumstances, it is hoped newspapers will forbear to criticize.[53]

Stuart also was wary of newspaper criticism and advised Robert to delay any proceedings against Mary until the facts and surrounding circumstances were "fully sustained and justified" by his friends and by the public.[54] By May 17, Robert and Swett had decided to wait until the physicians replied to Robert's queries about submitting their diagnoses in writing.[55] But the next day, Mary's condition was worse. Not only was she spending vast amounts of money on useless items, but the Pinkerton agent reported that she was being visited in her room by suspicious people; Mary also had sold some of her bonds and had $1,000 in cash on her person and was considering leaving Chicago for either California or Europe.[56] Swett advised that they act immediately.

The strain and difficulty under which Robert was placed at this time cannot be overestimated, yet it has been completely ignored in previous examinations of the case. Confronted with his mother's irrational acts, his need and desire to keep her safe, his considerations of manly duty and family privacy, and the admonishments of six medical experts, Robert now had to make the decision to act. Convinced he had no other option, he ordered Swett to act. On May 18, Swett personally visited all his trial witnesses, after which he found their case much stronger than he had first suspected. On May 19, Robert filed an affidavit in Cook County Court, after which an arrest warrant was issued, on application by Dr. Isham, to make Mary Lincoln appear in court to answer the charge of insanity.[57] Swett appeared at Mary Lincoln's hotel room at 1:00 P.M. to inform her of the warrant and the proceeding, which was scheduled to begin at 2:00 P.M., and to convey her to court.

The legal system under which Mary Lincoln was tried in May 1875 has received scant attention, which is surprising considering the number of historians who claim she was the victim of a "kangaroo court" full of "brazen injustice," a "high-handed denial of her civil rights," a "gross miscarriage of justice . . . a conspiracy, a frame-up, on the part of some of the sharpest legal minds in the country."[58] The circumstances of Mary's trial cannot be judged from a twenty-first-century viewpoint, but must be understood within the context of its contemporary time frame. In 1875 America, laws governing the treatment and commitment of insane people varied from state to state. The laws of Illinois guaranteed Mary Lincoln some of the most liberal personal protections in the country at that time, namely, a jury trial. Even if Robert and the former friends and colleagues of Abraham Lincoln had wanted to go on a male chauvinist rampage to railroad the perfectly sane widow into the asylum, the simple fact is, they could not have done so.

The State of Illinois began legislating for the care of insane people in 1823 with the "Act regulating the estates of Idiots, Lunatics, and persons distracted." This law gave any person accused of insanity the right to a jury trial. If the jury found the defendant insane, the law provided for the judge to appoint a conservator to control and safeguard his or her property. There were no state hospitals for the mentally ill in Illinois at this time, and the insane were kept at home, in prisons, in poorhouses, or at private asylums. The great crusade to improve the care and treatment of the mentally ill, begun in 1841 by Dorothea Dix, prompted the Illinois state legislature to create state mental hospitals and also to amend the 1823 statute. In 1851, a new law declared that married women and minor children could be placed in the state hospitals "on the request of the husband of the woman (or parent or guardian of the infant) without the evidences of insanity or distraction required in other cases."[59] Those "other cases," such as those involving the insanity of men, required an application to county court and a trial by jury.[60]

The catalyst for changing such a blatantly sexist system occurred in 1860, when a woman named Elizabeth Packard was forcibly removed to the Jacksonville (Illinois) State Hospital for the Insane. Her detainment was based solely on the words of her husband—a Calvinist preacher with whose beliefs she publicly disagreed—and his consultation with the hospital superintendent.[61] Her only medical exam was the taking of her pulse. After a three-year incarceration, Mrs. Packard was released, only to have her husband lock her in the house while he made plans to permanently commit her to an asylum in Massachusetts.[62] Such a house arrest was illegal in Illinois, and in the ensuing trial, at which Rev. Packard claimed his wife was a lunatic, she was declared sane.[63] Packard's husband then took the children and all the family belongings to Massachusetts, leaving his wife behind. Packard subsequently wrote several exposes and memoirs claiming that she was perfectly sane when committed to the asylum, as were many of the other women she encountered there. She used her intelligence and persuasive personality to crusade for a change in Illinois's insanity law. She successfully lobbied the state legislature—vociferously supported by Myra Bradwell in the pages of the popular *Chicago Legal News*—to require a jury trial for any persons subjected to commitment proceedings.[64] This 1867 "personal liberty" law was still in effect in 1875, thus giving Mary Lincoln a mandatory right to a jury trial.

Mental health experts generally did not support the new personal liberty law. The editor of the *American Journal of Insanity* decried Mrs. Packard as a "talkative and crazy woman" whose lobbying was "a pestilent commotion stimulated by an offence against female vanity." The new law, he claimed, was impractical because it made commitment more difficult. "There ought to be no more difficulty in getting a patient into a hospital for the insane than into a hospital for any other disease or accident." The belief that sane people were easily and commonly committed to, and trapped in, asylums was ridiculous, and even if it were true, the writ of habeas corpus was available in cases of unlawful confinement, he stated. Most important, a public trial made a spectacle of the insane, causing them unnecessary excitement.[65]

This was, in fact, the most common complaint of the medical experts: a public trial seriously hindered the insane from receiving help. "The horror felt by insane persons and their relatives at the general character of legal proceedings under the present law, has led to the establishment of private institutions just outside the borders of the state, of which many avail themselves, of those who are able to afford it," one critic wrote.[66] Those who could not afford it and whose relatives feared a public trial often received no treatment.[67] Another complaint was that the jury statute "failed to recognize the distinction between a trial and an inquest. The adjudication of insanity followed the line of criminal procedure. The unfortunate patient was 'accused' of insanity and if 'convicted,' taken into custody by the sheriff exactly as in criminal procedure," stated Richard Dewey, superintendent of the Kankakee (Illinois) State Hospital. The effect was often detrimental, with the patient believing "that the court proceedings were for the purpose of substantiating some charge against him, and when found insane believed himself innocently condemned."[68] Dewey also claimed that more sane people were declared insane by juries than ever had occurred under the previous system. Many physicians agreed with this position, this fear of juror ignorance. The Illinois State Medical Society's Committee on Medical Jurisprudence suggested in an 1873 report that a commission of experts, rather than laymen, should judge whether a person was insane.[69]

In fact, the uncertainty of convincing a jury of laymen was one of the main concerns of Robert's attorneys. "Robert was so careful to keep within the truth that the physicians doubted whether we would be able to make out a case sufficiently strong to satisfy *the general public*, and perhaps not strong enough to secure a verdict," Swett wrote.[70] The jury consisted of many of Chicago's most successful, capable, and respected men: Charles B. Farwell, member of the U.S. House of Representatives; Lyman J. Gage, cashier of the Merchants Loan & Trust Company and later treasury secretary under President William McKinley; S. C. Blake, physician and former Chicago city physician (and member of the Lincoln and Hamlin Club of Chicago); businessman J. McGregor Adams of Crerar, Adams & Company, a railway supply firm; insurance agent S. M. Moore of S. M. Moore & Company; grocer Henry C. Durand of Durands & Company; wholesale boot and shoe dealer C. M. Henderson of C. M. Henderson & Company; jeweler Thomas Cogswell of Cogswell, Weber & Company; crockery and glassware merchant S. B. Parkhurst of Parkhurst & Company; jobbing stationer and blank book manufacturer D. R. Cameron of Cameron, Amberg, Hoffman & Company; foundryman James A. Mason; and wholesale grocer William Stewart of Stewart, Aldrich & Company. These men were truly Mary's economic and social peers.[71] In fact, Judge Marion R. M. Wallace seems to have gone out of his way to find an unimpeachable jury for the widow of the martyred president—a sensible decision, since he undoubtedly was aware of the press scrutiny the case would garner. There is no evidence in the known historical record that Robert or his attorneys or advisers were friends with the judge or jury, communicated with the judge or jury, or sought to influence the decisions of the judge or jury.

Leonard Swett later wrote that his mission to bring Mary Lincoln to court on the afternoon of May 19, 1875, "presented more real terrors than anything I have ever undertaken. To have advanced on a battery instead would, it seems to me, have been a real relief."[72] It took Swett one hour to coax Mary into his carriage and convey her to court, during which time she attacked Swett with bitterness and sarcasm that wounded him "worse than bullets would [have]." Her bitter invective also extended to Robert, once she discovered the trial was his doing. Mary at times threw up her hands, with tears streaming down her cheeks, and prayed to the Lord to release her and drive Swett away. At one point, she asked Swett to leave her room while she changed her dress, but he refused, saying he was afraid if he left her alone she would leap out the window. Finally, after being threatened with the indignity of sheriff's deputies leading her to court in handcuffs, Mary acquiesced to ride with the attorney to the courthouse.[73]

The celerity with which Mary's trial was orchestrated gave few spectators the chance to be present although, of course, reporters for the major

Chicago newspapers were there. Mary sat at the defendant's table with Robert and her attorney, Isaac Arnold, who was not only a friend of her husband but one of the first biographers of the martyred president, as well as a former congressman. Robert had asked Mary's cousins, John Todd Stuart and Elizabeth Grimsley Brown, to come to Chicago and sit with his mother for moral support during the trial, but neither was able to be present.[74] Before the proceedings began, Arnold approached Swett and said he "doubted the propriety of defending her," since he too considered her insane. Swett, who by this time was all "used up" after his ordeal with Mary, snapped back, "That means that you will put into her head, that she can get some mischievous lawyer to make us trouble; go and defend her, and do your duty."[75] A fatigued Swett then told Robert's attorney, B. F. Ayer, to take charge of the case, immediately after which the trial began.

Swett's snippy retort to Arnold's conscience has been cited as proof of a male chauvinist conspiracy to railroad Mary Lincoln into the asylum; that Mary Lincoln was "robbed of any defense by her sex . . . and by her duplicitous legal counsel."[76] Yet, taken within the context of duty—as Swett even admonished Arnold—the statement takes on a deeper meaning. It was Robert's manly duty to protect his mother and the duty of Robert's advisers to the memory of their beloved friend Abraham Lincoln to help Robert do his duty. It is obvious that Swett did not want Mary's defense to put up a strong fight, but only because they believed they were acting in Mary's best interests and a protracted legal fight—which would create an unwanted media frenzy—would only prolong her exposure to danger and her lack of appropriate care.

The trial of Mary Lincoln lasted three hours, during which time eighteen witnesses testified to her derangement. As stated above, these included physicians, hotel employees, Chicago merchants, and Mary's only son. A grief-stricken Robert, looking pale and weepy-eyed, reportedly broke down crying twice while on the stand. "His face indicated the unpleasantness of the duty he was about to perform and his eyes were expressive of the grief he felt," one newspaper reported.[77] In addition to his testimony stated above, Robert said he had no idea why his mother thought he was sick in March, as he had not been sick in ten years. She had always been exceedingly kind to him, but he had "no doubt" that she was insane. "She has been of unsound mind since the death of father; has been irresponsible for the past ten years." He regarded her as "eccentric and unmanageable," in the habit of meeting with strange people, spending lavishly on useless items, and ignoring his advice. "She has long been a source of much anxiety to me."[78]

The newspaper coverage of Mary's defense is far from conclusive, but Arnold's defense reads as rather perfunctory. The *Inter Ocean* showed only three cross-examinations by him, the *Times* showed only one, and the *Tribune* mentioned only that he recalled Robert to the stand to ask whether insanity was hereditary in the family. But would a more forceful defense have mattered? Eighteen witnesses, including seven medical experts and her own son, built the case against Mary. Swett later stated that the evidence of Mary's insanity was so overwhelming that they did not even put in their whole case.[79] In fact, the testimony covered only a small portion of Mary's acts and the evidence of her unbalance. Robert allowed only the barest minimum of evidence necessary to establish the case to be introduced at court in order to minimize public exposure and embarrassment.[80] From a historical perspective, it leaves one wondering just how much he kept private and how much documentary evidence he later destroyed, as he admittedly did.[81] One thing not said during the trial but stated in correspondence with his aunt was that Mary once suggested to a lady the idea of kidnapping Robert's five-year-old daughter.[82] Months after the trial, Mary plotted her son's murder.[83]

It is interesting that, despite Robert's belief that part of his mother's problem was her belief in Spiritualism, the issue never was specifically declared during the trial. Dr. Danforth's testimony that Mary heard voices, listened to table rappings, and was protected by her husband's spirit, certainly smacked of Spiritualism, and some newspapers reported that Mary's insanity was partly caused by her belief in Spiritualism; but it was never explicitly stated in court as a cause of her madness.[84] This may have been a legal decision considering that the legal connection—if there was one—between Spiritualism and insanity was too nebulous. The Maine Supreme Court had only months prior to this trial refused to decide whether a belief in Spiritualism was an insane delusion or not, while the Connecticut Supreme Court hesitated on the subject as late as 1882.[85] Contemporary mental health experts were divided on the relationship between Spiritualism and insanity.[86]

Mary Lincoln did not testify in her own defense; in fact, she never uttered a single word during the entire trial.[87] Swett concluded his case by simply stating that all Mary's family and friends considered her insane ever since the assassination of her husband and that the weight of so much tragedy in her life had been too much for her to bear. Robert applied to the court only after consultation with his father's friends and numerous medical experts, and everyone involved or interested had approved of his action. After that, the jury adjourned. During the hiatus, when Robert approached his mother, trying to comfort her, she exclaimed, "O Robert, to think that my son would ever have done this!"[88] This exchange was published widely in contemporary newspapers, has been quoted often in subsequent histories of the case, and has done much to create and perpetuate Robert's reputation as a cold man.

Within ten minutes of its adjournment, the jury returned a verdict of insanity.[89] Robert was appointed conservator of Mary's estate.[90] Forty-six years after the trial, juror Lyman Gage told historian William E. Barton that while Mary Lincoln did not appear violently insane to the jury, it was clear that she "suffered from phobias and occasional insane delusions," such as her fear of fire and her manic purchasing. "There seemed no other course than for the jury to find the lady guilty as charged," Gage wrote. He also stated that after the trial, "the leading physician who testified against" Mary—probably Willis Danforth, judging from time on the stand—privately told him there was "no doubt whatever of the fact of her mental aberration. . . . that it was a case of dementia, or degeneration of the brain tissue," and that within two years, she would die from it.[91] There can be little doubt that Danforth—or whoever Gage's physician was—gave the same diagnosis to Robert Lincoln, which adds yet another layer of understanding to his motivations for the trial.

It is important at this point to take a step back and consider Robert Lincoln on this most horrible day. When it comes to Robert's emotions concerning the trial, his detractors consider him cold as flint and devoid of sentiment. Yet, the newspaper coverage described his appearance and testimony as grief-stricken and weepy-eyed. The *Inter Ocean* described him on entry into the courtroom as "pale" and that his eyes "bore evidence of weeping." It reported that he broke down in tears twice during his personal testimony, and that after his mother's final accusation, he turned away "to conceal his grief." The *Tribune* likewise reported that his eyes were "suffused with tears" upon his entry into court; it also stated that "his eyes were expressive of the grief he felt" when he took the stand to testify, and that after his mother's final words to him, "His response was stifled by the [illegible] of tears."[92]

As for Robert's motives, none of the major Chicago newspapers observed or accused him of insincerity or cruelty. The *Times* stated he "discharged his delicate and unhappy task with filial thoughtfulness."[93] The *Inter Ocean*'s more complete coverage reported the opening statements of Robert's attorney, B. F. Ayer, who said the proceedings were instituted by Robert "through feelings of concern for his mother's safety."[94] Ayer stated that Mary Lincoln's friends and family "feared some harm might befall her unless she is placed under restraint. They do not intend that she shall be sent to a State Asylum but to a private asylum where she will be cared for properly."[95] This latter statement is especially intriguing and noteworthy as refutation of the conspiracy theorists because the Illinois insanity statute assumed placement in the State Hospital for the Insane, although it allowed the family of "non paupers" to place them in another facility. Surely, if Robert was as heartless as he has been accused, he would have left Mary to the state, rather than invest time and money in finding a private sanitarium for her.[96]

The *Tribune* likewise reported that the proceedings were instituted "to protect her from her own hands, and to secure her from bodily harm." It reported Robert as testifying that he had instituted the trial "in the interest of his mother. He did not want any money from her."[97] The *Inter Ocean* also reported "He did not want any money from her."[98] The papers show Robert's statement was made at his own instigation, not in response to a question. So why did he make that statement? It has come to be regarded as a beacon of subterfuge and insincerity: evidence that he really did want her money. Yet, given Robert's keen experience with sensationalist newspapers, and the fact that they could make even noble deeds sound avaricious, he knew a petition to take charge of her estate and confine her would be regarded as rapacious. Therefore, his statement was preemptive. If it had seemed insincere or the trial appeared duplicitous, surely the eager—and often sensationalist—press would have reported it so.

Robert, in fact, spent more than $1,000 to commit and care for his mother at Dr. R. J. Patterson's privately run Bellevue Place Sanitarium in Batavia, Illinois, from May through October 1875.[99] Perhaps this is a nominal amount compared to the $84,035 he eventually inherited at Mary's death in 1882, but Robert actually fully expected his mother to cut him out of her will—in fact, he even recommended it.[100] To Mary's mind, however, her last surviving son and the men her husband trusted above all others had robbed and betrayed her. After losing her parents, her friends and family, her children and husband, her social position and public respect, Mary Lincoln had now lost her freedom, and, more important to her monomaniacal mind, her money. This final loss, permeated by indignity, was so acutely painful, so horribly overwhelming, that the next morning, after evading the guards outside her hotel room, Mary Lincoln tried to kill herself.

5 *Mrs. Lincoln Admitted Today*

TODAY, THERE IS MUCH DISAGREEMENT as to whether or not Mary Lincoln was in fact "insane" in May 1875 and, if she was, from which disease she suffered and to what degree. Moreover, the term *insanity* is a troublesome one with various meanings, which also muddles the discussion. Typically, it is used as a lay term for crazy thought or behavior, and this episode in Mary's life has become established as the "Insanity Episode" in the Lincoln literature. The term *insanity* has also come to be used as a legal term, where an insanity defense argues that the accused suffered a mental condition that rendered that person not responsible for his or her actions. In this context, Mary could be dubbed "insane," because her trial declared her sufficiently irresponsible as to be unfit to control her person or her property.

Twenty-first-century mental health professionals, however, dislike the term *insanity*, which has largely been replaced by *psychosis* in modern psychiatric terminology. In fact, the words *insanity* and *insane* do not even appear in the index to the most up-to-date official listing of acceptable psychiatric diagnoses, the Diagnostic and Statistical Manual IV-TR, published by the American Psychiatric Association.[1] *Psychosis* basically means any condition that causes the affected person to lose contact with reality. The most common of these breaks with reality are delusions (fixed beliefs in something that is untrue) and hallucinations (sensations of sound, sight, etc. of something that is not really there). The evidence shows that Mary suffered from both, such as her stories of the Wandering Jew, the Indian spirit, and the voices in the walls and floor.

Psychoses are not the only serious psychiatric illnesses, however. Patients who are severely depressed may not have delusions or hallucinations, but they may be extremely unhappy in a sustained way, lose their ability to enjoy things, lose their energy and motivation, stop doing their usual activities, feel irretrievably helpless and hopeless, and even cease functioning. Mary had both psychotic and severe depressive symptoms at various times in her life, not just in 1875, suggesting she suffered from what came to be known as Manic-Depressive Illness, now called Bipolar Disorder.

Since these episodes recurred, she actually suffered numerous "insanity episodes," and not simply one episode that resulted in her commitment. In this respect, it would be more medically accurate to describe the events beginning in March 1875 as Mary's "Institutionalization Episode," rather than her "Insanity Episode."[2]

In spite of the technical classifications of insanity, or perhaps because of them, historians have offered radically different conclusions and interpretations of Mary's actions and mental condition, utilizing the exact same evidence. This has caused one historian to wonder "whether evidence matters in matters of historical importance."[3] In the days following Mary's trial, however, no one was terribly surprised at the tribunal or its verdict. The news spread rapidly across the country. Public opinion and newspaper editorials generally supported Robert in his action and at the same time lamented that it had been necessary. They sympathized with Mary Lincoln, found her blameless, and attributed her derangement to the murder of her husband.[4]

"Nothing but an imperative sense of duty and of filial devotion could have compelled the institution of the inquiry," the *Chicago Tribune* editorialized.

> It has been generally known in the circle of the lady's acquaintances and personal friends that something of this kind would eventually be necessary. As will be seen from the evidence, Mrs. Lincoln's mind has been for ten years prey to growing madness, and this fact, now made public, will cast a new light on many of her past actions, which were harshly criticized by those who did not know her, and which, while understood by her personal friends, could not be explained by them, since to have done so would have been to have exposed her mental condition, which it was then hoped might improve.[5]

The *Chicago Inter Ocean* called it "one of the saddest trials that has ever appeared on the docket of any court in this or any other country." It stated the witness testimony was "conclusive as to her insanity," which began with her husband's assassination and increased after Tad's death in 1871, and it was the "sorrowful duty of her son" to institute proceedings against her.[6] The *Chicago Times* called Mary "a woman of refinement and education" and stated, "Her talk and conversation betoken her a lady, and one of no ordinary culture. It is sad to think that she has fallen a victim to the dread malady, insanity."[7] The *Times* also praised Robert, editorializing that "trying as was the position of the only one of her name left to counsel and protect her, he discharged his delicate and unhappy task with filial thoughtfulness."[8]

The *New York Tribune* offered a long paean to Mary—anonymously written by John Hay, President Abraham Lincoln's former secretary—in its editorial pages.[9]

> The sympathy of the nation which has been too grudgingly given to the widow of Abraham Lincoln, will certainly no longer be withheld now that a court of justice has declared her bereft of reason. It has long been known to those nearest to her that her mind never entirely recovered from the shock of the President's assassination. . . . But everything she did or said in that delirium of despair was wickedly and shamefully used against her afterward. . . . There is no doubt that this treatment had its effect in preventing her recovery from the great shock which had shattered her life.[10]

The *Chicago Times* also chastised Americans who "sneered, jested, laughed at her waywardness, without doing her the justice to inquire into its cause."[11] The *Chicago Tribune*, revisiting the case on May 21, obviously having spoken with attorneys Leonard Swett and Isaac Arnold, clearly sympathized with Mary for breaking under a strain nobody could have endured. It praised her for maintaining her ladylike dignity and character, but stated that her breakdown "had long been foreseen by her intimates; that it was postponed as long as affectionate regard could do so with safety to herself."[12]

Friends and colleagues of Abraham Lincoln also commented on Mary's trial. Of course, prior to the trial, David Davis, Leonard Swett, and John Todd Stuart unabashedly declared their belief as to Mary's insanity. Davis and Stuart were not present at the trial, but both were pleased by the outcome. "I am very glad that it is over and so far as I am able to judge from the newspapers everything was done that the melancholy occasion required of you," Stuart wrote to Robert on May 21. "The presence of Mrrs. Swett and Arnold was especially fortunate and the character of the jury not less so."[13] Davis wrote, "It is a source of deep thankfulness that the matter passed off so well. The terrible strain on you will be removed and you can go to work. Some good comes out of almost everything & the necessity of confining your mother in an asylum will go very far toward removing the unfavorable impressions created by her conduct since your father's death."[14]

Senator Orville Hickman Browning of Illinois said, "As for poor Mrs. Lincoln I have for several years past considered her demented."[15] John Hay, President Lincoln's private secretary, was characterized in a newspaper as believing there was "no question as to Mrs. Lincoln's insanity."[16] Gideon Welles, Lincoln's navy secretary, told Robert that he believed the widow's hospitalization was long overdue.[17] Mary's cousin, Elizabeth Grimsley Brown, whom Robert consulted in March 1875, had told Robert she believed Mary to be insane but objected to the idea of putting her in an asylum. However, she believed her failure to prevent the trial was an act of Providence. Brown was thankful "That perhaps strangers could accomplish that in which relatives might fail. Neither you, cousin John or myself could have *induced* your mother to have gone voluntarily before a jury and our presence perhaps would have rendered her violent."[18]

In subsequent years, other intimates of the Lincolns offered further opinions. William Herndon believed Mary was "in part an unbalanced woman—her mind is . . . unhinged, and has been for years."[19] John G. Nicolay stated that Mary "was very eccentric there is no doubt. . . . The shock of the assassination did ultimately disturb Mrs. Lincoln's sanity."[20] Albert S. Edwards, Mary's nephew, stated that his aunt "was insane from the time of her husband's death until her own death."[21] Mrs. John Todd Stuart, the wife of Mary's cousin, and Mrs. B. S. Edwards, Mary's sister-in-law, both said they had always believed the anxiety of Lincoln's reelection campaign caused Mary's "mental trouble."[22] Adam Badeau, aide-de-camp to General Grant during the Civil War, wrote that the trial finally illuminated circumstances until then publicly unknown. "It relieved Mrs. Lincoln herself from the charge of heartlessness, or mercenary behavior, or indifference to her husband's happiness. It approved the action of the son, which, in some quarters, had been gravely misunderstood; and, above all, it showed the suffering Abraham Lincoln must have endured all through those years in which he bore the burden of a struggling nation on his shoulders, whether he knew or only feared the truth."[23]

Robert Lincoln, in his disrespect for newspapers and editorialists, expected the outpouring of public judgment. As he wrote to John Hay two weeks after the trial:

> I knew that on the next day after my action the whole country would be flooded with criticisms, kind or unkind as might happen, but all based on a short press dispatch, which could not sufficiently give the facts. Yet I could not wait any longer when six of our most eminent physicians assembled in council, after hearing the statements in writing of most of the witnesses who afterwards testified at the Inquisition, gave me to understand that by longer delay, I was rendering myself responsible for a probable tragedy of some kind.

He also wrote that it would be "impossible" for anyone to understand "the distress and anxiety of my mind for the two months before that time."[24]

Just one week earlier, Robert had similarly explained his motivations—and the necessity of a jury trial—to Sally Orne, one of his mother's closest friends. Orne was also the only one of Mary's friends known to have requested from Robert an explanation for the trial. Robert wrote:

> If you have since seen any detailed account of the occurrences which forced me to place my mother under care, I think, indeed I know, you could not but have approved my action. Six physicians in council informed me that by longer delay I was making myself morally responsible for some very probable tragedy, which might occur at any moment. Some of my eastern friends have criticized the public proceedings in Court which seemed to them unnecessary. Against this there was no help, for we have a statute in this state which imposes a very heavy penalty on any one depriving an insane person of his liberty, without verdict of a jury. My mother is, I think, under as good care and as happily situated as is possible under the circumstances. She is in the private part of the house of Dr. Patterson and her associates are the members of his family only. With them she walks and drives whenever she likes and takes her meals with them or in her own rooms as she chooses, and she tells me she likes them all very much. The expression of surprise at my action which was telegraphed East, and which you doubtless saw, was the first and last expression of the kind she has uttered and we are on the best of terms. Indeed my consolation in this sad affair is in thinking that she herself is happier in every way, in her freedom from care and excitement, than she has been in ten years. So far as I can see she does not realize her situation at all. It is of course my care that she should have everything for her comfort and pleasure that can be obtained. . . . The responsibility that has been and is now on me is one that I would gladly share if it was possible to do so, but being alone as I am, I can only do my duty as it is given me to see it, trusting that I am guided for the best.[25]

While nearly all secondary works about the trial quote Robert's letter to Sally Orne in part or full, her reply is nearly always neglected. This is unfortunate because her remarks provide strong evidence against the notion of Robert's heartlessness. Orne wrote:

> It is a great comfort to hear from your own self, of the loving care and wise guidance which your dear Mother is under. Not that I ever had one doubt of that, for I know too much of your goodness as a son from her own lips to ever allow the first thought or suggestion to have any influence over me. . . . I only wish all the States had the same 'Statute.' It is a blessed one.[26]

Mary Lincoln's friends and acquaintances, apologists and critics, may have admired Robert for his strength and felicity in the face of such a painful circumstance, but Mary herself did not. *She* did not believe she was crazy, and in her pain and resentment over the proceedings, she told Robert there was now a breach between them that would never be closed; and that he "was no longer her son who would thus treat the mother who bore him and loved him."[27] This statement, in addition to her pre-verdict cry of "O Robert, to think that my son would ever have done this!" sounds as though Mary were irreparably angry at Robert. The newspapers, however, reported that she quickly apologized for her outbursts and seemed acquiescent to her fate. Robert himself wrote to John Hay that the Chicago newspaper accounts were factually accurate, except that they implied that Mary was angry. "This really lasted for a moment only. She has since been extremely cordial with me."[28]

As part of the verdict, Mary was deemed incapable of controlling her property, and the court appointed Robert as the conservator of his mother's estate.[29] He now had sole power to collect her income, pay her debts, and spend her money. The day of the trial, Robert filed an inventory of Mary's estate totaling $73, 454.18.[30] Mary, however, was indignant at the prospect of relinquishing her property, and at first she refused to surrender her $56,000 in bonds to Robert. She put off the moment at court and lasted until she, Swett, and Arnold had returned to her hotel room. Finally she rose up to Swett, the tears streaming from her eyes, and said, "And you are not satisfied with locking me up in an insane asylum, but now you are going to rob me of all I have on earth. My husband is dead, and my children are dead and these bonds I have saved for my necessities in my old age; now you are going to rob me of them."[31] Mary yielded her bonds only after Swett threatened to have the sheriff forcibly remove them from her.

Mary was left in her hotel room that night with one woman and two men to guard her, who had instructions to not let her leave.[32] She spent the evening quietly packing and went to bed early.[33] The next morning, Robert visited his mother on his way to work.[34] Later in the afternoon, as Robert and Swett were preparing for Mary's departure that night for Bellevue Place Sanitarium, Mary escaped.

The details of Mary's suicide attempt show it was accomplished with cunning and with more than a degree of intrepidity. "It is perfectly frightful to think how near she came to poisoning herself," Leonard Swett exclaimed four days later, describing the incident to David Davis.[35] According to Swett and to the contemporary reporting in the *Chicago Tribune*, *Chicago Times*, and *Chicago Inter Ocean* (all of which agree generally but vary slightly in certain details) , sometime in the late morning of May 20, Mary convinced her guards to let her leave her room and descend to the lobby.[36] The female guard was stationed inside Mary's room to prevent the widow from jumping out the window, while the two male guards—one of whom was a Pinkerton agent—were stationed outside in the hallway. All three were specifically instructed not to let Mary leave "on any pretense," but also not to physically restrain her in any way.

Mary hurried downstairs to the Squair & Company drugstore, located in the Grand Pacific Hotel, and ordered a two- or possibly four-ounce concoction of laudanum and camphor, ostensibly to apply to her shoulder for neuralgic pain.[37] The owner, Mr. Squair, knew of Mary's trial and mental condition, suspected her real purpose to be suicide, and, in order to put her off until Robert Lincoln could be called for, told her it would take half an hour for him to prepare it.[38] Mary said she would return at that time, stepped onto the sidewalk in front of the hotel, hailed a cab, and rode one block to the drugstore of Rogers & Smith, at the corner of Adams and Clark Streets.

Suspecting that Mary would seek the poison someplace else, Squair followed her to Rogers & Smith, accompanied by the Pinkerton agent, who had followed Mary downstairs. Mary ordered the same concoction from Mr. Smith, but Squair quickly entered, pulled Smith aside, explained the situation, and told him not to give her any drugs. Smith made some excuse and refused to give her the mixture.[39] Mary then talked her way past the Pinkerton agent again and directed her cab two blocks farther down Clark Street to the pharmacy of William Dale. Squair preceded Mary into Dale's store, however, and told the pharmacist not to give her any drugs. Rebuffed again, Mary took her cab back to Squair's drugstore in the Grand Pacific Hotel to see if her first order was completed.

The druggist at Squair's, faced with Mrs. Lincoln and still awaiting the arrival of Robert, created a harmless mixture of camphor, burnt sugar, and water. He labeled it "laudanum and camphor" and gave it to her. Mary had scarcely exited the store before she opened the three-ounce bottle and drank the entire solution. She then returned to her room to await her expected demise. By this time, the hotel manager had become aware of what was transpiring, and he also sent a messenger for Robert Lincoln.

Mary waited in her room for ten minutes, but, feeling no effects of the supposedly lethal drink, returned to Squair & Company. She said the mixture was too weak to ease her shoulder pain and asked for more laudanum. She also stepped behind the counter to watch the druggist mix the actual compounds.[40] Thinking quickly, Squair said the laudanum was kept in the basement. He descended downstairs, made another mixture of the innocuous burnt sugar and water, labeled it "Laudanum poison," warned her to be careful, and gave it to her. Once again, Mary downed the liquid as soon as she stepped out of the store and then returned to her room. Robert arrived shortly thereafter, followed by Leonard Swett, and both stayed with her until it was time to depart for Bellevue Place Sanitarium in Batavia. Finally, finding her efforts at self-destruction futile, Mary apparently submitted to her circumstances.

For the next few hours until her departure, Mary was "cheerful and kind," Swett reported, and "apologized for many things she said to me the day before."[41] The *Chicago Times* reported that Mary's demeanor was so cordial to the friends who accompanied her to the train station that no one suspected the "terrible determination" of her previous actions.[42] The *Inter Ocean* dubbed it a fortunate circumstance that Mary's first attempt to obtain poison was at Squair's store, "for through his activity the nation was spared an additional sorrow, and a life was saved which may yet in the fullness of her God-given reason appreciate the kindly action of her son and her friends."[43]

The fact that Mary Lincoln, an unstable but never violent woman, attempted suicide the morning after a jury declared her insane has shocked people since it was first reported on May 21, 1875. It certainly adds another layer of complexity to the disagreement over Mary's mental state. John Hay, writing anonymously (and apparently without Robert Lincoln's knowledge) in a *New York Tribune* editorial, bespoke the general contemporary perception that the suicide attempt "was a terrible confirmation of the justice of the decree of the Court."[44] The question, however, still is asked to this day: did Mary Lincoln attempt suicide because she was insane, or because she was a sane woman being committed against her will?

Suicide can occur under a number of circumstances. Most commonly, people who commit suicide are not psychotic but depressed. They grow tired of their misery, see no hope for recovery, and decide to end their lives. Likewise, people suffering from chronic pain and illness also may attempt suicide to end their suffering. Some suicides are motivated by psychosis, such as hearing voices that tell them to kill themselves, or developing delusions that someone is coming to torture them, so they avoid the torture by killing themselves. There also is an entire range of parasuicidal behaviors—suicide threats or attempts that likely will fail but that make a statement or gain attention.[45]

Of these circumstances, the possibility of Mary's drinking poison to gain attention is the least likely. There is no evidence to suggest this was her intention, and it certainly was not typical of her character. The notion that Mary's attempt was a reasonably sane response to her unjustifiable situation also is unlikely. A saner reaction would have been to simply escape: leave her room, hire a carriage, and leave town. Her guards were told not to forcibly restrain her, and considering the ease with which she visited three separate drugstores, an attempt to flee Chicago might well have succeeded. Mary clearly understood Robert's aversion to publicity, and she could easily have caused enough of a public spectacle, or threatened to, to make Robert reconsider his plans. Of course, tales of the perfectly sane being railroaded into an asylum by impatient spouses and greedy heirs, followed by the struggle of the hero to escape such unjust afflictions, makes for compelling drama. It happened to Elizabeth Packard (who subsequently changed the law) and doubtless to others. But as an institutional norm, the overwhelming majority of such accusations and stories have been disproved since at least the time of Mary's trial.[46]

But, when considering all the evidence—Mary's delusions, hallucinations, mood swings, incapacitating depressions, chronic illness, the public humiliation of her trial, the perceived theft of her money and property, the perceived betrayal by her son and her husband's closest friends, her impending loss of personal freedom, her willful ingestion of what she believed were two lethal doses of medicine, and, perhaps, as two medical historians have theorized, a posttraumatic stress reaction to her husband's assassination—the case in favor of this being a serious attempt to take her life is overwhelmingly convincing.[47] The theory that the suicide was a false story planted in the newspaper is rebutted by the fact that no less than five newspapers reported the incident, as did Leonard Swett in a private letter, and every source contains minor differences in detail, indicating no single origin for the story.[48] Likewise, Mary's room windows at the sanitarium were protectively covered to prevent suicide, specifically because of her May 20 suicide attempt.[49] The reason Mary never again attempted suicide can only be surmised, but it may very well have been "a measure of her tenacity and strength of character," as Dr. Norbert Hirschhorn stated in his excellent examination of the suicide episode.[50] The afternoon of May 20, however, Robert Lincoln took no chances, and he and Swett stayed with Mary until the 5:00 P.M. departure for Bellevue Place.

Mary, Robert, and Swett went together to the train station. Mary was allowed to take all the baggage she wanted, so she brought five trunks with her and another dozen were to follow later.[51] Besides all the clothing, curtains, and jewelry Mary had hoarded, she also brought a number of carpetbags filled with "a considerable number" of carpet-covered footstools, a situation Robert considered bizarre, but he said nothing and let her take them.[52] At the train station, Mary was "kind and uncomplaining" to Swett, the previous day's bitterness apparently gone.[53] She took his arm as they approached the station, and she even urged him to come visit her. Swett then left, and Isaac Arnold, Mary's attorney, and Dr. Richard J. Patterson, superintendent of Bellevue Place Sanitarium, arrived to accompany Mary and Robert to Batavia. The party traveled in an elegant special car, proffered as a courtesy to Mary by the directors of the railroad, complete with cooking and sleeping conveniences.[54] At the end of the ninety-minute journey, Mary Lincoln beheld her new home. In the span of ten years, the former First Lady had gone from the White House, to a boarding house, to living as a homeless wanderer, and now, to an insane asylum.

Bellevue Place Sanitarium was a well-respected private asylum for "a select class of lady patients of quiet unexceptionable habits." It was established in 1867 as a retreat for the treatment of nervous and mental diseases, using the most modern "moral" treatment of "rest, diet, baths, fresh air, occupation, diversion, change of scene, no more medicine than . . . absolutely necessary, and the least restraint possible."[55] Located on the banks of the Fox River, thirty-five miles west of Chicago, Bellevue Place welcomed new patients to a rural setting of twenty acres of secluded grounds with manicured lawns, large, shady evergreens and elm trees, and numerous flowers beds (Bellevue was well-known for its unparalleled rose bushes) and ornamental shrubs, all interwoven by concrete walkways and driveways, studded with hammocks and lawn chairs. Bellevue's property also boasted forty thousand square feet of greenhouses, also with wide walks and ample seating. There also were carriages and sleighs available for patients to use for daily outings.[56]

The main building of Bellevue Place was a massive, three-story limestone structure, complete with ivy creeping up its walls. The interior was bright and spacious, with hallways one hundred feet long and twelve feet wide, high ceilings, and large, well-lit rooms. The décor, with elegant furniture, potted plants, and vases of fresh flowers, was designed "to give a bright, cheerful and homelike expression," one of Bellevue Places's brochures advised, because "in all its appointments, [Bellevue] is intended to create an atmosphere of home, with its restfulness, freedom and seclusion." In keeping with its calming aesthetics, Bellevue Place admitted only the best of patients as well. Typical patients—all of whom were female—were nervous invalids who were "not insane" and "those who occupy a border-land between undoubted insanity and doubtful sanity"; and incurable patients who either could not gain admission to state hospitals, or whose families preferred a more private retreat. The majority of patients were depressed, some were suicidal, but all were quiet, as Dr. Patterson did not admit patients who were "habitually noisy, violent or destructive."[57]

Bellevue was equipped for twenty-five to thirty patients, but there were only twenty inmates in mid-1875. As a residence, Bellevue housed both its doctors and its patients, and, almost as if it were an ersatz bed-and-breakfast, was run by the Patterson family. Dr. Patterson served as primary physician and superintendent; his wife acted as matron; his son, Dr. Paul Patterson, was his father's medical assistant and partner; his daughter, Miss Blanche, also worked there, probably as assistant to her mother. There also were a dozen attendants and nurses.[58] It is probably only due to the later controversy over Mary's confinement that posterity knows so much about Mary's living conditions and treatment at Bellevue. Succinctly, as stated by historian Rodney Ross (whose father was once superintendent of Bellevue Place), "No other patient received such favored consideration."[59]

Mary had her own private suite of two rooms on the second floor, including a private bath, in the part of the house reserved as the Pattersons' private residence. The larger room was Mary's sitting room and bedroom. It was carpeted and plainly furnished with a bureau, rocking chair, lounge, plain bedstead, and elegant bed.[60] The smaller room of Mary's suite was occupied by a personal attendant, a young former schoolteacher, selected for the position "on account of her kindness and intelligence."[61] Charges were later made that Mary suffered barred windows and locked doors; this was untrue. Every room in the house had windows fitted with a protective covering to prevent falling. Patterson called it a "light ornamental screen"; Robert Lincoln referred to it as "a white wire netting such as you may see often to keep children from falling out of the window"; a journalist who toured the hospital described it as "merely an ornamental screen of steel wire, with a six inch mesh, woven in a diamond pattern, not at all suggestive of bars."[62] This covering was removed from Mary's room at Robert's request, but was later reinstalled by Patterson after he remembered Mary's attempted suicide the day after her trial.[63]

Mary's door was locked only at night, with the key kept by her personal attendant, who slept in the second room of Mary's suite. During the day, Mary kept her room key and could walk or drive anywhere she chose on or off the grounds, while accompanied by an appropriate attendant, usually her personal attendant, or Miss or Mrs. Patterson.[64] She was allowed to receive visitors and also to visit friends in the nearby town of Batavia.[65] Mary often visited the Patterson family in their personal rooms on the first floor, sometimes taking her meals with them, the rest of the time eating in her room.[66]

Mary's stay at Bellevue Place was documented formally by sanitarium staff in what has become known as the "Patient Progress Reports for Bellevue Place," a commercially bound volume, 9 × 12 ½ inches in size, with entries written in ink by two separate people. These reports are invaluable to the study of the case and reveal much about Mary's condition. "Mrs. Lincoln admitted today," reads the first entry, May 20, 1875. "Case is one of mental impairment which probably dates back to the murder of President Lincoln—More pronounced since the death of her son, but especially aggravated during the last 2 months."[67]

The daily entries from then until the end of June show Mary gave her attendants little trouble, slept well, was always pleasant, but usually depressed.[68] Evidence of her depression can be found in her inactivity, which is a typical result. During her first ten days in the sanitarium, Mary took a walk or carriage ride nearly every day. By the beginning of June, however, she became more inactive, refusing to go out more often than not. In a period of thirty-three days—from May 29 to June 30—she declined to go for a carriage ride (and usually to even leave the building) twenty-two times, or approximately 70 percent of the time. Mary also had trouble completing activities she said she would do. On June 10, she tried to pack a trunk of her possessions to send back to Robert but failed to complete it. On July 2, the report noted Mary would "habitually" make an appointment for a morning carriage ride, postpone it until night, then refuse to go, and repeat the same performance the next day.[69] This behavior also is typical of depressed people who are urged to be active.

Robert Lincoln visited his mother every week, often bringing his five year-old daughter Mamie with him. For the first month, he found his mother quite friendly to him. "While she will not in words admit that she is not sane, still her entire acquiescence in absolutely everything, while it arises in part from the plain enfeebled condition of her mind, makes me think that she is aware of the necessity of what has been done," he wrote to John Hay in early June.[70] On June 17, Robert's visit was marked with a reception "not quite so cordial in her manner . . . as at previous visits."[71]

Privately, Robert Lincoln received numerous letters from the general public, offering both sympathy and criticism over his mother's insanity trial.[72] He noticed in all of them, however, the impression that his mother was in "close confinement," the writers "using the word 'asylum,' with a notion of straightjackets, cells and brutal keepers."[73] He and Leonard Swett both felt it necessary to correct this misunderstanding in the public perception. Robert wrote to John Hay, his good friend and an editor at the *New York Tribune*, to ask him to write "a short article . . . containing a statement of the actual situation," in the form of a letter from the

Children of Robert T. and Mary Harlan Lincoln (clockwise from top): Abraham II, Mary (Mamie), and Jessie. Courtesy Friends of Hildene, Inc.

newspaper's Chicago correspondent. Robert's reasoning for his request shows his lifelong distrust of journalists. "We think it better to be started in your paper for several reasons. One is on account of the broad field you cover. A negative reason is the sensational character of our local papers." But, he wryly commented, "It will be a 'triumph of journalism' for there isn't a lie in it, but you must not tell the personal column man so, or he wouldn't touch it with a pair of tongs."[74]

Robert's request of his friend Hay has never been recorded in the insanity case historiography, nor has Hay's response. His anonymous editorial explained that Robert's action was taken only after consultation with family friends and six medical experts. It described Mary's situation as related above: private rooms, friendly attendants, and personal freedom. "Such has been the influence of the quiet and pleasant surroundings that nothing whatever has occurred to render necessary anything more than a prudent supervision, and this is given by pleasant companionship, without any appearance of restraint. At present her derangement exhibits itself mainly in a general feebleness and incapacity, and it is not yet possible to give an opinion as to her restoration."[75]

By early July, Mary was growing restless. She started waking multiple times in the night, and on July 5 had a fit of crying. Then on July 8, a reporter for the *Chicago Post and Mail* arrived at Bellevue, hoping to update the paper's readers on Mary's condition, her treatment, and how she passed her time at the sanitarium. The journalist, a Mrs. Rayne, was impressed by Dr. Patterson, whom she found friendly and gracious, and also by the beauty and warmth of Bellevue itself, which she thought could easily be imagined as "a cozy hotel."[76] She did not expect to see the former First Lady, since, in her seven weeks at Bellevue, Mary had absolutely refused to see any visitors and even kept to her room when visitors were in the house or on the grounds.[77] To the surprise of both Mrs. Rayne and Dr. Patterson, Mary agreed to see her.[78]

The *Post and Mail* article, published July 13, 1875, is an amazing piece of historical evidence regarding Mary Lincoln's time at Bellevue Place. Not only does it corroborate the physical attributes of the inside and outside of the sanitarium and some of the patient progress report entries, it offers descriptions of things otherwise unknown, such as the appearance and contents of Mary's room and general descriptions of the other twenty patients. But what is most impressive is that Rayne reported aspects of Mary's behavior and physical appearance, as well as Dr. Patterson's impressions of Mary's possibility for recovery, not recorded in the patient progress reports or anyplace else. Of Mary, she wrote:

> She was dressed in ordinary black, have worn, with white ruches edged with black in the neck and sleeves; her dark hair, fast turning gray, was carelessly coiffed in a knot at the back with coronet braid. She looked worn and ill and her hands, ringless and uncared for, were never at rest. I could plainly see in her lusterless eyes and in the forced composure of her manner, evidences of a shattered mind. She was perfectly ladylike in manner, but rambling and diffuse in her conversation. She alluded rationally, however, to the past, spoke tenderly of Mr. Lincoln, once as "my husband" and again as "the President."[79]

Rayne reported that, in general, Mary's dress was "at all times plain, even to shabbiness, and no one could be more indifferent to effects of the toilet." This is a relevant observation, since nineteenth-century doctors considered neglectful or slovenly dress by a person ordinarily well groomed an indication of insanity.[80] And yet, shortly after her arrival at Bellevue, despite having ten trunks of personal possessions, Mary ordered a morning dress "of black French cambric, quite elaborately made with white basque and pockets, and a black and white striped laun." She never wore these clothes, however, "or evinced any disposition to even try them on," but immediately after they were completed asked for samples of black alpacea [sic] from which to select a suit. "Her mind was diverted from this, as it was only a form of her malady to accumulate material."[81]

Rayne found herself overcome with sympathy for the poor, traumatized widow and could detect a soupçon of her previous society manner. What really touched her, however, was the pathetic nature in which Mary would sit alone in her room and imagine herself in company with her husband, senators, and ambassadors; and the way she would sit at her table and hold conversations with her dear dead boys, Willie and Tad. It seems Mrs. Rayne did not witness these scenes, but was probably told them by one of the Bellevue Place staff, for they were accompanied in print by the explanation that they were "the result of scenes photographed on the brain" that only death could erase and were not a development of Mary's belief in Spiritualism.[82] The journalist found Dr. Patterson reluctant to discuss Mary's condition, but he conceded she was quiet, rested well, and was "quite satisfied with her surroundings." He did say, or at least intimate, that he had little hope for Mary's permanent recovery.[83]

Interestingly, out of everything that Mrs. Rayne heard and experienced during her visit to Mary Lincoln at Bellevue Place, it was the most nominal of things that changed the course of Mary's situation. Apparently, the reporter was acquainted with some of Mary's Chicago friends, and it seems their interest in the widow may have been the instigation for the visit. Mary and Mrs. Rayne discussed these friends before anything else, much to Mary's pleasure.[84] At one point in the conversation, Mary "alluded very feelingly to her attachment to Judge Bradwell's family."[85] Had Dr. Patterson known the brouhaha that was about to erupt, signaled by those ten words, he never would have allowed the reporter inside Bellevue Place.

6 *It Does Not Appear That God Is Good*

Myra Bradwell has become known as the woman who orchestrated Mary Lincoln's release from Bellevue Place Sanitarium, and not without reason. She was somewhat of a female icon in her day. Bradwell was an activist for numerous causes, such as female suffrage and fair legal treatment for women, and counted among her friends such luminaries as Susan B. Anthony and Mary Livermore. Not only was she America's "first" woman lawyer but also was the founder, publisher, and editor-in-chief of the prestigious and widely read *Chicago Legal News.* "Myra Bradwell did more to create rights for women and other legally handicapped persons than did any other woman of her day, and perhaps any day," stated her sole biographer.[1] But in July 1875, this feminist hero was not looking for another cause or a fight with either Dr. Patterson or Robert Lincoln.

In fact, despite her friendship with Mary Lincoln, Myra Bradwell seems to have made no attempt to write to or visit Mary Lincoln at Bellevue Place during the widow's first two months there. The reason is unknown. Perhaps Bradwell was preoccupied publishing the *Chicago Legal News*; or maybe she simply believed (as she later explicitly stated) that her friend was insane, so she chose to give the physicians time to ply their trade. What is now known, however, due to the discovery of Mary Lincoln's lost insanity letters, is that Myra Bradwell was not the instigator she has come to be credited as. She certainly was a willing and extremely able accomplice, but it was Mary herself who created and directed her plot for freedom.

Inside Bellevue Place, Mary Lincoln sequestered herself from most of society, as she did during her European sojourn in 1868 and would do again after being declared sane in 1876. Initially, she did not reach out to Myra Bradwell. Both Dr. Patterson and the *Post and Mail* reporter attested that Mary refused all visitors during her first two months at the sanitarium; and the eagerness with which she asked the reporter about her Chicago friends indicates she was not in communication with them. Mary had, up to that point, expressed no displeasure at being at Bellevue

Place during her time there, and while she suffered bouts of depression, she had made no mention of being uncomfortable, confined, or in any way desirous of freedom from her situation. Robert even reported more than once that his mother was always happy to see him and seemed pleased with her surroundings.[2]

Then suddenly on July 15, after a visit from Robert and his daughter, Mary told Dr. Patterson she wanted to live with her sister, Elizabeth Edwards, in Springfield, Illinois. The notation in the Bellevue daily patient progress report suggests Mary's statement was regarded skeptically. "This sister we understand she might have lived with anytime but has not even felt kindly toward her—Mrs. L said—'It is the most natural thing in the world to wish to live with my sister—She raised me and I regard her as a sort of mother.'"[3] This last was certainly true. After the death of their mother, Elizabeth Todd, the oldest child by five years, played a motherly role to her younger siblings, even to the point of finding husbands for three of them.[4] Yet, in the later White House years, Mary had become estranged from Elizabeth due to a family feud regarding government patronage, and the two barely spoke throughout the following decade.[5]

So why did Mary suddenly change her mind about her situation, and did she change her mind about living at Bellevue or about keeping quiet about not wanting to live there? No known evidence gives an explicit answer. The Bellevue patient log shows she had no visitors and received no mail. Mary's seclusion likely was motivated by her embarrassment at being declared insane and her resulting self-pity from feelings of abandonment by family and friends. What seems likely is that upon learning her Chicago friends were thinking of her, Mary realized she was not alone after all.

In fact, her friends were powerful people. James Bradwell, Mary's unofficial legal adviser, was a former county court judge and current member of the state legislature; Myra Bradwell was a renowned activist and publisher; and John Franklin Farnsworth, a Chicago attorney originally from nearby St. Charles, Illinois, had been a Union general during the Civil War and a member of the U.S. House of Representatives from 1857 to 1861 and 1863 to 1873 (and had been present at Abraham Lincoln's deathbed in 1865). Mary must have decided that if these people were thinking of her, then perhaps they would help her. Robert Lincoln said more than once that his mother would do anything to accomplish a goal once she decided on it.[6] After Mrs. Rayne's visit, Mary realized a newfound (or newly emerged) sense of victimization, which caused her to begin a campaign to secure her freedom.

When Robert next visited his mother on July 28, Mary told him of her desire to live in Springfield. Robert did not think it prudent for Mary to leave Bellevue, but he did think a visit was a good idea. He had, in fact, been telling his mother for years that she needed to make amends with her sisters. He encouraged her to write to Elizabeth Edwards and suggest a visit. After Robert left Bellevue that day, Mary asked Dr. Patterson if she could mail the letter to her sister. At the post office, Mary got out of the carriage and deposited the letter herself, an otherwise nominal item probably noteworthy in the daily patient progress report only because the staff saw her increased initiative as a sign of improvement.[7] Later events would show, however, that Mary's initiative at the post office was actually an act of deceit.

The next day, Mary received three visitors suddenly concerned about her incarceration. Both Dr. Patterson and Robert Lincoln believed Mary must have mailed multiple letters to various people the evening before, rather than one letter to her sister, as she said.[8] Subsequent historians have repeated this contention.[9] The discovery of Mary's lost letters, however, proves this to be untrue. The earliest found letter from Mary's stay at the sanitarium was, in fact, the first letter she wrote to the Bradwells, dated July 28, 1875, the day Robert visited and Mary practiced her deceitful mailing. The letter shows that Mary Lincoln did not write multiple letters that day, but just one, to James Bradwell. "May I request you to come out here just so soon as you receive this note. Please bring out your dear wife, Mr. Wm. Sturgess and any other friend. Can you not be *here*, tomorrow on the noon train. Also bring Mr. W. F. Storey with you. I am sure you will not disappoint me. Drive up to the house. Also telegraph to Genl. Farnsworth to meet you here."[10] Mary's anxious state of mind is evident in her uncharacteristically large and shaky handwriting, the presence of ink spots (or possibly wiped tear drops) on the page, and in her postscript in which she offers to pay for Judge Bradwell's travel expenses—an abnormal offer from the usually penurious widow.

The fact that Mary Lincoln addressed her call for help to the Bradwells makes sense. James Bradwell was her attorney, Myra Bradwell was her good friend, and both were influential people. One interesting revelation from this letter is Mary's request for Wilbur F. Storey. Storey was the editor of the *Chicago Times*, the most sensationalist newspaper in Chicago. He had been an antiwar Copperhead during the Civil War and made the *Times* one of the most vituperative critics of the Lincoln administration. Postwar, the *Times* was an outspoken reporter and critic of Chicago society. Storey's motto was "to print the news and raise hell."[11] Mary's request to speak with the controversial editor shows that she understood

Mary Lincoln's first letter from Bellevue Place Sanitarium seeking help in obtaining her release, July 28, 1875. Frederic N. Towers Collection, Library of Congress. Photo courtesy Towers family.

Also bring Mr W. F.
Storey with you.
I am sure you will
not disappoint me
Drive up to the house.
Also telegraph to Genl
Farnsworth to meet
you here —
    With much love
to Mrs Bradwell,
believe me,
        Truly yours

If your trip M.L.

                Mary Lincoln
Please pardon me if I mention
that I will meet the expense

the need to harness the power of the press in her cause. It also shows that the inception of the frontal public assault on her incarceration was Mary's idea, and not Myra Bradwell's idea, as has been previously supposed.[12] For her to rely on a man who had previously criticized her idolized husband shows to what lengths she would go to achieve her goal.

Mary's friends did not arrive at Bellevue all at once, however, leading to the erroneous surmise that she had written separate letters. Farnsworth was the first to appear at Bellevue during the afternoon of July 29. He stated that Mary "wants her liberty and she wanted him to help her," although she did not complain about her treatment. Farnsworth thought she looked better than the last time he saw her. "He thinks *she does not talk like a sane woman* but still she would hardly be called insane by those who used to know her—He thinks she has been on the border of insanity for many years," the patient progress report noted. Farnsworth suggested Mary be set free but Robert maintain control of her money and property, under which arrangement she could "not do much harm."[13] That afternoon Mary wrote a letter she said was to her old washerwoman, but in reality it contained letters to other past friends seeking help. Dr. Patterson forwarded the letter to Robert Lincoln. During the evening, James and Myra Bradwell arrived at Bellevue. Myra told Dr. Patterson that even though she believed Mary was "not quite right," she thought the widow should be allowed to "be at home and have 'tender loving care.'"[14]

Dr. Patterson did not seem to be upset by the visits of Farnsworth or the Bradwells. He was probably accustomed to family and friends of his patients offering suggestions about treatment and early release. The patient progress report shows Mary was "very much afraid" Dr. Patterson would never trust her again because of her letter-writing deceit, and the day after the Bradwells' visit, she asked that she be allowed to send a letter to Myra Bradwell. Dr. Patterson told Mary she was "at liberty to write where she pleased and to whom she pleased—but that she ought to be open about it."[15] He also said he felt it proper to forward any letters she wrote to persons unknown to him to her legal conservator, Robert, for review. Mary "thought this fair and right."[16] The next day, July 31, Mary stayed in her room and did nothing worth noting in the Bellevue daily report.

James and Myra Bradwell were not idle on their return from Batavia. The next day, they wrote letters to Mary's sister Elizabeth Edwards and her cousin John Todd Stuart. These letters—among the cache of newly discovered materials—suggest that either Mary greatly exaggerated her suffering to the Bradwells or the Bradwells wrote with hyperbole. Most likely, it was a little of both. James Bradwell told Stuart that Mary "feels lonesome and that the restraint of the place is unendurable."[17] Myra Bradwell told Elizabeth Edwards that Mary "feels her incarceration most terribly and desires to get out from behind the *grates and bars.*"[18] This last, which was untrue, is a charge both Bradwells would later make to newspapers as well. The Bradwells suggested their correspondents visit Mary at the sanitarium, and that Mary accompany her sister back to Springfield for a short visit. "I cannot feel that it is necessary to keep her thus restrained," Myra Bradwell wrote. "Perhaps I do not look at the matter rightly, but let this be my excuse—I love her most tenderly and feel sorry to see one heartache added to her already overburdened soul."[19]

Mrs. Edwards's reply to Myra Bradwell, also found amid the "lost letters," shows that Elizabeth felt the same as the Bradwells and General Farnsworth; namely, that Mary was not sane, but that it was improper to place her in a sanitarium. "Had I been consulted, I would have remonstrated earnestly against the step taken," Edwards wrote. She thought her sister simply needed a personal attendant and companion. "The judgment of others must now, I presume, be silently acquiesced in, for a time, in the hope, that ere long, her physical and mental condition, will be improved, by rest and medical treatment."[20] Elizabeth could not visit Mary, since she was recovering from a recent surgical operation, but felt it would do her sister good to visit friends. No response from John Todd Stuart to James Bradwell is known to exist.

Now, with a sympathetic friend with whom to commiserate and a goal to achieve, Mary kept in close contact with Myra Bradwell, pouring out her sorrows and frustrations and continually requesting help. Mary was trying to amass an army of supporters to come to her aid, and she repeatedly asked Myra to contact old friends. On August 2 alone, Mary asked Myra to contact six people. She also lamented, "It does not appear that God is good, to have placed me here. I endeavor to read my Bible and offer up my petitions three times a day. But my afflicted heart fails me and my voice often falters in prayer. I have worshipped my son and no unpleasant word ever passed between us, yet I cannot understand why I should have been brought out here." Most interesting, however, is that the letter shows Mary's mania for clothing had not abated, for she asked that Myra on her next visit bring samples of black alpaca, "a best quality without luster and without cotton," as well as samples of heavier black woolen goods.[21]

Mary's agitation is obvious in the next letter she wrote to Myra Bradwell, which, although undated, appears to have been written also on August 2. It sounds much the same as the first letter. It frantically repeats, and demands, and even begs, five times, for Myra and James Bradwell to come visit Bellevue; and again requests Myra to contact three of Mary's old friends and her sister, Elizabeth Edwards. "Without doubt, you will not forget me," Mary wrote. "God will not fail to reward you if you do not *fail* to visit the widow of Abraham Lincoln in her solitude. . . . *Come, come,* is the watchword." This letter is interesting as well in that it is the first letter that offers insight into Mary's feelings about her son. "If I have used excited words in reference to my son, may God forgive me, and may *you both* forget it." The widow's repentance shows that she was very excited when telling the Bradwells of her situation but also that her feelings for Robert were not calloused. However, she knew that Robert thought her desire for clothing was symptomatic of mania, and so she closed her letter to Myra with the warning to keep her request for dress materials a secret, writing, "you will understand."[22]

Mary's recently discovered letters do much to illuminate the inception of her quest for freedom from the sanitarium and the public controversy that was about to erupt. In particular, they reveal the inner machinations of Mary and the Bradwells, the tenor of their conversations during visits, and Mary's growing antipathy toward Robert. Perhaps most important, Mary's tendency to be agitated and her preoccupation with buying new clothing were still present and were even being aggravated by the Bradwells. There is no doubt that Myra Bradwell was advocating for Mary's release, fomenting thoughts of it in the widow's mind, and cooperating with her in laying plans for a public campaign. On August 6, during a visit to Bellevue, Myra had a long discussion with Dr. Patterson, during which "She told the doctor distinctly that she had no doubt that Mrs. Lincoln was insane and had been for some time—but she doubted the propriety of keeping her in an asylum for the insane."[23] She spent the night with Mary in her room, and the next morning again advised Dr. Patterson that Mary should be allowed to live at the Edwardses' home in Springfield.

By this point, Robert and Dr. Patterson had become suspicious of the effects of the Bradwells' visits. Myra had become so bold in her assertions of the need for Mary's freedom that she even showed Dr. Patterson the letter she had received from Elizabeth Edwards condemning Mary's commitment and told him to show it to Robert. This caused Robert to write the longest, most revealing letter of the entire episode to his aunt, explaining his actions. "There is no need of my rehearsing ten years of our domestic history. If it has caused you one tenth of the grief it has caused me, you will remember it," Robert wrote.[24] He considered it a "blessing" to put his mother at Bellevue, the facility and superintendent of which he described at length. Robert also criticized the interference of Myra Bradwell, saying he felt the quiet and absence of any chance of excitement at the sanitarium had improved his mother's condition. Dr. Patterson, however, who was in Chicago to consult with Robert that very day, was afraid that the Bradwells' visits and manner would "tend to undo the good that has been accomplished."[25]

"What trouble Mrs. Bradwell may give me with her interference I cannot foretell," Robert wrote. "I understand she is a high priestess in a gang of Spiritualists and from what I have heard it is to their interest that my mother should be at liberty to control herself and her property."[26] This was, of course, one of the reasons Robert had his mother committed in the first place. His mother's "feebleness of mind," as Robert called it, and her belief in Spiritualism made her susceptible to thieves and sharpers. But he also feared for his mother's safety, saying that if she were freed she would immediately go to Europe, "and such a thing in her present state of mind would be productive of the most disturbing events to us all."[27] Robert reiterated that he had no objection to Mary's visit to Springfield, in fact he thought it would be beneficial, and he invited his aunt to visit Bellevue to see the place for herself, rather than rely on the word of Myra Bradwell.

By early August, Robert had become so concerned about Myra Bradwell's conduct that he proposed a conference with her.[28] Little did Robert know, however, to what extent the Bradwells truly were aiding and abetting his mother. On the very day Robert consulted Dr. Patterson in Chicago and explained his motivations to his aunt, Saturday, August 7, Mary Lincoln had a meeting of her own. After spending Friday night in Mary's room, Myra Bradwell left Saturday morning for Chicago, but returned at 1:00 P.M. with someone the patient progress report described as a "Mr. Wilkie of Chicago." Mary, Myra, and Mr. Wilkie then spent two hours in private conversation.[29] "Mr. Wilkie," in fact, was Franc B. Wilkie, the principal writer (editorial and otherwise) for the *Chicago Times* newspaper. He was described in 1868 as a man of large imagination, who wrote with ease and rapidity, preferred sentiment to dry logic, and "hesitates at no subject."[30] He was best known for his descriptive writing about individuals: his artistic and minute elaboration of details and his ability to illuminate the character of anyone he chose.[31] Wilkie's visit was the fruition of Mary's initial July 28 request to bring *Times* editor Wilbur F. Storey to Bellevue. At the time of his visit, with Dr. Patterson absent, none of the employees at the sanitarium knew who Wilkie was, although it did not take them long to find out.[32]

Dr. Patterson and Robert Lincoln were furious that Myra Bradwell had brought a man who was a complete stranger to them to visit Mary.

Myra Bradwell. Library of Congress, LC-USZ62-21202.

Their indignation was magnified by the fact that the visit was purposely arranged for a Saturday, when both women knew Dr. Patterson would be away from the sanitarium. "I can but regard this as a breach of hospitality, and of common courtesy to me," Patterson wrote to Myra Bradwell the next day.[33] He told her that she needed thereafter to get Robert Lincoln's approval for any future visits, especially when accompanied by a stranger, as well as for mailing or conveying any of Mary's letters. Robert called Myra "a pest and a nuisance," and "characterized her introduction of Mr. Wilkie . . . as an outrage."[34]

In only one week, beginning with the first visit of Myra Bradwell to Bellevue Place, Mary Lincoln, who had previously been characterized as one of the best patients Dr. Patterson had ever treated, gathered her friends to foment for her freedom, practiced deceit and trickery upon the staff regarding her mail, and allowed an interview with a sensationalist journalist on a day she knew the doctor would be away. What other personal and professional stresses Dr. Patterson may have been under at the time are uncertain, but Myra Bradwell's meddling certainly affected him. Although Robert Lincoln told his aunt on August 7 that Dr. Patterson felt the Bradwells' influence was damaging Mary's progress, on August 9 the doctor told Robert that Mary was "both mentally and physically greatly improved," and he saw no reason medically why she should not be allowed to leave Bellevue and go live with her sister in Springfield, "unless her condition should change for the worse."[35] This sudden change of attitude and diagnosis is strange, unless he was so exasperated by the Bradwells, and/or possibly afraid of the publicity in the notorious *Chicago Times*, that maybe he was ready to wash his hands of the whole affair.

But the worst was yet to come. Over the ensuing two weeks, a flurry of activity occurred, with letters and visits being variously traded between all the principal people involved: Robert Lincoln, Mary Lincoln, Myra Bradwell, James Bradwell, Dr. Patterson, and Elizabeth Edwards. Robert and Myra had an apparently cordial conference on August 10, at which Myra conceded that Mary was "not entirely right," but repeated her contention that Mary should not be confined to a sanitarium. Robert wryly noted in a letter to his aunt, "How completely recovered my mother really is is shown by Mrs. B's saying she was to take out to her samples of dress goods she wants to buy. She has with her *seven* trunks of clothing and there are stored here *nine* more." He told Mrs. Bradwell that any experiment of releasing his mother "would be interesting to those who have no responsibility for the results. They can afterwards dismiss the matter with a shrug of the shoulders." He also told his aunt that Myra Bradwell convinced him she was not a Spiritualist, as he had supposed.[36]

Despite her statements to Robert Lincoln, Myra Bradwell wrote to Elizabeth Edwards on August 11 that Mary had "not one symptom of insanity." She urged the older sister to accept Mary into her home. "I am so sorry for the dear woman, shut up in that place. When they tell me she is not restrained, I want to ask how they should like it themselves?"[37] Elizabeth Edwards, however, understood the game the Bradwells were playing, and between August 11 and August 14, she wrote Robert four letters, in which she never once suggested that Mary be released. Elizabeth apologized to Robert for her letter to Myra Bradwell of August 3, which Myra clearly had taken as an affirmation of her belief that an injustice had been done and explained that she had only promised to visit Bellevue out of sympathy and kindness.[38]

Elizabeth truly was recovering from surgery and had no intention to visit, nor did she intend to allow Mary to come live with her. She told Robert on August 12 that she assumed any visit by Mary would be just that, a visit, accompanied by a nurse, and then a return to Bellevue. "The peculiarities of her whole life have been so marked and well understood by me, that I have not indulged the faintest hope, of a permanent cure. The painful excitement of the *past years*, only added to the malady, [which was] . . . apparent to her family for years, before the saddest events, occurred." Elizabeth closed the August 12 letter with the clear and ingenuous statement, "I am unwilling to urge any steps, or assume any responsibility, in her case. My present feeble health, causing such nervous prostration, as would render me, a most unfit person, to control an unsound mind. I am now satisfied, that understanding her propensities, as you do, the course you have decided upon, is the surest and wisest." [39]

Elizabeth Edwards showed herself to be somewhat of a coward regarding her sister. She lied to her about coming to visit Bellevue, simply to indulge Mary, and she twice asked Robert not to tell her sister her true feelings about her mental state. She suggested instead that he say Dr. Patterson, County Court Judge Wallace, or Leonard Swett was to blame for Mary not being allowed to live in Springfield.[40] "I am unwilling to excite her by intimating anything unpleasant, when she seems disposed to be amicable."[41] When she later met with Myra Bradwell and said the opposite of what she wrote to Robert Lincoln, she practically called her nephew a bully and a liar.[42] Subsequent historians have accused Robert of glib deceit when, on August 14, he informed Myra Bradwell that Mary could not make a visit to Springfield because Elizabeth Edwards was too ill to receive her.[43] Robert told Myra what he had said numerous times previously: that he regretted the situation as he hoped a visit and renewed acquaintance with her sister would do his mother good.[44] To be fair, Elizabeth's letter explaining her recovery from a surgical operation was unknown until its recent discovery, but to accuse Robert Lincoln of an outright lie to keep his mother locked up seems quite unfair. The historical evidence already showed clearly that Elizabeth Edwards wanted no responsibility for her sister's keeping at all.

Robert Lincoln did not confine himself to excuses, however, when communicating with Myra Bradwell on August 14. "I visited my mother on yesterday and I could not help observing with pain, a renewal in the degree of the same appearances which marked her in May and which I had not noticed in my last few visits. I do not know of any outside cause for this unless it is the constant excitement she has been in since your first visit." While he had told her when they met on August 10 that he did not object to her visiting his mother, his last visit convinced him that Myra's influence had created "a partial destruction of the good accomplished by two months and a half of quiet and freedom from all chance of excitement."[45] He asked her to visit less often and not to bring people whom he did not know; nor did he want her to aid his mother in corresponding with anyone other than family.

During this time, Mary Lincoln was not idle. On August 8, she wrote a letter to James Bradwell that was perceptibly different from all her other correspondence to either him or his wife:

> Knowing well your great nobleness of heart, I can but be *well* assured, that you will soon see that I am released from this place. Mrs. Bradwell will explain every thing. I am sleeping very finely and as I am perfectly sane, I do not desire to become insane. I pray you to see that justice is done immediately to me, for my mind is entirely clear and my health is perfectly good. With a high appreciation of yourself and your wife, son, and daughter, whom I love very much, believe me, very truly, your friend, Mary Lincoln.[46]

What is most interesting about this letter is that it is so clear, succinct, and cogent, not rambling or erratic, and written in a very steady hand. Yet, its utter restraint, professionalism, and lack of overt emotionalism, so prevalent in Mary's other letters to the Bradwells, as well as the fact that it was addressed to James and not Myra Bradwell, suggest a deeper purpose than mere correspondence. In fact, this letter was written with such purposeful intent, it is not fanciful to call it almost a press release; for it easily could have been intended for inclusion in Wilkie's *Chicago Times* article as testimony to Mary's unjust imprisonment. This letter is another indication of Mary's strength of character, her resolve to achieve her goal, and her complete command of her freedom campaign. It does not suggest, however, that she was "completely sane," because she could have had continuing symptoms and still created a clear statement such as this, as long as she avoided her typically delusional topics such as clothing and money.

Around August 8, Mary told Myra Bradwell that Robert had written to Elizabeth Edwards about the possibility of a visit. Mary's resentment of Robert was growing, however, and she wrote, "I rather think he *would* prefer *my* remaining *here* in his heart."[47] She feverishly requested the Bradwells not to forget to visit her and twice told them to write to Elizabeth Edwards. This letter, part of the cache of recently discovered correspondence, plainly shows Mary's agitation, with its large and shaky letters, its eleven underlines, its repetitions, and the anxious impatience evident in her repeated use of the words *urgent* and *urgently*. It also offers further proof that her clothing mania continued, for she requested Myra to bring an exchange of Mary's trunks as well as a small key to another trunk.

In Mary's next letter to Myra Bradwell, written the following day, she was even more agitated, repetitious, and rambling, paranoid that the Bradwells would forget to visit, forget her, and abandon her. Her paranoia also extended to the trunks full of clothing she requested. "Come to me Mrs. B. bring your husband also bring those 2 trunks I wrote you about. A long Russian leather trunk and the tall blk trunk marked M.L. *fail me not*. Come to me. I long to see you both. Bring me also the key of the middle sized trunk. I must have you near me again."[48]

Mary's agitation, so evident in her letters, also was evident to her doctors and attendants at Bellevue Place. The patient progress reports stated her to be more discontented since Myra Bradwell's July 7 visit with Franc Wilkie than during the past week.[49] She wrote many letters, practically confined herself to her room, continued her capricious behavior of ordering, but then not taking, carriage rides, and disavowed any knowledge of when the Bradwells would visit. "Mrs. Lincoln is frequently untruthful in her statements, and exceedingly deceitful. Her lying and deceit should be put down to insanity," the report noted on July 16.[50] Mary also was distressed about "an important paper" that belonged to her that Judge Bradwell had in his possession. "She desired very much to see him about it."[51] Perhaps this explains one reason for Mary's dire fear of the Bradwells' forgetting to visit or neglecting her.

Robert perceived his mother was reverting to her previous nervousness; and perhaps he even knew that she was beginning to resent him. He wrote her a tenderly worded letter explaining that Elizabeth was too ill to consent to a visit, but he would try to arrange it soon, as there was nothing he thought would do her more good. "You must trust me that I can and will do everything that is for your good and you must not allow yourself to think otherwise, for in that way you will only retard the recovery I am looking for," he concluded. "Your stay with Dr. Patterson has plainly benefited you and you must not undo all that has been done."[52] Robert Lincoln here seems to have miscalculated the strength of his mother's resolve, as well as her growing resentment. He also had not learned something his aunt would later tell him: that his mother did not regard herself as insane, and every time he alluded to her mental state it simply upset her.

Robert Lincoln also seems to have underestimated Myra Bradwell's tenacity, which is strange since, as a Chicago attorney himself, he should have been well aware of her fight to be accepted at the bar and her legal activism. Despite his rebuke of August 14 and his limitations on her visits, Myra Bradwell did not relent. Instead, she went on the offensive. She still had the unpublished story written by Franc Wilkie of the *Chicago Times*, which she was apparently holding for the appropriate time. She also paid a visit to Elizabeth Edwards. Elizabeth has been called the unsung hero of the insanity affair, but her inconsistent actions do not bear this out.[53] Myra's silver lawyer's tongue, combined with Elizabeth's cowardice and fear of confrontation, caused Mary's sister to backpedal.

Elizabeth wrote Robert on August 17—who was at this time vacationing at Rye Beach, New Hampshire—to say that he had misunderstood her previous letters. "It may be that a refusal, to yield, to her wishes, at this crisis, will greatly increase her disorder. . . . I now say, that *if you will bring* her down, *feeling perfectly willing*, to make the experiment, I promise to do all in my power, for her comfort and recovery."[54] On the same day that he received his aunt's capricious letter, Robert received upsetting news from Dr. Patterson:

> On yesterday Judge and Mrs. Bradwell spent an hour in private consultation with Mrs. L. [and] they remained in my office about five minutes only—just long enough for the judge to say that "Mrs. L. ought not longer to remain in confinement and that it was injuring her health." I showed them your letter from Mrs. Edwards and they intimated that improper influences had been brought to bear upon Mrs. E. that had caused her to write such a letter. I presume they will continue their mission. If Mrs. E. shall change her [illegible] purpose, shall I remand the patient to her?[55]

The Bellevue Place patient progress report for that day contained this entry:

> So much discussion with the patient about going away, tends to unsettle her mind and make her more discontented and should be stopped. She should be let alone and this I have told Judge Bradwell. She should never have been subjected to this unnecessary excitement. It is now apparent that the frequent visits of Mrs. B have tended to stir up discontent & thus do harm.[56]

Finally, Robert Lincoln had had enough. He responded to Dr. Patterson with a terse telegram: "Contents of letters sent by you show that your patient must not be allowed to leave you now. Cut off absolutely all communication with improper persons. I write today to you and Mrs. Edwards."[57] Upon receiving Robert Lincoln's telegram, Dr. Patterson immediately wrote to James Bradwell and courteously informed him that, at least until Robert's return in early September from New Hampshire, the Bradwells would not be allowed to visit Mary Lincoln. "I am quite willing to believe that the objects of your visits and the numerous letters of Mrs. Bradwell are well meant and not designed to promote unrest and discontent. But I have become fully convinced that such is their tendency and result," Patterson wrote. He said that the possibility of Mary's removal from Bellevue never should have been discussed with her and promises never made, especially by people not in control of the situation. Such conversations had put Mary's mind in a "constant ferment."[58]

James Bradwell replied by calling Dr. Patterson a hypocrite, since he also had discussed Mary's possible removal with her. But, more than that, Bradwell was clearly incensed at what he called Mary's "close confinement." He said she "pines for liberty" and that it was "shameful" to keep her locked up. "I believe that such confinement is injurious to her in the extreme, and calculated to drive her insane," Bradwell wrote. He closed his letter with a threat: "Should you not allow her to visit Mrs. Edwards, and insist on keeping her in close confinement, and I should be satisfied that the good of Mrs. Lincoln required it, as I certainly shall unless there is change in her condition, I, as her legal advisor and friend, will see if a habeas corpus cannot open the door of Mrs. Lincoln's prison house."[59]

Whether or not Mary was aware of her son's order is unclear. Patterson told the Bradwells they could write to her and create an explanation, although there is no evidence they did so. The patient progress report does show, however, that on August 18 Mary was "more capricious and [has] a little tendency to irritability," and on August 19, she was "in a perturbed state of mind" and "shows great capriciousness about her food and her washing." The report said Mary asked every morning for cornbread and then did not eat it, but called for rolls; she then ordered griddle cakes for every supper, but did not eat them and called for rolls.[60]

Robert Lincoln's decision to bar the Bradwells from Bellevue Place was one he could not help but make. Both he and Dr. Patterson considered Mary's progress to be receding, and it is clear that Robert also perceived his mother's growing anger and suspicion toward him. Her resentment obviously was fueled, if not incited, by the Bradwells, as was her growing belief that the sanitarium had changed from a retreat to a prison. The evidence shows that Mary was complacent about her situation until the arrival of the Bradwells. The two lawyers, whom Robert considered meddlers in affairs that were none of their business, also offended his sense of family privacy. Yet, in seeking to drive the Bradwells away, Robert greatly misapprehended their indefatigability and sheer audacity. It was a mistake he would shortly be made to regret, as they forcibly transformed the battle over his mother's situation from a private family affair to an indecent public spectacle.

7 *No More Insane than I Am*

THAT MARY LINCOLN AND THE BRADWELLS knew they must harness the power of the popular press and public sentiment to aid in the widow's release was evident in Mary's first request to speak with the *Chicago Times* in July 1875; yet, between the July 13 *Post and Mail* story and James Bradwell's acrimonious reply to Dr. Patterson's August 18 letter, the papers were strangely devoid of any mention of the widow's plight at Bellevue Place. Even *Times* editor Franc Wilkie, after two hours of conversation with Mary on August 7, had published nothing. All of this changed, however, when the Bradwells found their suggestions rejected and their visits and letters forbidden by Robert Lincoln. Since they could no longer lobby privately for Mary's release, they decided to do so publicly. For the next two weeks, Mary Lincoln's situation was in the local and national newspapers almost every day.

Without consulting Dr. Patterson or Robert Lincoln, the Bradwells leaked to the *Post and Mail* that Mary Lincoln was partially restored to health, would go visit her sister in Springfield, and might not return to the sanitarium at all. The paper's August 21 edition stated, "A legal lady of Chicago and her husband" had taken steps for Mary's release, "it being implied that her contemplated visit to Springfield was the result of their friendly, if not professional, intercourse."[1] The Associated Press repeated the news the next day, as did the *Chicago Tribune*, saying it would be "received with pleasure by everyone," especially by those friends of Mary who opposed her incarceration in the first place.[2]

Leaking this false information to the press was only the opening effort. On August 23, Judge Bradwell gave an interview with the *Post and Mail*, during which he repeatedly complained that Mary was the sane victim of an unjust confinement.

> Mrs. Lincoln ought not to be where she is now, and never ought to have been placed there. It was a gross outrage to imprison her there behind grates and bars, in a place understood to be for mad people. Why to be so shut up and guarded, and locked up at night, with the feeling that it may last for life, is enough to make almost any aged

and delicate woman crazy. She is no more insane today than you and
I are.[3]

Bradwell said Mary had asked him what she had done to deserve such
a fate; complained that she was not insane, but soon would be; and insisted that she did not want to be a prisoner. Interestingly, Bradwell did
not attack or blame Robert Lincoln in any way during his interview,
but instead denounced Dr. Patterson as a man with suspicious motives
who needlessly censored Mary's mail and was opposed to her freedom.
Bradwell also tempered his rhetoric to say that he hoped Mary's release
could be achieved amicably, but that he was prepared to initiate "startling
developments" if she stayed at Bellevue Place much longer. He modestly
declined to specify what those developments would be, saying, "Let her
get out of danger first."[4]

With this interview, James Bradwell showed himself to be a formi-
dable adversary. He made Mary's case sound dire and desperate, implying
that she was suffering and in "danger," and that her jailer was needlessly
apathetic. He characterized himself as a concerned friend who was acting with candor and credibility but was too much of a gentleman to
offer threats. Perhaps most important, he set his condemnation on Dr.
Patterson and not Robert Lincoln. This was a plan executed with acu-
men. The American public would not have tolerated an attack on Robert
Lincoln. He was the only surviving son of the martyred president who
had endured his father's assassination and his mother's insanity trial
with nothing but sympathy and respect from the public. He also was
a well-respected Chicago attorney who would have defended himself
much more deftly than Dr. Patterson did, and Robert would have been
supported by numerous political luminaries, including President Ulysses
S. Grant.[5] No, to accuse Dr. Patterson of mistreatment was a clever, and
much safer, plan to evoke sympathy for the widow's cause.

The next day, August 24, Franc Wilkie published in the *Chicago Times*
the account of his July 7 interview with Mary Lincoln. The headline
read, "REASON RESTORED: Mrs. Lincoln Will Soon Return from
Her Brief Visit to the Insane Asylum; for Her Physicians Pronounce Her
Sane as Those Who Sent Her There; and She Is Only Awaiting Robert's
Return from the East to Set Her Free Again." The story purported to be
an independent analysis of Mary's health through "scientific facts" based
on "personal observation" by a reporter who went to Bellevue Place "not
as a newspaper man but as a gentleman who knew her history and took
a friendly interest in all that pertained to her welfare." Of course, the
historical evidence proves that Wilkie was invited there by Mary Lincoln

and Myra Bradwell to carry out a specific agenda as a reporter to condemn the sanitarium and exonerate the beleaguered widow from the accusation of insanity. The *Times*'s disingenuousness went even further, however, when it farcically claimed "a mutual friend who happened to be there at the same time" had introduced its reporter to Mary.[6]

As Mary and Myra intended, the story was written and timed for maximum impact and did not disappoint in its sensationalism. The *Times* declared that its correspondent "became convinced that [Mary's] mind was in a perfectly sound and healthy condition," and there was "not a sign of weakness or any abnormal manifestations of mind visible." It reported that Mary attributed her pretrial behavior in Florida to fever and a shattered nervous system, but that now she was in perfect mental and physical health and "ought not to be deprived of her liberty."[7] The story also contained an interview with Myra Bradwell, who avowed that she was "extremely reluctant" to talk about such a private subject, but who then proceeded to echo her husband's statements that Mary was the sane victim of a cruel doctor. "I was inexpressibly shocked when I learned of her alleged insanity and of her confinement in an asylum at Batavia," Bradwell said. "During her stay in Florida I received many long and beautifully-written letters from her. . . . I wondered what could have occurred to have unbalanced her mind so suddenly."[8]

Here, Myra Bradwell cleverly did not judge Mary's state of mind at the time of the trial but simply said that by late August she considered Mary recovered. "She is no more insane than I am," Myra declared. She also repeated her husband's statements that Elizabeth Edwards was prepared to receive her sister into her home, and all that was needed was the return of Robert Lincoln from the East. Myra slyly added that Robert had told her he would allow his mother's release, and that she had "no reason in the world to doubt Mr. Robert Lincoln's word."[9] Myra Bradwell was being especially selective with her word choice here. Robert's letters all show he consented to a visit, not a release. Myra's words took on added weight that day when the *Chicago Times*, calling her "a lady of prominence and unquestioned veracity," espoused her case on its editorial page. "The case is a peculiarly sad one," the paper declared, "But if [Mrs. Lincoln] has since recovered her right mind, and is being held in duress unlawfully, and without good cause, the public will unite in a demand for her release."[10]

As her husband had done, Myra Bradwell showed that she, too, was a shrewd antagonist. She upheld the contemporary standard of appropriate female decency and reticence by regretting the publicity of Mary's case at the same time that she continued the accusations against Dr. Patterson.

Most important, she not only avoided condemning Robert Lincoln but praised him as an honorable man, making it impossible for Robert to oppose his mother's freedom without dishonoring himself.

As it happened, Robert's rebuttal was unnecessary. Newspapers across the country, echoing public sentiments, immediately attacked the Bradwells—and the *Chicago Times*—for their meddling. The *Springfield (Illinois) Journal* called the Bradwells "busybodies" whose attacks upon Mary's family, friends, and physicians were "an extremely injudicious, as well as an unfeeling and gratuitous outrage."[11] The *Boston Globe* agreed and said the Bradwells' accusations were "not borne out by the facts, and . . . [are] known to be utterly untrue."[12] The *Chicago Tribune* called the situation "an atrocious libel" upon Mary's family and friends. It decried the "scandal" that had been "set afloat by over-officious and intermeddling mischief-makers, who interfered in a matter which did not concern them, for purposes of sensation."[13] Another newspaper called the story "a contemptible fiction" and "foul scandal" that insulted Robert Lincoln and recommended that he contemplate legal action.[14]

The *St. Louis Republican* reported that Mary's relatives in Springfield, Illinois, were "greatly annoyed" by the Bradwells' public statements, and that Myra Bradwell's visits were worsening the widow's condition.[15] Mary's relatives were, in fact, "indignant" at the Bradwells, according to Dr. Patterson. He wrote Robert that Elizabeth Edwards's two daughters visited Mary on August 19 and told the physician that they "are satisfied with what has been done in Mrs. Lincoln's case, and would feel obliged to Mrs. B if she would mind her own business and not meddle with Mrs. L. They say also that Mrs. B. wrote a very mean letter to Mrs. Edwards, and I understood them to intimate that she charged unkind or improper treatment toward Mrs. L. while here."[16]

Mary's old friend and pastor, Professor David Swing, tried to be a voice of moderation in the debate. He called Mary's "weakness of mind" a temporary occurrence during the spring and said she was sufficiently recovered to leave Bellevue Place. He tried to dispel the accusations of conspiracy by saying that attorneys Leonard Swett and Isaac Arnold were too noble to do such a thing. He also defended Robert. "There is room in this matter for an immense amount of injustice to be done Robert Lincoln, and we hope the public will decline accepting the opportunity," Swing wrote.[17]

The *Chicago Times* supported Swing's statement and editorialized that since Mary's episode was only temporary, to continue her confinement would be nothing less than "unlawful restraint." The *Times* also took a swipe at the *Chicago Tribune*, saying it had been "guilty of scandalous vituperation" of the trustworthy Bradwells, while it ignorantly persisted in calling Mary a lunatic. "The *Tribune* will do well not to permit its zeal to outrun decency and discretion," it stated. Most interesting, however, was the degree to which the *Times* had become invested in the story. It warned the *Tribune* (and, indirectly, Robert Lincoln) that there were many facts in reference to Mary Lincoln's "prolonged confinement" that, if made public, "would not reflect credit upon parties who are closely related to it as principals."[18]

At this point, Dr. Patterson decided to enter the fray with a letter to the editor of the *Chicago Tribune*. One by one, Patterson rebutted every accusation made by the Bradwells concerning improper incarceration, locked doors, barred windows, and unnecessary restraint. He called their assertion that he signed a certificate declaring Mary fully recovered as untrue. "She is certainly much improved, both mentally and physically; but I have not at any time regarded her as a person of sound mind," he wrote. "I believe her to be now insane." Patterson also said he was not opposed to Mary going to Springfield to live with her sister, but her condition was such that he did not think it would work. "The experiment, if made, will result only in giving the coveted opportunity to make extended rambles, to renew the indulgence of her purchasing mania, and other morbid mental manifestations," he wrote. Judge Bradwell's August 19 letter threatening a writ of habeas corpus clearly did not intimidate Patterson. In fact, Patterson practically dared Bradwell to try it, for he concluded his letter by saying, "Mrs. Lincoln has been placed where she is under the forms of law, and, if any have grievance, the law is open to them."[19]

Not to be outdone, the Bradwells responded by releasing the correspondence between Judge Bradwell and Dr. Patterson, which was published in the *Chicago Tribune* the next day.[20] It seems to have had little, if any, effect, however, as no articles or editorials about the controversy occurred in the Chicago papers over the next few days. That did not mean that the Bradwells were done fighting. They simply switched to a different tactic. As public sentiment had turned against them, the Bradwells' next publicity effort was anonymous and in a different newspaper. It was their most sensationalist, mendacious, and audacious endeavor to date, headlined "MRS. LINCOLN: Is the Widow of President Lincoln a Prisoner? No One Allowed to See Her Except by Order of Her Son." The article was a first-person narrative by "a lady of this city, who has, for many years, been an intimate friend of Mrs. Lincoln."[21]

The narrator stated it was her first visit to Bellevue Place and her first attempt to contact Mary Lincoln since before the trial. "I had no object in my view in making this visit except to *satisfy myself* in regard to Mrs.

Lincoln's insanity, of which so many of late have expressed doubts."[22] Yet when, at the front door, she asked Dr. Patterson's permission to visit the former First Lady, his expression became "flinty," and he refused unless she had permission from Robert Lincoln. "She may be out in a few days and you can see her to your heart's content," he said. He also would not allow the anonymous narrator to leave a note, saying it would only disturb his patient's mind. "If she is only permitted to see such persons as you choose, and not permitted to receive letters except from such, she is virtually a prisoner, is she not?" the narrator accused. "Madam, she is no more so than any other patients I have under my care," Patterson supposedly replied.[23]

The narrator then sat, first on the outside stoop and then inside a parlor, to pass the time until leaving to catch her train back to Chicago. She wondered at the emptiness of the place, supposing the stories that Patterson's patients were free to roam his house "must be an erroneous impression of a good-natured public." She also decided that if she were placed in such a place by friends or family either to "get rid" of her or because they truly believed her insane, "it would take but a few days to make a raving maniac of me."[24] Other newspapers quickly exposed Myra Bradwell's ruse, however, and her meddling was again publicly condemned.[25]

When Robert Lincoln returned to Chicago on September 1, he was confronted by what he termed "the extraordinary performances of the Bradwells." He had not even had time to "digest" them, however, before writing a letter to Dr. Patterson asking for the physician's opinion on the safety of moving Mary Lincoln to Springfield.[26] It is unlikely that the actions of the Bradwells precipitated this letter; as Robert said, he hadn't read the newspapers yet. Most likely, Robert had been considering the "experiment" of his mother's move to Springfield for the entire two weeks of his vacation.[27] Robert Lincoln was not the type of man to be pressured by others. He was intelligent, self-assured, well-connected, and, as one historian wrote, "he had his father's fine farseeing judgment, one of the rarest of human qualities."[28] Rather than being afraid of, or outwitted by, the Bradwells, as some have contended, Robert simply realized that there was no return to a simple, quiet stay at Bellevue Place for his mother.[29] Mary was now constantly agitated by the promise of Springfield and would only continue to be agitated, even if all communication with and knowledge of the Bradwells were stopped. In such a state of constant ferment, her health would fail to improve and perhaps would decline. Even Dr. Patterson told Robert, "Now that so much is said about Mrs. Lincoln's removal to Springfield, I think it would be well if she could go at once."[30]

For such a step as removing his mother from professional care, Robert did not want to rely solely on Dr. Patterson's opinion of Mary's condition. He wrote to Dr. Andrew McFarland, superintendent of the Jacksonville, Illinois, State Hospital for the Insane, and Dr. Alexander McDill, superintendent of the Madison, Wisconsin, State Hospital for the Insane, requesting they examine Mary Lincoln and offer their opinions on the safety of her removal from Bellevue Place.[31] "As a guest of her sister, I do not think it possible that the same restraint could be exercised over possible irrational acts, should they occur as if she remained under the care of Dr. Patterson," Robert wrote, "but I am anxious that she should visit my aunt, if it is not probable that harm to her may come of it."[32]

McDill could not travel to Bellevue Place in a timely manner, but McFarland arrived four days after receiving Robert's letter.[33] He found Mary's condition such as to cause him "grave apprehensions as to the result unless the utmost quietude is observed for the few ensuing months, beyond which all reasonable hope of restoration must be abandoned." McFarland did not think it wise to let Mary go to Springfield unless she was constantly under the care of an attendant, but even then he saw "no good results likely to follow beyond gratifying an ardent desire to go, in which she seems to have been prompted by others. My fears are that a desire for further adventure will take possession of her mind, as soon as beyond the control of the present guardians of her safety, that may be attended with hazard if gratified."[34] Despite McFarland's opinion, Robert decided to make the experiment immediately. He told Dr. Patterson to prepare Mary for the journey and to allow her to bring only three trunks of possessions.[35]

Mary Lincoln left Bellevue Place Sanitarium on September 10, 1875, a little less than four months after her trial and commitment. She was accompanied by one of the Bellevue Place female attendants to Chicago, where she met Robert, and another female attendant, sent by Dr. McFarland, met her at Springfield the next day to act as her personal nurse.[36] According to Myra Bradwell's granddaughter, Mary Lincoln "went directly to my grandmother's home [in Chicago] and remained there some time before joining her sister, Mrs. Edwards, in Springfield."[37] The historical evidence does not bear out this assertion, however; the *Chicago Tribune* reported that Mary Lincoln met Robert at the Chicago train station, spent the night, and arrived in Springfield on the morning of September 11.[38] While it is possible that Robert allowed his mother to spend her first night out of the sanitarium at the Bradwell home on Michigan Avenue, considering all the trouble the couple caused, it is highly unlikely that Robert would have taken his mother there.

Mary's trip to Springfield was a visit, not a relocation. It was, as all parties involved called it, an "experiment" to test Mary's reaction. Elizabeth Edwards thought it would be good for Mary to be with family and friends, but Robert did not expect much. He had been telling his mother for years that she should reconnect with estranged acquaintances but was always rebuffed. He told his aunt this and explained his negative expectations. "I cannot have any confidence in her sincerity in this & I do not believe that if her object was accomplished, she would receive a call from any one of her sisters. Keep this letter and see if I am not correct," he admonished.[39]

But, at first, he was not correct. After three days in Springfield, Mary was happy and agreeable, willing to take walks and rides, and overall seemed "delighted" to visit friends and family. "I can truly say, that she never appeared to better advantage than she does now," Elizabeth wrote her nephew.[40] Robert's aunt also revealed exactly why, after ten years of estrangement, she had accepted her sister into her home. "Insanity, although a new feature, in our family, first appeared within my knowledge, in the case of my own daughter, at the early age of thirteen," she confided. "At the birth of each child, the same symptoms were shown, and severely felt, particularly by her husband, and myself. . . . God pity those who are the victims, and who are the anxious sufferers in such terrible afflictions!"[41] Historian Michael Burlingame recently has uncovered evidence that psychiatric illness actually ran deep in the Todd family. Mary's grandfather Levi Owen Todd, brother Levi, niece Mattie Todd, and grandniece Georgie Edwards all died in insane asylums; fourteen members of the Canfield family (cousins) were in various asylums; Mary's brother George suffered depression; and her grandniece, Nellie Canfield, committed suicide.[42]

Dr. Patterson and Robert Lincoln, however, were more interested in Mary's health and well-being than in pitying her. They both had a duty to perform. For Robert, it was nothing less than deciding whether or not his mother was better served at Bellevue Place or at the Edwards home. On September 20, ten days into Mary's visit, he requested Dr. Patterson's opinion on Mary's condition and on the safety of her permanent removal to Springfield. "I am not able to report much change in the mental condition of Mrs. Lincoln since you last saw her," the physician wrote. "I do not hesitate to say that as a result of her intercourse with Judge and Mrs. Bradwell, she became worse; and since they have ceased their visits, she is again better and improving." As to her permanent removal to Springfield, since she had complied with all the conditions placed upon her to achieve the move, "I suppose the experiment ought to be made."[43] After this letter, the widow's return to Bellevue Place was postponed indefinitely.

Mary Lincoln may have achieved her freedom from the sanitarium, but her legal status remained the same. She still was legally insane, and Robert still was her conservator. Under state law, there was no way to change that fact until at least one year after her commitment trial. This fact bothered Mary; it constantly ate at her mind. Still, her first months at the Edwards home were characterized by an improvement in her condition. "We take daily rides, and your mother enjoys, without a doubt, the change in her habits," Elizabeth Edwards reported in late September. "She has dined at Mrs. Smith's, taken tea at our sister Francis's, and received every visitor, with a manifestation of cheerfulness, and pleasure, as has surprised me. . . . Thus far, she has shown herself very clear-headed."[44] These good tidings must have continued through October and into early November, as no letters from that period are known to exist.[45]

Robert may have been as surprised as his aunt concerning his mother's uncharacteristic goodwill to family and friends; but more than likely, he was not. "Her course since the Inquisition has shown that in general she is able to control her impulses if she has an object in doing so," Robert wrote to David Davis in November.[46] In this case, her object was to spite the son who had locked her up and, to a lesser degree, the physician who kept her locked up. Both men made it clear they did not expect Mary's temperament or condition to change in Springfield, and Robert explicitly told his aunt to expect his mother to isolate herself. No doubt Elizabeth Edwards shared Robert's assessment with her sister. As Robert stated, since the trial, his mother "constantly kept in view her discharge," and her actions since then were calculated to facilitate that discharge.[47] By September, with her discharge achieved, Mary's next goal was to prove Robert's opinions about her wrong. Her resentment toward her son was visibly growing, and Elizabeth Edwards suggested that Robert stop alluding to his belief in his mother's insanity where she could hear it or read it, as it only upset her.[48]

By November 1875, Mary had a new goal: the return of her right to control her property. Robert's conservatorship was "very galling" to Mary's proud spirit, Elizabeth Edwards told her nephew, and she suggested that Mary should be allowed to control her own interests. "Surely, the evidence of derangement exhibited last spring, must have arisen from physical disorder. She informs me that her health was poor before going to Florida, and during her stay there, and on her return, was often conscious, of the presence of fever—moreover, had used chloral very freely, for the purpose of inducing sleep. Those causes, had doubtless much to do, with producing the sad result." In fact, in her two months with the Edwardses, Mary had acted "more reasonable and gentle, than in former years," her sister reported. "I have no hesitation in pronouncing her sane."[49]

Elizabeth also reported that Mary's purchasing of unnecessary items was not excessive, compared to what the widow could afford. She suggested Robert "assume indifference" to his mother's spending and thereby regain her affection and, ultimately, some influence in her pecuniary affairs. "Above all, do everything, that will conciliate and make her as happy, as it would be possible to render her—for she has indulged her morbid ways so long, that it is impossible to prevent frequent reactions, to extreme sadness."[50] Elizabeth here—unwittingly—offered further testimony to Mary's Bipolar Disorder, describing classic symptoms of recurring episodes of depression ("frequent reactions to extreme sadness") punctuated by periods of normalcy; and still demonstrating, at least at times, a mania to shop.

By early November, Mary grew increasingly agitated, even irritable, whenever the subject of her property was broached. This issue was the Edwardses' only concern, and it began to surface, much like Mary's ardent desire for freedom the previous July, with a letter to James Bradwell. Unlike the Bradwells' summer intervention at the sanitarium, their damning influence in November was not because of their care for Mary, but because of their neglect. They had not written or visited Mary once in the two months since her release from Bellevue Place. Mary reopened communication with the Bradwells on November 11. "A long & weary time has passed since I last saw you," she wrote. "Knowing well the interest you have taken in my sad fate, I feel assured that you will be pleased to hear that I am in perfect health."[51] The purpose of her letter was to request Judge Bradwell to send her the will he had drawn up for her in 1873, in which she gave Robert and his children all her possessions. This was the "important document" that Dr. Patterson asked Bradwell to return to Mary in mid-August.[52] There is no indication in the letter why Mary wanted her will, but Elizabeth Edwards assumed, and the extant documentary record suggests, it was so she could cut Robert out.[53]

"What can I say to your dear wife?" Mary rhapsodized. "The sorrow which has been mine for the last six months, has been in a measure alleviated, by the friendship of such noble hearts as yours." This letter contains the only evidence suggesting that perhaps one of the "conditions" put on Mary by Robert and Dr. Patterson in exchange for her removal from Batavia to Springfield was a termination of her association with the troublemaking Bradwells. "I feel assured you will reply to this note at once without even mentioning that you have heard from me," Mary wrote, suggesting her communication was in fact illicit. She closed her letter with the postscript "*Write* me—quietly—both of you."[54] Given the Bradwells' zealous efforts to advocate Mary's sanity and release from Bellevue, the fact that James Bradwell waited one month to respond to Mary's letter is difficult to comprehend. Was he abiding by an agreement, or, as critical newspapers had charged he would, had he lost interest in Mary's situation because the sensation was over?

Whatever the reason, his silence clearly piqued Mary. She posted him a second, more terse note three weeks later, repeating her request for the will, coldly signing it "Mrs. A. Lincoln" rather than her usual "Mary Lincoln."[55] This reaction was in keeping with Mary's petulance. As Julia Taft Bayne said of Mary during the White House years, "She wanted what she wanted when she wanted it."[56] In this case, she wanted to renew communication with her old friends. Whether James Bradwell's silence was well- or ill-intentioned, the fact that he was not doing what Mary wanted him to do offended her. Bradwell did finally send her the document in mid-December.[57] After that brief exchange, no further correspondence had ever been found.

The couple's silence has created one of the enduring mysteries of the insanity case: After their enormous efforts to free Mary from the sanitarium, why did Myra and James Bradwell abandon her? None of the previously known Insanity File materials or any of Mary's known letters explained why. The discovery of Mary's lost letters, however, finally illuminates the truth. The Towers trunk contained ten letters from Mary Lincoln to Myra Bradwell during a period of more than two years after the conclusion of Mary's institutionalization episode, proving that their friendship did, in fact, continue. It strengthens a surmise that the Bradwells agreed to a cessation of communication with Mary Lincoln for as long as she was considered legally insane. The theory further is bolstered by the fact that *the day after* Mary Lincoln was declared sane in June 1876, Myra Bradwell immediately broke her nine-month silence and wrote her vindicated friend a letter. The two women then kept in contact until at least July 1878 (the date of the final letter discovered in the Towers trunk) and probably until Mary's death in 1882.

But in November 1875, Judge Bradwell's silence, in essence another abandonment, combined with her anger over Robert's conservatorship, precipitated Mary's next psychotic episode. After her letters to Judge Bradwell, Mary grew increasingly upset at her son. Her behavior thereafter could almost be dubbed compartmentalized. She was cheerful, polite, affectionate, and agreeable, often taking rides and making visits, and "gives less trouble than any person I ever knew," until the subject of her property came up, according to Ninian Edwards.[58] The idea that

Robert controlled her bonds and had possession of most of her trunks made her impatient and incensed. "I am convinced, that the only alternative in this case, for the sake of peace and quietness, will be to yield your mother the right to control her possessions," Elizabeth wrote Robert in mid-November. "You will understand, that she is now pressing this matter, until the unpleasantness is such, that I am constrained to make the plea." Mary had even suggested that if returned to her, she would leave her bonds in possession of Jacob Bunn, a prominent Springfield banker, "to be undisturbed during her life."[59]

This last matter was Robert's main concern. He did not trust his mother's judgment in financial matters and would not allow her the "power of impoverishing herself."[60] As her son and male head of the family, and temporarily her conservator, he was responsible for her conduct and her physical and financial security. "There is no person upon whom lies the responsibility and duty of protecting her when she needs it, except myself," Robert wrote his uncle. But he agreed that he wanted "every liberty and privilege" restored to his mother as soon as it was safe to do so. "I want to do everything I can which is really for her happiness and I have no wish to interfere with her expenditures further than to ensure her having money to expend as long as she lives," Robert continued. "But if there is danger of her expending her capital and we should countlessly ignore it or imprudently contribute to it and she should impoverish herself we would be severely censured."[61]

There were not only emotional issues involved in changing his mother's situation but legal, financial, and social issues as well. First of all, it was not even clear if Robert legally could return his mother's power of possession to her. The entire point of the conservatorship was to keep the responsibility away from those declared insane. Second, Robert had posted a bond as conservator, backed financially by two sureties for $150,000. This was insurance against his mother's estate. If Robert, as the conservator, spent all his ward's money, that $150,000 bond would repay the loss. Robert was concerned that if Mary regained control of her estate while he was still conservator, she could spend her entire fortune before she was legally released from the conservatorship.[62] If that happened, Robert and his friends would be obligated to repay that bond to Mary.

Not only could the widow bankrupt herself due to her mental illness, Robert knew that in her exasperation at him she also could do it out of spite.[63] Her anger toward Robert was undeniable by this time, and what better way to make him pay for her commitment than to publicly humiliate him by bankrupting him and his friends? There was also the social issue of Robert's duty to his mother. He could not allow her to impoverish herself, nor, more simply, to make a public spectacle of herself, as she had done during the Old Clothes Scandal; such a spectacle would embarrass her, her husband's memory, and her son. The amount of pressure Robert felt at this time must have been enormous. He was dealing with his mother, his law practice, his family, and, in early November, the birth of his third child, Jessie Lincoln.[64]

Robert did not wish to decide his mother's future without the advice of others, so he once again turned to his father's friends, David Davis, Leonard Swett, and John Todd Stuart. "You know the whole story and you can judge as well as anyone what would be the consequences to my mother of erroneous action on my part at this time," he wrote to Stuart.[65] To Davis, Robert wrote with more candor, saying his aunt clearly did not understand the severity of his mother's condition and even blaming her for Mary's release from Bellevue Place. Elizabeth Edwards's mention of Mary's purchases, wrote Robert, was a clear indication to him that "no radical change has taken place since last Spring but only opportunity is wanting to develop the same trouble."[66] Robert and Swett had discussed four possible actions to take, which he explained to Davis:

1. To remove all restraints upon travel and residence.

2. To pay to her to be expended by herself without scrutiny of any kind her whole income in monthly installments, at the present rate of gold & including a payment from me to her of $125 per month which will end April 1881. This monthly income will be about $700.

3. To have a competent person make an estimate on the annuity principle of what monthly sum can be paid her during her life so as to leave nothing at her death and if Judge Wallace will consent, to pay such sum to her monthly.

4. In addition to 1 & 2 or to 1 & 3, to deliver to her as being necessary for her comfort all of her personal effects which consist of clothing and jewelry.[67]

The problem with number 3, Robert believed, was that the permanence of her yearly pension provided by Congress was uncertain.[68]

Robert's correspondence with Davis at this time gives further insight into his sense of manly duty toward his mother. Essentially, his aunt had advised him to let his mother do whatever she wanted, be it shopping, controlling her money, or traveling. Life had taught her, she said, that when you have done all you could for people, let them be.[69] "The trouble in my case is that I cannot abandon the matter if I would," Robert complained. "The time will not come when I can end the trouble by saying I have done what I can, & if I let it alone, it would not let me alone."[70]

Davis agreed with Robert on all counts. "You cannot escape responsibility if you wanted to, and it would be esteemed by the world bad conduct if you should try," Davis wrote. Elizabeth Edwards had no conception of Mary's real troubles, and her advice of indifference was grounded on a "total misapprehension of the relations between parent and child." He recommended that Robert remove all restraints on his mother's travel and residence, return all her personal effects, and pay her the monthly income from her bonds. "If she had remained undisturbed at Batavia there might have been a chance for her recovery, but I fear the intermeddling will prove disastrous to her, as it has already added to your trouble," Davis wrote. "I think your mother would rest satisfied, if unrestrained & paid her income in monthly installments."[71]

Robert took Davis's advice and gave his mother everything she requested of him (including eleven trunks of clothing and a box of jewelry), except the power to control her bonds.[72] But this did nothing to lessen her anger or excitability. "Your mother for the last two or three weeks has been very much embittered against you," Ninian Edwards told Robert, "and the more you have yielded the more immeasurable she seems to be."[73] She also was demanding more money and more of her trunks from Robert and continuing her unnecessary purchases. What concerned the Edwardses, however, was that Mary was giving away money and possessions that either belonged to Robert or would be part of his eventual inheritance. Both Ninian and Elizabeth were shocked by this behavior and mentioned in separate letters they believed Robert should not be robbed of his future.[74]

Ironically, subsequent historians have accused Robert of being the thief—motivated in the insanity case solely out of rapaciousness to control his mother's money and protect his inheritance.[75] His letters prove this to be a fallacy. In a letter to David Davis, whom Robert considered a second father, and whom he trusted above all others, he said he had "no interest" in her property and assumed she had already arranged to cut him out of her will.[76] In response to his aunt and uncle's concerns about Mary's property, he wrote, "I do not desire that any interest of mine or my children in the ultimate disposition of her property should be consulted and the only object I wish attained by any plan is her own protection."[77] Five months later, when Robert was told his mother planned to bankrupt herself to prevent her son's inheritance, he suggested that "the sane way" to punish him would be to cut him out of her will.[78] This possibility of disinheritance did not affect Robert, who achieved his own financial stability as a Chicago attorney, nor would it dissuade him from doing his duty. "She has always been exceedingly generous to me," he told his uncle. "I am exceedingly gratified to her for it all and shall never hesitate to acknowledge it but being grateful merely will not discharge my duty to her even if necessary against her will."[79]

By December, as Mary's anger continued to grow, she threatened to hire an attorney to overturn Robert's conservatorship, and, in the legal process, make public the past ten years of their personal relations.[80] She threatened to expose bad business investments Robert had sought to involve her in as a way to embarrass him, but Robert was unconcerned since the accusation was not true.[81] Ninian Edwards tried to dissuade Mary from taking such a legal route, but by late December she had arranged for attorney John M. Palmer, a former Illinois governor, to relieve her of her situation.[82] Despite what both Robert and Ninian Edwards told her, she simply would not believe that Robert had no legal discretion to restore her rights. Her fixation on the subject was increasing so feverishly that Robert not only asked Palmer to explain a conservator's rights to his mother but also offered to resign his position if Palmer was willing to replace him.[83] With this offer, Robert once again proved he would do whatever was necessary to relieve his mother of her mental burdens.

By the end of the year, Mary's major aggravation, in the eyes of Ninian and Elizabeth Edwards, was the subject of her bonds. "It is impossible to reason with her on the subject," they wrote Robert. "She is much exasperated against you."[84] In all other ways, she was cheerful, gregarious, social, and active, although her amount of shopping was increasing. They both repeatedly told Robert that only restoring Mary's bonds to her possession would calm her and diminish her bitterness. Still, Elizabeth and Ninian Edwards considered the widow completely restored to sanity, and they seemed relatively unconcerned by her behavior. That is, until they found her gun.

8 *A Deeply Wronged Woman*

MARY LINCOLN WAS A WOMAN who knew how to hold a grudge, or, as one historian aptly characterized her, she was always "a good hater."[1] Her treatment and criticism during the White House years of her sister Ann Todd Smith and social rivals Frances Seward and Kate Chase are but a few well-known examples of her rancor.[2] By the beginning of 1876, Mary's animosity was focused fully and solely on Robert for his unforgivable act of having her declared insane, and everything concomitant to it. Her increasing anger was paralleled by a dramatic increase in her shopping. She spent at least half of every day with dressmakers and in stores, hid the actual extent of her purchasing from her sister and brother-in-law, and instructed the merchants to do the same.[3] But her anger toward Robert ultimately reached such an alarming and unmitigated zenith that Ninian and Elizabeth Edwards felt compelled to warn Robert that his life might be in danger.

"I am sorry to say that your mother has for the last month been very much embittered against you, and has on several occasions said that she has hired two men to take your life," Ninian Edwards wrote Robert in mid-January. "On this morning we learned that she carries a pistol in her pocket. . . . She says she will never again allow you to come into her presence. We do not know what is best to be done."[4] The next day, Robert's uncle wrote that Elizabeth thought she could get the gun away from Mary. But one day later, Elizabeth suggested that Robert write to his mother and confront her about it; this would give Ninian an excuse to demand the weapon without either of the Edwardses incurring her wrath.[5] "Your uncle is perhaps unnecessarily excited upon the subject of the *pistol*," Elizabeth wrote in her typical attempt at conciliation. "There may be danger to herself and others."[6] She suggested, again, that only the return of her bonds would alleviate Mary's anger.

Where Mary got the pistol has never been definitely proven, but it seems likely it was Tad's old revolver, which Mary and Abraham had given him in 1863.[7] Robert's reaction to the threat was surprisingly altruistic. "Your letters . . . give me great concern, not for myself but I fear that something unforeseen may happen," he wrote. Robert added, as a subtle jab at the Edwardses for their meddling, "The doctors whom we consulted last spring were very urgent in expressing their opinion that no one could foretell the possible freaks which might take possession of my mother & that she should be placed where no catastrophe could happen."[8]

Robert saw his mother's worsening spending mania and her devolution to threats of physical violence as a deterioration of her condition. He had heard from one of his Springfield friends, in an unsolicited letter, that his mother was making large and unnecessary purchases and incurring debts with various Springfield merchants. As these actions had worried Robert in March, they now worried him again as evidence of impending trouble. "I am afraid the present situation will as it did last spring move from bad to worse," he wrote. "If it would get better it would relieve me from an anxiety which is overwhelming. She was removed from the care of Dr. Patterson against my judgment as to the safety of such a step and she remains out of professional care contrary to my judgment. No catastrophe has yet occurred, but remembering what was told me by the physicians last spring, I live in continual apprehension of it."[9] Robert also suggested—indirectly to his uncle and directly to his aunt—that if his mother's condition did not improve, he might have to return her to Bellevue Place. "If your influence cannot restrain her what are we to do?" he asked, suggesting that aside from the *idea* of the sanitarium, it was not an unpleasant place for Mary to be.[10]

Mary's agitation over control of her bonds soon subsided after her attorney told her there was no legal way for Robert to return her property until a minimum of one year had passed from the date of his appointment as her conservator.[11] Her anger at Robert did not subside, however, and she carried out a previous threat to remove all items she considered her property from her son's house. On February 7, Robert sent his mother so many boxes of her demanded possessions—paintings, household items, and books—that Elizabeth Edwards complained of the clutter in her house.[12]

Robert apologized but was undeterred in his course of accommodating his mother, even though her demands offended and hurt him. "Although I considered these things as much my own as though I had bought them, I gave them to her desiring to gratify her as far as I can," he explained. But as soon as he sent her the boxes, Mary immediately sent another letter, more than a dozen pages long, filled with more demands. "Everything that we can recognize was a present at one time or another, many things neither my wife nor I remember ever seeing, many other (dress goods & the like) are worn out & forgotten. Apart from these considerations the whole demand is so unreasonable in the light of any service that the things could be to her or that she could properly make of them in her situation that it is plainly irrational and the emanation of an insane mind." Robert again intimated that he might have to return Mary to Bellevue Place.[13]

Despite the clamoring for Robert to return his mother's power of property, no one was willing to legally remove the responsibility of conservatorship from him. John Palmer ignored Robert's offer to resign if Palmer would take his place; Springfield banker Jacob Bunn, who suggested he would be willing to oversee Mary's finances once they were returned to her power, also was unwilling to substitute himself as conservator.[14] Without a legal substitute, and without the consent of his legal sureties to remove himself without a substitute—which he requested but did not receive—there was nothing Robert could do but await his discharge.[15] Despite this impasse, or perhaps because of it, by mid-April Mary began getting agitated again about the return of her property.[16]

By the middle of May, Mary was threatening to bankrupt herself and depend solely on government support for the rest of her life, simply to spite Robert. "I should hardly think her as sound in mind as you do," Robert wryly commented to his aunt, "as the sane way of punishing me for trying to take care of her, would be to make a will and give me nothing." Robert used the news to point out, again, that if his mother was so exasperated at him, it would be absurd for him to return financial power to her, as she could simply spend all her money and then call him and his sureties to account for double the value of her property. "No scandal or trouble will be avoided by my doing or not doing anything," Robert concluded. "Plenty of it will probably come and I can only hope that my aunts, who now have charge of her, will have less trouble on that score than I have had for many years."[17]

Robert remained convinced that his mother was mentally ill, and he seems to have been entirely unconvinced about the propriety of restoring her rights to her at the end of the first year of conservatorship. His letters make it clear that he feared the worst if she were allowed to travel and spend money as she wished. Once again, he wrote to David Davis for advice. "I am satisfied, that you had better consent to the discharge of your mother at the end of the year," Davis replied, suggesting that even if she squandered all her money, she would still have her $3,000 yearly pension to live on. "I have after mature reflection come to the conclusion that it is better for your happiness to give a free consent to the removal of all restraint on her person or property and trust to the chances of time."[18]

On June 15, 1876, at 2:00 P.M., Robert Lincoln, as his mother's conservator, Leonard Swett as Robert's attorney, Ninian Edwards as a witness on his sister-in-law's behalf, the county court judge, the court clerk, and a jury attended an unpublicized hearing at the Cook County courthouse to declare Mary Lincoln a fit person to control her property. This was not a trial to declare her sane, as it has subsequently come to be misinterpreted. It was a hearing to remove her conservator and to restore her rights and property. It was a simple affair that consisted only of Mary's submitted petition asking for the discharge of her conservator, the testimony of Ninian Edwards as to Mary's fitness for the discharge, the consent of Robert for his removal as conservator and his accounting of her estate. As was typical of Robert's private nature, he asked the judge, court clerk, and Ninian Edwards to keep the hearing a secret to prevent "a large crowd of loafers [who] would be on hand expecting some sensation."[19]

According to reports by the *Chicago Tribune* and *Chicago Times*, the hearing took less time than the actual empanelling of the twelve-member jury.[20] Ninian Edwards read Mary's petition stating that she was "the proper person to have the care and management of her own estate."[21] Swett then told the judge that Mary's "friends" (meaning Robert) long had been anxious to restore her rights and property to her, but could not because the legal statute forbade it.[22] This was a clever move to put Robert's benevolence into the public record and was clearly a preemptive action against any later unseemly accusations by the embittered Mary. Edwards gave brief testimony to his sister-in-law's condition, saying she had been in his home for nine or ten months and "her friends all think she is a proper person to take charge of her own affairs."[23] Robert then "waived process," which allowed for his immediate discharge as conservator rather than imposing the usual ten-day wait.[24]

The jury, composed of no distinguished Chicago citizens, unlike its 1875 predecessor, deliberated just long enough "to attach their respective signatures to a verdict."[25] It declared Mary Lincoln "restored to reason and . . . capable to manage and control her own estate."[26] Robert presented to the court his official accounting of his mother's estate, which totaled $81,390.35 in cash, stocks and bonds, and personal possessions—an increase of nearly $8,000 under his stewardship.[27] At the end of the trial, Ninian Edwards immediately sent Mary a telegram about her bonds, stating, "All right. We will send them."[28] Thus ended the second trial of Mary Lincoln.

Robert Lincoln was not a flawless man, but throughout the entire fifteen-month period of Mary's institutionalization episode, he acted with concern, compassion, and benevolence toward his mother, and its finale only strengthens that conclusion. Robert agreed to the second trial even though he considered his mother still mentally ill; he waived the ten-day notice period because he knew his mother was impatient for the verdict; he increased his mother's estate by $8,000; and he refused his entitled compensation as conservator. And yet, the notion held by subsequent historians that Robert Lincoln sought his mother's commitment out of malice and greed somehow persists.

But why did Robert and Swett allow the jury to declare Mary "restored to reason" when they clearly did not believe that she was and that it was not what the jury was empanelled to decide? Unfortunately, the county court records offer no explanation. Two insanity case historians have astutely observed that Robert's notice of waiver was labeled "In the matter of Mary Lincoln to be declared to be a proper person to have the charge of her property," while Ninian Edwards's affidavit, handwritten by the court clerk, was labeled "In the matter of the restoration to reason of Mary Lincoln."[29] The Illinois lunacy statute stated that only a person who was declared restored to reason could have his property restored to him.[30] The Illinois Supreme Court had ruled in 1872 that the statute voided all contracts made by persons declared insane.[31] These two points of law make clear that Mary's property could not be restored until she was declared sane. Therefore, a logical conclusion as to Mary's case would be that the court clerk, who drew up the verdict and presumably understood the law, was the one who included the phrase "restored to reason."

Of course, this does not answer the question of why Robert or Swett did not object. If the verdict was read aloud in court, which would have given opportunity for objection, neither the *Chicago Times* nor the *Chicago Tribune* mention anything about it. They simply state the jury "returned" its verdict. No subsequent letters by either Robert or Swett ever mention anything about the wording of the verdict. Both men were, however, able attorneys, so one logical assumption is that they both understood the law and simply accepted the wording despite their personal beliefs about her condition.

Yet a letter from Ninian Edwards to Robert Lincoln just two days after the hearing—and one day after newspaper reports of the hearing—suggests that all parties involved in it were surprised by the jury's verdict. "They were not called upon to try the question of her sanity, and [I] regret very much that the verdict stated that she was 'restored to reason,'" Edwards wrote. Mary was upset the day after the verdict because of that wording, Edwards stated, since it implied that she had regained a sanity that she never conceded she had lost.[32] This only added to her angst, and her legal emancipation and the return of her bonds did nothing to appease her anger at her son.

The morning after the trial, Robert went to Springfield to personally return his mother's bonds to her. If he was hoping for reconciliation, he did not find it. Instead, he was confronted by a woman filled with rage and hate, who refused to even approach him. Mary accused Robert of bringing "false charges" against her in order to steal her money, told him he would not be allowed to approach the rest of the family—especially his father—in heaven, and commanded him to look upon her gray hair, which "he *had entirely* created" by his actions over the past year. "When I looked into his face (at a slight distance you may be sure), I saw the reluctance, with which he yielded up what he so ignominiously fought for—my poor pittance, as the world goes—so far as wealth is concerned—'a widow's mite,' my bonds. Prayers will scarcely avail in his case I think," she wrote to Myra Bradwell.[33]

Her vituperation did not end there. Three days later, she wrote Robert a letter that has become legendary in Lincoln lore, a vicious, hurtful letter in which she again denounced her son as a treacherous thief and demanded return of all her property in his possession, specifically enumerating laces, jewelry, engravings, and books:

> I am now in constant receipt of letters, from my friends denouncing you in the bitterest terms, six letters from prominent, *respectable*, Chicago people such as you do not associate with. . . . Two prominent clergy men, have written me, since I saw you—and mention in their letters, that they think it advisable to offer up prayers for you in Church, on account of your wickedness against me and High Heaven. In reference to Chicago you have the enemies, & I chance to have the friends there. Send me all I have written for, you have tried your game of robbery long enough. On yesterday, I received two telegrams from prominent Eastern lawyers. You have injured yourself, not me, by your wicked conduct.[34]

Mary stated that she and two attorneys had drawn up a list of all her property that Robert had stolen and said it would be published in the newspaper in a few days. This letter has long fueled salacious speculation that Mary's lost insanity letters contained still more denunciations of Robert, vindictive revelations of his secrets, and perhaps even evidence that the entire trial and insanity episode was the "kangaroo court" some historians have claimed.[35] This is partly true.

Despite the ten-month abeyance in communication, Myra Bradwell had not forgotten the friend she worked so hard to free from the sanitarium. She ran a notice of the hearing restoring Mary Lincoln's rights and property in the *Chicago Legal News*.[36] She also wrote Mary a letter immediately after the June 15 hearing.[37] Mary's reply, found amid the lost insanity letters, is shocking in its intensity and vitriol against Robert. It was written on June 18, 1876, one day before Mary's famous letter to Robert, and not only presaged but also elaborated on many of the sentiments in that letter. Mary's intense state of mind is apparent in her clear, bold handwriting; her refusal to write Robert's name but only his initials, or to call him "the young man"; the profusion of words underlined (thirty-seven words total, some multiple times); and her repetition both of statements against Robert and requests for Myra Bradwell's assistance. "The most villainous plot, has come to a close," Mary wrote. "God is just, *retribution*, must follow those who act wickedly in *this* life."[38]

Besides relating her confrontation of Robert, Mary's letter to Myra Bradwell also sought vengeance.

> I have my dear friend, a very great favor to ask of yourself[,] your good husband & the gentleman who called with you at B. the City Editor, of the Times [Franc B. Wilkie]. If I were to tell you *three, all* the utterances of this man R.T.L. you would *not refrain* from writing the *latter* person up, *without* a day's delay. Your pen is sharp, so is Judge Bradwell's, so is the Editor's, just named, of course you would not wish your names to appear, but you will not fail me, I am sure, *now* is the time, have justice rendered me, my dearly loved friend, see the City Editor of the Times, before the close of the day, when you receive *this* letter. I have been a deeply wronged woman, by one, for whom I would have poured out, my life's blood.
>
> R.T.L.'s *imprecations* against you all, have been very great, only on account of your being my true friends. *Do not* allow a day to pass, before this writing *is done* and forwarded in every direction. Let not *his wickedness* triumph.[39]

The *Times* never published an article about Robert. Mary's denunciations, however, did not go unnoticed or unanswered. For the ensuing two weeks, Mary and Robert fought a war of words and accusations, using Ninian Edwards and Leonard Swett as proxies. The subject, still, was Mary's property. Her bonds had been returned to her, but she was demanding the return of everything she considered her property in Robert's house—this included every present she ever gave Robert and his wife, which Mary was now claiming they had stolen from her. Robert had acquiesced to his mother's irrational demands for objects over the previous year, but by June 1876, his magnanimity was at an end.

Springfield Ill
June 18 '76

Burn this scrawl —

any mail, especially
on the last page to decipher
unable to decipher
dear Jean

My dear Mrs Bradwell:

Your most wel-
-come letter, was received
last evening and I
am quickly demonstr-
-ating the pleasure
it afforded me, by
replying at once.
God is just, _retribution,_

First four pages of Mary Lincoln's June 18, 1876, letter seeking revenge against her son Robert for her commitment. Frederic N. Towers Collection, Library of Congress. Photo courtesy Towers family.

must follow those who act
wickedly in this life,
Sooner or later, Compen-
-sation Surely awaits
those, who Suffer un-
-justly, if not here, in a
brighter & happier one.
The most villanous plot,
has come to a close, but
on Friday Morning, when
the young man, who her

-petrated, it came down to S— when I looked into his face (at a slight distance you may be sure) I saw the reluctance, with which he yielded up, what he so ignomin--iously fought for — my poor pittance, as the world goes — So far as wealth is concerned — "a widow's mite" my bonds — Prayers will scarcely

avail in his case I think.
My heart fails me, when I
think of the contrast be_
_tween himself and my
noble, glorious husband,
and my precious sons,
who have only "gone be_
_fore," and are anxiously
I am sure, awaiting the
reunion, where no more
separation comes — and
as I told him (R. T. L.) he
could not approach us in
the other world — on account

Robert showed his mother's letter to Leonard Swett, his attorney and adviser. Swett was so incensed that he wrote a withering response to Ninian Edwards laying out the absurdity—and clear insanity—of a woman who was "exceedingly kind" and lavishly generous to her children, gave them gifts, told them to take and use anything of hers in storage, wrote to ensure they did so, and then turned around and accused them of thievery.[40] She now was demanding the return of those gifts, which rightfully belonged to Robert, and was threatening lawsuits and "scandalous" publicity. Edwards knew that Mary spent all her money on dresses and curtains, making and fitting them, then folding and placing them in her trunks, never to be removed. This was fine as long as the widow had enough money to live on during her life, especially as Robert was unconcerned about receiving any inheritance.

But now, after ten years of enduring his mother's vicissitudes, bearing the "terrible burden of his mother's approaching insanity," acting only when seven physicians warned him of the danger of Mary "jumping out of her window every week," returning her bonds and other items that, in Swett's opinion, he should not have returned, and doing all that was necessary for his mother's health and safety, "I say with such a son and such a mother, shall we, friends of the family, permit her to go about with a pistol, avowing her purpose to shoot him, or shall we permit her to break him down and ruin him by harassing and annoying him?" Swett wrote.[41]

Swett would not tolerate Mary's threats after all Robert had done and sacrificed for her, and he concluded his letter with a threat of his own. If Mary tried to ruin Robert, "I shall, as a citizen, irrespective of Robert, or any one, . . . have her confined as an insane person, whatever may be the clamor or consequences." Adding to Swett's resolve, before he sent his letter, Robert received another letter from his mother demanding the return of still more property and calling him a "monster of mankind."[42] Swett showed his letter to David Davis, who approved it. Both Ninian and Elizabeth Edwards also approved of Swett's letter.[43] They not only agreed with everything he wrote but twice wrote to reassure Robert and his attorney that their nephew had their "confidence and sympathy" and they "never for one moment" believed he had acted from selfish motives but only for his mother's interest and happiness.[44] Ninian also sought to lessen Swett's accusations by saying he now had reason to believe that the "story" about Mary having a pistol was "not true."[45]

Swett's letter enraged Mary, and she decried it as being "filled with voluminous falsehoods."[46] The attorney's threat worked, however, for Mary promised to both the Edwardses that she would "neither bring suit against

Robert nor make any attacks on him."[47] Ninian Edwards stated that all Mary wanted was the return of some paintings and a case of silverware, and Robert could keep the rest; and she planned to return to Robert a collection of Charles Dickens's works that had his name inscribed in them.[48] This, however, still was unacceptable to Swett. He and Robert had a long conference about his mother's demands and decided not to comply. One reason was that the items she demanded did not belong to her, they belonged to Robert. Another reason to refuse was based more on principle, namely, that Mary's recent letters to Robert were "such as none but an insane mother would write to her son," and plainly showed "the utter wreck of Mrs. Lincoln's mind" and wounded Robert deeply. Swett concluded:

> While of course, owing to her condition of mind, this unkindness is to be forgiven and forgotten, the fear of being misunderstood by strangers has induced Robert—and I think wisely—in reference to the things referred to in your letters, not to return them, demanded as a matter of right, accompanied with the assertion that they were obtained improperly. Therefore if Mrs. Lincoln shall desire these things under the terms named in my first letter, she must ask for them, recognizing the fact that they were given to her children, and that they are rightly in their possession.[49]

After this, Mary stopped the demands for her possessions, although she was not happy about it. The entire debate was a "weak 'invention of the enemy' united with villainous falsehood," she wrote to Myra Bradwell. "That Swett, should become so debased as to try and drag down to his own debased standard the son of the noblest, most honest man, who ever lived. None of my treasures in the way of rich & rare presentations, that were made me, have been returned to me. As I truly told R.T.L. villains, could not venture to approach my dearly beloved husband in the other world. *His* reply I gave you."[50]

Mary's lost insanity letters reveal for the first time that there was more at stake in this argument than her possessions. There also was a matter of money as it related to her old house at 375 West Washington Street in Chicago, which she had sold to her son in April 1874 for $10,000.[51] Robert paid no money up front, but paid a monthly mortgage to Mary (which she called "rent") beginning April 27, 1874, to be completed by May 1, 1881.[52] His payments, which did not include interest, began at $125 per month but were increased to $150 at Mary's request.[53] Robert rented out the house to various tenants. In his first letter, Swett had claimed the house title was unclear and in litigation. Mary perceived his statement as proof of some conspiracy to deprive her of her monthly payments. She immediately wrote to James Bradwell, asking him to examine the lease on the house. "There is beyond question, the most unmitigated villainy in the case," she wrote.[54]

That Mary suffered paranoia over losing this monthly income and a continued delusion that Robert was intent to defraud her is obvious. Besides instructing James Bradwell to investigate the matter, Ninian Edwards mentioned it to Leonard Swett twice in two days and also wrote Robert that Mary was "afraid" that he would not pay; while Jacob Bunn none-too-subtly informed Robert that he now had power of attorney over Mary's bonds and the power to collect the rent.[55] Mary twice wrote to Myra Bradwell about the house issue in July 1876, checking the judge's progress on it and execrating both Swett and Robert in the process, calling them "two of the greatest scoundrels of the age."[56]

Judge Bradwell must have found nothing wrong with the title, as no other correspondence to him about it has been found, although according to Mary he did not think it a good arrangement.[57] For his part, Robert repaid every cent he owed his mother, making the final payment more than four months early, in December 1880.[58] In addition to her financial paranoia, Mary's fear of abandonment, which was so prevalent in her letters to Myra Bradwell while in Bellevue Place, also resurfaced during this time. "I have received no letter from you, am I forgotten?" she asked on July 7; then, after receiving a response one week later, Mary chastised, "Write and do not act *quite so mean* by your silence."[59]

With the conclusion of her institutionalization episode, Mary Lincoln was free to live where and how she wanted. She chose to stay in Springfield, but, just as after the assassination, she could not bear to be there. Not only did the place hold too many painful memories, she also felt everyone regarded her as a lunatic. "I feel it in their soothing manner," she told her sister. "If I should say the moon is made of green cheese they would heartily and smilingly agree with me. I love you, but I cannot stay. I would be much less unhappy in the midst of strangers."[60] Three months after her legal release, Mary Lincoln, accompanied by her nephew Edward Lewis Baker, traveled via Lexington and Philadelphia to New York City. There, on October 1, 1876, she boarded the steamer *Labrador* and, as she had in 1868, headed for self-exile in Europe.[61]

The trip was concealed from the newspapers in order to keep it secret from Robert, whom Mary believed would stop her and possibly have her committed again, although her sister assured her he would not.[62] According to Elizabeth Edwards, Mary's "resentful nature" made it necessary for her to "place an ocean" between herself and her son. "I go an exile, and alone!" Mary dramatically exclaimed as she left the Edwards's home; Elizabeth predicted Mary would weary of isolation and return soon.[63] In fact, it was four years before Mary returned to America, and five years before she forgave Robert for having her committed. Mary's time in Europe has been shrouded in darkness due to the lack of any of her personal correspondence during those years. With the discovery of Mary's lost insanity letters, however, her life in Europe finally can be illuminated.

9 Resignation Will Never Come

BEFORE THE DISCOVERY OF Mary Lincoln's lost insanity letters, very little was known about her time abroad, from 1876 to 1880. There were approximately one hundred known letters from this period, with the majority being to Mary's banker, Jacob Bunn, and containing only financial matters. She also wrote more personal letters to her nephew, Edward Lewis Baker, supplying information about her life and travels and her continued antipathy toward her son. It was known that Mary's central residence was the resort town of Pau, France, which she had previously visited during her 1868–71 trip, and where she already had friends.[1] Based out of Pau, Mary traveled less than she did on her first European sojourn, confining herself to various cities in France and Italy.

In Europe, Mary was for the most part happy. She was at times treated anonymously, which pleased her, and at other times treated like aristocracy, which she adored. Her health continued as it had been, with fatigue, neuralgia, frequent spells of cough and cold, bodily pain and soreness, boils, and, in 1879, significant weight loss. Some physicians have theorized this weight loss, as well as Mary's other symptoms, were the effects of untreated diabetes.[2] Mary characterized it as a positive occurrence, writing, "My great bloat has left me & I have returned to my natural size."[3] Mary kept an astute eye on Jacob Bunn's handling of her finances. She did not bankrupt herself or go into debt, but she did spend her entire income as she received it.[4] In fact, the compilers of her collected letters, Justin and Linda Turner, found in Mary's letters to Bunn that she showed "an astonishing degree of perspicacity and control" over her finances. In light of Mary's history of frequent, uncontrolled spending, the Turners found the Bunn correspondence "an even greater source of wonder."[5]

Ten of Mary's newly discovered letters date from 1876 to 1878 and reveal significant facts about, and insights into, her European years. The most striking aspect of all the letters, like the Bunn correspondence, is that Mary sounds calm, rational, and cogent, inquiring about friends and events and offering descriptions of her travels. Mary herself explained her peace of mind in a December 1876 letter to Myra Bradwell, stating, "I am allowed tranquility here and am not harassed by a demon."[6] The demon, of course, was Robert Lincoln, whom she later referred to as "That wretched young man, but *old* in sin."[7] Mary also seemed to have realized that her forced isolation from friends was not conducive to happiness or social propriety. She told her nephew, "I am aware, it is entirely my own fault, as in *NY* and *Phil*, in keeping myself aloof from dear friends, who love me well. I propose to act in a more *civilized* manner in the future."[8] Elizabeth Edwards too noticed the beneficence of Mary's social intercourse, for she told Robert that "the improvement in her social feeling, was quite manifest, during her stay here, and among strangers, she will yearn for home ties."[9]

But while Mary corresponded with her sister and her nephew, her true yearning for home ties was in her correspondence with Myra Bradwell. Mary's letters to her friend clearly show her love and gratitude, and the constant refrain is a desire to see her and hear from her. "Close your doors some day, my bright appreciative friend, take your husband's arm, bring your talented daughter and son with you [to Europe] and rest," she wrote in December 1876.[10] "You have no friend, I believe, who loves you *half* so well as myself."[11] Myra Bradwell did, in fact, travel to Europe to visit with her friend in summer 1878, attesting even further to the strength of their relationship.[12]

But Mary's letters to Myra Bradwell go even deeper and are much more interesting than simple exclamations of love and gratitude. Mary described her physical health, twice mentioning boils under her left arm and pain over her entire body. In one letter, she noted that the spa waters of Vichy "did me no good."[13] She only mentioned her son once, when she referred to the "demon," although he was still in her thoughts. As she wrote her sister, "My 'Gethsemane' is ever with me."[14] Mary also mentioned her husband, often in terms of apotheosis, although her statements do not match the historical facts, and she inflates her own importance in relation to him. "My darling husband, who worshipped me so greatly, that often he said, that I was his weakness," she reminisced in July 1876.[15] Such inflated self-esteem and grandiosity may have been a symptom of mania; at the very least, it shows her lack of insight into how burdensome she could be to those who loved her.[16]

In April 1877, when a vacancy opened on the U.S. Supreme Court, Mary encouraged Myra to secure the seat for her husband, James Bradwell. "You with your great talents and diplomacy, could so well arrange affairs," Mary wrote. "A wife can do so much for her husband which you have undoubtedly done."[17] This last sentence is again a subtle way of inflating her own importance in her husband's rise to greatness. While visiting Sorrento, Italy, in 1878, Mary mused about how "My beloved husband

and myself for hours would sit down and anticipate the pleasant time, we would have in quietly visiting places and halting in such spots as this, when his official labors were ended."[18]

Mary's letter from Sorrento is perhaps the most intriguing of all her recently discovered European correspondence. She spent two months in Italy in early 1878, visiting Naples, Rome, and Sorrento. Practically nothing is known of that trip. Only three letters during that period previously have been published, all to Mary's banker and mostly about financial matters.[19] Mary's letter to Myra Bradwell is the first known letter from Sorrento and the first known detailed account of her actions and thoughts in Italy. She visited tourist attractions, such as Herculaneum and the "Castle of St. Elmo," and stopped at the Hotel de Rupie to view Mount Vesuvius and the Bay of Naples.[20] "But nothing equals, I think, the charming scenery of Sorrento. Even Mrs. [Harriet Beecher] Stowe's imaginative pen has scarcely done it justice," she wrote.[21]

The 566-word letter also gives insight into Mary's mental state; while it is clear and impressive in its narrative quality, it also is suffused with a great sadness indicative of a possible depressive episode. "It is my season of sadness and Naples with its noise, was unendurable," she wrote. Her sadness was felt even keener, however, because she was revisiting places she first visited in 1866, while in the midst of her bereavement for her husband. "My heart was then filled with great sorrow, but since that time the crushing hand of bereavement has been laid so heavily upon me, that it is only by a strong effort of will that I revisit places." As was typical in her lower moods, Mary also wondered at the meaning of God's plan for her, although "to some of us, *resignation* will never come."[22] She also, again, implored the Bradwells to come visit her in Europe.

During these later years of her life abroad, indicators other than her letters to Myra Bradwell showed the return of Mary's depression. She told Jacob Bunn, in a letter from Naples one week after her Sorrento letter, that her grief since her 1866 European trip had "greatly intensified" and, "consequently, I take no interest whatever in fresh scenes & objects."[23] She appears to have reneged on her vow to be more sociable and civilized. Over the years, her letters tell how she lived a life of quite retreat, sometimes sitting in a darkened, solitary room and feeling isolated from the world.[24] "I live, very much alone . . . have a few friends & prefer to remain secluded," she wrote her sister.[25] By October 1879, Mary was pining to return to America, saying that to such an "oppressed, heart broken woman" as herself, her long absence from the United States was "simply an exile."[26]

First page of Mary Lincoln's letter to Myra Bradwell from Sorrento, Italy, April 22, 1878. Frederic N. Towers Collection, Library of Congress. Photo courtesy Towers family.

Robert during this time was continuing to make a success of his own life. By 1876, with three children and a wife to support, he focused on building his law practice, which continued to grow more prestigious. He remained in contact with his aunt, Elizabeth Edwards, who, in late 1876, apologized if her actions regarding her sister had upset him. "The truth is I only, from the beginning of this unpleasant matter, wished to do my duty, depending upon the judgments of others for guidance. It may yet turn out, that all parties have been too indulgent, if so, the consolation will be, in having erred on the side of humanity." She also revealed to Robert her true feelings about Mary's shopping mania, stating, "Her recovery from it, seems so utterly hopeless."[27]

In 1877, Robert was offered the position of assistant secretary of state by President Rutherford B. Hayes, but declined, and was appointed by the Illinois governor to the Board of Railroad and Warehouse Commissioners and to the Stephen Douglas Monument Commission.[28] By 1879, Robert was being mentioned as a possible presidential candidate. Mary read one such press notice while in France and, despite railing against Robert for his treachery, was so "elated" about the possibility of him as president that she fantasized about the formation of his cabinet and imagined how her granddaughter would "grace" the White House.[29]

But still, three years after her legal exoneration, Mary and Robert did not communicate. In 1877, Robert replied to a letter asking about his mother that she was "somewhere in Europe," but he did not know her address.[30] Robert would have written to his mother, but he did not think such a missive would be well received. "If I could persuade myself otherwise, I would write to her at once & not think I was making any concession, for I have not allowed her anger at me to have any other effect upon me than regret that she should so feel and express herself towards me," he wrote his aunt in 1879. Robert was glad, however, that his mother sent presents to her granddaughter despite the rift with him, giving hope that one day her animosity toward him would end. "I am very anxious that it should. Its existence has been very distressing to me."[31]

Despite her sister's reassurances, Mary feared a return to America, thinking Robert would immediately interfere in her life and possibly seek her commitment once again. Robert asked Elizabeth to tell his mother that "under no possible circumstances" would he do so. "I have no reason to think that such interference is now or will hereafter be proper but that whatever I might think hereafter, I would under no circumstance do anything," he stated. Robert also revealed just how upsetting the entire institutionalization episode had been to him, telling his aunt, "If I could have foreseen my own experience in the matter, no consideration would have induced me to go through with it, the ordinary troubles and distresses of life are enough without such as that."[32]

By 1880, Mary's physical maladies of headaches, bodily pains, neuralgia, incontinence, and severe cough were compounded by a much more serious affliction. In December 1879, she had fallen off a stool while hanging a painting and seriously injured her spine, causing her intense pain on her left side and difficulty walking.[33] The doctors set her back in plasters, but this did not alleviate the suffering of what she referred to as her *"almost* broken back."[34] Then, in June 1880, due to the pain and weakness in her left side, Mary fell down a flight of stairs, further injuring her back, which the doctor set in plasters once again.[35] After four years of exile, and now lonely and in great pain, Mary Lincoln decided to go home.

On October 15, 1880, Mary sailed from Le Havre, France, aboard the steamer *L'Amerique* to return to the United States. During the twelve-day journey across the Atlantic, the celebrated actress Sarah Bernhardt famously saved Mary from falling headfirst down a stairway. "You might have been killed, Madame," Bernhardt said. "'Yes,' [Mary] answered with a sigh of regret, 'but it was not God's will.'" Bernhardt then realized that "I had just done this unhappy woman the only service I ought not to have done her—I had saved her from death."[36] Upon the ship's arrival in New York on October 27, huge crowds met Bernhardt on the docks, while some one hundred distinguished and invited guests came aboard ship to welcome her with flowers, speeches, and music. Mary Lincoln, a quiet, old woman dressed "plainly and almost commonly," with a rip in her cloak and hair streaked with white, waited with the rest of the passengers for Bernhardt and her fans to depart. Mary then disembarked "almost unnoticed"; she was so anonymous that a policeman even made her stand back while Bernhardt ascended into a carriage and left the docks.[37]

Mary felt ill on her arrival and asked her nephew, Edward Lewis Baker, who met her at the dock, to take her to the Clarendon Hotel.[38] There, she saw no visitors except Dr. Louis A. Sayre, a world-renowned orthopedic physician and childhood friend.[39] Sayre told a newspaper reporter the widow suffered from inflammation of the spine, kidney trouble, and a "great mental depression," none of which was serious as long as she received the proper treatment and the sympathy of family and friends.[40] After a few days of rest, Mary returned to the Edwards home in Springfield.

The last two years of Mary's life were full of physical and mental suffering. Her physical health had so deteriorated, she claimed, that she needed assistance to walk, could not descend the stairs, suffered terrible headaches and swelling, and was losing her eyesight. Elizabeth Edwards, Robert Lincoln, and others considered Mary's great suffering to be at least partly imaginary.[41] She rarely left her room, preferring to remain in the dark lit only with candles, even during the daytime.[42] This exasperated her sister, who wrote that Mary's "enjoyment of a darkened room, does not accord with my ideas of enjoying life. . . . I have suffered from indulging her with my company until I can scarcely see to guide my pen."[43] Mary accepted visitors, although she did not return visits. One of her old friends stated that during her final years she was "bright and sparkling" in conversation, and her memory remained sharp until the day she died.[44] She read very little, although her chief gratification was reading and rereading newspaper articles that stated "that she was lying at the point of death."[45]

Mary's mania for material possessions had not abated. She brought sixty-four trunks of clothing with her to the Edwards home, which she would go through, unpack, and repack, for hours every day.[46] Mary's niece, who lived in the Edwards home during Mary's final stay there, said her mother, Elizabeth Edwards, thought it funny that Mary was "so sick" but was still able to spend all day bending over trunks.[47] Mary had so many trunks in the Edwardses' storeroom—weighing about eight thousand pounds—that the maid resigned, being afraid to sleep in her quarters under the storeroom for fear the floor would collapse.[48] Mary's niece later remembered her aunt was "a lot of trouble" to the Edwards family, although she was told not to say anything unkind about the widow in her last years "because she wasn't herself."[49]

Mary also continued to have delusions and hallucinations. She would sleep only on one side of her bed to leave "the president's place" on the other side undisturbed and asked her visitors if they heard her husband's voice.[50] Her biggest fear, however, had to do with Robert. She finally reconciled with him in May 1881 after five years of estrangement, although it is unknown how and why their reconciliation came about.[51] It seems likely that Elizabeth Edwards had a hand in it; as the mother figure who understood the stubborn Mary and the matriarch who respected Robert and always regretted the mother-son rift, she was probably the only person who could have reunited them. When Mary heard that President-elect James A. Garfield had appointed Robert secretary of war, she was terrified. According to one report, she would often sit and repeat, "Secretary of war? Secretary of war? Then he'll be shot sure! That's always the way in war!"[52] After Garfield's assassination, it was reported that Mary began suffering "the most intense mental anguish," being so clearly reminded of her husband's murder, and became frantically afraid that Robert would be murdered as well.[53]

Garfield's assassination—or, more specifically, Congress's pending award of a $5,000 per year pension to Mrs. Garfield—also reinvigorated Mary's delusions of poverty. In October 1881, she returned to New York City for further medical treatment by Dr. Sayre. He told a reporter that her spinal and kidney trouble was very serious, although improving, but it was difficult for her to walk and impossible for her to go up or down stairs.[54] The main point of Sayre's publicity, however, was to announce Mary's poverty to the country, saying that her $3,000 annual congressional pension was inadequate to pay for her necessary medical care. Sayre also used the occasion to indignantly refute suggestions that Mary was insane. "She is no more insane than you or I are," he declared, in a phrase reminiscent of Myra Bradwell's from 1875.[55]

Like so many aspects of and events throughout Mary Lincoln's life, the suggestion that she was practically destitute created national headlines. Some newspapers accused Sayre of meddling in others' affairs, seeking only his own publicity; other newspapers accused Mary of succumbing again to the same embarrassing delusions of poverty that led to the 1867 Old Clothes Scandal.[56] The *Illinois State Journal* indignantly dismissed the notion that Mary was neglected, suffering, and living in poverty. It editorialized that "while Mrs. Lincoln is, undoubtedly, physically and mentally ill, she is a hypochondriac as to her health and a monomaniac on the subject of money."[57] Some people even accused Robert of filial neglect for not taking care of his mother. Mary herself refuted that allegation, telling a reporter that both Robert and his wife had repeatedly suggested they take care of her, but Mary had refused and "insisted it was her duty to live upon her own resources."[58]

Mary enlisted the help of old friends to once more lobby Congress, but this time for an increase in her pension to equal Mrs. Garfield's $5,000 per year, as well as interest and back payments. Robert and Mary Harlan Lincoln helped Mary's endeavor by convincing influential businessman Cyrus W. Field to lobby Congress on Mary's behalf.[59] U.S. House member William M. Springer also furthered her cause when he requested Dr. Sayre and three other eminent physicians—experts in ophthalmology, neurology, and kidney diseases—examine the widow's case and give a report of her physical condition to Congress.[60] The physicians declared she suffered from chronic inflammation of the spinal cord, chronic disease of the kidneys, and commencing cataract of both eyes; the ultimate effect of her maladies would be paralysis of her lower limbs and loss of eyesight. Her condition would never improve, considering its nature and her age, they stated.[61] Unlike the fight about Mary's first pension, Congress supported the bill without much fuss; but like the first time, Mary was "very ill with anxiety" because of it.[62] The Congress not only increased Mary's pension but also paid her $15,000 in back payments.[63]

Of Mary Lincoln's final financial crusade and her lonely condition, her old nemesis, William Herndon, wrote in January 1882, "As to Mrs. Lincoln, she has plenty of her own friends to keep her for life—say 20 thousand dollars besides her pension. Her friends here are wealthy and well willing to take care of her if she will only let them. Mrs. Lincoln is a curious woman—an unfortunate one, and to a certain extent a despised one. Mrs. Lincoln is in part an unbalanced woman—her mind is . . . unhinged, and has been for years."[64] During her medical treatment in New York, Mary spent two months at Dr. E. P. Miller's medical baths establishment, still under Dr. Sayre's primary care, undergoing electrical therapy, massages, baths, and bed rest.[65] Sayre reported that during her time at Miller's, her eyesight began to fail, and while not blind, she found it difficult to read or write, and she usually kept her room dark.[66] Robert and his wife visited Mary in New York every two or three weeks.[67]

Mary returned to the Edwards home in March 1882. At first, she refused medical treatment but then allowed the Edwardses' personal physician, Dr. Thomas W. Dresser, to attend her.[68] A recently publicized oral tradition states that the Hospital Sisters of the Third Order of St. Francis nursed Mary Lincoln in the Edwards home during the final months of her life from March to July 1882. "I did all that she wanted or needed all day and all night," remembered Sister Francis Dreisvogt. "At night, I sat on the chair and laid my head near her pillow. She could call me any time by touching me."[69] Mary's health continued to fail, and by July, in addition to her spinal pain and poor eyesight, she was suffering from large boils over her entire body.[70]

Mary Lincoln died, most likely from a stroke, on July 16, 1882, at the age of sixty-four, one day after the eleventh anniversary of Tad's death.[71] Some physician-historians have theorized that her final illness and death were caused, at least in part, by untreated diabetes. This diagnosis was suggested by her symptoms of urinary incontinence, attacks of boils, and dramatic weight loss beginning in 1879.[72] Dr. W. A. Evans, in his landmark psychological (and to some extent physiological) study of Mary Lincoln, suspected that she suffered a diabetic coma during the final week of her life.[73] Based on his reading of contemporary newspaper reports, and the fact that diabetes damages the walls of blood vessels, he agreed with Dr. Dresser's opinion that Mary died of stroke, "probably due to the rupture of a blood vessel in the brain."[74] Recently, the theory that

Mary suffered and died from syphilis has been propounded, although with only circumstantial evidence.[75]

Mary's final wishes were fulfilled by Robert. Her body was laid out in the parlor of the Edwards home, the same room in which she was married, in a white silk dress. Ironically, despite her sixty-eight trunks full mostly of clothing, Elizabeth Edwards had to send to Chicago for a suitable one.[76] During her final days, Mary's fingers became so tumescent she had to take off her wedding ring. In death, the ring, inscribed "A. L. to Mary, Nov. 4, 1842. Love is Eternal," was replaced on her finger.[77] Mary had so often pined for death during the seventeen years since her husband's murder that some onlookers felt her corpse seemed not only calm but almost happy, even to the point of a "faint semblance of a smile" on her lips.[78]

Mary's funeral was held in the First Presbyterian Church of Springfield, attended by a crowd so large that not everyone was able to enter the church.[79] Rev. James A. Reed gave a eulogy extolling Mary's virtues, saying, "While she, no doubt, had her faults like other women, and made mistakes, yet she had excellence and her virtues which shone with a luster all her own." As the partner of Abraham Lincoln, Mary deserved thanks for her wifely devotion. Reed likened the Lincolns to two great trees whose roots were intertwined, and when one had been blasted away, the other also died, only much more slowly.[80] Mary's casket was then conveyed to the Lincoln tomb in Oak Ridge Cemetery and placed in the vault alongside her husband and sons Eddie, Willie, and Tad.

Mary Lincoln received a sympathy and compassion in death that eluded her in life, although her mental troubles were far from ignored. "By the death of Mary Todd Lincoln . . . there is removed from the stage of life a figure always invested with a certain historic and tragic interest," the *New York Times* editorialized. "It would be well for those who have been disposed to judge harshly of some of the personal characteristics of Mrs. Lincoln to remember that few women have ever been more devoted to their husbands, and that few have ever suffered so awful a shock as she when he was killed by her side."[81] The *Chicago Tribune* said sorrow over her death would be felt around the country, although the death itself was her relief from years of pain. "The world knows how she suffered, and how her mind at times was clouded, but it can never know how desolate her life was for the fifteen years that followed [Lincoln's] death," the paper declared.[82]

Mary's friends also mourned her loss and defended her legacy. Jane Grey Swisshelm said Mary was a person "[to] whom the people of this country owe a great reparation." While she was "never entirely sane"

ILLINOIS. — OBSEQUIES OF MRS. ABRAHAM LINCOLN, AT SPRINGFIELD, JULY 19TH.

Sketch of Mary Lincoln's funeral, July 19, 1882. Courtesy Abraham Lincoln Presidential Library.

after the shock of the assassination, on most subjects Mary's mind was "perfectly clear."[83] Howard Glyndon, who knew Mary slightly during the war years, stated that no matter how she acted during those terrible times, she could win no approval from Washington society. She "refused to play the martyr" and did things her own way, which caused the American press and people to treat her unkindly. "Her erratic behavior has been commented upon in a spirit which will not show well when all the events connected with her life have become history."[84] Adam Badeau, an officer on Grant's staff during the Civil War, declared that the verdict of her insanity vindicated her from "the odium for which she was not responsible" and made her "an object of commiseration."[85] David Davis, who perhaps knew her better than most, quite simply and feelingly wrote of her, "Poor Mrs. Lincoln! She is at last at rest. She has been a deranged woman, ever since her husband's death. In fact she was so, during his life."[86]

While Mary Lincoln remained friends with James and Myra Bradwell through the end of her life, there is no evidence they attended her funeral. Their roles in Mary's legacy, however, did not end with her death. Not only did they have more than thirty letters of personal correspondence and many gifts from their friend when she died, they also were in possession of her July 1873 will, which James Bradwell had drawn for her. Part of this will was found in the Towers trunk along with the other lost letters. The matter of Mary's will is an intriguing one and mysterious, for Mary Lincoln was considered to have died intestate.[87] Robert, as her only surviving son and sole heir, had to apply to the Sangamon County Court for letters of administration in order to receive her estate, which totaled $84,035.[88]

So what happened to Mary's will? As previously stated, James Bradwell helped Mary draw one up between 1872 and 1873. Documents found in the Towers trunk show that in that will, executed July 23, 1873, Mary gave Robert her house at 375 West Washington Street in Chicago, while the remainder of her estate was left to Judge David Davis and her cousin John Todd Stuart as trustees, to be distributed among Robert's children.[89] In a codicil dated January 3, 1874, Mary made a special bequest of a one-thousand-dollar U.S. savings bond to her infant grandson, Abraham Lincoln II, known by the family as "Jack," to be paid to him on his twenty-first birthday, with the interest to be paid semiannually for pocket money.[90]

Also on July 23, 1873, Mary wrote a letter, to be delivered to the Cook County judge upon her death, to inform him that her will was completed and located in the Fidelity Bank.[91] This letter was indeed delivered to County Court Judge Mason B. Loomis on July 20, 1882, four days after Mary's death. Loomis could not find Robert Lincoln, so instead he opened the letter at the Isham & Lincoln law office, in the presence of Robert's partner, Edward Isham. Both men declined to make public the contents of the letter.[92] As that letter and envelope were found in Robert Lincoln's personal Insanity File, he obviously received it and looked in the bank's safety deposit box.[93] The will, however, was not there.

First and last pages of Mary Lincoln's "lost" will. Frederic N. Towers Collection, Library of Congress. Photo courtesy Towers family.

of the United States

In witness whereof I Mary Lincoln the testatrix have this twenty third day of _____ A.D. 1873 affixed my seal and subscribed my name to this my will consisting of nine pages

Mary Lincoln [seal]

We do truly certify that the above named testatrix Mary Lincoln signed sealed and acknowledged the above instrument to be her last will and testament in our presence and we at her request _____ _____ _____ _____ as witnesses on this twenty third day of July A.D. 1873

James B Bradwell
Myra Bradwell.
Js B Bradwell

It is known that Mary sought to amend her will in January and July 1874 and then requested that Bradwell send her the will in December 1875, presumably so she could disinherit Robert.[94] Ninian Edwards verified that Bradwell sent her the will in December 1875 and told Robert it gave $20,000 specifically to Robert's daughter, Mary, and the rest to Robert and his family.[95] So if Mary did get her will back, why was it never probated? She must have, at some point over the ensuing years, sent it back to Judge Bradwell for his keeping, and he never returned it to the Fidelity Bank safety deposit box. Bradwell's granddaughter, Myra Pritchard, verified in her unpublished manuscript that her grandfather did indeed have possession of Mary's will at the time of her death in 1882. Pritchard wrote that James Bradwell did not reveal the document because "it would have brought on another clash with Robert Lincoln . . . and reopened the old, unpleasant controversy," and "he saw no reason why he should needlessly subject his family to further unpleasant publicity."[96] No doubt at this point, James Bradwell feared Robert Lincoln more than he had in 1875, as in 1882 Robert was President Chester A. Arthur's secretary of war and was being mentioned as a possible presidential candidate. "The story of Mary Lincoln, her insanity trial, her incarceration, all the old rancor and heartaches would have been bared to public view again and [my grandfather] was convinced that silence was the better way," Pritchard wrote.[97]

Robert Lincoln spent the rest of his life carving his own niche in history, separate from his illustrious father. His law firm grew to become one of the most prestigious in Chicago, working cases that ranged from local issues up to the U.S. Supreme Court. They represented some of the most important businesses and individuals in America, such as the Pullman and Commonwealth Edison Companies, millionaires Marshall Field and Walter L. Newberry, and *Chicago Tribune* editor Joseph Medill.[98] Besides secretary of war, Robert also served as President Benjamin Harrison's minister to Great Britain. The Republican Party tried five times to nominate Robert to run for president, but each time he declined.[99] "The Presidential office is but a gilded prison. The care and worry outweigh, to my mind, the honor which surrounds the position," Robert famously declared in 1887.[100] Robert eventually became president of the Pullman Car Company and then its chairman of the board. He died in 1926, at age eighty-two, a self-made multimillionaire.

James and Myra Bradwell spent the rest of their lives in Chicago, raising their children and attending to their individual interests. Myra continued to support women's rights and female suffrage and to publish the *Chicago Legal News* until her death in 1894, making it the most widely circulated legal newspaper in America.[101] James continued as a practicing attorney, legislator, and social advocate. Upon his wife's death, he became editor and publisher of the *Chicago Legal News*. In the late 1890s, he gave an interview to Lincoln biographer Ida Tarbell in which he mentioned the numerous Mary Lincoln letters and gifts in his possession.[102] James Bradwell died in 1907.[103]

Mary Lincoln's story did not end with her death in 1882, or even with Robert's death in 1926. In fact, the conclusion of Mary's insanity story resided with the woman Mary Lincoln alienated and called a thief, a woman who did not even attend Mary's funeral, and about whom historians know very little—Robert's wife, Mary Harlan Lincoln.

10 *To Be Destroyed Immediately*

ROBERT LINCOLN WAS A PRIVATE MAN who did not believe that personal facets of his parents' lives should be made public. As the last male Lincoln, he owned all of his father's personal and political papers. There was a famous claim by Nicholas Murray Butler, a friend of Robert's and president of Columbia University, that he witnessed Robert burn his father's letters.[1] Subsequent historians have generally discredited this allegation, although Robert Lincoln's attorney, Frederic N. Towers, made a similar claim of being witness to correspondence burning.[2] Robert did admit to burning a number of his mother's letters written during the "period of her mental derangement," as he called it.[3] But the eldest Lincoln son was not ignorant of his father's historical importance, nor was he averse to sharing his family with posterity; however, he did insist on choosing which parts of his family's history would be preserved.

Robert occasionally lent some of his father's papers to museums for special exhibits, but mostly he kept them securely locked away in his home.[4] Prior to his death in July 1926, Robert Lincoln bequeathed all of his father's papers to the American people, to be held in trust by the Library of Congress.[5] A condition of his deed was that the papers would be sealed from public view until twenty-one years after his death. Robert stated this was because some of the people mentioned in the papers were still living, and it would not be proper to expose them to public scrutiny. Many historians believe the condition was a way for Robert to thwart historian Albert Beveridge's access to the papers, about which Beveridge had been pestering Robert for years.[6]

After her husband's death, Mary Harlan Lincoln continued Robert's tradition of upholding and augmenting the public memory and legacy of Abraham Lincoln by donating more family materials to the Library of Congress and also by denying public access to private family materials.[7] The one historian Mary Harlan Lincoln did trust was Robert's cousin and Mary's dear friend, Katherine Helm. Helm, the daughter of Mary Todd Lincoln's half-sister, Emily Todd Helm, was writing the first and only authorized biography of Mary Todd Lincoln, which she commenced with Robert's approval and continued with his and his wife's aid. They often gave her access to family papers and letters only a handful of other people had ever seen, including some materials that have since disappeared and, therefore, now can only be found in her book.[8]

Given this closeness and trust, it is therefore no surprise that when Mary Harlan Lincoln received an unexpected visitor in October 1927 bearing news of the impending publication of a history of her mother-in-law's insanity case, she wrote a letter to Katherine Helm to inform her. At that time, Helm was still in the process of writing her biography. "My dear Miss Helm: We had quite a surprise party last Wednesday, and Mrs. Lincoln has asked that I write to you and tell you about it," the letter, written by Lincoln attorney Frederic Towers, began. It continued:

A Mrs. Stuart (Myra) Pritchard called here with her attorney. . . . it seems that Mrs. Pritchard is the grand-daughter of Judge Bradwell, of Chicago; to whom and to whose wife, Myra Bradwell, Mrs. Abraham Lincoln addressed many letters during her lifetime. Now, the point is this: Mrs. Pritchard contemplates the publication of this material, in the form of a biographical sketch; and while, of course, she does not have to ask anyone's permission to do so, the purpose of her visit here was to inform Mrs. Lincoln of her intention; which, I think, is very decent of her. She tacitly agreed to submit to Mrs. Lincoln's inspection anything she might wish to publish; and Mrs. Lincoln, I believe, rather feels as I do,—namely, that it is better to have Mrs. Pritchard as a friend than to offend her. So she has agreed, tentatively, to see Mrs. Pritchard in Washington.[9]

In fact, Mary Harlan Lincoln not only agreed to meet with Mrs. Pritchard in Washington, D.C. and inspect the 111-page manuscript but also suggested that she might be able to add information from her own files.[10] This statement, as borne out by later events, was intended to keep her in Myra Pritchard's good graces while she decided how best to handle the situation. Yet, far from aiding Myra Pritchard in her publication endeavors, Mary Harlan Lincoln thwarted her.

Towers and his partner, Norman B. Frost, upon their meeting with Myra Pritchard in December 1927, were confronted with the most unprecedented cache of materials relating to Mary Todd Lincoln ever found.[11] It must be noted that up to 1927, no book had been published that was written solely about Mary Lincoln, and there was only one book about Abraham Lincoln that even mentioned his wife's insanity trial.[12] Myra Pritchard, Myra Bradwell's granddaughter, purportedly owned thirty-seven letters of correspondence from Mary Todd Lincoln to Myra and James Bradwell.[13] These letters spanned the period from 1872 to 1878,

Mary Harlan Lincoln. Courtesy Friends of Hildene, Inc.

the majority of them directly relating to Mary's 1875 commitment to the sanitarium. Myra Pritchard also owned Mary Todd Lincoln's 1873 will, the one written by James Bradwell and never probated. From these materials, Myra Pritchard had written her book, "The Dark Days of Abraham Lincoln's Widow, as Revealed by Her Own Letters." She already had secured a publishing contract from J. H. Sears & Company to print her work in nine installments in *Liberty* magazine, for which she was paid $5,000.[14]

Towers and Frost entered their meeting knowing Robert Lincoln had, for a while, sought to collect and destroy all his mother's letters relating to her mental illness.[15] He did this to protect not only his mother's reputation but also his own; for he knew, as no one else did, the malicious,

Myra Helmer Pritchard. Courtesy James Gordon.

hurtful, and even untrue statements his mother made to and about him as revenge for his actions. As Frost and Towers saw, Pritchard's letters revealed exactly what Robert had tried to suppress: a woman of dramatic mood swings and temperament, whose letters varied from tender and loving, to hectic and neurotic, to accusatory, paranoid, and downright vicious. As Myra Pritchard later wrote, "One can readily see why the Robert Lincolns would not want these letters published."[16]

After two days of meeting with Myra Pritchard and reading through the materials, Frost and Towers found three letters written by Mary Todd Lincoln they found "objectionable to print." Initially, Frost and Pritchard discussed the possibility of "eliding" these letters from her manuscript because Mary Harlan Lincoln felt it would be "unfair and . . . objectionable" to print them.[17] Pritchard agreed to give the objectionable letters to the attorneys on the condition that they agreed not to press any legal rights they might have under the *Wilson* case, a recent court decision that the writer of a letter and his or her succeeding heirs, and not the recipient, was the actual owner.[18]

After taking a night to think it over, Pritchard told Frost that taking out the three letters in question "would somewhat divest the story of its commercial value." Since Mary Harlan Lincoln would not consent to publication of the article without revisions, Frost suggested that the entire manuscript, original letters, and any copies should be sold either to the Lincoln family or to "some friendly publishing company, to be revised, printed or destroyed as might be seen fit."[19] Pritchard then left Washington to discuss the proposal and the matter of price with her attorney.

One can only imagine the dejection the pressure to give up her manuscript must have caused Myra Pritchard, especially considering it was a situation of her own creation. Scholarship concerning Abraham Lincoln still was in its infancy in 1927, and, aside from occasional newspaper articles, practically nothing had been written about Mary Todd Lincoln, especially not about her insanity trial. Pritchard, therefore, was sitting on a gold mine of historical material, both from a financial and a literary standpoint. The publication of her manuscript would not only garner her a handsome royalty check but also would immediately catapult her name and her writing into national prominence.[20] Chicago judge Henry Horner, one of the great collectors of Lincolniana, told Pritchard after he examined her grandparents' correspondence with Mary Lincoln that it would have "an unquestioned bearing on the phases of history in which [Mary Lincoln] played a part."[21] As Pritchard's attorney, Otis Rockwood, wrote to Towers at the end of the year, "Of course Mrs. Pritchard is very anxious to become better known as an authoress and therefore she desires keenly to have this article published."[22]

Yet one week later, the two sides had agreed to a full sale of the material and all copies for the price of $22,500—a compromise between the $20,000 Mary Harlan Lincoln felt appropriate and the $25,000 Myra Pritchard thought reasonable.[23] The sale was conditional upon authentication of the letters by a handwriting expert, which was secured and confirmed in late January 1928 from the examiner of questioned documents at the U.S. Treasury Department.[24]

The actual contract of sale, executed on January 31, 1928, set the conditions that the manuscript, all connected letters, and all copies in Myra Pritchard's possession be turned over to Mary Harlan Lincoln; that no other person had any copies of the materials; that no other copies of the materials existed; that if Myra Pritchard subsequently obtained any other Lincoln family letters, they would be turned over to the Lincoln family; that Myra Pritchard would not publish, permit, or cause to be published any of the manuscript or letters in her possession; and that if any of the materials were published or offered for sale, in whole or part, by anyone who secured possession through Myra Pritchard, the contract would be voided and she would be required to repay the Lincoln family the amount of purchase.[25]

The contract "sews her up as tight as a drum," observed Karl Harriman, the vice president of Myra Pritchard's publishers, J. H. Sears & Company, once he was informed of it. "In point of fact I think if she is apprehended reading a book about Lincoln, or mentioning his name or the name of his lady, she is likely to subject herself thereby to imprisonment for life, if indeed not summary execution."[26] Myra Pritchard and the general manager of Liberty Weekly, Inc., signed a contract dissolving their previous publishing agreement in January 1928.[27]

Myra Pritchard was unhappy about the sale, and in March 1928, drew up a statement regarding her disposal of the Mary Lincoln letters. "These letters along with some other Lincoln relics were given to me some eight or nine years before my mother's death, with the stipulation that I should write about them but not until both my mother and Robert Lincoln should have passed on," the statement reads. "My mother was most anxious that these letters be published because she felt that Mrs. Abraham Lincoln had been maligned and that these letters would explain much of the real Mrs. Lincoln to the world and place her in a more favorable light."[28]

Of course, Pritchard understood why the Lincoln family did not want the letters published, as they offered intimate and embarrassing views into the private lives of a very private family, but still she tried her best to convince the Lincolns to release the publication rights. "I finally sold them to Frost and Towers, attorneys for Mrs. Robert Lincoln, for $22,500," she wrote. "The value of these letters would have been infinitely more before Robert Lincoln's death in 1926."[29] She did not know what Mary Harlan Lincoln intended to do with the letters, but she assumed they would be destroyed.[30]

Interestingly, the Pritchards and the Lincolns were not the only people to know of the existence of the insanity letters. Myra Bradwell showed the letters to at least one other person; and Myra Pritchard had either spoken of them or shown them to at least three other people.[31] Other historians also discovered their existence through hearsay. In late November 1928, Pritchard received letters from two different people, one asking for access to the letters, the other asking for their donation to the Library of Congress.[32] Pritchard wrote to Frederic Towers and asked him how she should respond, stating, "it is my desire to protect your interests in every way I can."[33] Towers suggested she answer honestly and simply say the papers "have passed out of your hands."[34]

Myra Pritchard also continued to uphold her part of the contract agreement when, in 1932, she donated other Lincoln items in her possession on a call-loan basis to the Chicago Historical Society for public display. Pritchard loaned the society a number of authentic Lincoln-related items that Mary Todd Lincoln had given to Myra Bradwell, including President Lincoln's "Definition of Democracy" in his own handwriting; a gold pen with which, Mary claimed, Abraham Lincoln had signed the Emancipation Proclamation; a bloodstone seal presented by the sultan of Turkey to President Lincoln; as well as a legal document and message to Congress in Abraham Lincoln's handwriting.[35] Eleanor Gridley, a longtime friend of Myra Bradwell's, submitted a sworn affidavit to the effect that the items were genuine.[36] Pritchard wrote in a letter to L. H. Shattuck, Chicago Historical Society director, that if the affidavit mentioned the insanity letters, "I should not want that on record or any public comment made of it. If it does mention these items I will get another affidavit from Mrs. Gridley . . . omitting the Mrs. Lincoln correspondence."[37]

At 12:01 A.M. on July 26, 1947, the Robert Todd Lincoln Collection of the Papers of Abraham Lincoln, stored in the Library of Congress since 1919, were opened to the public. The opening caused nationwide interest and media coverage, as no historians had examined the complete collection since John Hay and John Nicolay in the late nineteenth century. After all the excitement and the furor of the opening, and all the revelations of the materials in the collection, one big disappointment was that the papers contained only one letter either to or from Mary Todd Lincoln. An article in *Life* magazine asked the trenchant question, "What then has happened to [her letters]?"[38]

The insanity letters, in fact, still existed. Not only were many in the possession of Frederic Towers, the Lincoln family attorney, but they also were in the possession of Myra Pritchard, who, despite the stringent agreement she had signed with Mary Harlan Lincoln, had kept typewritten copies of all the Mary Lincoln letters and her own unpublished manuscript.

Upon Myra Pritchard's death in February 1947, her daughter, Margreta Pritchard, opened her mother's safety deposit box and found within a parcel labeled "In case of my death this is to be destroyed immediately." The parcel contained the entire 1928 *Liberty* magazine manuscript. After

Margreta Pritchard read the manuscript, she told her family members her intention and "personally burn[ed] the contents and entirely consumed the same in flames."[39]

She did not, however, burn the typewritten copies of the letters. Instead, she approached Oliver R. Barrett, a prominent Chicago attorney and one of the foremost Lincoln collectors in America, to ask his advice on whether or not she should publish the letters her mother had kept secret for nineteen years. There are no records explaining why Margreta Pritchard considered publishing the letters despite her mother's previous contract with the Lincoln family, and there is no way to know how the Lincolns would have reacted. Mary Harlan Lincoln had died in 1937, but her children and grandchildren were still alive, as was Frederic Towers, the attorney who negotiated the deal and still had the papers in his possession.[40]

Barrett advised Margreta Pritchard that the letters should not be published, that they had "absolutely no historical value," and would be of benefit only to someone "who desired to read the rantings of an insane person." Barrett also told Margreta Pritchard's attorneys to thoroughly search her belongings to obtain the typewritten copies of the letters, the manuscript, and any evidence of the fact that the originals were sold to the Lincoln family. "He then feels that we should take these typewritten copies and tie them together securely and place a screw through the middle of them and then get in touch with the Librarian of the Library of Congress and the President of the Chicago Historical Society and in their presence have the same destroyed."[41]

Barrett felt it would not be "exactly morally right" to publish letters that Robert Lincoln so aggressively sought to keep private and unpublished during his life, and which his family had taken the time and expense to purchase, presumably so they could be destroyed. He also felt such destruction would increase the value of the Robert Lincoln collection that had recently opened at the Library of Congress. Its value had been cast into doubt by the above-mentioned *Life* magazine article, which had questioned whether the Library of Congress actually had the complete collection of Lincoln papers left by Robert Lincoln, or whether they had purged it of detrimental items such as the insanity letters. Barrett suggested that destroying the letters would "be rendering a great service" and would "put the question to rest once and for all."[42]

Margreta Pritchard's attorneys agreed with Barrett, for the same reasons, and urged her to destroy the letters, which she ultimately did.[43] The lore and lure of the letters continued, however. In September 1949, while in the midst of composing her Mary Lincoln biography, Ruth Painter

Randall received word of the letters in the possession of the Pritchard family. Randall's friend, Henrietta Horner, the wife of Lincoln scholar Harlan Hoyt Horner, wrote to her, "Perhaps you have gotten on the trail of a series of letters written by Mrs. Lincoln to Mrs. Myra Bradwell, the woman who secured Mrs. Lincoln's release from Batavia. Mrs. Eleanor Gridley wrote me about the existence of these letters which she had been allowed to read, and which she was sure were preserved by the Bradwell family in Chicago. None of them have ever been published or quoted so far as I know."[44] No evidence has been found suggesting Randall made any effort or had any luck finding or securing the letters, other than the statement in her book that the letters had "vanished."[45]

So what did Mary Harlan Lincoln do with the letters and the manuscript once she acquired them? As with so many historical actions—and so many things regarding the family of Abraham Lincoln—it remains a mystery. The fact that they were not included in Robert Lincoln's personal Insanity File, nor found at the Lincolns' Vermont home, indicates Mary Harlan Lincoln did indeed destroy them, as Myra Pritchard supposed. But if she did destroy them, then why did her attorney, Frederic Towers, keep copies of them, and did Mary Harlan Lincoln know of the copies he kept?

Numerous historians have wondered over and searched for the letters for decades, as evidenced in Myra Pritchard's attempt to publish the letters in 1928, the searches by Mary Lincoln biographers Evans (1928), Randall (1953), and the Turners (1972), as well as the current "Ghosts of the Library" presentation at the Abraham Lincoln Presidential Library and Museum. When I began my research for my impending biography of Robert T. Lincoln, I had no idea or intention of finding them.[46]

My initial discovery began in March 2005, while doing research on Robert at his home, Hildene, in Manchester, Vermont. I discovered two letters written by Frederic Towers about Myra Pritchard's visit to Hildene: the one quoted above to Katherine Helm, and another to Myra Pritchard arranging the Washington, D.C., meeting between the two parties. While looking for Bradwell/Pritchard family descendants, I read a biography of Myra Bradwell called *America's First Woman Lawyer*, by Jane M. Friedman, which contained an entire chapter describing the sale of the insanity letters, based on primary Pritchard family information.[47] Friedman described in her prologue how she tracked down Myra Pritchard's distant relative, James Gordon, who had legal documentation concerning the letter sale episode and its aftermath.[48] Mr. Gordon did not have the insanity letters or the book manuscript but still had the legal correspondence and files relating to the materials and the Mary Harlan Lincoln episode.

Frederic N. Towers, Robert T. Lincoln's attorney. Courtesy Towers family.

Realizing that the story was a legal affair, and knowing none of the insanity materials were anywhere in any Lincoln collections that I could find, I wondered about the files of the Lincoln family attorneys. Could they have kept something? A few months later—a total of five months after I found the first two letters at Hildene—I spoke with Frederic C. Towers on the telephone in early August 2005. He told me that during a recent move he had uncovered an old steamer trunk, labeled "F. N. Towers Lincoln Papers," that belonged to his father. The trunk was filled with hundreds of legal papers of Robert T. and Mary Harlan Lincoln; but included as well were materials pertaining to Mary Todd Lincoln's insanity episode. Towers had found not only photographic and hand-written copies of numerous letters by Mary Lincoln but also all the legal

Steamer trunk owned by Frederic N. Towers in which Mary Lincoln's "lost insanity letters" were discovered in 2005. Photograph by Jason Emerson.

documentation of the sale by Myra Pritchard to Mary Harlan Lincoln, as well as Pritchard's entire unpublished manuscript. Towers and his siblings were at that point deciding what to do with them—whether to keep them, sell them, or donate them to a Lincoln-related museum.

After much discussion and follow-up, Frederic C. Towers and his siblings allowed me to write the story of their letters. I asked Towers why he thought his father kept copies of the insanity letters and whether he believed Mary Harlan Lincoln knew he had them. He had no firm answer, yet he supposed that his father probably kept the documents, the letters, and the Pritchard manuscript without Mary Harlan Lincoln's knowledge or consent. He did not believe his father did this out of spite but rather out of a sense of duty to posterity. More than likely, the reason was that Robert Lincoln's attorney, Frederic N. Towers, according to his son, personally witnessed Robert Lincoln burning family letters, and as he vehemently opposed such destruction, he may have decided to save the insanity materials to prevent still more historical loss.[49] The truth most likely will never be known.

Frederic Towers's preservation of what have since become known as Mary Lincoln's "lost insanity letters" was, in fact, an enormous contribution to posterity, and for that, he and his family should be thanked, and his spirit should be rightly proud.

Epilogue

THE MENTAL ILLNESS OF MARY LINCOLN is a fascinating historical study that has rarely been explored from a psychiatric viewpoint. Despite a historiography of some eighty years, most historians and writers have eschewed the medical perspective, focusing instead on historical, moral, legal, political, and social viewpoints. A true understanding of her illness cannot be understood, however, without determining what her mental aberrations consisted of. The historical evidence shows that Mary Lincoln most likely suffered from Manic-Depressive Illness, now called Bipolar Disorder. She suffered intense mood swings during her youth and early adulthood, which increasingly transformed into periods of depression and, during acutely traumatic episodes such as the death of a loved one, severe depression that went beyond the bounds of what psychiatrists would call a normal grief reaction.

Numerous sources offer evidence that during Mary's marriage to Abraham Lincoln her symptoms escalated to include delusions and hallucinations (such as her constant fear of fires and burglars) and the compulsive spending that so characterized her later life. This continued during the White House years, along with the emergence of delusions of persecution and poverty. The assassination of her husband clearly unhinged Mary, and her mood swings and depressive episodes became more intense and more frequent. Her delusions and hallucinations became more pronounced, as did her spending, until her commitment to Bellevue Place Sanitarium. Her symptoms then turned to violence, first with her 1875 suicide attempt, and then in the form of threats against Robert's life and her acquisition of a pistol. What little is known about her years in Europe seem to show a lessening in the severity of her condition, but her mood swings, depressive episodes, and senseless spending continued. (For a professional psychiatrist's viewpoint on Mary Lincoln's condition, see appendix 3.)

The first attempt to psychiatrically examine Mary Lincoln's mental state was Dr. W. A. Evans's, *Mrs. Abraham Lincoln: A Study of Her Personality and Her Influence on Abraham Lincoln*, published in 1932. Evans, a physician and medical school professor who also consulted other specialists in mental diseases, sought to examine and diagnose Mary's mental state through her psychology. His belief was that to truly understand Mary's life and actions one must understand her personality, which included her mentality and even her physical health. Evans did not limit himself to the actual instances of Mary's "insanity" but also examined her family background, life history, life traumas, and physical health, to explain what he concluded to be an emotional, but not mental, insanity. Mary had a "mild, emotional insanity which caused her to act as does a case of schizophrenia—living alone, apart, and letting the world take care of itself," Evans wrote.[1] Yet, because she was a victim of her emotions, she was not responsible for what she said or did or for what people said about her, he concluded.

Evans's conclusions for Mary's insanity were weakened, however, by his defense of her. In fact, Evans nearly contradicted himself and unwittingly gave ammunition to later Mary defenders as his conclusions about the degree of her mental instability were marred by caveats, rationalizations, and nuances that grew as the book moved toward its end. He stated that her mania for money, extravagance, and miserliness were "well known" to psychiatrists and "present in many people who are accepted as normal." And while not denying her mental condition, Evans also stated that Mary's belief in Spiritualism, thought at that time by some doctors to be both a cause and a manifestation of insanity, "militated" against her at the time of her trial.[2]

In January 1941, Lieut. James A. Brussel, U.S. Army Medical Corps, the chief psychiatrist at Fort Dix, New Jersey, published a psychiatric study of Mary Lincoln in the *Psychiatric Quarterly*.[3] Brussel studied Mary's life from childhood to death and stated that her case was difficult to diagnose, as it was "replete with etiological factors, running the gamut from congenital defects to adverse living conditions and complicating trauma."[4] Brussel found psychotic symptoms of hallucinations, delusions, terror, depression, suicidal intentions and attempts, ideas of persecution, and outbursts of irritability, rage, and overactivity. His diagnosis was that Mary was a victim of migraine, although he stated that epilepsy, "or at least an 'epileptic equivalent,'" was possible. He ruled out psychoneurosis, Manic-Depressive psychosis, and schizophrenia.[5]

Twenty-five years later, another psychiatrist, John M. Suarez, published a case study of Mary Lincoln in the *American Journal of Psychiatry*.[6] Suarez concluded that Mary had a lifelong personality disorder that erupted in 1875 into full-blown paranoid psychosis with manic, schizophrenic, and involutional features.[7] While the successive tragedies in Mary's life led to her breakdown, Suarez declared, there was "not enough evidence to support the hypothesis that there was a serious, overt psychopathology at least up until her time at the White House."[8] Robert's part in the insanity episode lay in his emotional distance from his mother, Suarez found. "Her great anger toward him for abandoning her, which became so apparent during and after the commitment, was hinted [at] earlier in her obsessive concern for his health despite lack of evidence and in the face of bona fide assurances," Suarez wrote. "There is little doubt that she would be committed by any court today. She was clearly a danger to herself and others."[9]

The articles by both Brussel and Suarez, with their expert psychiatric diagnoses, are invaluable resources for any study of Mary Lincoln's illness and build upon Evans's foundation with increasingly modern understandings of psychiatry. Sadly, both studies have lain completely unknown or ignored by subsequent historians and in historiographies of the topic.

The only other medical examination of Mary's case occurred in a 1999 article in the *Journal of the History of Medicine and Allied Sciences*, "Mary Lincoln's Final Illness: A Medical and Historical Reappraisal," by Norbert Hirschhorn and Robert G. Feldman. This article was an important contribution to the insanity trial historiography because it appraised Mary Lincoln's illness from a physiological viewpoint, something only slightly touched upon by Evans and Suarez. Based upon Mary's medical history, as written by her physicians, observations from friends and relatives, and Mary's own words, Hirschhorn and Feldman concluded that in the last decade of her life she suffered intense pain from a progressive and fatal disease that was "misinterpreted as madness."[10]

Mary suffered from a syndrome known as tabes dorsalis, a form of chronic spinal cord disease, they concluded. This disease would account for all of Mary's physiological symptoms during the 1870s: lancinating pain throughout her body; incoordination in walking, especially down stairs; narrowing of vision; ulcers on her feet; urinary incontinence; and swelling of joints. The disease could have been caused by syphilis or, more probably, by prolonged and untreated diabetes, Hirschhorn and Feldman stated. How did this physical condition affect her mental state? "Given the wide spectrum of classifiable mental and character disorders, the question has no meaning," they wrote. "In any case, no global diagnosis is feasible only from the historical data." Yet, the authors did see her behavioral and physical symptoms, imputed as insanity during her trial, as having their origins in tabes dorsalis. They do not use this diagnosis to excuse her bizarre behavior and, in fact, attribute her acute anxiety, insomnia, and delusions to a condition that "most resembles post-traumatic stress disorder," probably coinciding with the tenth anniversary of President Lincoln's assassination.[11]

In recent years, some nonmedical historians have suggested their own diagnoses for Mary's condition as well. Michael Burlingame declared she suffered from manic depression, although she showed symptoms of borderline personality disorder as well.[12] Deborah Hayden declared Mary's symptoms to be the result of syphilis.[13] Jean Baker asserted that Mary's delusions in March 1875 were not medically based but actually a "premonition," or a Spiritualistic "self-induced trance," caused by her use of chloral hydrate, with the vindictiveness of a male chauvinist society to blame for her commitment.[14] Mark E. Neely and R. Gerald McMurtry, in the most detailed examination of Mary's case up to that point, avoided any sort of medical diagnosis or understanding altogether. Instead, they contented themselves with Mary's own "confession" that she was insane in the spring of 1875 due to her use of chloral hydrate and the effects of her physical illnesses.[15] Like Baker, they also faulted the contemporary medical profession's prejudice against women, although they did not fault the medical evidence used against her.

Interpretations of the part Robert played in his mother's insanity episode have varied from indifference, to support, to downright animosity. The current interpretation that holds sway in the popular mind is that Robert was a rapacious, avaricious, coldhearted snob who detested his mother and put her away to rid himself of her and steal her money. The historical evidence, however, completely disproves this. That evidence, found in letters and papers spread among archival repositories and seldom, and then only selectively, used and edited in disparate secondary sources, attests to Robert Lincoln's beneficent intentions toward his mother in 1875. It proves him to have been a man of his time, with a reticent demeanor, a private personality, and a Victorian sensibility of manly duty. It proves that his motives were not vile but honorable; that he took action only as a last resort, and that it was an action that pained him considerably.

Of course, Robert was not a perfect man and should not be so construed. His patience was not infinite; and at times, his exasperation at his mother was evident. His refusal to unconditionally lavish concern and attention on her, as she both desired and, to a certain extent, emotionally and psychologically needed, may be faulted as too much emotional reserve—a manifestation, perhaps, of his staunch Victorian sensibilities—that certainly did not help the situation. His logical lawyer's mind also made mistakes that a more seasoned man might not have made, such as his intention to have his mother arrested before her trial and his way of dealing with Myra and James Bradwell.

The varied opinions and explanations for Mary's mental illness show that her case still intrigues laymen and historians one hundred and twenty-five years after her death. In fact, one of the few things nonhistorians know about Mary Lincoln today is that she was "crazy." Regrettably, the academic debate about Mary's insanity and its causes has devolved in recent years to a disrespectful argument of he-said/she-said between defenders of Mary and defenders of Robert. This is not only unfortunate but unnecessary.

To declare Robert an honorable, loving son is not to attack or demean Mary Lincoln. This is one of the primary roadblocks to a true understanding of the insanity event that has been a part of the popular thinking for decades: to defend either Robert or Mary does not make it a requirement to defile the other. Mary Lincoln deserves understanding for her horribly traumatic life and her psychiatric illness. She deserves empathy, and not a little pity, for the trials she endured, which began with the death of her mother and ended only in her own death. Mental illness is not something actively sought, and we cannot blame Mary for her irrationalities; nor can we blame Robert for dealing with his mother in a way he deemed most necessary and proper.

The student of history must not make conclusions outside of historical context. This is the principal mistake made in regard to Robert Lincoln. His personality, his motivations, have never been considered in their proper Victorian attire, but when they are, and when he is given a fair standard to measure against, there can be no doubt that Robert Lincoln was an honorable man who loved his mother. Likewise, when examining the evidence, there can be no doubt that Mary Lincoln suffered from serious mental illness. Her family, friends, and doctors treated her with love and respect, but they were firm in their commitment to the alleviation of her troubles.

Would Abraham Lincoln have committed his wife to an asylum if he had lived past his presidency? If necessary, it is possible that he would have. We know that he once threatened her with commitment. The natural course of Manic-Depressive illness is that it worsens over time, so Mary's illness might have progressed even if her husband had lived. However, it was his presence that supported her through many trials and traumas, and if he had lived, Mary might never have spun out of control as she did. Not only did the assassination dramatically unhinge her but in losing Lincoln she lost her most solid anchor to sanity. As she said, for more than twenty years, Lincoln was "Always—lover—husband—father & *all all to me*—Truly my all."[16] And as Rev. Reed said in Mary's eulogy, when Abraham died, Mary died as well, only much more slowly.

Appendixes
Notes
Bibliography
Index

Unpublished Mary Todd Lincoln Letters

THESE TWENTY-FIVE LETTERS SPAN THE YEARS 1872 to 1878, from three years before to three years after Mary Lincoln's institutionalization. Mary wrote twenty of these letters: seventeen to Myra Bradwell, and three to James Bradwell. Of the remaining five letters, two were written by Myra Bradwell, one by James Bradwell, one by Elizabeth Edwards, and one by Dr. R. J. Patterson. Also included is part of Mary Lincoln's 1873 will, drafted by James Bradwell, which, like the letters, had disappeared from history's view.

Of the twenty-five letters, there are photographs of seven of Mary's handwritten originals, in whole or in part; copies of eight in Myra Bradwell's handwriting, written on *Chicago Legal News* letterhead, dating to sometime in or prior to 1894, when she died; and copies of three in Myra Pritchard's handwriting, dating probably to 1928. The other seven letters are found only in the unpublished Pritchard manuscript, "The Dark Days of Abraham Lincoln's Widow, as Revealed by Her Own Letters," based on the letters Mrs. Pritchard had in her possession until 1928. None of the letters are originals in Mary Todd Lincoln's handwriting, although their authenticity is not in doubt. Mary Harlan Lincoln hired Bert C. Farrar, examiner of questioned documents with the U.S. Treasury Department, to examine the letters and ascertain their legitimacy.[1] Mr. Farrar obviously concluded the letters genuine, as Mary's purchase of the letters from Myra Pritchard was subject to that authentication.

Interestingly, and sadly, Myra Pritchard owned even more Mary Lincoln letters than quoted in her manuscript or found in the Towers trunk. She explained in part 9 of her manuscript that those letters, written after 1878, "add nothing to the record I have sought to perpetuate here. They are sweet, chatty letters of her travels and her friends. In none of them does she mention the gray days of the past and to publish them would, I think, be inexcusable prying into Mary Todd Lincoln's intimate affairs."[2] Myra Pritchard's daughter, Margreta, destroyed all the Mary Lincoln letters in her family's possession in 1951.[3] (For more on the sale and destruction of these letters, see appendix 2.)

These letters derive importance not only from their relation to Mary's insanity trial but also to their mere existence, for, as the compilers of Mary's collected letters wrote, "Letters written by Mary Lincoln in the period between 1871 and 1876 today are the rarest of items."[4] Prior to the finding of the letters in the Towers trunk and the Pritchard manuscript, only ten such letters were known to exist.

Some of the people mentioned in these letters are referred to nowhere else in the entire historiography of Mary Lincoln's life, including her collected letters. My own research, as well as consultation with the curators of the Abraham Lincoln Presidential Library and other Lincoln experts, has uncovered some, but unfortunately not all, of these identities.

In January 2007, the Towers family donated their father's Lincoln papers to the Library of Congress, being desirous that the general public should have access to this unprecedented cache of materials. Mary Lincoln's lost letters, as well as hundreds of documents pertaining to Robert Todd Lincoln, his family, and his work to preserve his father's memory, now can be viewed in the library's Manuscripts Division Reading Room.

Note on the text: All transcriptions are based on photographs of letters and handwritten copies where possible and otherwise on the text of Myra Pritchard's manuscript, with her edits and punctuation changes.

November 1, 1872[5]
My dear Mrs. Bradwell,
Please inform me, what has become of your own dear self. I am very anxious to see you and I wish you would call in a day or two. I can scarcely understand your neglect, dear kind friend. Come *very soon*, and present my kindest regards, to your good husband, and your daughter. Before *3* days have passed I want to have, one of our old fashioned chats together. With ever so much love, Believe me, Always, truly yours,

Mary Lincoln

January 26, 1873[6]
My dear Mrs. Bradwell,
How much I regret to say to you that I am suffering for the last two days with a severe headache, which the Doctor[7] tells me may settle in my head if I do not remain very quiet. I rise out of bed to tell you this—for it is quite a source of annoyance to me that I shall not be able to see you tomorrow; but you may be sure, dear Mrs. Bradwell, that so soon as I shall be able I will call for you to claim you for a few hours.

You cannot begin to know what a treat it is for me to hear you converse and be near you. The doctor objects to my calling to see dear Mrs. Swisshelm[8] at present lest it may renew my nervousness in recalling past and happier times. Before the week closes we will surely meet.

> Most affectionately your friend,
> Mary Lincoln

May 6, 1874[9]
My dear Mrs. Bradwell,

Your kind note from Mobile was received several days since and I would have sent you an earlier reply had it not been for quite a severe attack of illness and this is the first day I am out of bed for five days. Such terrible weather we have had! I am delighted that you are enjoying yourself so very much and trust that you will return to us with your health entirely restored. Today is lovely here and I am even anticipating the Dr.'s[10] afternoon call with his sugar pellets and harmless draughts as a pleasant variety to the monotony of the day. Our good friend, Mrs. Swisshelm has been confined to the house with severe quinzy and you may be sure that I am missing her greatly. Her quaint style is perfectly charming to me and such a relief to me from my *remembrance* of the artificial world, with which in former and *so much* happier days I was constantly surrounded. This note I fear will scarcely reach—ere you are leaving for C. [Chicago]

> With a world of love, believe me, your devoted friend,
> Mary Lincoln

St. Augustine, Fla., February 20, 1875[11]
My dear Mrs. Bradwell,

Your kind letter was received some time since & although I have not replied to it, believe me truly that you are very frequently in my thoughts—and I, have so often wished we could be together in this "Sunny clime." I am now looking down upon a yard with its roses, white lilacs and other flowers. (Although it is raining and we have had a good deal of rain in its soft, dreamy, light fashion,) since the middle of January, I remained too much out, on my balcony, took a severe cold, had much inward and outward fever for three weeks and one day when it was raging at its height I told my nurse[12] to pack up a small trunk and valise and we would leave town. So, on the 11th of Feb. we started for this place five hours distant from

Jacksonville by boat and railway. On board the steamer I met three or four choice Philadelphia friends, ladies and gentlemen and they insisted on my joining them and instead of a modest journey of five hours to St. A. it proved four days and nights on the boat. If these *comme il faut* persons from the north generally and the most charming scenery on the celebrated Ochlawahs river could give pleasure, then it certainly was mine. Words would fail in description going from the broad St. John's into the narrow streams. With scenery such as is seldom met with in this world such pens as W.C. Bryant and others have given minute details of the voyage. Scribner's November monthly speaks of it and Harper dwells at great length upon it. How much we will have to say to each other when we meet. From this most unexpected excursion I came here. I have been here five days, three of which have been passed in bed. For you may be well assured that the fever in my veins, must run its course. But two bright days I have emerged from it wandering over this quaint and most interesting place. My first visit was of course to the ancient Fort[13] and my wondering head was in every prison nook until we came to the one whose entrance was excavated I believe, in 1835, where two iron cages were found, one, now said to be in the Smithsonian Institute in Wash. Hooked to the wall, where history records, and the Sergeant repeats, the story that two prisoners were enclosed in these same cages walled in, left to their fate, with God alone to be merciful to them! The prison of course is in darkness except the dim light held by the sergeant. I entered the fearful place and how I came out of it and how I have suffered in mind since our merciful Heavenly Father alone knows the wrongs of time will be redressed in a brighter world! My son[14] writes me that the winter has been terribly cold and my good friend and your dear husband, how is he getting along and how is his health this winter? What would I not give to see you again. My pen *as you perceive*, refuses its office.

With much love to you and yours
believe me, most affectionately yours,
Mary Lincoln

Wednesday, July 28th, 1875, Batavia, Ill[15]
My dear Friend:
    Judge Bradwell
    May I request you to come out here just *so* soon as you receive this note. Please bring out your dear wife, Mr. Wm Sturgess,[16] and

any other friend. Can you not be *here*, tomorrow on the noon train. Also bring Mr. W. F. Storey,[17] with you. I am sure you will not disappoint me. Drive up to the house. Also telegraph to Genl Farnsworth[18] to meet you here.

With much love to Mrs. Bradwell, believe me, truly yours,
Mary Lincoln

Please pardon me, if I mention that I will meet the expenses of your trip. M. L.

[sideways on front page] In the event of Judge B. not receiving this note in time, please come out on at afternoon train. —M. L.

CHICAGO LEGAL NEWS COMPANY
151 & 153 Fifth Ave.
Chicago, July 30, 1875[19]
Hon. John T. Stuart[20]
Dear Sir,

I saw Mrs. Lincoln at Batavia on yesterday. She desired me to write to you and say that she very much wants to see you, and would like you to visit her as soon as you can as she feels lonesome and that the restraint of the place is unendurable. I believe a visit from you would do her good and I hope you may be able to make it.

Mrs. Lincoln's general health has greatly improved. She spoke of Mrs. Edwards[21] in the kindest terms, and expressed the wish that she might visit her at Batavia and said that she would like to return to Springfield with her and make a visit. I believe such a visit would result in good to Mrs. Lincoln, and do no one any harm. Dr. Patterson[22] said of all the patients he ever had at the retreat, Mrs. Lincoln had given him the least trouble. I am,

Very truly yours,
James B. Bradwell

CHICAGO LEGAL NEWS COMPANY
151 & 153 Fifth Ave.
Chicago, July 30, 1875[23]
Mrs. Edwards.
Dear Madam:

I have just returned from a visit to your dear sister, Mrs. Lincoln. She desires me to write to you asking you to come up and visit her and expresses a wish to return with you to Springfield. She feels her incarceration most terribly and desires to get out from behind the *grates and bars*.[24] I cannot feel that it is necessary to keep her thus restrained. Perhaps I do not look at the matter rightly, but let this be my excuse—I love her most tenderly and feel sorry to see one heartache added to her already overburdened soul.

She has always spoken most tenderly of you and I do believe it would do her good to meet you and receive a sister's loving tenderness.

Pardon the liberty I have taken in addressing you and believe me, your sister's friend

Myra Bradwell

Springfield, Aug. 3 [1875][25]
Mrs. Bradwell,
Dear Madam:

I haste to reply to your kind note, relative to my unhappy sister. My heart rebelled at the thought of placing her in an asylum; believing that her sad case merely required the care of a protector, whose companionship, would be pleasant to her. Had I been consulted, I would have remonstrated earnestly against the step taken.

The judgment of others must now, I presume, be silently acquiesced in, for a time, in the hope, that ere long, her physical and mental condition, will be improved, by rest and medical treatment.

The sorrows that befell her in such rapid succession and *the one, so* tragic, was enough to shatter the nerves, and infuse the intellect of the bravest mind and heart. I regret to say that I cannot just now visit Mrs. Lincoln, being prostrated from the effects of a recent surgical operation.[26] But will at once write to her, and soothe her burdened heart, if possible, with words of love and sympathy.

It is my opinion, that she should be indulged in a desire to visit her friends as the surest means of restoring her to health and cheerfulness.

Accept my thanks, for your interest, in my sister, and the suggestions you have made me.

Yrs truly
Mrs. N. W. Edwards

Batavia, Illinois [August 2?, 1875][27]
My Dear Mrs. Bradwell:

Last evening I received your two most welcome letters. It is impossible to express the delight they afforded me and yet my disappointment is great that you do not propose coming out here until Friday. Your short stay prevented my doing what I had proposed or rather what I had mentioned to you. Please write a letter to Mrs. Robert Anderson[28] of St. Louis, also Mrs. Judge May. I most *earnestly* entreat you, my very kind friend to come out on *Friday morning*, fail not, I beg of you.

It does not appear that God is good, to have placed me here. I endeavor to read my Bible and offer up my petitions three times a day. But my afflicted heart fails me and my voice often falters in prayer. I have worshipped my son and no unpleasant word ever passed between us, yet I cannot understand why I should have been brought out here.

I must see some of my friends and your noble, kind hearted husband will see to this, I am sure, immediately. May I trouble you to write a letter to *Mrs.* Henry T. Blow[29] with a request that it will be forwarded to her in the event of her absence from St. Louis.

Mrs. Bradwell, my dearest friend, I love you very much. Go to my friends, go and see Mrs. Harriet Farlin[30] and her son Mr. Farlin, a partner of a Mr. Wing, real estate agents. Go to Mrs. F., she resides at 505 Michigan Avenue. Write a note when you receive this to Gen'l Farnsworth requesting him to come and see me on tomorrow afternoon at four o'clock.

Pray for me that I may be able to leave such a place as this. Let me see Judge Bradwell. I beg you to come *Friday morning*. I should like to see *Dr. Evarts*.[31] I feel that I must have some further conversation with him. Write me, your heartbroken friend, frequently, *daily*. But come to me. Will you kindly bring me out some samples of black alpaca a best quality without luster and without cotton. Also some samples of heavier black woolen goods.

Mary Lincoln

Batavia, Wednesday, Aug. [2?, 1875][32]
My dear Mrs. Bradwell:

Your letter was received on yesterday. You did not state in what manner your Sabbath was passed. I am sure it was in a profitable way. I shall certainly trust to hear from you very soon, and without doubt, you will not forget me. God will not fail to reward you if you do not *fail* to visit the widow of Abraham Lincoln in her solitude. Does not Judge Bradwell's business bring him to the country *this* week and surely you will accompany him. Do not fail in coming to me when you receive this letter. Dear friend, as you love your Heavenly Father, come to me, bring your husband, the best of men. See Mrs. Farlin and Mrs. Davis her daughter. Please write at once to my sister, Mrs. N.W. Edwards to come out here to see me. Explain everything. And if I have used excited words in reference to my son, my God forgive me, and may *you both* forget it. *Come,* come, is the watchword. You will when you receive this. Write to my sister. She is a sweet, intelligent, loving woman. And *Mrs. Blow* is nobleness itself. Write and do not forget my pleading. With kindest love to your husband and children, believe me,

> Most affectionately yours,
> Mary Lincoln

Say nothing to these people or any one else about the alpaca—you will understand.

August 8th, 1875[33]
My dear friend
Judge Bradwell:

Knowing well your great nobleness of heart, I can but be *well* assured, that you will soon see that I am released from this place. Mrs. Bradwell will explain every thing. I am sleeping very finely and as I am perfectly sane, I do not desire to become insane.

I pray you to see that justice is done immediately to me, for my mind is entirely clear and my health is perfectly good.

With a high appreciation of yourself and your wife, son, and daughter, whom I love very much,

> Believe me,
> Very truly,
> Your friend
> Mary Lincoln

Batavia, Ill., Friday Aug. [8?] 1875[34]
My dear friend
Mrs. Bradwell:

My son has just left me after making me a short call. He mentions that he wrote on yesterday, to my sister Mrs. N. W. Edwards of Springfield, requesting information of her, whether she would be willing to receive me as a visitor. I showed him, her letter and he [begin photo page] considered it a little cool & perhaps general. I rather think he *would* prefer *my* remaining *here* in his heart. *Myra* Bradwell—write to my sister Mrs. E. *at once* the moment you read this [end of M.B. handwritten copy] letter and beg & pray her as a Christian woman—to write him (R.T.L. *urgently* requesting a visit from him. [end of photo page] A moment since Dr. P. returned from the drive to the depot and came to my door and announced that the Physician and Matron of the Elgin *Asylum*,[35] requested to be shown my room—and I am now expecting them every moment. I submit this to you both. Hoping and praying that the visit of to-morrow will not be *forgotten*. God in his mercy will not forget you. Also bring an exchange if you please, also that small key. Use your own judgment regarding the trunks. *When* we meet and I trust you will remember my desolation—much I shall tell you. It is necessary to see Judge Bradwell also. I wish I could kneel down for *one* hour; my heart faints within me. Write at once a most urgent letter to my sister, tell her to write urgently to R.T.L. My sister Mrs. C.M. Smith[36] has also written me begging me to come to her. Mrs. E. appears to be his specialty, fail me not.

With much love,
I remain truly yours,
Mary Lincoln

Batavia, Ill., Saturday Aug. [?] 1875[37]
My dear friend
Mrs. Bradwell:

I enclose this note to you—hoping my good, kind sister—Mrs. E.—will write you just when this is received and enclose this. Come to me Mrs. B. bring your husband also bring those 2 trunks I wrote you about. A long Russian leather trunk and the tall blk trunk marked M. L. *fail me not*. Come to me. I long to see you both. Bring me also the key of the middle sized trunk. I must have you near me again. Write me more plainly than you do. Write again to Henry T. Blow & his wife and on the envelope request that the letter may be directed wherever they are.

Tell Judge B.—your husband—that dependence is placed upon him and he must not forget to come to me. Write to Mr & Mrs. C. M. Smith of Springfield.

Tell Mrs. S. she must not go to C. come to [end of copy]

CHICAGO LEGAL NEWS COMPANY
151 & 153 Fifth Ave.
Chicago, Aug. 11th, 1875[38]
Dear Mrs. Edwards:

I came in from Batavia last Saturday afternoon. Stayed with your sister Friday night. Slept with her and saw not one symptom of insanity. She slept as sweetly and as quietly as a kitten. Robert tells me if you will take her, he will bring her down to Springfield. I do hope you will for she must be at liberty. Do please take her and love her and I am sure you will not have any trouble with her for Dr. Patterson told Mr. Bradwell and myself that he never had a patient that made him so little trouble.

I am so sorry for the dear woman, shut up in that place. When they tell me she is not restrained, I want to ask how they should like it themselves?

I hope to hear from you soon,

Kindly, Myra Bradwell

Batavia, Ill., Aug. 12, 1875[39]
To Mrs. Bradwell:

In reply to your note of yesterday, I regret that your "Mrs. Edwards letter" has not reached you.

In writing to R. T. Lincoln a few days ago, I enclosed the letter, properly addressed to you, and stamped asking him to hand it to you, at a visit I knew he proposed to make you, or to drop it in the mail box. I shall "do as I agreed" and see that you have it as soon as possible.

Respectfully,
R. J. Patterson

Springfield, Ill, June 18th, 1876[40]
My dear Mrs. Bradwell:

Your most welcome letter, was received last evening and I am quickly demonstrating the pleasure it afforded me by replying at once.

God is just, *retribution*, must follow those who act wickedly in *this* life, sooner or later compensation surely awaits those, who suffer unjustly, if not here, in a brighter & happier world. The most villainous plot, has come to a close, but on Friday morning, when the young man, who perpetrated it came down to S. [Springfield] when I looked into his face (at a slight distance you may be sure, I saw the reluctance, with which he yielded up what he so ignominiously fought for—my poor pittance, as the world goes—so far as wealth is concerned—"a widow's mite," my bonds. Prayers will scarcely [end of photo] avail in his case I think. My heart fails me, when I think of the contrast between himself and my noble glorious husband, and my precious sons, who have only "gone before" and are anxiously I am sure, awaiting the reunion, where no more separation comes—and so I told him (R. T. L.) he could not approach us in the other world—on account of his heartless conduct, to the wife of a man who worshiped me—as well as my blessed sons did. *This one* as my beloved husband always said was so very different from the rest of us. Prided himself on his philosophical nature—not satisfied with the fortune I bequeathed him *in one* morning,[41] desiring the rest, brought false charges against me. The only trouble about me, in all my sorrows and bereavements has been that my mind has always been too *clear* and remembrances have always been too keen, in the midst of my griefs. As to *Swett*[42] he has proved himself to be, the most unmitigated scoundrel & *hell* will be his portion & *doubtless*, he will have company. Never could such a creature approach my husband, who loved me so devotedly—in the other life—I have my dear friend, a very great favor to ask of yourself[,] your good husband & the gentleman who called with you at B. the City Editor, of the Times.[43] If I were to tell you *three, all* [underlined twice] the utterances of this man R. T. L. you would *not refrain* from writing the *latter* person up, *without* a day's delay. Your pen is sharp, so is Judge Bradwell's, so is the Editor's, just named, of course you would not wish your names to appear, but you will not fail me, I am sure, *now* is the time, have justice rendered me, my dearly loved friend, see the City Editor of the Times, before the close of the day, when you receive *this* letter. I have been a deeply wronged woman, by one, for whom I would have poured out, my life's blood.

R. T. L.'s *imprecations* against you all, have been very great, only on account of your being my true friends. *Do not* allow a day to pass, before this writing *is done* and forwarded in every direction. Let not *his wickedness* triumph. It appears there is no law for the widow—in this land, and I solemnly pledge you my word as an honorable woman, that *not one* [underlined three times] word shall ever escape my lips—not a person in *this* [underlined twice] house or elsewhere about any article or the probable author, that may be published. My sister Mrs. E. sat by me on Friday for about an hour & a half and in a quiet composed & I trust lady like manner I gave expression to my feelings as to sins he had committed against a broken hearted woman who had been called upon to give up, all her dearly beloved ones, for *the time* being only—and I asked him to look upon my bleached hair—which he *had entirely* created caused with the past sorrowful year.

Write, fail me not, I pray you, *any delay* will be grievous, I assure you. So much I have to tell you. Kiss your sweet lovely daughter

for me. Would to heaven, I could see you. Best regards to your husband—*fail me* not.

Always your most affectionate friend,

Mary Lincoln

I enclose this article from yesterday's journal. Phillips,[44] I believe
wrote it—write stronger. I am sure you will. M. L.

[on front of letter]: Burn this scrawl. You will, especially on the last
page, be unable to decipher it, I fear.

Springfield, Ill., June 22nd 1876[45]

Judge Bradwell

My dear friend:

Swett—has written a letter to Mr. Edwards, which has been received this morning, filled with the most voluminous falsehoods.
Amongst other things Swett writes—that the title to the house 375
West Washington St.[46] is in litigation, the title being imperfect. You
remember well the article I showed you, which Robert T. Lincoln
drew up—in regard to this house which I gave him, subject to the
rent to be paid for seven years, from the time I deeded it to him. It
is evident that after these long years—it is rather late for a flaw to
be in the lease.

May I employ your services to examine this lease. It is evidently
gotten up to prevent the monthly payment of the rent. *Ascertain
correctly* and write me all the facts in the case. The lease was examined and considered perfect at the time of the purchase. It was purchased from a man by the name of *Cook*, who resides near Batavia,
Ill. I presume the people who reside in the same block feel very easy
as to their titles—Cook—building all the houses. There is beyond
question, the most unmitigated villainy in the case. *Do not* delay
an hour, my dear Judge Bradwell, in regard to this involving such a
loss. It appears that I must see yourself and Mrs. Bradwell. Pardon
blots and everything—fail me not—*at once* write.

Your friend

Mary Lincoln

Springfield, Ill., July 7, 1876[47]

My dear Mrs. Bradwell:

I have received no letter from you, am I forgotten? If you ascertain
any facts in relation to 375 West Washington St. please inform me.

A weak "invention of the enemy" united with villainous falsehood. That Swett, should become so debased as to try and drag

down to his own debased standard the son of the noblest, most honest man, who ever lived. None of my treasures in the way of rich & rare presentations, that were made me, have been returned to me. As I truly told R. T. L. villains, could not venture to approach my dearly beloved husband in the other world. *His* reply I gave you.

My husband always told me, that he only liked those whom I did and when I remember the contrast between R. T. L. and my other blessed sons, the latter so lovely, gentle and noble and my darling husband, who worshipped me so greatly, that often he said, that I was his weakness.

We conversed very unreservedly together when you were in S. Anything you said to me will be held sacred—some little communications I made you *please* breathe to no living soul. We discussed Prof. S.[48] who between ourselves I think amounts to very little. The subject of Mrs. E. etc please erase from your memory, as an honorable woman I entreat you to cast *all thoughts* of either of these persons from your mind or *mention* [underlined twice].

What are your plans, believe me, I am deeply interested in them, for the next *six weeks or two* months. Write me dear friend, when you receive this scrawl I am so anxious to hear from you.

My pen is refusing its office, so I must bid you adieu, until I hear from you. Please present my love to all your family whilst I remain
Your very affectionate friend
Mary Lincoln

Springfield, Ill., July 14th, '76[49]
My dear Mrs. Bradwell:
Your expected letter has been received. As to the abstract, I suppose R. T. L. has it. Mr. Cook from whom 375 West Wash. St. was purchased, resides somewhere in the country, near Chicago, doubtless transacts business in the latter place.

Mr. Phillips made me a very pleasant call a few evenings since. Is very vehement against two of the greatest scoundrels of the age R. T. L. and Swett. The last of whom he pronounces a very profligate man and says that my husband had become thoroughly disgusted with S. (Swett and so expressed himself to P.) Certainly as the wife I heard enough against S.

We speak of you so frequently. Would that we could daily meet, converse together. Will not Judge Bradwell return west by way of Springfield? I, so much wish to see him before the sail, "down the

bay." If you still have Mrs. Ellen Johnson[50] (colored) address—
please forward it to me—also, please drop her a note to call to see
you—as she would like to hear—that a *faithful, devoted* son failed
in his attempt to render a deeply bereaved mother *insane. Do* see her
for my sake, my dear friend.

Will write you again soon. My sister is well and cheerful—Too
much kindness of heart is the only trouble of the *other party*—I assure you—easily imposed upon an innocent by those who make a
representation of want of means. Others justly require what is thus
bestowed. Much love to you and yours. Write and do not act *quite
so mean* by your silence.

Affectionately yours,
M. L.

Pau, France, Dec. 1, 1876[51]
My dear Mrs. Bradwell:

You have been so frequently in my thoughts of late that I feel I
must give vent to them in words which will be but a faint expression of the love and gratitude I feel towards you. When we parted
in Springfield last summer I scarcely thought it possible that we
would not again meet, ere my departure across the waters, but
such has been the case, but that will be no reason that we cannot
frequently hear from each other. I think often of you leading the
occupied life you do yet sweetened by the presence of your devoted
husband and two most interesting children filling your home with
so much happiness.

Your daughter[52] I suppose still remains at school destined to become one of the most learned young ladies in our country. Kiss her
sweet face for me and tell her that she must not apply herself too
much to her books. Doubtless she enjoyed her visit east very much.
Did you visit the Centennial?

I believe I told you that I already had some friends residing at
Pau. They received me with the greatest affection and I have made
some new acquaintances whom I like very much but if I could *only*
see you, dear precious friend, this day, not to speak of your dear
noble husband, I will not allow myself to dwell on so pleasant a picture. This place is very beautiful to me surrounded by the Pyranees
whose distant peaks are already covered with snow. I sleep under
four soft blankets, the air growing a little *cool*, yet, during my six
weeks stay, I have never heard the least wind. One of the peculiarities I am told of the climate.

The *drives*, are simply enchanting, two days since I drove out six miles to Gau and returned, and the lovely Chateaus built upon the hills all facing the mountains I cannot attempt to describe clearly. I am situated at one of the finest hotels, most accommodating landlord, very near the chateau of Henry 4th[53] where I frequently wander through the grand rooms, so filled with historical interest, and beyond a park of miles—with seats under the beautiful old trees.

Close your doors some day, my bright appreciative friend, take your husband's arm, bring your talented daughter and son with you and rest. I have received some delightful letters from friends, and some distinguished ones who dwell in this land and most of them are natives, who give me so cordial a welcome to their shores. On my table, lies a card received today from a gentleman and his wife who reside at Pau. An Austrian, Baron de Brenneke,[54] who was in Washington while we were there. They often visit me and are very accomplished people—plain and *so elegant* and consequently so unassuming. I fear that I am wearying you with so long a letter.

Would that I could see you again but I am allowed tranquility here and am not harassed by a *demon*. I wrote Mrs. Ellen Johnson 1425 Butterfield St. recently a letter. *Will you* see her. Do write me without the least delay. I am very anxious to hear from you. Remember me to the Judge. *Always* your affectionate, *deeply* grateful friend.

Mary Lincoln

Write and tell me everything. M. L.

Pau, France. Basses, Pyranees. April 12, 1877[55]
My dear Mrs. Bradwell:

It has been some time since I had the pleasure of receiving your most welcome letter yet, notwithstanding the lapse of *time*, you have been frequently in my thoughts and most fondly remembered. I have been much saddened within the last two months with hearing from my sister Mrs. Edwards of the loss of two sweet little grandchildren, one, the only child of Charles Edwards, a very bright and promising little girl and Albert, the other brother, has lost a little girl—both with scarlet fever. Naturally, it has cast a great gloom over their households.

When you wrote me you had just returned from Springfield and Gen. Logan[56] was in a state of great suspense. I suppose he consoles himself with the hope of the possible *future* presidency. Speaking of these things, my dear friend, why is it with your husband's great legal ability, noble heart, and name, why do you not turn your attention to securing *that* place on the Supreme Bench at Washington for him.[57] You with your great talents and diplomacy, could so well arrange affairs. Judge B. is far too modest for the age in which he lives, and so much care and work would be spared him by the *change*. A wife can do so much for her husband which you have undoubtedly done. It would gratify me so much to have that *vacant* place assigned him. I believe a few quiet words would secure it. You know how greatly I prize you both and what interest I take in you and yours.

When you see Mrs. Ellen Johnson please say to her that I wrote her in Nov. last and not a line have I yet received from her. I suppose your dear daughter (to whom present much love) still continues in college. Only a very great man will be her husband, be assured. I hope soon to hear form you. Please address me by name and write "Poste Restante" on left hand corner. Remember me to the Judge.

I remain your affectionate friend

Mary Lincoln

I write this very hastily. My address is Mrs. Abraham Lincoln, Pau, Basses Pyranees, France.

Sorrento, Italy, April 22nd, 1878[58]

My dear Mrs. Bradwell:

In the quiet of this beautiful place, I have been thinking a good deal of you and have concluded to inflict a letter upon you, so that *I* too, may not be entirely forgotten by yourself & the Judge. A few weeks since, I came round by sea, from Marseilles to Naples, and as it was my second visit to the latter place [end of photo] within the last few years, I remained there only a week, but will return there in a few days.

It is my season of sadness and Naples with its noise, was unendurable. With guide book in my hands, some years since I visited all places that were considered to be of interest, and it is well for me that I did so for I could not interest myself *now* as I did *then*, in visiting each place. My heart was then filled with great sorrow, but since that time the crushing hand of bereavement has been laid so heavily upon me, that it is only by a strong effort of will that I revisit places.

I went to Herculaneum,[59] before I left Naples also to the "Castle of St. Elmo."[60] Stopped at the Hotel de Rupie which commands the finest view of Vesuvius and the Bay of Naples but nothing equals, I think, the charming scenery of Sorrento. Even Mrs. Stowe's imaginative pen has scarcely done it justice.[61] In front of my Hotel in full view lies a grand chain of mountains, Vesuvius, rising above them all. The Bay in full view, and orange and lemon grove within these grounds, trees bowed down with their fruit, of so much larger size and better flavor than we have with us. The villa of Aristides was the sole object of interest to me at Herculaneum.

Close up some day your dear daughter's books, bring her to these lands, so filled with historical associations, have the Judge accompany you for a rest and you will find yourselves, so well repaid, for your journey. My beloved husband and myself for hours would sit down and anticipate the pleasant time, we would have in *quietly* visiting places and in *halting* at such spots as this, when his official labors were ended.[62] God works in such a mysterious way and we are left to bow to His will. But to some of us, *resignation* will never come. But perhaps for the tears shed *here*, compensation will succeed the grief of the *present time.*

Would that I could see you all once more, for you are very dear to my heart. My sister, Mrs. Edwards, writes me quite frequently and today I have written her a long letter. When you receive this letter, dear Mrs. Bradwell, sit down and write me a long one in reply. Please remember me to your family. If you remember you are owing me a letter. What has become of Mrs. Ellen Johnson? She was a faithful friend to me and I hope she is doing well. I wrote her a year since and have received no reply. I miss her good washing. I assure you when you see her remember me to her. Tell her I have a whole trunk of clothes for her, she will understand. Do write my dear friend.

Direct to Pau, France Basses Pyranees.

Poste Restante
Always your affectionate friend
Mary Lincoln

Pau, France, July 4, 1878[63]
My dear Mrs. Bradwell:

Your letter of July 2nd is just this *moment* received. I am greatly surprised that you have not received the letter I wrote you, at least *ten* days since from Vichy,[64] in reply to your *most* welcome one, dated Chicago, making the pleasant announcement that you were to sail for Europe, on the 12th of June. I addressed the letter to the care of Mrs. Walker,[65] Beverly, England. You did not give me the name of your hotel. Please enquire at the post office at Beverly for it.

I am so anxious to see you and would go anywhere to meet you, but have been laid up in bed for the last two days with boils under my left arm.[66] Address me *poste Restrante* Pau, France. I find on my return the usual beautiful hotel closed for the summer season where I have stopped but am in plain comfortable quarters at Hotel de l'Europe. I cannot contain myself this solitary 4th of July, knowing that you are *so near* and yet *so far*. It cannot be that you are not to receive the letters I write you, my *very, very* dear friend. The Vichy waters did me no good. However, I was not very much in need of them.

Write me at once. I cannot do anything today. My thoughts are so much with you. Very affectionately your friend

Mary Lincoln

Pau, France, July 6th, 1878[67]
My dear Mrs. Bradwell:

By this time you must be receiving my frequent letters. In looking over your last letter, I perceive that the date is June 27th. I wrote you on the 4th of July. Where are you now? An Englishman told me on yesterday that Beverly was in Yorkshire, consequently not so near London as I had supposed.

Vichy waters, have brought out several disagreeable boils under my left arm and the pain extends over my whole body. With the *very very* warm weather we are having, I am not spending a very pleasant time.

Do write me at once my dear friend. I am so anxious to hear from you, you are well aware how near you are to my heart, You have no friend, I believe, who loves you *half* so well as myself. I write with difficulty owing to the pain.

Affectionately yours
Mary Lincoln

Pau, France, July 19, 1878[68]
My dear Mrs. Bradwell:

This morning's mail brought me an envelope enclosing two letters for yourself from Beverly. Of course, I will retain them until you arrive. I cannot express to you, with what pleasure I look forward to *your* coming. I hope when you receive this letter, your health will have improved. I fear with your indisposition you have seen very little of London. However, *in the future*, you have time enough for it all.

It is a pity you did not bring your very sweet and interesting daughter over with you. I am longing greatly to see you, my very dear friend and I am sure you will feel anxious for your two letters—when you write to your dear noble husband, please present my kindest regards. I feel very tenderly attached to yourself and family—*the intolerable heat* prevents my inflicting a long letter upon you. When you come, we will direct our way very soon to the beautiful Pyranees. Four hours by sail brings us to the heart of them. I trust a breeze is refreshing you this morning, which *Pau* does not dream of. Do write me at once. Ever yours, most affectionately

Mary Lincoln

Mary Todd Lincoln's last will and testament, July 23, 1873, signed by Mary Lincoln and witnessed by James and Myra Bradwell.[69]

In the name of God Amen I Mary Lincoln of the City of Chicago County of Cook and State of Illinois widow of the good and lamented Abraham Lincoln the martyred president of the United States realizing the uncertainty of life and the certainty of death being of sound mind and memory and having fifty-six thousand dollars in United States Registered Bonds a house and lot in the City of Chicago in the State of Illinois known as known as number three hundred and seventy-five (375) West Washington Street: valuable clothing jewelry and various other articles of property which I wish to dispose of at and after my decease do make and publish this my last will and testament in manner following that is to say: I give devise and bequeath unto my beloved son Robert T. Lincoln my house and lot known and described as follows to wit: number three hundred and seventy-five (375) West Washington Street in the City of Chicago in the County of Cook and State of Illinois but in case my said son Robert T. Lincoln shall die without having sold and conveyed said house and lot then and in that event said house and lot shall be equally divided between the children of my said son Robert T. Lincoln[70] as they each arrive at the age of twenty one years, [end first photo page]
. . . of the United States

In witness whereof I Mary Lincoln the testatrix have this twenty third day of July A.D. 1873 affix my seal and subscribe my name to this my will consisting of nine pages.

Mary Lincoln

We do hereby certify that the alive named testatrix Mary Lincoln signed sealed and declared the above instrument to be her last will and testament in our presence and we at her request and in her presence subscribe our names then as witnesses on this twenty third day of July A.D. 1873.

James B. Bradwell

Myra Bradwell

Tos B. Bradwell[71]

APPENDIX 2

Legal Documents Pertaining to the Sale and Destruction of the Mary Lincoln Insanity Letters

1) Contract of sale between Myra Pritchard and Mary Harlan Lincoln, January 31, 1928. Originals located in both the Towers Lincoln Papers and the Pritchard Family Papers.

KNOW ALL MEN BY THESE PRESENTS That—
WHEREAS Myra Helmer Pritchard, party of the first part, is the owner of and has in her possession certain original letters written by the late Mrs. Abraham Lincoln, which said letters have been copied, elaborated upon and incorporated into a narrative, hereinafter referred to as "manuscript," which letters and manuscript it is the desire of the party of the first part to sell and dispose of; and
WHEREAS Norman B. Frost and Frederic N. Towers, co-partners, hereinafter referred to as "Frost & Towers," parties of the second part, are desirous of purchasing said original letters, manuscript and all photostatic or other copies thereof, together with the exclusive right to publish them, it or any thereof;
NOW, THEREFORE, this agreement witnesseth that in consideration of the premises and the sum of Twenty-two Thousand Five Hundred Dollars ($22,500.00), Eleven Thousand Two Hundred Fifty Dollars ($11,250.00) of which is hereby acknowledged and Eleven Thousand Two Hundred Fifty Dollars ($11,250.00) of which shall be paid by said parties of the second part to said party of the first part on or before July 15, 1928, said party of the first part has granted, bargained, sold and assigned, and by these presents does grant, bargain, sell and assign unto said parties of the second part, their heirs, executors and assigns, said original letters and manuscript, together with all photostatic and other copies thereof, to all of which said party of the first part warrants her title to be good, sufficient and free of encumbrance, and all of which are her sole and separate property and estate.
Said party of the first part hereby warrants that there are no copies of said letters or of said manuscript in the possession of any indi-

179

vidual, individuals or corporation, of which she has knowledge, and that there are no additional copies thereof, photostatic or otherwise in her possession.

Said party of the first part further warrants that there are no further or original letters of the said Mrs. Abraham Lincoln, or copies thereof, in her possession; and that she will not publish, permit or cause to be published, any thereof that may hereafter come into her possession, it being mutually agreed and understood between the parties hereto that any such letters or copies thereof hereafter coming into her possession will be delivered by her to the parties of the second part to be added to and become a part of those sold hereunder and hereby for and in consideration of the premises and the purchase price now paid to her by said parties of the second part.

Said party of the first part further warrants, covenants and agrees that if said manuscript, letters or copies thereof be published or offered for sale, in whole or in part, by any person, persons or corporation into whose possession it, they, or any thereof, at any time came through her act, and, it appearing that said parties of the second part or their principal, grantee or agent have not authorized such publication or given said manuscript, letter or any thereof into the possession of such person, persons or corporation, then, and in that event, the purpose of this sale giving the exclusive and absolute right in and to said manuscript and letters to the parties of the second part having been defeated, the purchase price thereof, or so much of it as shall have then been paid to said party of the first part, shall be returned by her forthwith to said parties of the second part.

And the said party of the first part further covenants and agrees that a breach of any warranty or warranties herein contained shall become and have the effect of breach and nullification of this entire agreement, and shall immediately result in an obligation upon her part to return to the parties of the second part the money consideration paid to her by them for said letters and manuscript.

IN WITNESS WHEREOF said parties of the first and second parts have hereunto set their hands and affixed their seals this 31st day of January, 1928.

Myra Helmer Pritchard
Norman Frost
Frederic N. Towers

On this 31st day of January, 1928, before me personally appeared Myra Helmer Pritchard, to me known to be the person described in and who executed the foregoing instrument, and acknowledged that she executed the same as her free act and deed.

Bertha P. Isaacs
Notary Public

On this 31st day of January, 1928, before me personally appeared Norman B. Frost and Frederic N. Towers, to me known to be the persons described in and who executed the foregoing instrument, and acknowledged that they executed the same as their free act and deed.

Bertha P. Isaacs
Notary Public

2) Receipt for services of Bert C. Farrar, examiner of questioned documents, U.S. Treasury Department, for examining authenticity of Mary Lincoln letters owned by Myra Pritchard, February 1, 1928. Original and duplicate located in the Towers Lincoln Papers.

Bert C. Farrar
Examiner of Questioned Documents
Room 112, Treasury Building
City of Washington
February 1, 1928

Mr. Frederic N. Towers,
Counselor at Law,
Hibbs Building,
Washington D.C.
My Dear Sir:

I beg to acknowledge the receipt of your check for One Hundred Dollars ($100.00), as payment in full for my services in the examination of certain letters written over the signature of Mrs. Mary Lincoln.

Very truly yours,
Bert C. Farrar

3) Affidavit re Destruction of Liberty Magazine Manuscript relative to Mary Lincoln Letters, September 18, 1947. Original located in Pritchard Family Papers.

State of Michigan
as
County of Calhoun
Margreta Pritchard, being duly sworn, did depose and say:

1. That she is the duly appointed, qualified and acting executrix of the estate of Myra Helmer Pritchard, deceased.

2. That as said executrix she had access to the safety deposit vault owned by Myra Helmer Pritchard during her lifetime and that after said box had been first examined by the Treasurer of Calhoun County she took from the same a parcel which bore on the exterior thereof in Myra Helmer Pritchard's handwriting the following instructions: "In case of my death this is to be destroyed immediately."

3. That after the death of Myra Helmer Pritchard, deponent did on the 14th or 21st day of July, 1947, after announcing to members of my family my intention, personally burn the contents and entirely consumed the same in flames.

4. I read the entire contents of this parcel and to the best of my recollection it contained the following: A typewritten manuscript of some twelve or fifteen chapters apparently compiled by Myra Helmer Pritchard setting up in narrative form the contents of numerous Mary Lincoln letters, constituting of an exchange of correspondence between her and the Bradwell family. This manuscript I believe was prepared for use by the Liberty Magazine.

Further deponent says not.

Margreta Pritchard
Subscribed and sworn to before me this 18th day of September, 1947
Marilyn Jones
Notary Public, Calhoun County, Michigan
My commission expires June 26, 1949

4) Affidavit Re: Destruction of Copies of Mary Lincoln Collection, March 15, 1951. Original located in Pritchard Family Papers. Note: The letter listed below as "Sat. Aug. 1875" was identified as "Robert T. Lincoln to Mrs. Bradwell," which appears to be in error; corrected, it should say, "Mary Lincoln to Mrs. Bradwell." Robert Lincoln never omitted dates from his correspondence, whereas Mary Lincoln often did. There was, in fact, a letter from Mary Lincoln to Myra Bradwell dated "Sat. Aug. 1875" in the Towers trunk, and most likely it is the same letter. Therefore, Robert's name has been replaced by Mary's below.

State of Michigan
as
County of Calhoun
Margreta Pritchard, being duly sworn, did depose and say that

on the 7th day of March, 1951, in the presence of W. R. Gordon, she personally destroyed by burning, every portion thereof, all the copies known to her of the following described letters, to-wit:

July 7, 1876	Mary Lincoln to Mrs. Bradwell	1 page
Aug. 13, 1875	Robert T. Lincoln to Mrs. Bradwell	1 page
Aug. 14, 1875	Robert T. Lincoln to Mrs. Bradwell	1 page
Aug. [?], 1875	Mary Lincoln to Mrs. Bradwell	1 page
Aug. 12, 1875	Dr. Patterson to Mrs. Bradwell	1 page
Aug. 3, 1875	C. C. Brown to Judge Bradwell	1 page
Aug. 18, 1875	R. J. Patterson to Judge Bradwell	1 page
Aug. 3, [?]	Mrs. Edwards to Mrs. Bradwell	1 page
Aug. 15, 1875	Robert T. Lincoln to Mrs. Lincoln	1 page
Sat. Aug. 1875	Mary Lincoln to Mrs. Bradwell	1 page
June 22, 1876	Mary Lincoln to Judge Bradwell	1 page
June 18, 1876	Mary Lincoln to Mrs. Bradwell	2 pages
Aug. 2, 1867	Mary Lincoln to Mrs. Bradwell	2 pages
Monday, Jan. 25, [?]	Mary Lincoln to Mrs. Bradwell	1 page
November 1st, [?]	Mary Lincoln to Mrs. Bradwell	1 page
October 10th, 1872	Mary Lincoln to Judge Bradwell	1 page
July 23rd, 1873	Mrs. Abraham Lincoln to County Judge of Cook County	2 pages
Jan. 18th, 1874	Mary Lincoln to Judge Bradwell	1 page

That this destruction was complete and final according to the agreement relative to destruction entered into with Robert Todd Lincoln to the best of the knowledge, information and belief of deponent.

Further deponent says not.

Margreta Pritchard

Subscribed and sworn to before me this 19th day of March, 1951

Marient Vanderwoort
Notary Public, Calhoun County, Michigan
My commission expires Aug. 29, 1952

State of Michigan

as

County of Calhoun

W. R. Gordon, being duly sworn, did depose and say that she witnessed the burning set out in the foregoing affidavit.

Further deponent says not.

Wilhelmena R. Gordon

Subscribed and sworn to before me this 20th day of March, 1951

Marient Vanderwoort
Notary Public, Calhoun County, Michigan
My commission expires Aug. 29, 1952

APPENDIX 3
The Psychiatric Illness of Mary Lincoln
James S. Brust, M.D.

To establish a psychiatric diagnosis of a historical figure long dead is a difficult task for anyone, psychiatrist or historian. Jason Emerson does a fine job in this book, *The Madness of Mary Lincoln*, and perhaps gets closer than any previous historian to revealing the true extent of Mary Lincoln's mental illness, and it was a pleasure to both learn from and advise him on his work. As a professional psychiatrist, I would like to elaborate on Emerson's conclusions from a medical perspective.[1]

The first question for the psychiatrist is, should we even attempt to diagnose someone out of the past? In those instances where an individual's psychiatric condition was a key factor in historical events, some understanding of his or her mental state would be important. We can cautiously try to gain such knowledge from contemporary accounts by the patient, as well as eyewitnesses. Fortunately, in the case of Mary Lincoln, the historical record may be richer than it is for most nineteenth-century American figures, especially with the addition of the newly discovered primary source material presented in this book. We must be aware of the limitations of such a backward-look diagnosis, but we do have some information on which to base it.

What, then, can we say of Mary Lincoln's psychiatric condition? One must proceed with caution: The mysteries of mind and brain are enormously complex, and scientific understanding is still in its relatively early stages. Diagnostic terminology and classification are continually changing, and the inherent limitations of relying solely on the historical record rather than live interviews greatly increase the difficulty.

In recognition of the complexity of attempting to understand how people think, act, and feel, the American Psychiatric Association changed to a multiaxial diagnostic system in 1980.[2] A full psychiatric diagnostic formulation now consists not only of the primary diagnosis (or diagnoses) on what is called Axis I, but also personality factors on Axis II, medical illness on Axis III, psychosocial and environmental problems or stressors on Axis IV, with Axis V being an assessment of the individual's overall level of functioning.

When applied to Mary Lincoln, this widened diagnostic system further illuminates her case. Psychosocial and environmental stressors (Axis IV) were marked, of course, with the early death of three of her four sons and her husband's brutal murder as she sat beside him. Medical illnesses (Axis III) seem to have been prominent as well, with issues such as migraine headaches, various pain syndromes, infections, likely diabetes with various complications, perhaps tabes dorsalis, and even the possibility of syphilis.

Personality factors are considered on Axis II. These are lifelong, enduring patterns of behavior and ways of perceiving, thinking about, and relating to others and oneself. If they deviate markedly from cultural norms and lead to long-standing distress and impairment, they can be classed as Personality Disorders. Personality traits that might be maladaptive can be considered as part of the diagnostic formulation even if they are not pervasive enough to constitute a full-blown Personality Disorder. A number of such traits, described throughout this book, might be attributed to Mrs. Lincoln, including paranoid traits (distrustful and suspicious of others, seeing malevolence in their motives), histrionic traits (attention seeking, using self-dramatization and exaggerated expression of emotions), narcissistic traits (a grandiose sense of self-importance and need for admiration), and borderline traits (exaggerated fears of abandonment, inappropriate and intense anger, and unstable relationships that alternate between idealization and devaluation).[3]

Before looking at the question of what, if any, psychiatric diagnosis Mary Lincoln might have had on Axis I, a word is in order on general trends in American psychiatry over the past fifty years. In the nineteenth century and before, those who cared for the mentally ill were essentially asylum keepers, struggling to deal with the bewildering and poorly understood array of serious disorders that beset their patients. As answers were sought and new theories tested, American psychiatry over the first half of the twentieth century took a turn toward the psychological and away from the biological—influenced first by Sigmund Freud's psychoanalytic theory, and then by Adolf Meyer, whose influential psychobiological model saw psychiatric illness as a "reaction" to life events.[4] But over the past fifty years, psychiatry in this country has turned to a much more biological and biochemical viewpoint—one that sees the more serious psychiatric illnesses as rooted more in brain chemistry than in life events. The impetus for change was probably the development of medications since the mid-1950s that have proved effective in treating specific psychiatric disorders. If a chemical could enter the brain and alter psychiatric symptoms, then it would seem those symptoms must have significant biochemical correlates. This moved psychiatric illnesses closer to general medical conditions—products of abnormal or altered physiological processes, not moral or personal failings.

Previous students of Mrs. Lincoln's case, including most of the physicians who have weighed in, seem to have been more comfortable concentrating on factors of loss and grief, or on her physical ailments, skirting issues of "mental illness." This isn't surprising. Even today—though undeserved—psychiatric disorders are seen in a pejorative light. So the key question for this study is whether or not Mary Todd Lincoln had a biologically based psychiatric disorder—one that might have come and gone on its own internal schedule rather than in response to life events and that would have been outside of her conscious control. What evidence do we have for such an illness?

There can be no question that Mary Lincoln suffered from episodes of depression; she acknowledged that herself. The severe grief reactions following President Lincoln's assassination and the deaths of sons Eddie (1850) and Willie (1862) are well documented in this book. While depression is expected following a loss, the severity and duration of Mrs. Lincoln's symptoms exceeded the usual grief reaction. Depression occurred at other times as well. Her sister Elizabeth Edwards said of Mary, "it is impossible to prevent frequent reactions, to extreme sadness." Dr. Willis Danforth, her physician in 1873, described "melancholia" as one of her symptoms. Upon her return from Europe in October 1880, her physician, Dr. Louis Sayre, who usually emphasized her physical symptoms, said Mrs. Lincoln was suffering from "great mental depression." Her tendency to stay in darkened rooms during the last two years of her life was far more likely a sign of depression than the product of any medical abnormality of her eyes.[5]

Mary Lincoln's psychiatric symptoms were not limited to depression. Another interesting aspect, well documented throughout this book, was her extravagant spending of money, often on unnecessary items. This is a symptom not usually associated with depression but rather with what we now refer to as *mania*, or a *manic state*. Mania is often seen as the opposite of depression, with elevated or euphoric mood rather than sadness, and associated behaviors that tend to be more active, outgoing, and talkative, as opposed to the quiet isolation of depression. If Mary Lincoln experienced manic episodes, our diagnostic speculation turns in an important new direction, toward what for years was known as Manic-Depressive Illness but is now called Bipolar Disorder. Official diagnostic criteria for a manic episode require "A distinct period of elevated, expansive or irritable mood lasting at least one week."[6] Given the existing historical record, we might be hard-pressed to show the required intervals of elevated or expansive mood in Mary Lincoln. But not all people in manic states are happy, and it would not be a stretch to imagine her, at various times, in a persistently irritable mood for a week or more.

Abnormal mood alone is not enough to establish the diagnosis of a manic state; other symptoms are required. These can include "inflated self esteem or grandiosity" and "engaging in unrestricted buying sprees"— based on this book, a case can certainly be made for the presence of these signs in Mrs. Lincoln. Other symptoms of a manic episode, such as decreased need for sleep, being more talkative than usual, and racing thoughts and distractibility, *may* have been present, though not specifically described by witnesses.[7] We can no longer ask those who knew her, of course, nor observe Mrs. Lincoln ourselves—these are among the difficulties in attempting to diagnose someone long dead. We will not be able to diagnose Mrs. Lincoln by strict current criteria. But we may have enough for informed speculation.

Other evidence points toward Bipolar Disorder. One characteristic is that this illness tends not to be chronic, at least until its very later stages. The episodes, be they manic or depressed, will come on periodically, perhaps with a regular cycle, but then remit, leaving the affected individual relatively normal again until the next spell. We know that Mary Lincoln seemed fine at times. Even her son Robert noted that her episodes tended to "blow over."[8] Mary Lincoln herself saw her depressions as cyclical, coming in April, which she called "my season of sadness."[9] April, of course, was the anniversary of President Lincoln's assassination and near the February deaths of sons Willie and Eddie. Though there is ample evidence of depression in other seasons as well, the possibility of a cycle is important.

So we have evidence of depression, of mania, of a relapsing-remitting course, and even of a regular cycle. These are consistent with Bipolar Disorder. There is often a family history of the disorder as well, though it can be especially difficult to find when looking back more than one hundred years. But Mary Lincoln's full sister, Elizabeth Edwards, revealed that her daughter, who would have been Mary's niece, first showed signs of "insanity" at age thirteen, and "at the birth of each child, the same symptoms were shown, and severely felt."[10] We lack details of the niece's symptoms, but if described as "insanity," they must have been severe. The picture described sounds consistent with full-blown post partum psychosis, rather than milder postpartum depression, and women with such episodes in their childbearing years often turn out to be Bipolar.[11]

There is further evidence of serious psychiatric illness in Mary Lincoln's family. As scholar Michael Burlingame shows in his upcoming biography of Abraham Lincoln, one of Mary's brothers, Dr. George Todd, suffered from depression, while another brother, Levi Owen Todd, died in an insane asylum. Also institutionalized were niece Mattie Todd and a grandniece (the daughter of Mary's nephew Albert Edwards). Another grandniece, Nellie Canfield, committed suicide. Together, these cases point toward an inheritable, biological component to Mary Lincoln's mental illness.

Bipolar Disorder has a high suicide rate. We know Mary Lincoln made a serious suicide attempt the day after her commitment hearing.

There is one final piece of Mary Lincoln's overall psychiatric picture that is perhaps the most important of all. She was, at times, clearly psychotic. Psychosis can be roughly defined as a grossly impaired ability to test reality. The most common manifestations are delusions and hallucinations. Delusions are fixed beliefs in things that others know to be highly unlikely or even impossible and that are impervious to any attempts at logical, alternative explanation. Hallucinations are sensations falsely perceived to be arising outside the affected individual, when in fact they exist solely within that person's brain. A common example is hearing voices when no one is talking.

One need look no further than this book's descriptions of Mary Lincoln's mental state on her arrival in Chicago in March 1875 to see graphic examples of severe psychosis. She delusionally believed that a man had poisoned her coffee on the train, that the city of Chicago was burning, that a "wandering Jew" had stolen her purse, and that people in the hotel would harm or kill her. She had auditory hallucinations, listening to the voice of the "wandering Jew" and others talking to her through the wall and fearing "strange sounds" in her room.

These symptoms, and Mary Lincoln's frightened response to them, were the main reasons that hospitalization was necessary, but what caused them? Manic-Depressive Illness/Bipolar Disorder is predominantly a condition of abnormal mood, not abnormal thinking. Marked delusions and hallucinations are more commonly associated with Schizophrenia, or other severe psychiatric illness.[12] But while psychotic symptoms are not required in order to establish a diagnosis of Bipolar Disorder, they are, in fact, common in that illness. Manic patients are often paranoid (as Mary Lincoln was) and can show a full range of psychotic symptoms. Even patients in the depressed state can have delusions, usually negative toward themselves—for example, that they have done something wrong, have a deadly illness, or, in Mrs. Lincoln's case, that they are impoverished.

It cannot be "proved" that Mary Todd Lincoln had Bipolar Disorder, but the evidence presented in this book makes it seem very possible. And if she did, it has important implications for understanding not only her commitment and hospitalization in 1875 but also many other aspects of her life. The illness we now call Bipolar Disorder has been described for some 2,500 years. Though given different names through the ages, there is evidence of a clinical entity whose essential features have been similar for centuries. It is not something unique to a given individual or period of time.[13] Modern psychiatric thought sees Bipolar Disorder as biologically based. Though episodes may be precipitated or worsened by unhappy or stressful life events, they will not occur at all without the requisite biological and biochemical underpinnings, and the depression or mania can even come on as totally internal events, without significant external factors. So, the illness cannot be "caused" solely by a series of losses, and there was more to Mary Lincoln's psychiatric illness than the tragic deaths she endured. And perhaps most important, the affected person cannot bring the episodes and symptoms on, nor make them go away, just by his or her own conscious will. The most serious manifestations of her illness were not her "fault," but they were severe, and those around her had no choice but to deal with the situation as best they could.

The story of Mary Lincoln's psychiatric illness and treatment is not an antiquated tale from a bygone era. It is actually quite timely. People still get sick in the same way, and though available treatment, especially with medication, is now much more effective, they and their families often continue to misunderstand the biological basis of the problem, fruitlessly search for some key external factor to fix, and resist any treatment labeled "psychiatric." Were she alive today, Mary Lincoln would still require psychiatric hospitalization in the face of the symptoms she suffered in 1875, and her family would confront the same dilemma if she declined it.

One final irony in the debate over the "Insanity Episode" is that Mrs. Lincoln improved while at Bellevue Place, and while not fully well when she left, was certainly more stable and better able to carry on with life than when she first entered. One might have expected that point to be raised in the historical literature, but it is virtually never mentioned. Though by today's standards, available treatment was meager in that era, the psychiatric profession, when finally given a chance, acquitted itself well in Mrs. Lincoln's case, and perhaps more frequent stays at a sanitarium might have eased rather than aggravated Mary Lincoln's suffering.

Notes

ABBREVIATIONS

ALPL   Abraham Lincoln Presidential Library, Springfield, Illinois

DDFP   David Davis Family Papers (Manuscripts Division, ALPL)

FTC   Frederic N. Towers Collection of Lincoln Papers (Manuscripts Division, LC)

H-WC   Herndon-Weik Collection of Lincolniana (Manuscripts Division, LC)

IF   Insanity File, Lincoln Museum, Fort Wayne, Indiana

JMHC   John Milton Hay Collection, John Hay Library, Brown University, Providence, Rhode Island

LB   Letterpress Books, Robert Todd Lincoln Papers (Lincoln Collection, ALPL)

LC   Library of Congress

PFP   Pritchard Family Papers, privately owned by James Gordon

WEBS   William E. Barton Scrapbook, Barton Collection, Department of Special Collections, University of Chicago Library

INTRODUCTION

1.   Mark E. Neely and R. Gerald McMurtry, *The Insanity File: The Case of Mary Todd Lincoln* (Carbondale: Southern Illinois University Press, 1986), 132–33.

2.   Ibid.; James T. Hickey, *The Collected Writings of James T. Hickey from Publications of the Illinois State Historical Society, 1953–1984* (Springfield: Illinois State Historical Society, 1990), 173.

3.   W. A. Evans, *Mrs. Abraham Lincoln: A Study of Her Personality and Her Influence on Abraham Lincoln* (New York: Alfred A. Knopf, 1932), 27.

4.   Ruth Painter Randall, *Mary Lincoln: Biography of a Marriage* (Boston: Little, Brown, 1953), 434.

5.   Justin G. Turner and Linda Levitt Turner, *Mary Todd Lincoln: Her Life and Letters* (New York: Alfred A. Knopf, 1972), 612.

6.   James Bradwell, interview by Ida Tarbell, n.d., Ida M. Tarbell–Lincoln Collection, Pelletier Library, Allegheny College, Meadville, Pa.

7.   Turner and Turner, *Mary Todd Lincoln*, 595.

1. MUCH LIKE AN APRIL DAY

1.   Mary Lincoln, interview by William Herndon, Sept. 1866, 2:227–28, LN 2408, Ward Hill Lamon Papers, Huntington Library, San Marino, Calif.; Mary Lincoln, interview by William Herndon, 1866, in "Lincoln's Religion: Answer of William H. Herndon, Esq., to Mrs. Lincoln," Springfield, Ill., Jan. 12, 1874, typescript in frame

1728, microfilm reel 9, group 4, H-WC; Mary Lincoln to Mary Jane Welles, Oct. 14, 1865, and Mary Lincoln to James Smith, Dec. 17, 1866, in Turner and Turner, *Mary Todd Lincoln*, 276–78, 399–400; Mary Lincoln to Myra Bradwell, Sorrento, Italy, Apr. 22, 1878, FTC; "Mrs. Lincoln's Presentiment," *New York Times*, May 1, 1865, 5.

2.   Mary said they had decided to move to Chicago, but others have said Lincoln was determined to return to Springfield. Mary Lincoln, interview by William Herndon, Sept. 1866, Ward Hill Lamon Papers; Mary Lincoln, interview by William Herndon, 1866, in "Lincoln's Religion: Answer of William H. Herndon, Esq., to Mrs. Lincoln," Springfield, Ill., Jan. 12, 1874, H-WC; Mary Lincoln to Mary Jane Welles, Oct. 14, 1865, and Mary Lincoln to James Smith, Dec. 17, 1866, in Turner and Turner, *Mary Todd Lincoln*, 276–78, 399–400; Mary Lincoln to Myra Bradwell, Sorrento, Italy, Apr. 22, 1878, FTC; "Mrs. Lincoln's Presentiment," *New York Times*, May 1, 1865, 5; John Todd Stuart, interview by John G. Nicolay, June 24, 1875, in Michael Burlingame, ed., *An Oral History of Abraham Lincoln: John G. Nicolay's Interviews and Essays* (Carbondale: Southern Illinois University Press, 1996), 14; Mrs. John Todd Stuart, in "His Early Social Life and Marriage" (interview), *Chicago Tribune*, Patriotic Supplement no. 4, "Abraham Lincoln," Feb.12, 1900, 14, copy in Memoranda/Clippings folder: Research Material, 1860–1942, box 8, John G. Nicolay Papers, Manuscripts Division, LC; Marquis Adolphe de Chambrun, *Impressions of Lincoln and the Civil War: A Foreigner's Account*, trans. General Aldebert de Chambrun (New York: Random House, 1952), 33–34.

3.   Emphasis in original. Mary Lincoln to Francis Bicknell Carpenter, Nov. 15, 1865, in Turner and Turner, *Mary Todd Lincoln*, 284–85. While the accuracy of anyone quoting another's words is always suspect, in the next sentence Mary unwittingly offers credibility for the historian: "Every word, then uttered, is deeply engraven, on my poor broken heart." Lincoln's playfulness is also mentioned in Mary Lincoln to Mary Jane Welles, July 11, 1865, in ibid., 257.

4.   Harris, daughter of U.S. Senator Ira Harris, and her fiancé, Major Rathbone, accompanied the Lincolns to Ford's Theatre that night after General and Mrs. Grant declined the invitation.

5.   Helen (Bratt) DuBarry to "My dear Mother," Washington, D.C., Apr. 16, 1865, SC 425, Manuscripts Division, ALPL.

6.   Dr. Anson G. Henry to his wife, Apr. 19, 1865, Lincoln Miscellaneous Manuscripts, folder 8, box 4, Department of Special Collections, University of Chicago Library; Mary Lincoln to Edward Lewis Baker Jr., Apr. 11, 1877, in Turner and Turner, *Mary Todd Lincoln*, 633. Horatio Nelson Taft wrote in his diary on April 30, 1865, that Mary Lincoln's hand was on her husband's knee. "She says she saw the flash and heard the report of the pistol, thinking it was in some way connected with the play." John R. Sellers, ed., *Washington during the Civil War: The Diary of Horatio Nelson Taft, 1861–1865*, vol. 3, Manuscripts Division, LC, accessible at http://www.memory.loc.gov/ammem/tafthtml/tafthome.html.

7.   Numerous books and newspaper articles offer the firsthand statements of witnesses attesting to what Mary Lincoln and John Wilkes Booth said that night. For a good compilation, see Timothy S. Good, *We Saw Lincoln Shot: One Hundred Eyewitness Accounts* (Jackson: University Press of Mississippi, 1995).

8.   Leale was the first physician on the scene that night and wrote his reminiscence of the event only "a few hours" after leaving Lincoln's deathbed on the morning of April 15. Dr. Charles A. Leale, official statement regarding assassination of President Abraham Lincoln, to Maj. Gen. Benjamin F. Butler, chair of House Assassination Investigation Committee, New York, July 20, 1867, General Correspondence, box 43, Benjamin F. Butler Papers, Manuscripts Division, LC.

9. Robert declined his parents' invitation to accompany them to the theater that night. Nicholas Murray Butler later claimed Robert never forgave himself for staying at the White House, thinking he could have stopped Booth. Nicholas Murray Butler, *Across the Busy Years: Recollections and Reflections*, 2 vols. (New York: Charles Scribner's Sons, 1940), 2:379. See also Jason Emerson, "A Very Dreadful Night: Robert Todd Lincoln and His Father's Assassination," *Lincoln Forum Bulletin* 18 (Nov. 2005): 10–11.

10. Maunsell B. Field, *Memories of Many Men and Some Women* (New York: Harper & Brothers, 1874), 322; "Postscript, 4 O'Clock A.M.: Complete Details of the Great Calamity," *Chicago Tribune*, Apr. 17, 1865, 1.

11. Clara Harris to "My dear Mary," Washington, Apr. 25, 1865, Misc. Mss., Harris, Clara, New-York Historical Society.

12. Entry for Apr. 15, 1865, *Diary of Gideon Welles: Secretary of the Navy under Lincoln and Johnson*, 3 vols. (Boston: Houghton Mifflin, 1911), 2:288; "Our Late President," *New York Times*, Apr. 21, 1865, 1.

13. Historians have been misspelling Elizabeth Keckly's surname as *Keckley* since 1868. Jennifer Fleischner recently found her actual signatures and revealed the true spelling in her book *Mrs. Lincoln and Mrs. Keckly: The Remarkable Story of the Friendship between a First Lady and a Former Slave* (New York: Broadway Books, 2003), 7. I have chosen to follow Fleischner's findings when referring to Elizabeth Keckly in my text. However, in references to Keckly's published memoir—which began the misspelling of her name in 1868—I will continue to spell her name as it is on the book itself, *Keckley*.

14. Elizabeth Keckley, *Behind the Scenes; or, 30 Years a Slave and 4 Years in the White House* (1868; reprint, New York: Oxford University Press, 1988), 191.

15. Ibid., 195.

16. "Postscript, 4 O'Clock A.M.," *Chicago Tribune*, May 23, 1865, 1.

17. "Clouded Reason: Trial of Mrs. Abraham Lincoln for Insanity," *Chicago Tribune*, May 20, 1875, 1; "Mrs. Lincoln: The Widow of the Martyred President Adjudged Insane in County Court," *Chicago Inter Ocean*, May 20, 1875, 1; Robert Lincoln to Abram Wakeman, Nov. 8, 1908, in LB, 41:430, microfilm reel 71.

18. Emphasis in original. Mary Lincoln to Francis Bicknell Carpenter, Nov. 15, 1865, in Turner and Turner, *Mary Todd Lincoln*, 283. Interestingly, Mary Lincoln was not the only person who showed signs of mental illness after the assassination. Major Rathbone, years later, became criminally insane; he stabbed himself, shot and killed his wife, Clara Harris, and spent the rest of his life in a mental institution in Germany. See Michael W. Kauffman, *American Brutus* (New York: Random House, 2004), 385–86. Kauffman's facts came from his interview with the Rathbone grandchildren and from contemporary German newspapers.

19. Abraham was nine when his mother died of milk sickness; Mary was six when her mother died due to complications from childbirth.

20. Robert S. Todd married Elizabeth Humphreys in 1827, seventeen months after the death of his first wife, Eliza Todd. Eliza gave birth to six children, while Elizabeth Humphreys birthed nine. One clinical analysis of Mary Lincoln's personality attributed many of her later problems to this first trauma of her mother's death, theorizing that Mary was overindulged until her mother's death and then neglected in the chaos of a large second family. Evans, *Mrs. Abraham Lincoln*, 66–72.

21. Records show Mary had visited her sister Elizabeth Edwards's house as early as 1835. In that year, she witnessed a land deed for her brother-in-law, Ninian W. Edwards, who was selling land. Deed Record H, 310–11, Manuscripts Division, Illinois Regional Archives Depository, University of Illinois at Springfield. I am indebted to Wayne C. Temple for sharing this information with me.

22. Mrs. B. S. Edwards, interview in *Chicago Tribune*, Feb. 12, 1900, clipping in Nicolay Papers, LC.

23. William Herndon to Jesse Weik, Jan. 16, 1886, in *The Hidden Lincoln: From the Letters and Papers of William H. Herndon*, ed. Emanuel Hertz (New York: Viking, 1938), 136–37; William H. Herndon and Jesse W. Weik, *Herndon's Life of Lincoln*, ed. Douglas L. Wilson and Rodney O. Davis (Urbana and Chicago: University of Illinois Press, 2006), 134.

24. James C. Conkling to Mercy Ann Levering, Sept. 21, 1840, folder 1, box 1, Conkling Family Papers, Manuscripts Division, ALPL; Ninian Edwards quoted in Katherine Helm, *The True Story of Mary, Wife of Lincoln* (1928; reprint, Manchester, Vt.: Friends of Hildene, Inc., 2005), 81.

25. Elizabeth Edwards, interview by William Herndon, Jan. 10, 1866, 2:220–26, LN 2408, Ward Hill Lamon Papers, Huntington Library; Herndon and Weik, *Herndon's Life of Lincoln*, 135. Mary's sister-in-law also said Mary had a "prophetic vision" that she was destined to marry a man who would be president. Mrs. B. S. Edwards interview in *Chicago Tribune*, Feb. 12, 1900, Nicolay Papers, LC.

26. Elizabeth Edwards, interview by William Herndon, Jan. 10, 1866, Lamon Papers, Huntington Library; Mrs. B. S. Edwards, interview in *Chicago Tribune*, Feb. 12, 1900, Nicolay Papers, LC.

27. For a good examination of this broken engagement, see Douglas L. Wilson, *Honor's Voice: The Transformation of Abraham Lincoln* (New York: Random House, Vintage, 1999), 220–64.

28. C. E. L., "A Kindly Word for Abraham Lincoln's Widow," *Christian Register*, Sept. 7, 1872, 1.

29. Helm, *True Story of Mary*, 195; Jane Grey Swisshelm, "Tribute to the Dead from Mrs. Jane Grey," *Chicago Tribune*, July 20, 1882, 7.

30. Abraham Lincoln to Mary Lincoln, Washington, Apr. 16, 1848, in Roy P. Basler, Dolores Pratt, and Lloyd A. Dunlap, eds., *The Collected Works of Abraham Lincoln*, 9 vols. (New Brunswick, N.J.: Rutgers University Press, 1953–55), 1:465.

31. Mary Lincoln to Abraham Lincoln, Lexington, May —— 1848, in Turner and Turner, *Mary Todd Lincoln*, 38.

32. Such duality is often an indicator of Bipolar Disorder.

33. Helm, *True Story of Mary*, 32.

34. Orville Hickman Browning, interview by John G. Nicolay, Springfield, June 17, 1875, in Burlingame, *Oral History of Abraham Lincoln*, 1.

35. William O. Stoddard, *Inside the White House in War Times*, ed. Michael Burlingame (Lincoln: University of Nebraska Press, 2000), 33.

36. Evans, *Mrs. Abraham Lincoln*, 106.

37. James Gourley, interview by Jesse W. Weik, n.d., in *The Real Lincoln: A Portrait* (Boston: Houghton Mifflin, 1922), 121. Mary's cousin said she had "a very violent temper"; see John Todd Stuart, interview by John G. Nicolay, June 24, 1875, in Burlingame, *Oral History of Abraham Lincoln*, 15. For a detailed portrait of Mary's temper and negative side, especially as pertains to the Lincoln marriage, see Michael Burlingame, *The Inner World of Abraham Lincoln* (Urbana: University of Illinois Press, 1994), 268–355.

38. Herndon and Weik, *Herndon's Life of Lincoln*, 134.

39. John Hay to John G. Nicolay, Apr. 9, 1862, in Tyler Dennett, ed., *Lincoln and the Civil War in the Diaries and Letters of John Hay* (1939; reprint, New York: Da Capo, 1988), 41; William Herndon to Jesse Weik, Jan. 15 and 16, 1886, in Hertz, *Hidden Lincoln*, 134, 136.

40. Mary's collected letters have numerous references to her headaches. Further attestation comes from Abraham Lincoln, who wrote in 1848, "You are entirely free from headache? That is good—good—considering it is the first spring you have been free from it since we were acquainted." Abraham Lincoln to Mary Lincoln, Washington, Apr. 16, 1848, in Basler et al., *Collected Works*, 1:465.

41. Weik, *Real Lincoln*, 121. Gourley's statement to Weik on this subject is different from what he told Herndon in 1866.

42. James Gourley, interview by William Herndon, Feb. 9, 1866, 2:124–30, LN 2408, Ward Hill Lamon Papers, Huntington Library; Hertz, *Hidden Lincoln*, 384.

43. Keckley, *Behind the Scenes*, 235.

44. The Eighth Judicial Circuit covered fourteen counties in central Illinois, comprising eleven thousand square miles. The typical circuit term was three months in the spring and three months in the fall. Lincoln was the only lawyer who rode the entire circuit. Weik, *Real Lincoln*, 188–89.

45. James Gourley, interview by William Herndon, Feb. 9, 1866, Lamon Papers, Huntington Library; Hertz, *Hidden Lincoln*, 384.

46. Ibid.

47. One famous example is when Lincoln answered the door of their Springfield home in his shirtsleeves and told the female visitors that he would "trot the women folks out." Harriet Chapman, interview by Jesse Weik, 1886–87, in Douglas L. Wilson and Rodney O. Davis, eds., *Herndon's Informants: Letters, Interviews, and Statements about Abraham Lincoln*. (Urbana: University of Illinois Press, 1998), 646. See also Harriet Chapman to William Herndon, Charleston, Ill., Dec. 10, 1866, frames 1270–71, microfilm reel 8, group 4, H-WC; Herndon and Weik, *Herndon's Life of Lincoln*, 258; and Hertz, *Hidden Lincoln*, 417.

48. Shenk did not blame Lincoln's sad disposition on Mary but gave her influence credit for its "prosaic and salutary aspects." He did not offer an opinion of Abraham's psychological influence on Mary, only that it deserved its own study. Joshua Wolf Shenk, *Lincoln's Melancholy: How Depression Challenged a President and Fueled His Greatness* (Boston: Houghton Mifflin, 2005), 101.

49. Quoted in Margarita Spalding Gerry, ed., *Through Five Administrations: Reminiscences of Colonel William H. Crook, Bodyguard to President Lincoln* (New York: Harper & Brothers, 1910), 16.

50. Burlingame, *Inner World of Abraham Lincoln*, 280, 295–96. Another paternal moment can be found in Donn Piatt, "Lincoln the Man," in Allen Thorndike Rice, comp. and ed., *Reminiscences of Abraham Lincoln by Distinguished Men of His Time* (New York: Harper & Brothers, 1909), 347.

51. Keckley, *Behind the Scenes*, 236.

52. Emphasis in original. Mary Lincoln to Sally Orne, Dec. 12, 1869, in Turner and Turner, *Mary Todd Lincoln*, 534.

53. Abraham Lincoln to John D. Johnston, Feb. 23, 1850, in Basler et al., *Collected Works*, 2:76–77. The pain of the Lincolns' loss can be seen and felt in the anonymous poem "Little Eddie" that was published two days after the boy's death. Jason Emerson, "'Of Such Is the Kingdom of Heaven': The Mystery of Little Eddie," *Journal of the Illinois State Historical Society* 92, no. 3 (Autumn 1999): 201–21.

54. Mrs. John Todd Stuart, interview in *Chicago Tribune*, Feb. 12, 1900, Nicolay Papers, LC; Octavia Roberts, *Lincoln in Illinois* (Boston: Houghton Mifflin, 1918), 67.

55. Mrs. John Todd Stuart interview, in *Chicago Tribune*, Feb. 12, 1900, Nicolay Papers, LC.

56. William Wallace Lincoln was born Dec. 21, 1850; Thomas Lincoln, nicknamed "Tad" by his father because of his large tadpolelike head, was born Apr. 4, 1853. Family record in Abraham Lincoln's Bible, in Basler et al., *Collected Works*, 1:304.

57. Keckley, *Behind the Scenes*, 178.

58. Sellers, *Diary of Horatio Nelson Taft*, vol. 1, entry for Jan. 2, 1863.

59. Henry Villard, *Memoirs of Henry Villard: Journalist and Financier, 1835–1900*, 2 vols. (Boston: Houghton, Mifflin & Co., 1904), 148, 157; Turner and Turner, *Mary Todd Lincoln*, 97.

60. James A. Brussel, "Mary Todd Lincoln: A Psychiatric Study," *Psychiatric Quarterly* 15, supp. 1 (Jan. 1941): 16.

61. Sellers, *Diary of Horatio Nelson Taft*, vol. 2, entry for Feb. 20, 1862, and vol. 3, entry for Dec. 14, 1864.

62. N. P. Willis, "The President's Son," *Littell's Living Age* 933 (Apr. 19, 1862): 154.

63. Mercy Levering Conkling to Clinton Conkling, Springfield, Feb. 24, 1862, folder 18, box 2, Conkling Family Papers, ALPL.

64. The nurse, Rebecca R. Pomroy, first met the Lincolns when she was posted at the White House in February 1862 after the death of Willie Lincoln. Pomroy was called to help care for Tad, who was life-threateningly sick with the same typhoid from which his brother died, and for Mrs. Lincoln, whose illness at the time was more emotional than physical. Anna L. Boyden, *War Reminiscences; or, Echoes from Hospital and White House* (Boston: D. Lothrop & Co., 1887), 52, 78.

65. Keckley, *Behind the* Scenes, 181–82; Julia Taft Bayne, *Tad Lincoln's Father* (1931; reprint, Lincoln: University of Nebraska Press, 2001), 82.

66. Benjamin B. French diary, Mar. 2, 1862, 8:304, microfilm reel 2, P000359, Benjamin B. French Family Papers, Manuscripts Division, LC.

67. Keckley, *Behind the Scenes*, 104–5.

68. Mary Lincoln to Julia Ann Sprigg, May 29, 1862, and Mary Lincoln to Mrs. Charles Eames, July 26, 1862, in Turner and Turner, *Mary Todd Lincoln*, 127, 130.

69. Mary Lincoln to Julia Ann Sprigg, May 29, 1862, Turner and Turner, *Mary Todd Lincoln*, 127

70. Rebecca Pomroy recorded Mary as saying she was tired of being a slave to the world and "would live on bread and water" to feel happy again. Mary Lincoln to Mrs. Charles Eames, July 26, 1862, Turner and Turner, *Mary Todd Lincoln*, 130; Boyden, *War Reminiscences*, 79.

71. Mary Lincoln to Mary Jane Welles, Feb. 21, 1863, microfilm reel 35, miscellany, Gideon Welles Papers, Manuscripts Division, LC.

72. William Herndon to Jesse Weik, Springfield, Ill., Jan. 2, 1882, frames 1753–54, microfilm reel 9, group 4, H-WC.

73. *Washington Sunday Gazette*, Jan. 16, 1887, clipping in folder: "Barbee File, et al.," box 71, Randall Family Papers, Manuscripts Division, LC.

74. For an interesting examination of Lincoln's aloofness with most people and his private nature, even among friends, see David Herbert Donald, *"We Are Lincoln Men": Abraham Lincoln and His Friends* (New York: Simon & Schuster, 2003); and Hertz, *Hidden Lincoln*, 403.

75. Mary Lincoln to Josiah G. Holland, Chicago, Dec. 4, 1865, in Turner and Turner, *Mary Todd Lincoln*, 293.

76. Emily also noticed that Mary "has always a cheerful word and a smile for Mr. Lincoln, who seems thin and care-worn and seeing her sorrowful would add to his care." Diary of Emily Todd Helm, Oct. 1863, quoted in Helm, *True Story of Mary*, 223, 226.

77. Quoted in Helm, *True Story of Mary*, 250.

78. "Serious Accident to Mrs. Lincoln," *Washington Evening Star*, July 2, 1863, 2; "Accident to Mrs. Lincoln," *Washington Daily National Intelligencer*, July 3, 1863, 3; "News From Washington: Accident to Mrs. Lincoln," *New York Times*, July 3, 1863, 5; Boyden, *War Reminiscences*, 143–44.

79. "Serious Accident to Mrs. Lincoln," *Washington Evening Star*, July 2, 1863, 2; Boyden, *War Reminiscences*, 143–44.

80. Basler et al., *Collected Works*, 6:314.

81. Boyden, *War Reminiscences*, 143–44.

82. Ibid.

83. On July 11, Abraham Lincoln telegraphed Robert to come to Washington. A July 14 telegram irritably asks, "Why do I hear no more of you?" Robert arrived the next day. Basler et al., *Collected Works*, 6:323, 327.

84. While the majority of historians spell her name *Emilie*, Mrs. Helm often signed her name *Emily*, which is the spelling I will use. See, for example, Emily Todd Helm to Albert Edwards, Elizabethtown, Ky., Aug. 15, 1899, "Letters" folder, box 1, Ninian W. Edwards Papers, Manuscripts Division, ALPL. See also "Mrs. Lincoln's Mental Collapse," *Lincoln Lore* no. 1124, Oct. 23, 1950, in which the writer, *Lincoln Lore* editor Louis A. Warren, based his spelling on his personal interview with Mrs. Helm.

85. Helm, *True Story of Mary*, 225–26.

86. Alexander Todd, Mary's youngest brother, died serving with the Confederate army during a skirmish at Baton Rouge, La., in August 1862.

87. Helm, *True Story of Mary*, 227.

88. Mary's belief that Willie and Eddie visited her also can be attributed to her belief in Spiritualism, which is discussed in chapter 3.

89. Mary L. D. Putnam to her sons, St. Clair and Clement Putnam, Dec. 8, 1882, extract sent from Paul Angle to William E. Barton, Jan. 10, 1927, WEBS, vol. 63.

90. Mary Lincoln to Edward Lewis Baker Jr., 22 June 1879, in Turner and Turner, *Mary Todd Lincoln*, 683.

91. Keckley, *Behind the Scenes*, 182.

92. Ibid, 121–22.

93. Helm, *True Story of Mary*, 229–30.

94. Lincoln finally relented to Robert's desire to serve in early 1865, but he did so in a way that satisfied both his wife and his son. He wrote a personal note to Lt. Gen. Ulysses S. Grant asking for a place for Robert on the commander's personal staff, thereby giving Robert a chance to serve without exposure to any real danger. Abraham Lincoln to Lt. Gen. Ulysses S. Grant, Executive Mansion, Washington, Jan. 19, 1865, in *Abraham Lincoln Papers at the Library of Congress* (Washington, D.C.: American Memory Project, [2000–2001]), http://memory.loc.gov/ammem/alhtml/alhome.html; also in Basler et al., *Collected Works*, 8:223.

95. Quoted in Alvan F. Sanborn, ed., *Reminiscences of Richard Lathers: Sixty Years of a Busy Life in South Carolina, Massachusetts and New York* (New York: Grafton, 1907), 184.

96. Keckley, *Behind the Scenes*, 131.

97. Glyndon G. Van Deusen, *William Henry Seward* (New York: Oxford University Press, 1967), 338–39.

98. Adam Badeau, *Grant in Peace from Appomattox to Mount McGregor: A Personal Memoir* (Hartford: S. S. Scranton & Co., 1887), 356–60.

99. Badeau also claimed that Mrs. Grant's resentment at the Mrs. Ord incident was the real reason the Grants did not accompany the Lincolns to Ford's Theatre on April 14. Mrs. Grant denied that as well. John Y. Simon, ed., *Memoirs of Julia Dent Grant* (New York: G. P. Putnam's Sons, 1975), 146–47; Gen. William Tecumseh Sherman, *Memoirs of William Tecumseh Sherman*, 2 vols. (Bloomington: Indiana University Press, 1957), 2:332; Gen. Horace Porter, "Campaigning with Grant," *Century Magazine* 54, no. 4 (Aug. 1897): 600, 602.

100. Helm, *True Story of Mary*, 236.

101. Emphasis in original. Mary Lincoln to Charles Sumner, Apr. 10, 1865, in Turner and Turner, *Mary Todd Lincoln*, 216.

2. A MOST PAINFUL TIME OF ANXIETY

1. Mary Lincoln to Madame Berghmans, May 22, 1865, folder "May 22, 1865, Mary Lincoln to Madame Berghmans," Mary Todd Lincoln Collection, Lincoln Museum, Fort Wayne, Indiana. Many thanks to The Lincoln Museum for allowing me to be the first to quote from this previously unpublished letter.

2. Mary Lincoln to Mrs. Kasson, Chicago, Jan. 20, 1866, Lincoln Collection, ALPL, quoted in Thomas F. Schwartz and Kim M. Bauer, "Unpublished Mary Todd Lincoln," *Journal of the Abraham Lincoln Association* 17, no. 2 (Summer 1996), http://www.historycooperative.org/journals/jala/17.2/schwartz.html.

3. "News From Washington," *New York Times*, May 1, 1865, 1; "From Washington," *New York Times*, May 12, 1865, 1; untitled article, *Washington Star*, May 22, 1865, 2.

4. Benjamin B. French diary, May 24, 1865, 9:413–14, microfilm reel 2, P000666, Benjamin B. French Family Papers, Manuscripts Division, LC. Also, in a letter, French wrote that "the tragical death of her husband has made her crazyer [*sic*] than she used to be." Benjamin B. French to Pamela French, Washington, May 21, 1865, microfilm reel 6, P000084, ibid. See also "Some Curious Statements by Mrs. J. G. Swisshelm," *New York Times*, July 18, 1865, 3.

5. Keckley, *Behind the Scenes*, 208; "The West," *New York Times*, June 4, 1865, 3.

6. Presidential bodyguard William H. Crook traveled with the Lincolns to Chicago and stayed for one week, spending much time with Tad. Gerry, *Through Five Administrations*, 70–71.

7. Keckley, *Behind the Scenes*, 121–22; Helm, *True Story of Mary*, 227–30; Arthur G. Nuhrah, "A Commission for Robert," *Lincoln Herald* 66, no. 3 (Fall 1964): 143–48; Robert Lincoln to Winfield M. Thompson, Mar. 2, 1915, reprinted in "Robert Lincoln Letter, His First Published, Recounts Father's Quip on Law as Profession," *New York Herald Tribune*, Aug. 1, 1926, 1.

8. This last is pure speculation, but knowing that Robert's family, closest friends, and the girl he was courting all lived in the capital, it is a logical assumption.

9. Acceptance of Robert Lincoln's resignation, June 10, 1865, entry 158: Staff Papers, file: "Lincoln, Robert T.," Record Group 94: Records of the Adjutant General's Office, National Archives and Records Administration, Washington, D.C.

10. E. Anthony Rotundo, *American Manhood* (New York: Basic Books, 1993), 12–13.

11. Henry Villard, *Lincoln on the Eve of '61*, ed. Harold G. Villard and Oswald Garrison Villard (New York: Alfred A. Knopf, 1941), 55.

12. Keckley, *Behind the Scenes*, 122–23.

13. To name just a few examples, Robert sat on the boards of Commonwealth Edison, Chicago Telephone, Continental and Commercial Bank of Chicago, American Red Cross, and the Commercial Club; he was a trustee of Illinois Central Railroad in the 1870s and of the Mark Skinner Public Library (Manchester, Vt.) later in his life.

14. Rotundo, *American Manhood*, 13–14.

15. Mary Lincoln to Oliver S. Halstead Jr., Chicago, May 29, 1865, and Mary Lincoln to Harriet Howe Wilson, near Chicago, June 8, 1865, in Turner and Turner, *Mary Todd Lincoln*, 236, 243; "From Chicago . . . Mrs. Lincoln Again," *New York Times*, June 25, 1865, 3; Jim Stronks, "Mary Todd Lincoln's Sad Summer in Hyde Park," *Hyde Park Historical Society Newsletter* 20, no. 1 (Spring 1998), accessible at http://www.hydeparkhistory.org/mtlincoln.html.

16. Quoted in Keckley, *Behind the Scenes*, 212–13.

17. Mary Lincoln to Anson G. Henry, July 26, 1865, in Turner and Turner, *Mary Todd Lincoln*, 263.

18. Elizabeth V. Benyon, assistant law librarian, University of Chicago, to John Goff, Mar. 7, 1960, Goff Papers, Friends of Hildene, Inc., Manchester, Vt.

19. Mary Lincoln to Mary Jane Welles, Oct. 14, 1864, in Turner and Turner, *Mary Todd Lincoln*, 277.

20. Emphasis in original. Mary Lincoln to Mary Jane Welles, Dec. 6, 1865, in ibid., 294.

21. For an interesting study of the effect the memory of Lincoln had on Mary's post-assassination life, see Jennifer L. Bach, "Acts of Remembrance: Mary Todd Lincoln and Her Husband's Memory," *Journal of the Abraham Lincoln Association* 25, no. 2 (Summer 2004): 25–49.

22. Mrs. B. S. Edwards, interview in *Chicago Tribune*, Feb. 12, 1900, Nicolay Papers, LC..

23. Robert Lincoln to Mary Harlan, Oct. 16, 1867, quoted in Helm, *True Story of Mary*, 267–77. After a diligent search by this author through the Hildene archives and by the Lincoln curators at both the Abraham Lincoln Presidential Library and The Lincoln Museum in Fort Wayne, Indiana, the original of this letter could not be found. It is well documented that Robert and Mary Harlan Lincoln gave great encouragement and documentary assistance to their cousin, Katherine Helm, while she wrote her book. They even refused to help other would-be Mary Todd Lincoln biographers, always stating that they were helping Helm and no one else. Therefore, it is logical to assume that either Robert or Mary Harlan Lincoln actually gave this letter to Katherine Helm for her work. It is also likely, unfortunately, that either Robert or Mary destroyed it along with other personal papers.

24. James Gourley, interview by William Herndon, Feb. 9, 1866, Lamon Papers, Huntington Library.

25. Keckley, *Behind the Scenes*, 207.

26. Elizabeth Edwards to Robert Lincoln, Nov. 12, 1875, folder 16, box 2, IF.

27. Francis B. Carpenter, in "Met at a Dance: Romantic Story of President Lincoln's Courtship" (interview), *Boston Globe*, Feb. 17, 1895, 31.

28. "The West . . . Mrs. Lincoln and Family in the City," *New York Times*, June 4, 1865, 3; Keckley, *Behind the Scenes*, 203.

29. Keckley, *Behind the Scenes*, 207

30. Emphasis in original. Benjamin B. French to Pamela French, Washington, Dec. 24, 1861, microfilm reel 5, P000568, French Family Papers, LC. In his diary for Dec. 16, French described the episode slightly differently: The President "said it would stink in the land to have it said that an appropriation of $20,000 for furnishing the house had been overrun by the President when the poor soldiers could not have blankets, & he swore he would never approve the bills for *flub dubs for that damned old house!*" French diary, Dec. 16, 1861, 8:256–57, microfilm reel 2, P000334, ibid.

31. Randall, *Mary Lincoln*, 265–66.

32. Keckley, *Behind the Scenes*, 206–7; Mary Lincoln to Sally Orne, Jan. 13, 1866, Mary Lincoln to Alexander Williamson, Jan. 17 and 26, 1866, and Mary Lincoln to Oliver S. Halstead Jr., Jan. 17, 1866, in Turner and Turner, *Mary Todd Lincoln*, 326–30; "Remonstrance against Free Trade . . . Brutal Charges against Mrs. Lincoln," *Chicago Tribune*, Jan. 16, 1866, 1. Keckly explained that the boxes contained mostly presents given to the entire First Family during their four-year stay. David Davis, the administrator of Abraham Lincoln's estate, reportedly stated there were too many proofs against Mary Lincoln "to admit of doubt" about her guilt, that she was "a natural born thief; that stealing was a sort of insanity with her," and that she had taken numerous items of no value "only in obedience to her irresistible propensity to steal." Diary of Orville Hickman Browning, July 3, 1873, Manuscripts Division, ALPL.

33. Emphasis in original. Sellers, *Diary of Horatio Nelson Taft*, vol. 2, entry for Jan. 2, 1863, and vol. 3, entry for Dec. 14, 1864, LC.

34. Emphasis in original. Mercy Conkling to Clinton Conkling, Mar. 9, 1863, folder 20, box 1, Conkling Family Papers, ALPL.

35. Mary Lincoln to Elizabeth Todd Grimsley, Sept. 29, 1861, in Turner and Turner, *Mary Todd Lincoln*, 104–6.

36. Benjamin B. French diary entries, Jan. 8, 1862, 8:276, and Mar. 3, 1863, 9:58, microfilm reel 2, P000344 and P000468, and Benjamin B. French to Henry Flagg French, Washington, Oct. 13, 1861, and Sunday, Mar. 23, 1862, microfilm reel 5, P000559 and P000587, French Family Papers, LC.

37. *Congressional Globe*, 39th Cong., 1st sess., 1865–66, 1:99, 104, 172; Harry Pratt, *The Personal Finances of Abraham Lincoln* (Springfield, Ill.: Abraham Lincoln Association, 1943), 184; "The Cabinet Reported a Unit in Support of the President . . . Mrs. Lincoln's Appropriation," *Chicago Tribune*, Mar. 2, 1866, 1.

38. Mary Lincoln to David Davis, June 27, 1865, in Turner and Turner, *Mary Todd Lincoln*, 254. Harry Pratt's seminal book on Lincoln's finances states $85,000. See Pratt, *Personal Finances of Abraham Lincoln*, 131–41.

39. "A Homestead for Mrs. Lincoln," *New York Times*, May 6, 1865, 5; "The Late President Lincoln's Family," *New York Times*, June 10, 1865, 5; Dennett, *Lincoln and the Civil War*, 274.

40. Mary Lincoln to Alexander Williamson, Aug. 17, 1865, and Mary Lincoln to David Davis, Sept. 12, 1865, in Turner and Turner, *Mary Todd Lincoln*, 264–65, 274.

41. "A visit to Springfield & the Cemetery—where my beloved one's rest, last week—convinced me, that the further removed, I am, the better, it will be, for *my reason*, from *that* spot." Mary Lincoln to Mary Jane Welles, Chicago, Dec. 29, 1865, in ibid., 315.

42. Mary Lincoln to Alexander Williamson, May 11, 1866, Mary Lincoln to Simon Cameron, May 19, 1866, and Mary Lincoln to David Davis, Apr. 6 and June 30, 1867, in ibid., 364, 366, 424.

43. Ibid., 247. Jean H. Baker, Mary's most cited biographer, offers the figure of $10,000 debt, although she has no evidence to support it. Jean H. Baker, *Mary Todd Lincoln: A Biography* (New York: W. W. Norton, 1987), 258. Elizabeth Keckly stated a $70,000 debt, in *Behind the Scenes*, 204. See also Willard L. King, *Lincoln's Manager: David Davis* (Cambridge, Mass.: Harvard University Press, 1960), 235–37.

44. Robert Hendrickson, *The Grand Emporiums: The Illustrated History of America's Great Department Stores* (New York: Stein and Day, 1979), 36.

45. Robert Lincoln to David Davis, Dec. 22, 1865, folder A-109, box 7, DDFP.

46. Mary Lincoln to James H. Orne, Marienbad, Bohemia, May 28, 1870, quoted in Thomas F. Schwartz and Anne V. Shaughnessy, "Unpublished Mary Lincoln Letters,"

Journal of the Abraham Lincoln Association 11 (1990), http://jala.press.uiuc.edu/11/ schwartz.html; Michael Burlingame, "Mary Todd Lincoln's Unethical Conduct as First Lady," in *At Lincoln's Side: John Hay's Civil War Correspondence and Selected Writings* (Carbondale: Southern Illinois University Press, 2000), Appendix 2, 185–203. Burlingame's essay examines not only Mary's debts but also the White House furniture theft story and accusations of her influence peddling and bribery.

47. Emphasis in original. Mary Lincoln to Anson G. Henry, July 17, 1865, in Turner and Turner, *Mary Todd Lincoln*, 261.

48. Mary Lincoln to Elizabeth Blair Lee, Dec. 11, 1865, in ibid., 302.

49. Robert Lincoln to David Davis, Chicago, Nov. 16, 1866, folder A-109, box 7, DDFP.

50. Robert Lincoln to William Herndon, Chicago, Dec. 13, 1866, in LB, 1:23, microfilm reel 1; also in frame 1292, microfilm reel 8, group 4, H-WC.

51. Emphasis in original. Robert Lincoln to William Herndon, Chicago, Dec. 24, 1866, in LB, 1:26, microfilm reel 1; also in frames 1326–27, microfilm reel 8, group 4, H-WC.

52. "Mrs. Lincoln's Wardrobe," *Chicago Tribune*, Oct. 8, 1867, 2; Keckley, *Behind the Scenes*, 267–31.

53. Mary Lincoln to Elizabeth Keckley, Oct. 6, 1867, in Turner and Turner, *Mary Todd Lincoln*, 440.

54. Robert Lincoln to Mary Harlan, Oct. 16, 1867, quoted in Helm, *True Story of Mary*, 267–77.

55. David Davis to Miss Addie Burr, July 19, 1882, Adeline Ellery (Burr) Davis Green Papers, Rare Book, Manuscript, and Special Collections Library, Duke University, Durham, N.C.

56. "Mrs. Lincoln," *Illinois State Journal*, Oct. 10, 1867, 1; "Mrs. Lincoln: A Woman's Appeal," *Chicago Tribune*, Oct. 9, 1867, 2; editorial, *Chicago Tribune*, May 20, 1875, 4; editorial, *Chicago Inter Ocean*, May 20, 1875, 4.

57. "Mrs. Lincoln's Wardrobe," *Chicago Tribune*, Oct. 8, 1867, 2. Some people did defend Mary and instead blamed Washington and/or American society. See "Mrs. Lincoln's Wardrobe," *Independent* 19, no. 985 (Oct. 17, 1867): 4; and "The Widow of Lincoln," *Round Table: A Saturday Review of Politics, Finance, Literature, Society*, 6, no. 142 (Oct. 12, 1867): 240.

58. "Modern Culture," *Littell's Living Age* 8, no. 1591 (Dec. 5, 1875): 590.

59. Mary Lincoln to David Davis, Frankfort, Germany, Dec. 15, 1868, in Turner and Turner, *Mary Todd Lincoln*, 496–98.

60. Mary Lincoln to the United States Senate, Frankfort, Germany, Dec. 1, 1868, in ibid., 493.

61. *Congressional Globe*, 41st Cong., 2nd sess., 1870, 6:5559.

62. *Congressional Globe*, 40th Congress, 3rd sess., 1869, 2:1242–45.

63. *Congressional Globe*, 41st Cong., 2nd sess., 1870, 5:4540–41.

64. While with a twenty-first-century eye it might appear that Yates was accusing her of adultery, what he meant was that she sympathized with the Confederates during the rebellion. F. Lauristan Bullard, "Mrs. Lincoln's Pension," *Lincoln Herald* 49 (1947): 25. On Mary's alleged infidelities, see Burlingame, *Inner World of Abraham Lincoln*, 292.

65. Quoted in Bullard, "Mrs. Lincoln's Pension," 25.

66. Mary Lincoln to Sally Orne, Frankfort, Germany, Dec. 12, 1869, and Mary Lincoln to James H. Orne, Frankfort, Germany, Feb. 2, 1870, quoted in Schwartz and Shaughnessy, "Unpublished Mary Lincoln Letters."

67. Edward L. Pierce, *Memoir and Letters of Charles Sumner*, 4 vols. (Boston: Roberts Brothers, 1893), 4:420–21; *Congressional Globe*, 41st Cong., 2nd sess., 1870, 6:5560; Bullard, "Mrs. Lincoln's Pension," 26.

68. Mary Lincoln to David Davis, Nov. 9, 1871, and Mary Lincoln to Mary Harlan Lincoln, Frankfort, Mar. 22, 1869, in Turner and Turner, *Mary Todd Lincoln*, 597, 504. In the latter letter, Mary says Tad's presence "has become so necessary even to my life."

69. Ibid., 586. The Turners astutely characterized Tad as "the most tragic member of a family marked for tragedy."

70. Mary Lincoln to Mary Harlan Lincoln, London, Jan. 26, 1871, folder 1, box 1, IF.

71. Mary Lincoln to Mary Harlan Lincoln, London, Nov. 1870, in Turner and Turner, *Mary Todd Lincoln*, 581.

72. "Obituary: Death of Thomas Lincoln, Youngest Son of the Late President," *Chicago Tribune*, July 16, 1871, 3; John Hay, "Tad Lincoln," *Chicago Tribune*, July 19, 1871, 1.

73. Mary Lincoln to David Davis, Nov. 9, 1871, in Turner and Turner, *Mary Todd Lincoln*, 597; Robert Lincoln to David Davis, Sept. 21 and Nov. 9, 1871, folder A-109, box 7, DDFP; Pratt, *Personal Finances of Abraham Lincoln*, 184. Tad's estate consisted of $1,315.16 in cash and $35,750 in bonds.

74. Mary Lincoln to Eliza Slataper, July 27 and Aug. 13, 1871, in Turner and Turner, *Mary Todd Lincoln*, 591–92; Robert Lincoln to James H. Hackett, Chicago, Sept. 28, 1871, Robert Todd Lincoln Papers, Manuscripts Division, LC.

75. Emphasis in original. Mary Lincoln to Mary Harlan Lincoln, letter fragment, folder 1, box 1, IF.

76. Mary's half brothers Samuel Brown Todd died at the battle of Shiloh, April 7, 1862, Alexander Humphreys Todd died at the battle of Baton Rouge, August 5, 1862, and David Humphreys Todd died from wounds received at Vicksburg. Mary's brother-in-law, Benjamin Hardin Helm, husband of Mary's half sister Emily, died at the battle of Chickamauga on September 20, 1863. See Turner and Turner, *Mary Todd Lincoln*, 154–55.

3. NO RIGHT TO REMAIN UPON EARTH

1. Isaac N. Arnold, *The Life of Abraham Lincoln* (1884; reprint, Lincoln: University of Nebraska Press, Bison Book, 1994), 439.

2. Eddie Foy and Alvin F. Harlow, "Clowning through Life," *Collier's Weekly* 76, no. 26 (Dec. 25, 1926): 30.

3. Robert Lincoln to Mary Harlan Lincoln, July 15, 1871, quoted in Helm, *True Story of Mary*, 293–95.

4. Mary Lincoln to Eliza Slataper, July 27 and Aug. 13, 1871, in Turner and Turner, *Mary Todd Lincoln*, 591–92; Robert Lincoln to James H. Hackett, Chicago, Sept. 28, 1871, Robert Todd Lincoln Papers, LC.

5. Mary Lincoln to Rhoda White, Frankfurt, Germany, Dec. 20, 1869, in Turner and Turner, *Mary Todd Lincoln*, 536.

6. Mary Lincoln to Jesse K. DuBois, Cresson Penn, July 26, 1868, Lincoln Collection, ALPL, quoted in Schwartz and Bauer, "Unpublished Mary Todd Lincoln"; Mary Lincoln to Eliza Stuart Steele, Chicago, May 23, 1871, in Turner and Turner, *Mary Todd Lincoln*, 588.

7. Mary Lincoln to Francis B. Carpenter, Chicago, Nov. 15, 1865, Mary Lincoln to David Davis, Germany, Dec. 15, 1868, and Mary Lincoln to Mary Harlan Lincoln, Frankfort, Germany, Mar. 22, 1869, London, Nov. 1870, and London, Jan. 26, 1871,

in Turner and Turner, *Mary Todd Lincoln*, 283, 497, 505, 581, 583. See also the twenty-five letters from Mary Lincoln to Mary Harlan Lincoln, folder 1, box 1, IF.

8. Mary Lincoln to Mary Harlan Lincoln, Frankfort, Germany, Mar. 22, Nov./Dec., and Nov. 25, 1869, folder 1, box 1, IF; fragment of Mar. 22 letter also in Turner and Turner, *Mary Todd Lincoln*, 505. In all, Robert Lincoln's Insanity File contained twenty-five letters from his mother to his wife, nearly all of which contain evidence of gift giving. All these letters are printed in full in Neely and McMurtry, *Insanity File*, appendix, 147–82. As Neely and McMurtry astutely point out, the Robert Lincolns most likely kept these letters at first as cherished mementos of a beloved mother, although later they were necessary as evidence against the elder Mary's accusations of thievery.

9. Mary Lincoln to David Davis, Nov. 9, 1871, in Turner and Turner, *Mary Todd Lincoln*, 597; Robert Lincoln to Davis, Sept. 21 and Nov. 9, 1871, folder A-109, box 7, DDFP; Mary Lincoln to Mary Harlan Lincoln, Cronberg, Germany, Sept. 9, 1869, and undated fragments: "I hope to start . . . ," "It is double—and well . . . ," "If Grant had been in the least . . . ," and "I am troubled to hear . . . ," folder 1, box 1, IF.

10. Mary Lincoln to Mary Harlan Lincoln, London, Nov. 22, 1870, folder 1, box 1, IF.

11. Mary Lincoln to Eliza Slataper, Frankfort, Germany, Dec. 13, 1868, in Turner and Turner, *Mary Todd Lincoln*, 495.

12. Mary Lincoln to Eliza Stuart Steele, Chicago, May 23, 1871, in ibid., 588.

13. Robert Lincoln to Elizabeth Edwards, Aug. 7, 1875, in LB, 1:133–39, microfilm reel 1; "Clouded Reason: Trial of Mrs. Abraham Lincoln for Insanity," *Chicago Tribune*, May 20, 1875, 1; "Mrs. Lincoln," *Chicago Inter Ocean*, May 20, 1875, 1.

14. Robert Lincoln to Elizabeth Edwards, Aug. 7, 1875, LB.

15. Mary Lincoln to James H. Knowlton, Waukesha, Wisc., Aug. 3, 1872, Mary Lincoln to Norman Williams, Waukesha, Wisc., Aug. 8, 1872, and Mary Lincoln to John Todd Stuart, Chicago, Dec. 15, 1873, in Turner and Turner, *Mary Todd Lincoln*, 598, 599, 603; Kristine Adams Wendt, "Mary Todd Lincoln: 'Great Sorrows' and the Healing Waters of Waukesha," *Wisconsin Academy Review* 38, no. 2 (Spring 1992): 14–19; Lillian Krueger, "Mary Todd Lincoln Summers in Wisconsin," *Journal of the Illinois State Historical Society* 34, no. 2 (June 1941): 249–52.

16. For example, while complaining of severe chills, Mary once wrote to a friend, "You will not wonder, at my illness, when I mention, that last week, I visited, the resting place of my beloved husband." Mary Lincoln to Sally Orne, Chicago, Dec. 24, 1865, in Turner and Turner, *Mary Todd Lincoln*, 311.

17. I make this statement in agreement with the Turners, who also believed that Mary "learned the uses of illness" to garner attention and sympathy first from her husband and then, during her widowhood, from her son Tad and her few friends. See Turner and Turner, *Mary Todd Lincoln*, 32.

18. Eugene Taylor, *Shadow Culture: Psychology and Spirituality in America* (Washington, D.C.: Counterpoint, 1999), 137.

19. Ann Braude, *Radical Spirits: Spiritualism and Women's Rights in Nineteenth Century America* (Boston: Beacon, 1989), 5–6.

20. Ibid., 140.

21. "A Plea for Spiritualism," *Chicago Tribune*, Jan. 13, 1868, 2; "Spiritualism," *New York Times*, Jan. 26, 1873, 2; "A Decline in Spiritualism," *New York Times*, Feb. 23, 1875, 4; "Done with the Big Toe: Margaret Fox Kane Shows How Spirit Rapping Is Produced," *New York Times*, Oct. 22, 1888, 5. See also "Spiritualism or Insanity?"

New York Times, Feb. 3, 1892, 8, which described the court case of one Harriet C. Mantells, a woman of good social standing and high respectability whose neighbors claimed she was insane. The article referred to a courtroom full of people, especially physicians, "who were desirous of seeing how distinct a line could be drawn between Spiritualism and a diseased mind."

22. The inception of Mary's Spiritualism is difficult to trace, but her friend, Dr. Anson G. Henry, took credit for converting the First Lady to the Spiritualist doctrine. Anson G. Henry to his wife, Washington, May 8, 1865, SC 683, Anson G. Henry Papers, Manuscript Division, ALPL.

23. Turner and Turner, *Mary Todd Lincoln*, 122–24. For a good summary of Mary's Spiritualist beliefs, see Wayne C. Temple, *Abraham Lincoln: From Skeptic to Prophet* (Mahomet, Ill.: Mayhaven, 1995), 196–203.

24. John G. Nicolay to Jesse Weik, Washington, D.C., Nov. 25, 1894, frame 680, microfilm reel 13, group 5, H-WC; "Abraham Lincoln Not a Spiritualist," *Chicago Tribune*, Oct. 22, 1891, 4; "Lincoln's Alleged Spiritualism," *Chicago Tribune*, July 28, 1891, 10; Jay Monaghan, "Was Abraham Lincoln Really a Spiritualist?" *Journal of the Illinois State Historical Society* 34, no. 2 (June 1941): 209–32.

25. "Spiritual Photography," *Littell's Living Age* 1313 (July 31, 1869): 314.

26. Krueger, "Mary Todd Lincoln Summers in Wisconsin," 252.

27. "Recall Mrs. Lincoln," *Batavia Herald*, Mar. 6, 1909, clipping in Batavia Historical Society, Batavia, Ill.; "Mrs. Lincoln: A Visit to Her by 'The Post and Mail' Correspondent: How She Passes the Time at Dr. Patterson's Retreat," *Chicago Post and Mail*, July 13, 1875; Wendt, "Mary Todd Lincoln," 14–19; untitled article, *New York Observer and Chronicle*, July 22, 1875, 230.

28. Mary Lincoln to Charles Sumner, near Chicago, July 4, 1865, in Turner and Turner, *Mary Todd Lincoln*, 256.

29. Mary Lincoln to Sally Orne, Frankfort, Germany, Nov. 20, 1869, in ibid., 525–26.

30. "Insane Delusions: Can a Belief in Spiritualism Be Regarded as Such?" *New York Times*, May 23, 1875, 10.

31. Robert Lincoln to Elizabeth Edwards, Aug. 7, 1875, in LB, 1:133–39, microfilm reel 1.

32. "Spiritualism and Cash," *New York Times*, May 24, 1868, 4.

33. William H. Crook wrote that the Spiritualists "nearly crazed" Mary, who was "almost frantic with suffering" and "was so weakened that she had not force enough to resist the cruel cheat." Gerry, *Through Five Administrations*, 69–70.

34. Robert Lincoln to David Davis, Chicago, Nov. 16, 1875, folder 2, box 2, IF; Davis to Robert Lincoln, Washington, D.C., Nov. 20, 1875, folder 15, box 2, IF; untitled article, *Chicago Tribune*, Aug. 28, 1875, 8.

35. Eddie Foy, "Clowning through Life," 30.

36. More than thirty letters from Mary Lincoln to Sally Orne are known to exist, as well as numerous letters mentioning Mrs. Orne, testifying to their close relationship. It will also be shown later that she was Mary's only friend to inquire of Robert about the insanity trial. Mary Lincoln to James H. Orne, Frankfort, Germany, Feb. 2, 1870, quoted in Schwartz and Shaughnessy, "Unpublished Mary Lincoln Letters."

37. Eleanor Gridley, "Presentation of Bronze Bust of Mrs. Myra Bradwell, First Woman Lawyer of Illinois," reprinted from *Transactions of the Illinois State Historical Society* 38, no. 6 (May 1931): 6, Myra Pritchard Papers, Chicago History Museum.

38. Mary Lincoln to Jacob Bunn, Pau, France, Jan. 31, 1877, in Turner and Turner, *Mary Todd Lincoln*, 624.

39. *Myra Bradwell v. State of Illinois*, 83 U.S. 130 (1872); Jane M. Friedman, *America's First Woman Lawyer* (Buffalo, N.Y.: Prometheus, 1993), 18; Nancy T. Gilliam, "A Professional Pioneer: Myra Bradwell's Fight to Practice Law," *Law and History Review* 5, no. 1 (Spring 1987): 105–13.

40. Baker, *Mary Todd Lincoln*, 339; Friedman, *America's First Woman Lawyer*, 51; Neely and McMurtry, *Insanity File*, 59; Randall, *Mary Lincoln*, 433; Turner and Turner, *Mary Todd Lincoln*, 623–24. Prior to the discovery of the Towers Papers, only six letters written by Mary Lincoln gave primary proof of their acquaintance: Mary Lincoln to Jacob Bunn, Pau, France, Jan. 31, 1877, in Turner and Turner, *Mary Todd Lincoln*, 623–24; Mary Lincoln to James Bradwell, Oct. 10, 1872, Jan. 17 and 18, 1874, Nov. 11 and Dec. 1, 1875, folder 2, box 1, IF.

41. See the introduction and chapter 10.

42. Myra Helmer Pritchard, "The Dark Days of Abraham Lincoln's Widow, as Revealed by Her Own Letters" (unpublished manuscript, 1927), chap. 1, p. 14, FTC.

43. Affidavit of Eleanor Gridley, Mar. 8, 1929, PFP. It is strange that Gridley would state this, but Pritchard, who requested that Gridley write the affidavit, would not. Most likely, the Bradwells recounted Mary's stories of the Springfield and Washington years that, according to their granddaughter, they had heard. Gridley, age eighty-two in 1929, probably remembered incorrectly. She did thank James Bradwell for his assistance with her book, *The Story of Abraham Lincoln; or, The Journey from the Log Cabin to the White House* (New York: Eaton & Mains, 1900).

44. Gridley, "Presentation of Bronze Bust," 6.

45. "All Dabble in the Law: Ex-Judge James B. Bradwell and His Family of Legal Lights," *Chicago Tribune*, May 12, 1889, 26; "Mrs. Bradwell Dead," *Chicago Tribune*, Feb. 15, 1894, 12; "Pioneer Lawyer at Death's Door," *Chicago Tribune*, Nov. 29, 1907, 5. If either of the Bradwells were close acquaintants of Abraham Lincoln, their Chicago newspaper obituaries would have mentioned it, but they did not, although, strangely, Myra Bradwell's many eulogies never mention her connection to Mary Lincoln either. The more than two dozen newspaper articles I found by or about Eleanor Gridley, published between 1900 and her death in 1944, in which she discusses Abraham Lincoln also never mention any Bradwell–Lincoln connection. James Bradwell did write one letter to Abraham Lincoln in 1865 concerning the Northwestern Sanitary Fair in Chicago, but nothing in the quite formal letter gives any hint of friendship or even acquaintance. James B. Bradwell to Abraham Lincoln, Chicago, Jan. 16, 1865, series 1, general correspondence, 1833–1916, Abraham Lincoln Papers, LC, http://memory.loc.gov/cgi-bin/query/P?mal:1:./temp/~ammem_Rw4C. Historian Ida M. Tarbell , who interviewed James Bradwell while working on her Lincoln biography, called him Lincoln's "friend." Her interview notes, however, do not substantiate that characterization, as Bradwell's statements could easily have been based on information he was told by Mary Lincoln. Ida M. Tarbell, *In the Footsteps of the Lincolns* (New York: Harper & Brothers, 1924), 400; James Bradwell, interview by Ida Tarbell, n.d., Ida M. Tarbell–Lincoln Collection, Pelletier Library, Allegheny College, Meadville, Pa.

46. Mary Lincoln to James Bradwell, Oct. 10, 1872, folder 2, box 1, IF.

47. Mary Lincoln to Myra Bradwell, Nov. 1, 1872, FTC; also in Pritchard, "Dark Days," chap. 1, p. 15, FTC. Pritchard also stated in her manuscript that this was the earliest letter in her possession. She gave no explanation or supposition as to the fate of any letters previous to 1872.

48. Mary Lincoln to Myra Bradwell, Jan. 26, 1873, in Pritchard, "Dark Days," chap. 2, p. 2, FTC.

49. Mary Lincoln, last will and testament, July 23, 1873, FTC; and in Pritchard, "Dark Days," chap. 7, pp. 4–5, FTC; Mary Lincoln to County Judge of Cook County, July 23, 1873, folder 2, box 1, IF.

50. "Current Events," *New York Evangelist*, May 27, 1875, 8; "Clouded Reason," *Chicago Tribune*, May 20, 1875, 1; "Mrs. Lincoln," *Chicago Inter Ocean*, May 20, 1875, 1. The *Evangelist* article states Mary believed she would die on September 6, while the newspaper coverage of her insanity trial states she believed she would die "within a few days" of Dr. Danforth's September 16 visit.

51. Mary Lincoln to James Bradwell, Jan. 17, 1874, folder 2, box 1, IF.

52. Mary Lincoln to Robert Lincoln, Aug. 1874, Lincoln Collection, ALPL, quoted in Thomas F. Schwartz, "'My Stay on Earth Is Growing Very Short': Mary Todd Lincoln's Letters to Willis Danforth and Elizabeth Swing," *Journal of Illinois History* 6 (summer 2003): 130.

53. Danforth graduated Rock Island Medical College in 1849. He served as a cavalry captain and surgeon and later as medical director for the West Kentucky District during the Civil War. Later, he became a surgeon at Scammon Hospital in Chicago, a professor of surgery at Hahnemann Medical College in Chicago, president of the Chicago Academy of Medicine, president of the Illinois State Homeopathic Medical Society, president of the Wisconsin Homeopathic Society, and associate editor of *United States Medical and Surgical Journal*. "Numbered with the Dead," *Chicago Tribune*, June 6, 1891, 2; testimony of Dr. Willis Danforth, quoted in "Clouded Reason," *Chicago Tribune*, May 20, 1875, 1; "Mrs. Lincoln: The Widow of the Martyred President Adjudged Insane in County Court," *Chicago Inter Ocean*, May 20, 1875, 1.

54. Danforth testimony, quoted in "Clouded Reason," *Chicago Tribune*, May 20, 1875, 1; "Mrs. Lincoln: The Widow," *Chicago Inter Ocean*, May 20, 1875, 1; "Current Events," *New York Evangelist*, May 27, 1875, 8.

55. "The Action of Neurotic Medicines in Insanity," *American Journal of Insanity* 28 (July 1871): 114–15; J. B. Andrews, "The Physiological Action and Therapeutic Use of Chloral," *American Journal of Insanity* 28 (July 1871): 35–53; Charles F. MacDonald, "Hydrate of Chloral," *American Journal of Insanity* 34 (Jan. 1878): 360–67; "Large Dose of Bromide of Potassium," *American Journal of Insanity* 31 (Jan. 1875): 396; Stephen Snelders, Charles Kaplan, and Toine Pieters, "On Cannabis, Chloral Hydrate, and Career Cycles of Psychotropic Drugs in Medicine," *Bulletin of the History of Medicine* 80, no. 95 (Spring 2006): 95–114.

56. Elizabeth Edwards to Robert Lincoln, Springfield, Nov. 5, 1875, folder 16, box 2, IF; Baker, *Mary Todd Lincoln*, 314–45. The notion that Mary was physically addicted to laudanum also has been rejected in recent years. See Norbert Hirschhorn, "Mary Lincoln's 'Suicide Attempt': A Physician Reconsiders the Evidence," *Lincoln Herald* 105, no. 3 (Fall 2003): 97.

57. Mary Lincoln to Myra Bradwell, May 6, 1874, in Pritchard, "Dark Days," chap. 2, pp. 3–4, FTC.

58. Mary Lincoln to Willis Danforth, n.d., Lincoln Collection, ALPL, quoted in Schwartz, "'My Stay on Earth,'" 135.

59. Schwartz, "'My Stay on Earth,'" 127.

60. Ibid.

61. I am indebted to Dr. Eugene Taylor for making me aware of the difference between physical and psychological addiction.

62. I am indebted to Dr. James S. Brust for bringing this fact to my attention. Taylor, *Shadow Culture*, 102; Braude, *Radical Spirits*, 145.

63. Baker, *Mary Todd Lincoln*, 314, 324, 331.

64. Andrews, "Physiological Action and Therapeutic Use of Chloral," 35–53.

65. Chloral hydrate is still in use today, although it is not widely available or frequently prescribed. Typical doses today would be 7.5 grains to 30 grains per day (500 mg to 2,000 mg).

66. C. F. MacDonald, "Hydrate of Chloral," 360–67. MacDonald told the Association of Superintendents of Asylums for the Insane, to whom he presented his paper, that in the eight years he had been using chloral as treatment, he had never encountered a case of addiction, nor had any other physician whom he had asked.

67. Hirschhorn, "Mary Lincoln's 'Suicide Attempt,'" 97; Rodney A. Ross, "Mary Todd Lincoln: Patient at Bellevue Place, Batavia," *Journal of the Illinois State Historical Society* 63, no. 1 (Spring 1970): 5–34. Ross's article contains the only transcript of the Bellevue daily patient progress reports.

68. "President Lincoln," *Chicago Tribune*, Dec. 14, 1873, 2.

69. Mary Lincoln to John Todd Stuart, Chicago, Dec. 15 and 16, 1873, and Jan. 20 and 21, 1874, in Turner and Turner, *Mary Todd Lincoln*, 603–6; Robert Lincoln to John Nicolay, Dec. 16, 1873, in LB, 1:111, microfilm reel 1; Robert Lincoln to Isaac Markens, Apr. 16, 1908, folder 42, FTC.

70. Baker, *Mary Todd Lincoln*, 312.

71. "Springfield: A Correction—Mrs. Lincoln on Herndon's Lecture," *Chicago Tribune*, Dec. 19, 1873, 4.

72. W. H. Herndon, "Lincoln's Religion: Answer of William H. Herndon, Esq., to Mrs. Lincoln," Springfield, Ill., Jan. 12, 1874, published in *Illinois State Register*, Jan. 14, 1874, typescript in frames 1726–36, microfilm reel 9, group 4, H-WC; W. H. Herndon, "Mr. Lincoln," *Chicago Tribune*, Jan. 16, 1874, 2.

73. William Jayne to William Herndon, Springfield, Ill., Jan. 19, 1874, frames 1681–83, microfilm reel 9, group 4, H-WC.

74. Chauncey Black to William Herndon, York, Christmas morning, 1873, and York, Jan. 18, 1874, frames 1657 and 1677, microfilm reel 9, group 4, H-WC.

75. Mary Lincoln to Elizabeth Swing, Mar. 12, 1874, Lincoln Collection, ALPL, quoted in Schwartz, "'My Stay on Earth,'" 129; Mary Lincoln to Sally Orne, n.d., quoted in Schwartz and Shaughnessy, "Unpublished Mary Lincoln Letters."

76. Mary Lincoln to Myra Bradwell, St. Augustine, Fla., Feb. 20, 1875, FTC; and in Pritchard, "Dark Days," chap. 2, pp. 4–7, FTC.

77. Mary's "season of sadness" also raises the questions of whether she was affected by seasonal affective disorder and to what degree the time of year may have affected her psychology. Mary Lincoln to Myra Bradwell, Sorrento, Italy, Apr. 22, 1878, FTC.

78. Mary Lincoln to Edward Isham, Jacksonville, Fla., Mar. 12, 1875 (two telegrams), folder 3, box 1, IF; "Clouded Reason," *Chicago Tribune*, May 20, 1875, 1; "Mrs. Lincoln: The Widow of the Martyred President Adjudged Insane in County Court," *Chicago Inter Ocean*, May 20, 1875, 1.

79. J. J. S. Wilson, supt., to station manager, Jacksonville, Fla., n.d., John Coyne, manager, to Wilson, for Robert Lincoln, Jacksonville, Fla., Mar. 12, 1875, and Coyne to Wilson, Jacksonville, Fla., Mar. 13, 1875, folder 3, box 1, IF.

80. Mary Lincoln to Robert Lincoln, Jacksonville, Fla., Mar. 13, 1875, folder 3, box 1, IF.

4. OF UNSOUND MIND

1. Mary Lincoln's conduct and conversations from the time she arrived in Chicago on March 15 to the day of her sanity hearing on May 19 are recorded almost entirely in the trial reporting of contemporary Chicago newspapers. The following three articles form the basis for much of the account in this chapter: "Clouded Reason:

Trial of Mrs. Abraham Lincoln for Insanity," *Chicago Tribune*, May 20, 1875, 1; "Mrs. Lincoln: The Widow of the Martyred President Adjudged Insane in County Court," *Chicago Inter Ocean*, May 20, 1875, 1; and "A Sad Revelation: Mrs. Mary Lincoln, the Widow of the Late President, Adjudged Insane," *Chicago Times*, May 20, 1875, 2.

2. Exactly how long Robert slept nights in the room next to Mary's is unknown. As the trial testimony shows, it was at least until April 1, but it may have been all the way up to the May 19 trial.

3. The Wandering Jew is a figure from Christian folklore who taunted Jesus on the way to the crucifixion and was then cursed to walk the earth until Judgment Day. He is often characterized as a shoemaker. Columbia Encyclopedia, 6th ed., http://www.bartleby.com/65/wa/Wanderin.html.

4. It is interesting that Mary sought a "Mr. Shoemaker," since the Wandering Jew of legend, whom she believed she encountered on the train, was a shoemaker by trade. "Mrs. Lincoln Insane," *Illinois State Journal*, May 21, 1875, 2; "A Sad Revelation," *Chicago Times*, May 20, 1875, 2.

5. Seeing special meaning in neutral objects is a classic sign of psychosis. In its account of the incident, the *Chicago Times* identified the housekeeper as a Mrs. Harrington.

6. The *Chicago Times* identified the second waiter as one John Bessinger.

7. "Insanity's Freaks," *Chicago Times*, May 21, 1875, clipping in folder 31, box 2, IF.

8. Robert Lincoln to Leonard Swett, May 25, 1884, folder 3, box 2, IF.

9. Ibid.

10. The fact that Mary always recovered from her episodes—suggesting highs and lows in her temperament—indicates symptoms of Bipolar Disorder. Robert's letter has not been found, but Brown's response quotes from it. Elizabeth J. Todd Grimsley Brown to Robert Lincoln, Mar. 16, 1875, folder 10, box 2, IF.

11. Ibid.

12. Robert Lincoln to Ninian Edwards, Nov. 15, 1875, folder 2, box 2, IF.

13. Neely and McMurtry, *Insanity File*, 8. I was unable to find the primary source in the Insanity File for Robert's payment of a consultation fee to Dr. Patterson at that time, which Neely and McMurtry cite as miscellaneous expense accounts.

14. Robert Lincoln to Thomas Dent, Sept. 12, 1919, quoted in King, *Lincoln's Manager*, 244.

15. Robert Lincoln to Elizabeth Edwards, Aug. 7, 1875, in LB, 1:133–39, microfilm reel 1.

16. David Davis to Robert Lincoln, May 23, 1875, folder 15, box 2, IF. Swett was no stranger to legal cases involving insanity. In fact, he argued a case of insanity against Abraham Lincoln in 1855 and gained national attention in 1882 for using the insanity defense for a man accused of a double homicide in Colorado. Andrew McFarland, "Insanity as a Defense," *Chicago Tribune*, June 20, 1889, 7; "The Stickney Case," *Chicago Tribune*, Feb. 10, 1882, 2.

17. Robert so trusted Swett that he sought his advice and assistance again in 1876 during the attempt and aftermath of the plot to steal the body of Abraham Lincoln from its Springfield, Ill., tomb. "Violating the Tomb of Lincoln," *Prairie Farmer* 47, no. 46 (Nov. 11, 1876): 364; "Crime," *Chicago Tribune*, Nov. 20, 1876, 5; "Robbers in Lincoln's Tomb," *Boston Globe*, Nov. 22, 1876, 3. For a book-length account of the theft attempt, see John Carroll Power, *History of an Attempt to Steal the Body of Abraham Lincoln* (Springfield, Ill.: H. W. Rokker, 1890).

18. Mary did not state which friends she meant, but David Davis and Leonard Swett generally are considered two of Lincoln's closest associates. Mary Lincoln to Jesse

K. DuBois, Cresson Penn, July 26, 1868, Lincoln Collection, ALPL, quoted in Schwartz and Bauer, "Unpublished Mary Todd Lincoln."

19. Robert Lincoln to Ninian Edwards, Nov. 15, 1875, folder 2, box 2, IF.

20. David Davis to Leonard Swett, Indianapolis, May 19, 1875, folder 15, box 2, IF.

21. John Todd Stuart to Robert Lincoln, May 10 and 21, 1875, and Stuart to Leonard Swett, May 21, 1875, folder 26, box 2, IF. In an article titled "Mrs. Lincoln" (*Illinois State Journal*, Oct. 10, 1867, 1), it was reported of Mary's family and friends in Springfield at the time of the Old Clothes Scandal that "the most charitable construction that they can put upon her strange course is that she is insane."

22. The *Chicago Tribune* and *Chicago Inter Ocean* articles on the trial stated only that Robert had "a man" watching her, but Swett identified him as "Pinkerton's man." Leonard Swett to David Davis, Chicago, May 24, 1875, folder A-73, box 5, DDFP.

23. Baker, *Mary Todd Lincoln*, 323, 340, 341; Samuel A. Schreiner, *The Trials of Mrs. Lincoln* (New York: Donald I. Fine, 1987), 321, 325–26.

24. James Rhodes and Dean Jauchius, *The Trial of Mary Todd Lincoln* (Indianapolis: Bobbs-Merrill, 1959), 139–40. Rhodes and Jauchius's entire book, in fact, is one long excoriation of Robert Lincoln as a cold, calculating, selfish, apathetic man who would brutally and heartlessly commit his sane mother to an asylum by means of a kangaroo court. The book was so vicious, in fact, that the partners of Isham, Lincoln & Beale, the Chicago law firm cofounded by Robert Lincoln, sent a stern letter to the Bobbs-Merrill Company and both authors warning that the "fallacious and defamatory nature of the book" could subject them to legal action for criminal libel. Harry J. Dunbaugh to Hughes Miller, president, Bobbs-Merrill Co., Chicago, May 19, 1959, John Goff Papers, Friends of Hildene, Inc., Manchester, Vt.

25. Robert Lincoln to Elizabeth Todd Edwards, Aug. 7, 1875, in LB, 1:133–39, microfilm reel 1.

26. David Davis to Robert Lincoln, Washington, D.C., Nov. 20, 1875, folder 15, box 2, IF.

27. Kim Townsend, *Manhood at Harvard* (New York: W. W. Norton, 1996), 17.

28. "The Case of Mrs. Lincoln," *Chicago Tribune*, May 21, 1875, 4.

29. David Davis to Leonard Swett, Indianapolis, May 19, 1875, folder 15, box 2, IF; Swett to Davis, Chicago, May 24, 1875, folder A-73, box 5, DDFP.

30. Swett to Davis, May 24, 1875, DDFP.

31. "Gives Tribute to B. F. Ayer," *Chicago Tribune*, Apr. 9, 1903, 16; Swett to Davis, May 24, 1875, DDFP.

32. Davis to Swett, May 19, 1875, IF; Swett to Davis, May 24, 1875, DDFP; Robert Lincoln to Swett, June 2, 1884, folder 3, box 2, IF.

33. "Pioneer Surgeon Dead in Chicago," *Chicago Tribune*, May 29, 1904, 6.

34. Mary Lincoln to Rhoda White, Chicago, June 8, 1871, in Turner and Turner, *Mary Todd Lincoln*, 590.

35. "Dr. Hosmer Allen Johnson," in *Biographical Sketches of the Leading Men of Chicago* (Chicago: Wilson & St. Clair, 1868), 229–34.

36. "Noted Doctor Dies: Dr. Charles Gilman Smith Succumbs to Paralysis," *Chicago Tribune*, Jan. 11, 1894.

37. Bellevue Place advertising brochure, n.d., Batavia Historical Society, Batavia, Ill.

38. "Nathan Smith Davis," in *Biographical Sketches*, 81–89; "Give Banquet for Dr. Davis: Aged Physician Is Honored by His Fellow Medical Men in Chicago," *Chicago Tribune*, Oct. 6, 1901; "AMA's Founder," American Medical Association, http://www.ama-assn.org/ama/pub/category/12981.html.

39. "Obituary: Death of Dr. James S. Jewell, a Well-Known Chicago Physician," *Chicago Tribune*, Apr. 19, 1887.

40. Swett to Davis, May 24, 1875, DDFP.

41. A. E. MacDonald, "The Examination and Commitment of the Insane," *American Journal of Insanity* 32 (Apr. 1876): 509–10.

42. Ibid., 513.

43. Robert Lincoln to Leonard Swett, June 2, 1884, folder 3, box 2, IF.

44. A. E. MacDonald, "Examination and Commitment of the Insane," 507–8.

45. Robert Lincoln to Mrs. James H. (Sally) Orne, June 1, 1875, folder 2, Robert Lincoln Papers, Chicago History Museum; Robert Lincoln to John Hay, June 6, 1875, microfilm reel 8, JMHC.

46. Swett to Davis, May 24, 1875, DDFP.

47. See the letters of Nathan Smith Davis, Ralph N. Isham, James Stewart Jewell, Hosmer Allen Johnson, Richard J. Patterson, and Charles Gilman Smith to Ayer & Kales Law Firm, May 18, 1875, folder 24, box 2, IF.

48. Nathan Smith Davis to Ayer & Kales Law Firm, May 18, 1875, IF.

49. A. E. MacDonald, "Examination and Commitment of the Insane," 515; Orpheus Everts (superintendent at the Indiana State Hospital for the Insane), in "Insanity and Spiritualism" (interview), *Chicago Tribune*, Aug. 9, 1875, 3.

50. John Todd Stuart to Robert Lincoln, May 10, 1875, folder 26, box 2, IF; Elizabeth J. Todd Grimsley Brown to Robert Lincoln, May 19, 1875, folder 10, box 2, IF.

51. Stuart to Robert Lincoln, May 10, 1875, IF.

52. Davis to Swett, May 19, 1875, IF.

53. Ibid.

54. John Todd Stuart to Robert Lincoln, May 21, 1875, and Stuart to Leonard Swett, May 21, 1875, folder 26, box 2, IF.

55. Swett to Davis, May 24, 1875, DDFP.

56. Ibid.; Davis to Swett, May 19, 1875, IF.

57. Statement of Dr. Ralph N. Isham, May 18, 1875, Petition of Robert Lincoln to have Mary Lincoln declared insane, May 19, 1875, and Order to arrest Mary Lincoln, May 19, 1875, Cook County Court Documents, folder 33, box 2, IF.

58. James Rhodes and Dean Jauchius first espoused this theory in 1959, and it was subsequently picked up by numerous people, most prominently Jean Baker. Rhodes and Jauchius, *Trial of Mary Todd Lincoln*, 5; Schreiner, *Trials of Mrs. Lincoln*, 321; Baker, *Mary Todd Lincoln*, 321–22.

59. *Laws of the State of Illinois, Passed by the Sixteenth General Assembly, the Second Session, Commencing October 22, 1849* (Springfield, Ill.: Charles H. Lanphier, 1849), 98.

60. I. Ray, "American Legislation on Insanity," *American Journal of Insanity* 21 (July 1864): 21–56; Richard Dewey, "The Jury Law for Commitment of the Insane in Illinois (1867–1893), and Mrs. E. P. W. Packard, Its Author; also, Later Developments in Lunacy Legislation in Illinois," *American Journal of Insanity* 69 (Jan. 1913): 571–84; A. Wood Renton, "Comparative Lunacy Law," *Journal of the Society of Comparative Legislation*, n.s., 1, no. 2 (July 1899): 266–67.

61. Mrs. E. P. W. Packard, *Modern Persecution; or, Insane Asylums Unveiled*, 2 vols. (Hartford: Lockwood & Brainard, 1874), 1:51–63.

62. Ibid., 1:391.

63. *Packard v. Packard*, 27 FAM LQ 515 (1864).

64. "Legislation for Litigants: Changes in Practice in the Law Courts," *Chicago Tribune*, Mar. 2, 1867, 4; Dewey, "Jury Law for Commitment," 571–84; Albert Deutsch, *The Mentally Ill in America: A History of Their Care and Treatment from Colonial Times* (New York: Columbia University Press, 1946), 424–26; Friedman, *America's First Woman Lawyer*, 203–5; "Analysis of Legal and Medical Considerations in Commitment of the Mentally Ill," *Yale Law Journal* 56, no. 7 (Aug. 1947): 1192–93.

65. "Illinois Legislation regarding Hospitals for the Insane," *American Journal of Insanity* 26 (Oct. 1869): 204–29.

66. "Lunacy Law in Illinois," *American Journal of Insanity* 47 (Apr. 1891): 584–87.

67. Foster Pratt, "Insane Patients and Their Legal Relations," *American Journal of Insanity* 35 (July 1878): 182–85.

68. Dewey, "Jury Law for Commitment," 581–82. A similar argument also was made in Deutsch, *Mentally Ill in America*, 437–39.

69. The report was made by Dr. Andrew McFarland, former superintendent of the Jacksonville State Mental Hospital, who would play a later role in Mary Lincoln's case. "Transactions of the Twenty-Third Meeting of the Illinois State Medical Society: 1873," *American Journal of Insanity* 31 (July 1874): 120–21.

70. Emphasis added. Leonard Swett to David Davis, Chicago, May 24, 1875, folder A-73, box 5, DDFP.

71. They were not, however, her gender peers, since women were not allowed to serve on juries in the United States until the early twentieth century and the passage of the Nineteenth Amendment. For an excellent examination of female jury service, see Gretchen Ritter, "Jury Service and Women's Citizenship before and after the Nineteenth Amendment," *Law and History Review* 20, no. 3 (Fall 2002), http://www.historycooperative.org/journals/lhr/20.3/ritter.html.

72. The only contemporary firsthand account of Mary's conveyance to court is known through the correspondence: Swett to Davis, May 24, 1875, DDFP. The *Chicago Times* carried an account nearly identical to Swett's letter to Davis, which leads one to conclude that they must have interviewed him. See "Insanity's Freaks," *Chicago Times*, May 21, 1875, clipping in folder 31, box 2, IF.

73. Had Mary but known what was said in the pretrial discussions of Robert and his advisers, she might not have resented Swett so much for his appearance at her room. Robert, in fact, wanted to follow the law and send sheriff's deputies to his mother's room to arrest her and bring her to court in handcuffs. Swett convinced him that would be an error and instead went himself. "He took upon himself a most painful task and by his marvelous fairness and kindness accomplished it and saved me from the commission of a horrible blunder," Robert later admitted to John Hay. Robert Lincoln to John Hay, Chicago, June 6, 1875, JMHC; "Insanity's Freaks," *Chicago Times*, May 21, 1875.

74. Brown said she received Robert's telegram of May 18 too late to make the journey from Springfield to Chicago in time for the trial on May 19, while Stuart said he had to attend a meeting of the Penitentiary and State House Boards dealing with a problem that "My reputation was too much involved in . . . for me to leave." He added, moreover, "I did not think I could be of any service" at the trial. Both excuses seem rather thin. Most likely, while Brown and Stuart both considered Mary insane, neither consented to her commitment and probably did not want to publicly participate in the action. Elizabeth J. Todd Grimsley Brown to Robert Lincoln, May 19, 1875, folder 10, box 2, IF; John Todd Stuart to Robert Lincoln, May 21, 1875, and Stuart to Leonard Swett, May 21, 1875, folder 26, box 2, IF; "Mrs. Lincoln and Her Friends," *Illinois State Journal*, May 28, 1875, 2.

75. Swett to Davis, May 24, 1875, DDFP.

76. Baker, *Mary Todd Lincoln*, 322.

77. "Clouded Reason," *Chicago Tribune*, May 20, 1875, 1.

78. Ibid.; "Mrs. Lincoln: The Widow," *Chicago Inter Ocean*, May 20, 1875, 1.

79. Swett to Davis, May 24, 1875, DDFP.

80. Robert Lincoln to Elizabeth Edwards, Aug. 7, 1875, in LB, 1:133–39, microfilm reel 1; Swett to Davis, May 24, 1875, DDFP.

81. Robert Lincoln to Le Grand Van Valkenburgh, May 26, 1913, Robert Lincoln Papers, ALPL.

82. Robert Lincoln to Elizabeth Edwards, Aug. 7, 1875, LB.

83. Ninian Edwards to Robert Lincoln, Springfield, Ill., Jan. 14 and 15, 1876, folder 17, box 2, IF; Elizabeth Edwards to Robert Lincoln, Springfield, Jan. 16, 1876, folder 16, box 2, IF.

84. "A Sad Revelation," *Chicago Times*, May 20, 1875, 2; "Current Events," *New York Evangelist*, May 27, 1875, 8; untitled article, *Chicago Tribune*, Aug. 28, 1875, 8.

85. "Insane Delusions: Can a Belief in Spiritualism Be Regarded as Such?" *New York Times*, May 23, 1875, 10; "The Legal View of Spiritualism," *New York Times*, Jan. 13, 1882, 1.

86. Dr. Orpheus Everts, superintendent at the Indiana State Hospital for the Insane, said belief in Spiritualism was as sane as belief in any religion; but for a person to honestly believe they saw, felt, and spoke with dead spirits while practicing Spiritualism—or, for that matter, saw, felt, or spoke with Jesus while practicing Christianity—was an abnormal performance of sensory functions, indicating derangement. "Insanity and Spiritualism," *Chicago Tribune*, Aug. 9, 1875, 3. See also "Spiritualistic Madness," *American Journal of Insanity* 33 (Jan. 1877): 441–42. Leading neurologist Dr. W. A. Hammond, on the other hand, wrote a book called *Spiritualism and Allied Causes and Conditions of Nervous Derangement*, in which he declared that Spiritualism was both a cause of insanity and a manifestation of mental unsoundness; while Dr. R. Frederic Marvin, professor of psychological medicine and medical jurisprudence at the New York Free Medical College for Women, declared Spiritualism a symptom of "mediomania," a form of derangement. Evans, *Mrs. Abraham Lincoln*, 316; Braude, *Radical Spirits*, 158–59.

87. The preponderance of evidence points to Mary's silence and was reported as such in the *Tribune* and the *Inter Ocean* and in Swett's May 24 letter to David Davis, in which he wrote, "In the court room she never spoke." The *Chicago Times*, however, reported that Mary often consulted with her attorney during the trial, and that at one point, when a witness called her insane, she audibly asked the judge if witnesses were allowed to offer such a judgment.

88. "Mrs. Lincoln: The Widow," *Chicago Inter Ocean*, May 20, 1875, 1. The *Chicago Tribune* of the same day quotes Mary as saying, "Robert, I did not think you would do this."

89. The *Inter Ocean* reported the jury deliberating for "ten minutes," while the *Tribune* reported "but a few minutes." The *Chicago Times* did not give a time. Verdict of Jury Declaring Mary Lincoln Insane, May 19, 1875, Cook County Court Documents, folder 33, box 2, IF.

90. Appointment of Robert T. Lincoln as Conservator for Estate of Mary Lincoln, June 14, 1875, Cook County Court Documents, folder 33, box 2, IF.

91. Lyman J. Gage to William E. Barton, Point Loma, Calif., Jan. 20, 1921, in WEBS, vol. 47. I am indebted to Dr. Norbert Hirschhorn for directing me to this source, which was particularly elusive.

92. "Clouded Reason," *Chicago Tribune*, May 20, 1875, 1; "Mrs. Lincoln: The Widow," *Chicago Inter Ocean*, May 20, 1875, 1. The *Chicago Times* did not comment on Robert's emotional state.

93. "Mrs. Lincoln's Insanity," *Chicago Times*, May 23, 1875, 6.

94. "Mrs. Lincoln: The Widow," *Chicago Inter Ocean*, May 20, 1875, 1.

95. Ibid.; "Mrs. Lincoln Insane," *Illinois State Journal*, May 21, 1875.

96. State asylums were publicly funded, while Robert paid an average of $170 per month for Mary's care at Bellevue Sanitarium. Robert's expense records show he spent approximately $750 total (including travel, storage, and personal attendant expenses) to Bellevue from May through October. He paid these bills from Mary's estate, not his own. Robert Lincoln expense reports, folders 30 and 33, box 2, IF; copy also in WEBS, vol. 47.

97. "Clouded Reason," *Chicago Tribune*, May 20, 1875, 1.

98. "Mrs. Lincoln: The Widow," *Chicago Inter Ocean*, May 20, 1875, 1.

99. Robert Lincoln expense reports, IF; copy also in WEBS, vol. 47.

100. Final Report of Administrator to Judge of the County Court, Nov. 6, 1884, FTC; Robert Lincoln to David Davis, Chicago, Nov. 16, 1875, folder 2, box 2, IF, and in folder A-109, box 7, DDFP; Robert Lincoln to Elizabeth Edwards, May 17, 1876, in LB, 1:168–69, microfilm reel 1, and in folder 3, box 2, IF.

5. MRS. LINCOLN ADMITTED TODAY

1. American Psychiatric Association, *Diagnostic and Statistical Manual of Mental Disorders*, 4th ed., text revision (Washington, D.C.: American Psychiatric Association, 2000).

2. I am indebted to James S. Brust, M.D., for helping me understand this issue more clearly, both in general and in regard to Mary Lincoln.

3. Charles B. Strozier, "The Psychology of Mary Todd Lincoln," *Psychohistory Review* 17, no. 1 (1988): 15.

4. Untitled editorial, *Chicago Inter Ocean*, May 20, 1875, 4; untitled editorial, *Chicago Tribune*, May 20, 1875, 4; "Mrs. Lincoln Insane," *New York Tribune*, May 20, 1875, 12; "Mrs. Abraham Lincoln," *New York Times*, May 20, 1875, 1; "The Case of Mrs. Lincoln," *Chicago Tribune*, May 21, 1875, 4; "Mrs. Lincoln's Sad Condition," *Boston Globe*, May 25, 1875, 2; "Personal," *New York Observer and Chronicle*, May 27, 1875, 166.

5. Untitled editorial, *Chicago Tribune*, May 20, 1875, 4.

6. Untitled editorial, *Chicago Inter Ocean*, May 20, 1875, 4.

7. "Insanity's Freaks," *Chicago Times*, May 21, 1875, clipping in folder 31, box 2, IF.

8. "Mrs. Lincoln's Insanity," *Chicago Times*, May 23, 1875, 6.

9. John Hay worked mainly as an editorial writer for the Republican-leaning *Tribune* from 1870 to mid-1875. The generous sympathy of his editorial is interesting, given that he never got along with Mary Lincoln in the White House. However, Hay was a lifelong friend of Robert Lincoln, and it is only from one of Robert's letters that it is known Hay wrote the May 22, 1875, editorial. Robert Lincoln to John Hay, June 6, 1875, microfilm reel 8, JMHC. For Hay as journalist, see William Roscoe Thayer, *The Life of John Hay*, 2 vols. (Boston: Houghton Mifflin, 1929), 1:329–52; Richard Kluger, *The Paper: The Life and Death of the New York Herald Tribune* (New York: Alfred A. Knopf, 1986), 153–58.

10. "President Lincoln's Widow," *New York Tribune*, May 22, 1875, 6.

11. "Mrs. Lincoln's Insanity," *Chicago Times*, May 23, 1875, 6.

12. "The Case of Mrs. Lincoln," *Chicago Tribune*, May 21, 1875, 4. The article's statements regarding the trial, its aftermath, and Mary's own behavior align completely with Swett's and Arnold's writings on the subject. See Leonard Swett to David Davis, May 24, 1875, folder A-73, box 5, DDFP; and Arnold, *Life of Abraham Lincoln*, 439.

13. John Todd Stuart to Robert Lincoln, May 21, 1875, folder 26, box 2, IF. Stuart also told Leonard Swett, "I am glad it is over and so well done." Stuart to Swett, May 21, 1875, folder 26, box 2, IF.

14. David Davis to Robert Lincoln, May 23, 1875, folder 15, box 2, IF.

15. Orville H. Browning, interview by John G. Nicolay, June 17, 1875, in Burlingame, *Oral History of Abraham Lincoln*, 3.

16. Unidentified newspaper clipping, n.d., John Hay Scrapbook: Poems and Poetry Reviews, JMHC.

17. Gideon Welles to Robert Lincoln, Hartford, July 5, 1875, enclosed in Robert Lincoln to John G. Nicolay, Chicago, Nov. 11, 1876, quoted in Burlingame, *Inner World of Abraham Lincoln*, 297. The archivist was unable to locate this letter in the repository specified by Burlingame; however, I do not doubt its authenticity, as I found Robert's response to it: Robert Lincoln to Welles, Chicago, July 16, 1875, folder 9, box 3, Gideon Welles Papers, Connecticut Historical Society.

18. Emphasis in original. Elizabeth J. Todd Grimsley Brown to Robert Lincoln, May 19, 1875, folder 10, box 2, IF.

19. William Herndon to Jesse Weik, Springfield, Ill., Jan. 2, 1882, frames 1753–54, microfilm reel 9, group 4, H-WC.

20. Helen Nicolay, *Lincoln's Secretary: The Biography of John G. Nicolay* (New York: Longmans, Green, 1949), 193.

21. Albert S. Edwards to Samuel Inglis, Springfield, Feb. 20, 1897, SC 923, Albert S. Edwards Papers, Manuscript Division, ALPL.

22. Interviews with Mrs. John Todd Stuart and Mrs. B. S. Edwards, in *Chicago Tribune*, Feb. 12, 1900, John G. Nicolay Papers, LC.

23. Badeau, *Grant in Peace*, 355–56. A similar, yet differently worded, sentiment was printed in "Adam Badeau's Letter: A History of the Insanity of Mrs. Lincoln," *Chicago Tribune*, Jan. 17, 1887, 10.

24. Robert Lincoln to John Hay, June 6, 1875, microfilm reel 8, JMHC.

25. Robert Lincoln to Mrs. James H. (Sally) Orne, June 1, 1875, folder 2, Robert Lincoln Papers, Chicago History Museum. This letter is also printed in full in Helm, *True Story of Mary*, 295–96.

26. Sally Orne to Robert Lincoln, Aug. 8, 1875, folder 2, Robert Lincoln Papers, Chicago History Museum. This letter is also printed in full in Helm, *True Story of Mary*, 297–98.

27. "Insanity's Freaks," *Chicago Times*, May 21, 1875, clipping in folder 31, box 2, IF; "Mrs. Lincoln's Sad Condition," *Boston Globe*, May 25, 1875, 2; "Mrs. Lincoln and Her Friends," *Illinois State Journal*, May 28, 1875, 2.

28. Robert Lincoln to John Hay, June 6, 1875, JMHC.

29. Court of Cook County, Letters of Conservatorship, Estate of Mary Lincoln, June 14, 1875, folder 30, box 2, IF; photostats in "The Insanity of Mary Lincoln," WEBS, 47:13–16.

30. Inventory of Real and Personal Estate of Mary Lincoln, May 19, 1875, folder 33, box 2, IF; photostats in WEBS, 47:18–22.

31. Leonard Swett to David Davis, Chicago, May 24, 1875, folder A-73, box 5, DDFP.

32. Ibid.; "A Mind Diseased: The Evidence of Mrs. Lincoln's Mental Aberration," *Illinois State Journal*, May 29, 1875, 2; "Insanity's Freaks," *Chicago Times*, May 21, 1875, clipping in folder 31, box 2, IF.

33. "Mrs. Lincoln," *Illinois State Journal*, May 24, 1875; "A Mind Diseased," *Illinois State Journal*, May 29, 1875, 2.

34. "A Mind Diseased," *Illinois State Journal*, May 29, 1875, 2.

35. Swett to Davis, May 24, 1875, DDFP.

36. Ibid.; "Mrs. Lincoln: Attempt at Suicide," *Chicago Tribune*, May 21, 1875, 8; "Insanity's Freaks," *Chicago Times*, May 21, 1875; "Mrs. Lincoln," *Illinois State Journal*, May 24, 1875. The suicide attempt also was reported in an untitled article, *Chicago Inter Ocean*, May 21, 1875, 4; "Crime: Mrs. Lincoln Makes Persistent Effort to Commit Suicide," *Illinois State Journal*, May 21, 1875; and "Mrs. Lincoln Attempts Suicide," *Atlanta Constitution*, May 22, 1875, 1.

37. Stories diverge on this point: Swett reported two ounces, the *Inter Ocean* reported three ounces, and the *Chicago Times* reported four ounces—two of laudanum and two of camphor.

38. Stories diverge on this point as well: Swett and the *Chicago Times* both reported the mixture would be ready in ten minutes, while both the *Chicago Tribune* and the *Inter Ocean* reported thirty minutes.

39. The *Inter Ocean* reported that the pharmacist, Mr. Smith, told Mary his stock of laudanum had run out. No other reports explain Mr. Smith's excuse for refusing Mary's request.

40. All three newspapers, the *Tribune*, *Times* and *Inter Ocean*, agreed on this point.

41. Swett to Davis, May 24, 1875, DDFP.

42. "Insanity's Freaks," *Chicago Times*, May 21, 1875, clipping in folder 31, box 2, IF.

43. "Mrs. Lincoln," from the *Chicago Inter Ocean,* reprinted in *Illinois State Journal*, May 24, 1875.

44. "President Lincoln's Widow," *New York Tribune*, May 22, 1875, 6. Robert Lincoln's lack of knowledge about—and therefore lack of complicity with—the editorial is evident in that he only saw the piece after a friend gave him a copy. Robert Lincoln to John Hay, June 6, 1875, microfilm reel 8, JMHC.

45. Once again, I am indebted to James S. Brust, M.D., for his assistance in helping me understand suicide in general and specifically in regard to Mary Lincoln.

46. Then as now, mentally ill people sometimes claimed they were wrongfully hospitalized rather than acknowledge their illness because they knew that people who suffer from psychiatric illnesses are often judged negatively by society. See "Insanity and Its Treatment," *Scribner's Monthly* 12, no. 5 (Sept. 1876): 643–44; and Deutsch, *Mentally Ill in America*, 417, 424–26.

47. For the posttraumatic stress theory, see Norbert Hirschhorn and Robert G. Feldman, "Mary Lincoln's Final Illness: A Medical and Historical Reappraisal," *Journal of the History of Medicine and Allied Sciences* 54, no. 4 (1999): 525.

48. Jean Baker called the story a fiction by Robert Lincoln planted in the *Inter Ocean*, a newspaper owned by his former law partner, to "exculpate his filial treachery." Baker, *Mary Todd Lincoln*, 326. The implications of the minor discrepancies in each newspaper report were revealed to me by reading Hirschhorn, "Mary Lincoln's 'Suicide Attempt,'" 95.

49. R. J. Patterson, "Mrs. Abraham Lincoln," *Chicago Tribune*, Aug. 29, 1875, 16.

50. Hirschhorn, "Mary Lincoln's 'Suicide Attempt,'" 97.

51. "Mrs. Lincoln," *Illinois State Journal*, May 24, 1875.

52. Robert Lincoln to Leonard Swett, May 25, 1884, folder 3, box 2, IF.

53. Swett to Davis, Chicago, May 24, 1875, DDFP.

54. "Mrs. Lincoln," *Illinois State Journal*, May 24, 1875.

55. Ross, "Mary Todd Lincoln," 10. Ross's article is based on the Bellevue daily Patient Progress Reports, which Ross owns. Therefore, much of this information can be found only in his article.

56. Descriptions based on two Bellevue Place Sanitarium advertising brochures, one undated (2 pages), and one dated 1895 (15 pages), Batavia Historical Society, Batavia, Ill.; "Mrs. Lincoln: A Visit to Her by 'The Post and Mail' Correspondent: How She Passes the Time at Dr. Patterson's Retreat," *Chicago Post and Mail*, July 13, 1875, clipping in PFP.

57. Bellevue Place Sanitarium advertising brochures, Batavia Historical Society; "Mrs. Lincoln: A Visit to Her," *Chicago Post and Mail*, July 13, 1875, clipping in PFP.

58. "Mrs. Lincoln: A Visit to Her," *Chicago Post and Mail*, July 13, 1875, clipping in PFP; Ross, "Mary Todd Lincoln," 10.

59. Ross, "Mary Todd Lincoln," 11. For one nurse's recollections of Mary Lincoln at Bellevue, see Lutz White, "Now and Then: Before the Tardy Bell Rings," *Aurora (Ill.) Beacon-News*, Dec. 25, 1932, 6.

60. "Mrs. Lincoln: A Visit to Her," *Chicago Post and Mail*, July 13, 1875, clipping in PFP.

61. Robert Lincoln to Mason B. Loomis, n.d., folder 37, box 2, IF.

62. Patterson, "Mrs. Abraham Lincoln," *Chicago Tribune*, Aug. 29, 1875, 16; Robert Lincoln to Elizabeth Edwards, Aug. 7, 1875, in LB, 1:135, microfilm reel 1; Lutz White, "Now and Then: Before the Tardy Bell Rings," *Aurora (Ill.) Beacon-News*, Jan. 1, 1933, 6.

63. Patterson, "Mrs. Abraham Lincoln," *Chicago Tribune*, Aug. 29, 1875, 16; Robert Lincoln to Elizabeth Edwards, Chicago, Jan. 17, 1876, in LB, 3:382–83, microfilm reel 4; also in folder 1, box 2, IF.

64. Robert Lincoln to Loomis, n.d., IF; Robert Lincoln to Elizabeth Edwards, Aug. 7, 1875, LB; "Mrs. Lincoln: A Visit to Her," *Chicago Post and Mail*, July 13, 1875, clipping in PFP. For an interesting reminiscence of Mary Lincoln shopping in the nearby town of Aurora while a patient at Bellevue, see Lutz White, "Now and Then: Before the Tardy Bell Rings," *Aurora (Ill.) Beacon-News*, Dec. 18, 1932, 6.

65. Patterson, "Mrs. Abraham Lincoln," *Chicago Tribune*, Aug. 29, 1875, 16.

66. Robert Lincoln to Loomis, n.d., IF; Robert Lincoln to Mrs. James H. (Sally) Orne, June 1, 1875, Chicago History Museum; "Mrs. Lincoln: A Visit to Her," *Chicago Post and Mail*, July 13, 1875, clipping in PFP.

67. "Patient Progress Reports for Bellevue Place," 26, transcribed in Ross, "Mary Todd Lincoln," 26.

68. "Patient Progress Reports," 26–36, transcribed in Ross, "Mary Todd Lincoln," 26–28. A brief description of her first month can also be found in "Mrs. Lincoln: A Visit to Her," *Chicago Post and Mail*, July 13, 1875, clipping in PFP.

69. "Patient Progress Reports," 30, 37, transcribed in Ross, "Mary Todd Lincoln," 27, 28.

70. Robert Lincoln to John Hay, 6 June 1875, JMHC.

71. "Patient Progress Reports," 31, transcribed in Ross, "Mary Todd Lincoln," 27.

72. Robert kept at least three examples of such correspondence: J. M. Gibson to Robert Lincoln, May 21, 1875, L. M. McGinnis to Robert Lincoln, May 22, 1875, and Samuels (?) to Robert Lincoln, April 25, 1876, folders 18, 21, and 25, box 2, IF.

73. Robert Lincoln to John Hay, June 6, 1875, JMHC.

74. Ibid.

75. Editorial, *New York Tribune*, June 14, 1875, 6. Interestingly, and previously unrealized, this article is a verbatim reprint of Robert Lincoln to Loomis, n.d., IF. Loomis was a county judge and member of the Chicago City Council. No connection between him and the *Tribune* could be found.

76. "Mrs. Lincoln: A Visit to Her," *Chicago Post and Mail*, July 13, 1875, clipping in PFP.

77. Ibid.

78. Ibid.; "Patient Progress Reports," 40, transcribed in Ross, "Mary Todd Lincoln," 28.

79. "Mrs. Lincoln: A Visit to Her." Parts of the *Post and Mail* article also were reprinted in Roberta Campbell, "Reporter Visits with Mrs. Lincoln," *Batavia Herald*, Feb. 9, 1983, clipping in Batavia Historical Society.

80. It should be noted that inattention to hygiene, dress, and grooming can fit with both severe depression and psychotic illness. MacDonald, "Examination and Commitment of the Insane," 519–20.

81. "Mrs. Lincoln: A Visit to Her," *Chicago Post and Mail*, July 13, 1875, clipping in PFP.

82. Ibid.

83. Ibid.; "The Condition of Mrs. Lincoln: She Is Not Improving," *Boston Globe*, July 14, 1875, 5.

84. "Patient Progress Reports," 40, transcribed in Ross, "Mary Todd Lincoln," 28.

85. "Mrs. Lincoln: A Visit to Her," *Chicago Post and Mail*, July 13, 1875, clipping in PFP.

6. IT DOES NOT APPEAR THAT GOD IS GOOD

1. Friedman, *America's First Woman Lawyer*, 11.

2. Robert Lincoln to Sally Orne, Chicago, June 1, 1875, folder 5, box 2, IF, and in folder 2, Robert Lincoln Papers, Chicago History Museum; Robert Lincoln to John Hay, Chicago, June 6, 1875, microfilm reel 8, JMHC.

3. "Patient Progress Reports," 43, transcribed in Ross, "Mary Todd Lincoln," 29. On Mary's attitude toward her sister, see Robert Lincoln to Elizabeth Edwards, Aug. 7, 1875, in LB, 1:133, microfilm reel 1.

4. At nineteen, Elizabeth married Ninian Wirt Edwards, son of the former Illinois governor, and moved to Springfield, Ill. Ninian Edwards was a lawyer, businessman, and politician, and his home became the center of a coterie of Springfield's wealthiest, most fashionable, and influential people. Even from Springfield, Elizabeth continued her maternal disposition by inviting her younger sisters into her home and playing matchmaker for them. Her social soirees facilitated the meetings and marriages of Frances Todd to Dr. William Wallace, Ann Todd to Clark M. Smith, and Mary Todd to Abraham Lincoln (although the Edwardses objected to Lincoln as a suitable match for Mary). In 1862, after the death of Willie Lincoln, Elizabeth Edwards, again as a maternal comforter, spent two months at the White House consoling Mary. Elizabeth Edwards, interview by William Herndon, Jan. 10, 1866, 2:220–26, LN 2408, Ward Hill Lamon Papers, Huntington Library.

5. President Lincoln had appointed Democrat Ninian W. Edwards, Elizabeth's husband, as an Army commissary of subsistence in Springfield, Ill., in 1861. By 1863, Lincoln's local Republican friends were openly and vociferously accusing Edwards of corruption. Lincoln appears to have kept his faith in his brother-in-law's honesty, but

did transfer him to Chicago. See John Nicolay to Abraham Lincoln, Oct. 21, 1861, in Michael Burlingame, ed., *With Lincoln in the White House: Letters, Memoranda, and Other Writings of John G. Nicolay, 1860–1865* (Carbondale: Southern Illinois University Press, 2000), 60–61; Ozias M. Hatch to Lincoln, Springfield, May 25, 1863, Shelby M. Cullom to Lincoln, May 25, 1863, Jacob Bunn to Lincoln, May 25, 1863, Ninian W. Edwards to Lincoln, June 6, 1863, and Edwards to Edward Bates, June 6 and 18, 1863, Abraham Lincoln Papers, LC, transcribed and annotated by the Lincoln Studies Center, Knox College, Galesburg, Ill., http://memory.loc. gov/ammem/alhtml/alhome.html; Lincoln to Jesse K. Dubois and others, May 29, 1863, and Lincoln to Edward L. Baker, June 15, 1863, in Basler, *Collected Works*, 6:237–38, 275–76.

6. Robert Lincoln to Elizabeth Edwards, Aug. 7, 1875, LB, 1:138, microfilm reel 1; Robert Lincoln to David Davis, Chicago, Nov. 16, 1875, folder 2, box 2, IF, and folder A-109, box 7, DDFP.

7. "Patient Progress Reports," 46, transcribed in Ross, "Mary Todd Lincoln," 30.

8. Robert Lincoln to Elizabeth Edwards, Aug. 7, 1875, LB, 1:138, microfilm reel 1; "Patient Progress Reports," 47, transcribed in Ross, "Mary Todd Lincoln," 30.

9. See Neely and McMurtry, *Insanity File*, 58; Friedman, *America's First Woman Lawyer*, 51; and Schreiner, *Trials of Mrs. Lincoln*, 149.

10. Emphasis in original. Mary Lincoln to James Bradwell, Batavia, Ill., July 28, 1875, FTC.

11. "Wilbur F. Storey," in *Biographical Sketches*, 133–40.

12. Neely and McMurtry, *Insanity File*, 60; Baker, *Mary Todd Lincoln*, 339–40; Friedman, *America's First Woman Lawyer*, 54; Schreiner, *Trials of Mrs. Lincoln*, 158–59.

13. Emphasis in original. "Patient Progress Reports," 47, transcribed in Ross, "Mary Todd Lincoln," 30.

14. "Patient Progress Reports," 47, transcribed in Ross, "Mary Todd Lincoln," 31.

15. "Patient Progress Reports," 48, transcribed in Ross, "Mary Todd Lincoln," 31.

16. Ibid.

17. James Bradwell to John Todd Stuart, Chicago, July 30, 1875, in Pritchard, "Dark Days," chap. 3, p. 12, FTC.

18. Emphasis in original. Myra Bradwell to Elizabeth Edwards, Chicago, July 30, 1875, in ibid., 13, FTC.

19. Ibid. While James Bradwell suggested a "visit" to Springfield, Myra Bradwell was more cryptic. She simply wrote that Mary "expresses a wish to return with you to Springfield."

20. Elizabeth Edwards to Myra Bradwell, Springfield, Aug. 3, 1875, FTC.

21. Mary Lincoln to Myra Bradwell, Batavia, Ill., Aug. 2, 1875, in Pritchard, "Dark Days," chap. 4, pp. 2–4, FTC.

22. Emphasis in original. Mary Lincoln to Myra Bradwell, Batavia, Ill., Wednesday, Aug. [2?], 1875, in ibid., pp. 4–5, FTC.

23. "Patient Progress Reports," 51, transcribed in Ross, "Mary Todd Lincoln," 32.

24. Robert Lincoln to Elizabeth Edwards, Aug. 7, 1875, LB, 1:133–34, microfilm reel 1.

25. Ibid., 137.

26. Ibid.

27. Ibid., 136.

28. Dr. R. J. Patterson to Myra Bradwell, Batavia, Ill., Aug. 9, 1875, folder 23, box 2, IF.

29. "Patient Progress Reports," 52, transcribed in Ross, "Mary Todd Lincoln," 32.

30. "Franc B. Wilkie," in *Biographical Sketches*, 580–81.

31. Ibid.

32. "Patient Progress Reports," 55, transcribed in Ross, "Mary Todd Lincoln," 33.

33. Patterson to Myra Bradwell, Aug. 9, 1875, IF.

34. "Patient Progress Reports," 55, transcribed in Ross, "Mary Todd Lincoln," 33.

35. Dr. R. J. Patterson to Robert Lincoln, Batavia, Ill., Aug. 9, 1875, folder 23, box 2, IF.

36. Emphasis in original. Robert Lincoln to Elizabeth Edwards, Aug. 10, 1875, in LB, 1:141–42, microfilm reel 1.

37. Myra Bradwell to Elizabeth Edwards, Chicago, Aug. 11, 1875, in Pritchard, "Dark Days," chap. 4, pp. 8–9, FTC.

38. Elizabeth Edwards to Robert Lincoln, Springfield, Aug. 11, 1875, folder 16, box 2, IF.

39. Emphasis in original. Elizabeth Edwards to Robert Lincoln, Springfield, Aug. 12, 1875, ibid.

40. Elizabeth Edwards to Robert Lincoln, Springfield, Aug. 14, 1875, ibid.

41. Elizabeth Edwards to Robert Lincoln, Springfield, Aug. 13, 1875, ibid.

42. See Dr. R. J. Patterson to Robert Lincoln, Batavia, Ill., Aug. 17, 1875, folder 23, box 2, IF.

43. Neely and McMurtry, *Insanity File*, 63; Friedman, *America's First Woman Lawyer*, 58; Baker, *Mary Todd Lincoln*, 340.

44. Robert Lincoln to Myra Bradwell, Chicago, Aug. 14, 1875, folder 1, box 2, IF, and in LB, 1:143–44, microfilm reel 1, and in FTC.

45. Ibid.

46. Emphasis in original. Mary Lincoln to James Bradwell, Aug. 8, 1875, FTC.

47. Emphasis in original. Mary Lincoln to Myra Bradwell, Friday, Aug. [8?], 1875, FTC.

48. Mary Lincoln to Myra Bradwell, Batavia, Ill., Saturday, Aug. 1875, FTC.

49. "Patient Progress Reports," 55, transcribed in Ross, "Mary Todd Lincoln," 33.

50. "Patient Progress Reports," 56, transcribed in Ross, "Mary Todd Lincoln," 33.

51. Ibid. This paper was the will James Bradwell had drawn for her.

52. Robert Lincoln to Mary Lincoln, Chicago, Aug. 15, 1875, folder 1, box 2, IF.

53. Neely and McMurtry, *Insanity File*, 54.

54. Emphasis in original. Elizabeth Edwards to Robert Lincoln, Springfield, Aug. 17, 1875, folder 16, box 2, IF.

55. Dr. R. J. Patterson to Robert Lincoln, Aug. 17, 1875, IF.

56. "Patient Progress Reports," 57, transcribed in Ross, "Mary Todd Lincoln," 34.

57. Robert Lincoln to Dr. Richard J. Patterson (telegram), Rye Beach, N.H., n.d., folder 37, box 2, IF. Based upon the other evidence in the Insanity File, the logical date for this telegram is August 17—the same day Robert received Dr. Patterson's letter asking whether he should release Mary Lincoln, and the day before Patterson wrote to Judge Bradwell that he and his wife would no longer be allowed to visit Mary. Robert did telegram his aunt to tell her to "do nothing whatever about proposed visit until you receive my letter of today." Robert Lincoln to Mrs. N. W. Edwards (telegram), Rye Beach, N.H., Aug. 23, 1875, folder 17, box 2, IF.

58. Dr. R. J. Patterson to James Bradwell, Batavia, Ill., Aug. 18, 1875, folder 23, box 2, IF, and in FTC.

59. James B. Bradwell to Dr. R. J. Patterson, Chicago, Aug. 19, 1875, published in "Mrs. Abraham Lincoln: Correspondence of Dr. Patterson and Judge Bradwell," *Chicago Tribune*, Aug. 31, 1875, 8. The original letter has not been found.

60. "Patient Progress Reports," 58, transcribed in Ross, "Mary Todd Lincoln," 34.

7. NO MORE INSANE THAN I AM

1. *Chicago Post and Mail*, Aug. 21, 1875, quoted in "Mrs. Lincoln: Startling Interview upon Her Case with Judge Bradwell," *Chicago Post and Mail*, Aug. 23, 1875, clipping, folder 31, box 2, IF.

2. "Personal," *Chicago Tribune*, Aug. 22, 1875, 5.

3. "Mrs. Lincoln: Startling Interview," *Chicago Post and Mail*, Aug. 23, 1875, clipping in IF.

4. Ibid.

5. Robert served on Grant's staff in early 1865 during the Civil War. In later years, Grant always spoke highly of Robert and encouraged the younger Lincoln's appointment to President-elect James A. Garfield's presidential cabinet.

6. "Reason Restored: Mrs. Lincoln Will Soon Return from Her Brief Visit to the Insane Asylum," *Chicago Times*, Aug. 24, 1875, 4.

7. Ibid. Ironically, these statements could be regarded as evidence that her time at Bellevue was actually benefiting Mary Lincoln and had restored her health, even though she refused to admit it.

8. Ibid.

9. Ibid.

10. Editorial, *Chicago Times*, Aug. 24, 1875, 4.

11. "Mrs. Lincoln," *Springfield Journal*, Aug. 25, 1875, clipping, PFP

12. "Mrs. Abraham Lincoln," *Boston Globe*, Aug. 25, 1875, 1.

13. Untitled article, *Chicago Tribune*, Aug. 28, 1875, 8.

14. "Mrs. Lincoln," unidentified newspaper clipping, PFP.

15. *St. Louis Republican*, quoted in untitled article, *Chicago Tribune*, Aug. 28, 1875, 8.

16. Dr. R. J. Patterson to Robert Lincoln, Batavia, Ill., Aug. 20, 1875, folder 23, box 2, IF.

17. "Mrs. Abraham Lincoln: What Her Pastor, Prof. Swing, Says about Her Insanity," *Chicago Times*, Aug. 29, 1875, 1.

18. Editorial, *Chicago Times*, Aug. 30, 1875, 4.

19. R. J. Patterson, "Mrs. Abraham Lincoln," *Chicago Tribune*, Aug. 29, 1875, 16; "Poor Mrs. Lincoln," *Boston Globe*, Aug. 30, 1875, 1.

20. "Mrs. Abraham Lincoln: Correspondence of Dr. Patterson and Judge Bradwell," *Chicago Tribune*, Aug. 31, 1875, 8.

21. "Mrs. Lincoln: Is the Widow of President Lincoln a Prisoner?" *Chicago Morning Courier*, Sept. 4, 1875, clipping, PFP.

22. Emphasis in original. Ibid.

23. Ibid.

24. Ibid.

25. Argus Eye, letter to the editor, Sept. 4, 1875, and "Mrs. Lincoln's Friends Not Allowed to See Her," Sept. 4, 1875, unidentified newspaper clippings, PFP.

26. Robert Lincoln to Dr. R. J. Patterson, Sept. 2, 1875, folder 3, box 2, IF, and in LB, 3:349, microfilm reel 4.

27. Robert received his aunt's letter saying she would accept her sister as a houseguest not long after he arrived in New Hampshire.

28. Willard L. King to John S. Goff, Chicago, June 6, 1958, John Goff Papers, Friends of Hildene, Inc., Manchester, Vt.

29. For theories that Myra Bradwell had bested Robert Lincoln, see Baker, *Mary Todd Lincoln*, 341; and Friedman, *America's First Woman Lawyer*, 67.

30. Dr. R. J. Patterson to Robert Lincoln, Batavia, Ill., Sept. 7, 1875, folder 23, box 2, IF.

31. McFarland was the physician responsible for the commitment of Elizabeth Packard in 1860.

32. Robert Lincoln to Dr. Andrew McFarland, Sept. 4, 1875, in LB, 1:145–46, microfilm reel 1; photocopy in folder 3, box 2, IF. This letter was annotated at the top, "Letter exactly the same as this written to A. J. McDill, supt. State asylum for the insane, Madison, Wisconsin."

33. Dr. A .J. McDill to Robert Lincoln, Sept. 6, 1875, folder 19, box 2, IF; Robert Lincoln to McDill, Sept. 9, 1875, folder 3, box 2, IF; also in LB, 1:149, microfilm reel 1.

34. Dr. Andrew McFarland to Robert Lincoln, Sept. 8, 1875, folder 20, box 2, IF.

35. Robert Lincoln to Dr. R. J. Patterson, Chicago, Sept. 9, 1875, in LB, 1:147–48, microfilm reel 1; and photocopy in folder 3, box 2, IF.

36. Dr. Andrew McFarland to Robert Lincoln, Sept. 10 and 11, 1875, folder 20, box 2, IF.

37. This statement was based on the recollection of Eleanor Gridley, a close friend of the Bradwells, in Pritchard, "Dark Days," chap. 6, p. 10, FTC.

38. "Mrs. Lincoln," *Chicago Tribune*, Sept. 12, 1875, 12.

39. Robert Lincoln to Elizabeth Edwards, Aug. 7, 1875, in LB, 1:138, microfilm reel 1.

40. Elizabeth Edwards to Robert Lincoln, Springfield, Sept. 15, 1875 (two separate letters with same date), folder 16, box 2, IF.

41. Ibid., letter beginning, "I received your letter this morning . . . ," in a separate enclosure labeled "private."

42. Evans, *Mrs. Abraham Lincoln*, 44–50; Temple, *Abraham Lincoln*, 384, 421; Robert Lincoln to Ben [Helm], Chicago, Jan. 11, 1909, Robert Lincoln Papers, Chicago History Museum; Elizabeth Edwards to Emily Todd Helm, Springfield, June 22, [?], Emily Todd Helm Papers, Kentucky Historical Society, Frankfort, Ky. Michael Burlingame's findings regarding mental illness in the Todd family will be included in his upcoming four-volume biography of Abraham Lincoln. I am indebted to him for sharing his findings with me.

43. No known evidence tells whether Patterson traveled to Springfield to examine Mary or Mary's professional attendant wrote to him. Dr. R. J. Patterson to Robert Lincoln, Batavia, Ill., Sept. 21, 1875, folder 23, box 2, IF. Patterson wrote in his letter that he was responding to Robert's letter of Sept. 20, but that letter was not included in either the Insanity File or the Towers Lincoln trunk.

44. Elizabeth Edwards to Robert Lincoln, Springfield, Sept. 22, 1875, folder 16, box 2, IF.

45. This monthlong gap is strange, since Robert kept every piece of correspondence concerning his mother in his personal Insanity File.

46. Robert Lincoln to David Davis, Chicago, Nov. 16, 1875, folder 2, box 2, IF; and folder A-109, box 7, DDFP.

47. Ibid.

48. Elizabeth Edwards to Robert Lincoln, Sept. 22, 1875, IF.

49. Elizabeth Edwards to Robert Lincoln, Springfield, Nov. 5, 1875, folder 16, box 2, IF.

50. Ibid.

51. Mary Lincoln to James Bradwell, Nov. 11, 1875, folder 2, box 1, IF.

52. Dr. R. J. Patterson to James Bradwell, Batavia, Ill., Aug. 18, 1875, folder 23, box 2, IF; and in FTC.

53. Elizabeth Edwards recommended that Mary write to Bradwell and request the will. As her letters to Robert show, Mary was growing increasingly obsessive about her property and resentful of him. Elizabeth probably thought that regaining possession of the will, which Mary had been wanting to do for at least three months, would alleviate her anxiety. Robert Lincoln to Davis, Nov. 16, 1875, DDFP.

54. Emphasis in original. Mary Lincoln to James Bradwell, Nov. 11, 1875, IF.

55. Mary Lincoln to James Bradwell, Dec. 1, 1875, folder 2, box 1, IF.

56. Bayne, *Tad Lincoln's Father*, 20.

57. Ninian Edwards to Robert Lincoln, Springfield, Dec. 18, 1875, folder 17, box 2, IF.

58. Ninian Edwards to Robert Lincoln, Springfield, Nov. 17 and Dec. 1, 1875, ibid.; Elizabeth Edwards to Robert Lincoln, Springfield, Nov. 12 and Dec. 1, 1875, folder 16, box 2, IF.

59. Elizabeth Edwards to Robert Lincoln, Nov. 12, 1875, IF.

60. Robert Lincoln to Davis, Nov. 16, 1875, DDFP.

61. Robert Lincoln to Ninian Edwards, Nov. 15, 1875, folder 2, box 2, IF.

62. Robert Lincoln to Ninian Edwards, Chicago, Dec. 21, 1875, ibid.

63. Robert Lincoln to Elizabeth Edwards, May 17, 1876, in LB, 1:168–69, microfilm reel 1, and folder 3, box 2, IF.

64. Robert Lincoln to David Davis, Chicago, Nov. 22, 1875, folder A-109, box 7, DDFP.

65. Robert Lincoln to John Todd Stuart, Chicago, Nov. 15, 1875, folder 2, box 2, IF.

66. Robert Lincoln to Davis, Nov. 16, 1875, DDFP.

67. Ibid.

68. Robert was continually wary of Mary's reliance on her pension. He understood politics and fully expected his mother's foes, should they ever gain control of the House, to eliminate her pension. Ibid.; Robert Lincoln to Stuart, Nov. 15, 1875, IF.

69. Elizabeth Edwards to Robert Lincoln, Nov. 12, 1875, IF.

70. Robert Lincoln to Davis, Nov. 16, 1875, DDFP.

71. David Davis to Robert Lincoln, Washington, D.C., Nov. 20, 1875, folder 15, box 2, IF.

72. Ninian Edwards to Robert Lincoln, Springfield, Dec. 18, 1875, folder 17, box 2, IF; Robert Lincoln to Judge M. R. M. Wallace, Dec. 10 and 15, 1875, folder 33, box 2, IF, and in WEBS, 47:42–43, 45–46.

73. Ninian Edwards to Robert Lincoln, Springfield, Dec. 22, 1875, folder 17, box 2, IF.

74. Ninian Edwards to Robert Lincoln, Springfield, Dec. 18 and 22, and Jan. 15, 1875, ibid.; Elizabeth Edwards to Robert Lincoln, Dec. 1, 1875, folder 16, box 2, IF.

75. Baker, *Mary Todd Lincoln*, 323, 344, 369; Friedman, *America's First Woman Lawyer*, 50; Schreiner, *Trials of Mrs. Lincoln*, 324–25.

76. Robert Lincoln to Davis, Nov. 16, 1875, DDFP. In this letter, Robert also alluded to a similar remark he had made to his aunt in a previous letter. That letter appears to no longer exist.

77. Robert Lincoln to Ninian Edwards, Dec. 21, 1875, folder 2, box 2, IF.

78. Robert Lincoln to Elizabeth Edwards, May 17, 1876, in LB, 1:168–69, microfilm reel 1; and folder 3, box 2, IF.

79. Robert Lincoln to Ninian Edwards, Dec. 21, 1875, IF.

80. Ninian Edwards to Robert Lincoln, Dec. 1, 1875, folder 17, box 2, IF; Robert Lincoln to Edwards, Dec. 21, 1875, IF.

81. Ninian Edwards to Robert Lincoln, Dec. 18, 1875; Robert Lincoln to Edwards, Dec. 21, 1875, IF.

82. J. M. Palmer to Robert Lincoln, Dec. 21, 1875, folder 22, box 2, IF.

83. Robert Lincoln to J. M. Palmer, Chicago, Dec. 23, 1875, ibid.

84. Ninian Edwards to Robert Lincoln, Springfield, Dec. 18 and 28, 1875, folder 17, box 2, IF.

8. A DEEPLY WRONGED WOMAN

1. Willard L. King to John S. Goff, Chicago, June 6, 1958, John Goff Papers, Friends of Hildene, Inc., Manchester, Vt.

2. Mary resented her sister for criticizing her; she snubbed Frances Seward because she detested her husband, William Seward; and she hated Kate Chase for rivaling her as a Washington hostess and for harboring an ambition that her father, Salmon Chase, would replace Abraham Lincoln as president. Mary Lincoln to Elizabeth Todd Grimsley, Sept. 29, 1861, in Turner and Turner, *Mary Todd Lincoln*, 104–6; Van Deusen, *William Henry Seward*, 337; Mary Merwin Phelps, *Kate Chase, Dominant Daughter: The Life Story of a Brilliant Woman and Her Famous Father* (New York: Thomas Y. Crowell, 1935), 103–4.

3. Ninian Edwards to Robert Lincoln, Springfield, Jan. 14, 1876, folder 17, box 2, IF; Elizabeth Edwards to Robert Lincoln, Springfield, Jan. 16, 1876, folder 16, box 2, IF.

4. Ninian Edwards to Robert Lincoln, Jan. 14, 1876, IF.

5. Ninian Edwards to Robert Lincoln, Springfield, Jan. 15, 1876, folder 17, box 2, IF; Elizabeth Edwards to Robert Lincoln, Jan. 16, 1876, IF.

6. Emphasis in original. Elizabeth Edwards to Robert Lincoln, Jan. 16, 1876, IF.

7. Bayne, *Tad Lincoln's Father*, 56–57; Ruth Painter Randall, *Lincoln's Sons* (Boston: Little, Brown, 1955), 160–61. See also Abraham Lincoln to Mary Lincoln, Washington, June 9, 1863, in Basler et al., *Collected Works*, 6:256.

8. Robert Lincoln to Ninian Edwards, Chicago, Jan. 17, 1876, in LB, 3:379–81, microfilm reel 4.

9. Ibid.

10. Robert Lincoln to Elizabeth Edwards, Jan. 17, 1876, folder 1, box 2, IF, and in LB, 3:382–83, microfilm reel 4.

11. Elizabeth Edwards to Robert Lincoln, Springfield, Feb. 9, 1876, folder 16, box 2, IF; Ninian Edwards to Robert Lincoln, April 6, 1876, folder 17, box 2, IF.

12. Robert Lincoln to Mary Lincoln, Chicago, Feb. 7, 1876, folder 3, box 2, IF, and in LB, 1:162–64, microfilm reel 1; Elizabeth Edwards to Robert Lincoln, Feb. 9, 1876, IF.

13. Robert Lincoln to Elizabeth Edwards, Feb. 12, 1876, folder 3, box 2, IF, and in LB, 1:165–66, microfilm reel 1.

14. Robert Lincoln to Ninian Edwards, April 24 and 25, 1876, in LB, 3:415–16, 418–19, microfilm reel 4; Robert Lincoln to Elizabeth Edwards, May 17, 1876, folder 3, box 2, IF, and in LB, 1:168–69, microfilm reel 1.

15. Henry F. Eames to Robert Lincoln, April 25, 1876, and Robert Lincoln to Ninian Edwards, April 25, 1876, in LB, 3:417, 418–19, microfilm reel 4.

16. Ninian Edwards to Robert Lincoln, April 18, 1876, folder 17, box 2, IF.

17. Robert Lincoln to Elizabeth Edwards, May 17, 1876, IF, and in LB, 1:168–69, microfilm reel 1.

18. David Davis to Robert Lincoln, Bloomington, Ill., May 22, 1876, folder 15, box 2, IF.

19. Robert Lincoln to Ninian Edwards, May 24, 1876, in LB, 1:170, microfilm reel 1.

20. "A Happy Denouement: Mrs. Abraham Lincoln Restored to Her Reason and Freedom," *Chicago Times*, June 16, 1876, 3; "Mrs. President Lincoln: Her Restoration to Reason and Property," *Chicago Tribune*, June 16, 1876, 8.

21. Mary Lincoln petition to Cook County Court, June 1876, folder 33, box 2, IF; photostatic copy, in WEBS, 47:36.

22. "A Happy Denouement," *Chicago Times*, June 16, 1876, 3; "Mrs. President Lincoln," *Chicago Tribune*, June 16, 1876, 8.

23. Edwards's statement was so embarrassingly repetitive it mortified him, and he later wrote Robert Lincoln three letters in one day to explain its incoherence. Ninian Edwards testimony, folder 33, box 2, IF; photostatic copy, in WEBS, 47:337–38; Ninian Edwards to Robert Lincoln, Springfield, Ill., June 17, 1876 (three letters), folder 17, box 2, IF.

24. Robert Lincoln waiver, June 15, 1875, folder 33, box 2, IF; photostatic copy, in WEBS, 47:40; Robert Lincoln to Ninian Edwards, May 24, 1876, LB, 1:170, microfilm reel 1; Edwards to David Davis, June 8, 1876, folder 17, box 2, IF.

25. "Mrs. President Lincoln," *Chicago Tribune*, June 16, 1876, 8.

26. Verdict of the jury in the case of Mary Lincoln, June 15, 1876, folder 33, box 2, IF; photostatic copy, in WEBS, 47:48.

27. This increase was due in part to Robert's investment in additional government bonds and in part to the accumulated interest on her total bonds. Conservator of Mary Lincoln, Account of Receipts and Disbursements, June 15, 1876, folders 30 and 33, box 2, IF.

28. "A Happy Denouement," *Chicago Times*, June 16, 1876, 3.

29. Neely and McMurtry, *Insanity File*, 104.

30. Mason Brayman, *Revised Statutes of the State of Illinois* (Springfield, Ill.: Walters & Weber, 1845), 277.

31. Neely and McMurtry, *Insanity File*, 104.

32. Ninian Edwards to Robert Lincoln, June 17, 1876, IF.

33. Emphasis in original. Mary Lincoln to Myra Bradwell, Springfield, Ill., June 18, 1876, FTC. The fact of Robert's visit, along with what transpired that morning in the Edwardses' home, had never before been known until revealed by the finding of Mary's lost letters. Robert's visit was suggested by one sentence in a letter from Ninian Edwards to Robert, in which he stated he was "pained to hear of your mother's treatment of you." Ninian Edwards to Robert Lincoln, June 17, 1876, IF.

34. Emphasis in original. Mary Lincoln to Robert Lincoln, June 19, 1876, in Turner and Turner, *Mary Todd Lincoln*, 615–16.

35. Rhodes and Jauchius, *Trial of Mary Todd Lincoln*, 5.

36. "Mrs. Abraham Lincoln," *Chicago Legal News* 8, no. 39 (June 17, 1876): 309. The article was a reprint of the *Chicago Times* article, with one paragraph added to explain the legal process necessary to remove a conservator.

37. That letter was not included among those in the Towers Lincoln trunk and has never been found. Mary Lincoln did thank Myra Bradwell for her "most welcome letter" in Mary Lincoln to Myra Bradwell, June 18, 1876, FTC.

38. Emphasis in original. Ibid.

39. Emphasis in original. Ibid.

40. Leonard Swett to Ninian Edwards, June 20, 1876, folder 27, box 2, IF.

41. Ibid.

42. Ibid. Mary's letter has not been found but is quoted by Swett.

43. Ninian Edwards to Leonard Swett, Springfield, June 22, 1876, folder 17, box 2, IF.

44. Ibid.; Ninian Edwards to Robert Lincoln, Springfield, June 24, 1876, folder 17, box 2, IF.

45. Ninian Edwards to Leonard Swett, June 22, 1876, IF.

46. Mary Lincoln to James Bradwell, Springfield, June 22, 1876, FTC.

47. Ninian Edwards to Leonard Swett, June 22, 1876, IF.

48. Ibid.; Ninian Edwards to Leonard Swett, Springfield, June 24, 1876, and Edwards to Robert Lincoln, Springfield, June 26, 1876, folder 17, box 2, IF.

49. Leonard Swett to Ninian Edwards, July 1, 1876, in LB, 1:172–79, microfilm reel 1.

50. Emphasis in original. Mary Lincoln to Myra Bradwell, Springfield, July 7, 1876, FTC. Robert's reply has never been found.

51. Turner and Turner, *Mary Todd Lincoln*, 620 n.5; Mary Lincoln to Jacob Bunn, Pau, France, Jan. 31, 1877, in ibid., 623–24; "Mrs. Lincoln: She Corrects Some Reports concerning Her Financial Condition," *Illinois State Journal*, Nov. 29, 1881, 1.

52. Robert Lincoln to Jacob Bunn, Dec. 9, 1880, and Robert Lincoln to Edward L. Baker, Dec. 14, 1880, in LB, 3:766, 767–68, microfilm reel 5.

53. Mary Lincoln to Jacob Bunn, Pau, France, Oct. 23, 1877, in Turner and Turner, *Mary Todd Lincoln*, 620–21; Robert Lincoln to Edward L. Baker, Dec. 14, 1880, in LB, 3:766, 767–68, microfilm reel 5.

54. Mary Lincoln to James Bradwell, June 22, 1876, FTC.

55. Ninian Edwards to Robert Lincoln, June 26, 1876, folder 17, box 2, IF; Jacob Bunn to Robert Lincoln, June 24, 1876, folder 11, box 2, IF; Ninian Edwards to Leonard Swett, June 22 and 24, 1876, folder 17, box 2, IF.

56. Mary Lincoln to Myra Bradwell, Springfield, July 7 and 14, 1876, FTC.

57. Mary Lincoln to Jacob Bunn, Pau, France, Jan. 31, 1877, in Turner and Turner, *Mary Todd Lincoln*, 623–24.

58. Robert Lincoln to Jacob Bunn, Dec. 9, 1880, and Robert Lincoln to Edward L. Baker, Dec. 14, 1880, in LB, 3:766, 767–68, microfilm reel 5.

59. Emphasis in original. Mary Lincoln to Myra Bradwell, Springfield, Ill., July 7 and 14, 1876, FTC.

60. Helm, *True Story of Mary*, 298.

61. Elizabeth Edwards to Robert Lincoln, Springfield, Oct. 29, 1876, folder 16, box 2, IF.

62. Ibid.; Mary Lincoln to Edward Lewis Baker, Pau, France, June 22, 1879, in Turner and Turner, *Mary Todd Lincoln*, 682.

63. Elizabeth Edwards to Robert Lincoln, Oct. 29, 1876, IF.

9. RESIGNATION WILL NEVER COME

1. Elizabeth Edwards to Robert Lincoln, Springfield, Oct. 29, 1876, folder 16, box 2, IF; Mary Lincoln to Myra Bradwell, Pau, France, Dec. 1, 1876, in Pritchard, "Dark Days," chap. 9, pp. 1–4, FTC.

2. Evans, *Mrs. Abraham Lincoln*, 342; Hirschhorn and Feldman, "Mary Lincoln's Final Illness," 536.

3. She claimed her natural size was one hundred pounds. Mary Lincoln to Edward Lewis Baker, Pau, France, Oct. 4, 1879, in Turner and Turner, *Mary Todd Lincoln*, 690.

4. "Mrs. Lincoln: The True Condition of Her Financial Affairs," *Illinois State Journal*, Nov. 26, 1881, 6.

5. Turner and Turner, *Mary Todd Lincoln*, 620.

6.	Mary Lincoln to Myra Bradwell, Dec. 1, 1876, in Pritchard, "Dark Days," chap. 9, pp. 1–4, FTC.

7.	Emphasis in original. Mary Lincoln to Edward Lewis Baker, Pau, France, Apr. 11, 1877, in Turner and Turner, *Mary Todd Lincoln*, 633.

8.	Emphasis in original. Mary Lincoln to Edward Lewis Baker, Havre, France, Oct. 17, 1877, in Turner and Turner, *Mary Todd Lincoln*, 617–18.

9.	Elizabeth Edwards to Robert Lincoln, Oct. 29, 1876, IF.

10.	Mary Lincoln to Myra Bradwell, Dec. 1, 1876, in Pritchard, "Dark Days," chap. 9, pp. 1–4, FTC.

11.	Emphasis in original. Mary Lincoln to Myra Bradwell, Pau, France, July 6, 1878, in Pritchard, "Dark Days," chap. 9, pp. 12–13, FTC.

12.	Ibid.

13.	Mary Lincoln to Myra Bradwell, July 4, 1878, in ibid., pp. 10–12.

14.	Gethsemane was the garden—also called the Mount of Olives—where Jesus watched and prayed the night before he was crucified. According to Luke 22:43–44, Jesus's anguish in Gethsemane was so deep that "his sweat was like drops of blood falling to the ground." *Good News Bible: The Bible in Today's English Version* (New York: American Bible Society, 1976). Gethsemane was also where Judas Iscariot betrayed Jesus. Mary's use of the term clearly refers to her anguish at what she perceived to be Robert's betrayal and her own martyrdom. Mary Lincoln to Elizabeth Edwards, Pau, France, Mar. 19, 1877, Mary Todd Lincoln Collection, The Lincoln Museum.

15.	Mary Lincoln to Myra Bradwell, Pau, France, July 7, 1876, in Pritchard, "Dark Days," chap. 9, pp. 1–4, FTC.

16.	American Psychiatric Association, *Diagnostic and Statistical Manual*, 332.

17.	Mary Lincoln to Myra Bradwell, Pau, France, Apr. 12, 1877, in Pritchard, "Dark Days," chap. 9, pp. 4–6, FTC.

18.	While the Lincolns no doubt discussed this subject, that they sat "for hours" contemplating it in the midst of civil war seems unlikely and almost certainly was exaggerated in Mary's memory. Mary Lincoln to Myra Bradwell, Sorrento, Italy, Apr. 22, 1878, in ibid., pp. 12–13.

19.	Mary Lincoln to Jacob Bunn, Naples, Italy, Apr. 10 and 29, 1878, and Rome, Italy, May 22, 1878, in Turner and Turner, *Mary Todd Lincoln*, 665–67.

20.	Herculaneum was an ancient Roman resort town buried in lava in 79 A.D. from the eruption of Mt. Vesuvius that also buried Pompeii. It was discovered, in a state of preservation, in the late eighteenth century and excavated. The Castle of St. Elmo was a fourteenth-century castle in Naples, Italy.

21.	Mary Lincoln to Myra Bradwell, Apr. 22, 1878, in Pritchard, "Dark Days," chap. 9, pp. 12–13, FTC. Mary here referred to Stowe's 1861 romantic novel *Agnes of Sorrento*.

22.	Emphasis in original. Ibid.

23.	Mary Lincoln to Jacob Bunn, Apr. 29, 1878, in Turner and Turner, *Mary Todd Lincoln*, 666.

24.	Mary Lincoln to Jacob Bunn, Marseilles, France, June 5, 1878, in Turner and Turner, *Mary Todd Lincoln*, 668; Mary Lincoln to Edward Lewis Baker, Avignon, France, Jan. 16, 1880, and Pau, France, June 12, 1880, in Turner and Turner, *Mary Todd Lincoln*, 694, 699.

25.	Mary Lincoln to Elizabeth Edwards, Mar. 19, 1877, Mary Todd Lincoln Collection, The Lincoln Museum.

26.	Mary Lincoln to Edward Lewis Baker, Oct. 4, 1879, in Turner and Turner, *Mary Todd Lincoln*, 690–91.

27. Elizabeth Edwards to Robert Lincoln, Oct. 29, 1876, folder 16, box 2, IF.

28. Robert Lincoln to President Rutherford B. Hayes, Chicago, Oct. 10, 1877, and Robert Lincoln to Secretary of State William M. Evarts, Chicago, Oct. 10, 1877, in LB, 3:583–84, 585–86, microfilm reel 5; Lincoln to Hayes letter also in Rutherford B. Hayes Papers, Rutherford B. Hayes Presidential Center, Fremont, Ohio; untitled article, *Chicago Tribune*, Feb. 17, 1877, 4; "The Douglas Monument," *New York Times*, July 6, 1877, 2.

29. Mary Lincoln to Edward Lewis Baker, Pau, France, June 22, 1879, in Turner and Turner, *Mary Todd Lincoln*, 682.

30. Robert Lincoln to Rev. Henry Darling, Nov. 15, 1877, folder 38, box 6, Lincoln Collection, Miscellaneous Manuscripts, Department of Special Collections, University of Chicago Library.

31. Robert Lincoln to Elizabeth Edwards, Apr. 18, 1879, Robert Lincoln Collection, The Lincoln Museum.

32. Ibid.

33. "Mrs. Lincoln's Illness," *New York Times*, Oct. 31, 1880, 5; "Mrs. Lincoln in Want," *New York Times*, Nov. 23, 1881, 5; Helm, *True Story of Mary*, 298–99.

34. Mary Lincoln to Edward Lewis Baker, Pau, France, Jan. 19 and June 12, 1880, in Turner and Turner, *Mary Todd Lincoln*, 695, 699.

35. Mary Lincoln to Edward Lewis Baker, June 12, 1880, in Turner and Turner, *Mary Todd Lincoln*, 699.

36. Sarah Bernhardt, *The Memoirs of Sarah Bernhardt: Early Childhood through the First American Tour*, ed. Sandy Lesberg (New York: Peebles Press, 1977), 145–46.

37. "Sarah Bernhardt Beset," *New York Sun*, Oct. 28, 1880, 3.; Louis Verneuil, *The Fabulous Life of Sarah Bernhardt*, trans. Ernest Boyd (New York: Harper & Brothers, 1942), 128.

38. "Mrs. Lincoln's Illness," *New York Times*, Oct. 31, 1880, 5.

39. Dr. Lewis (sometimes spelled *Louis*) A. Sayre is considered the father of orthopedic surgery in the United States and introduced the practice of prolonged plaster fixation for diseases of the bones or joints. He received his medical degree from Transylvania University in Lexington, Ky., in 1842. After working as a surgeon at Bellevue Hospital and Charity Hospital, he became chair of orthopedic surgery at Bellevue Hospital Medical College, which he also helped found. He held his chair until 1898, when Bellevue Hospital Medical College was united with New York University. He then became emeritus professor of orthopedic surgery at the consolidated institution. Sayre was one of the founders of the New York Academy of Medicine, the New York Pathological Society, and the American Medical Association. "Dr. Lewis A. Sayre Dead," *New York Times*, Sept. 22, 1900, 14; Henry P. Plenk, ed., *Medicine in the Beehive State, 1940–1990* (Salt Lake City: Utah Medical Association, 1992), 324; "Mrs. Lincoln's Illness," *New York Times*, Oct. 31, 1880, 5.

40. "Mrs. Lincoln's Illness," *New York Times*, Oct. 31, 1880, 5.

41. Elizabeth Edwards to Emily Helm, Springfield, Mar. 3, 1881, quoted in Turner and Turner, *Mary Todd Lincoln*, 705; Robert Lincoln to Sally Orne, June 2, 1881, Robert Lincoln Papers, ALPL; "Mrs. Lincoln's Health," *New York Times*, July 22, 1881, 3; J. C. A., "Mrs. Abraham Lincoln," *Chicago Tribune*, Aug. 6, 1881, 6.

42. "Mrs. Lincoln's Health," *New York Times*, July 22, 1881, 3; Thomas W. Dresser to Jesse Weik, Jan. 3, 1889, in Wilson and Davis, *Herndon's Informants*, 671.

43. Medical historians Norbert Hirschhorn and Robert Feldman attributed Mary's extreme sensitivity to light (as well as her other physical symptoms of lancinating pain, difficulty walking, ulcers, urinary incontinence, and swelling) to the

syndrome tabes dorsalis (spinal degeneration), which they theorized was a result of diabetes, the disease most likely responsible for her terminal illness and death. It should be noted, however, that patients with severe depression often will isolate themselves in darkened rooms as well. Even if Mary did suffer from the Argyll Robertson pupils feature of tabes dorsalis (light sensitivity), she still could have left her room at night, but she did not. Special thanks to Dr. James S. Brust for pointing this out to me. Elizabeth Edwards to Emily Helm, Mar. 3, 1881, quoted in Turner and Turner, *Mary Todd Lincoln*, 705; Hirschhorn and Feldman, "Mary Lincoln's Final Illness," 511–42.

44. Thomas W. Dresser to Jesse Weik, Jan. 3, 1889, in Wilson and Davis, *Herndon's Informants*, 671.

45. "Mrs. Lincoln's Health," *New York Times*, July 22, 1881, 3.

46. Mary Edwards Brown, interview by Dorothy Kunhardt, n.d., in Philip B. Kunhardt Jr., Philip B. Kunhardt III, and Peter W. Kunhardt, *Lincoln: An Illustrated Biography* (New York: Alfred A. Knopf, 1992), 396–97; J. C. A., "Mrs. Abraham Lincoln," *Chicago Tribune*, Aug. 6, 1881, 6.

47. Mary Edwards Brown interview, in Kunhardt, *Lincoln: An Illustrated Biography*, 396–97.

48. Ibid.; Thomas W. Dresser to Jesse Weik, Jan. 3, 1889, in Wilson and Davis, *Herndon's Informants*, 671; "Mrs. Lincoln's Health," *New York Times*, July 22, 1881, 3.

49. Mary Edwards Brown interview, in Kunhardt, *Lincoln: An Illustrated Biography*, 396–97.

50. Mary L. D. Putnam to her sons St. Clair and Clement Putnam, Dec. 8, 1882, extract sent from Paul Angle to William E. Barton, Jan. 10, 1927, WEBS, vol. 63.

51. The *Illinois State Journal* reported Robert was on an official War Department visit to Fort Leavenworth, Kans., as secretary of war and stopped in Springfield May 26–27, 1881, for a short visit. Robert's preserved letters verify this trip. Tradition holds that Robert went on a personal visit and brought his daughter "Mamie" with him, whom Mary adored, as a way to help smooth the peace with his mother. This appears to be a case of historical hearsay, as no primary evidence exists to suggest that was the case. Historians W. A. Evans and Carl Sandburg began the Mamie story in separate 1932 biographies, both without citation. Sandburg's account was especially egregious, however, as he claimed Robert's entire family went to Springfield to see Mary. The newspaper accounts and Robert's letters prove this untrue. In 1953, Ruth Painter Randall, who cited Evans, repeated the Mamie story, and it has been considered authentic by subsequent historians. Untitled article, *Illinois State Journal*, May 27, 1881, 6, and May 28, 1881, 4, 6; Robert Lincoln to George C. Clark, May 23, 1881, and to General O. O. Howard, June 2, 1881, and to Benjamin Richardson, June 3, 1881, and to George J. Hagar, June 3, 1881, LB, 4:344–45, 365, 374, 376–77, microfilm reel 6; Robert Lincoln to Sally Orne, June 2, 1881, Robert Lincoln Papers, ALPL; Evans, *Mrs. Abraham Lincoln*, 53; Carl Sandburg and Paul M. Angle, *Mary Lincoln: Wife and Widow* (New York: Harcourt, Brace, 1932), 158; Randall, *Mary Lincoln*, 440.

52. J. C .A., "Mrs. Abraham Lincoln," *Chicago Tribune*, Aug. 6, 1881, 6.

53. "Mrs. Lincoln's Distress," *Chicago Tribune*, Oct. 2, 1881, 2; "Mrs. Lincoln Going to Canada," *New York Times*, Oct. 10, 1881, 4.

54. "Mrs. Lincoln in Want," *New York Times*, Nov. 22, 1881, 5.

55. Ibid.

56. "Mrs. Lincoln: Broad Denial of the Stories Set Afloat by Dr. Sayre," *Chicago Tribune*, Nov. 24, 1881, 3; "News in Brief," *Chicago Tribune*, Nov. 24, 1881, 1; "Mrs. Lincoln's Pecuniary Condition," *Illinois State Journal*, Nov. 26, 1881, 4.

57.　"Mrs. Lincoln's Pecuniary Condition," *Illinois State Journal*, Nov. 26, 1881, 4.

58.　"Mrs. Lincoln: Broad Denial," *Chicago Tribune*, Nov. 24, 1881, 3; "Mrs. Lincoln: She Corrects Some Reports concerning Her Financial Condition," *Illinois State Journal*, Nov. 29, 1881, 1.

59.　Cyrus West Field was an American businessman and financier who led the Atlantic Telegraph Company, which successfully laid the first telegraph cable across the Atlantic Ocean in 1858. He had previously raised more than $300,000 in public subscriptions for Mrs. Garfield. "Mrs. Lincoln in Want," *New York Times*, Nov. 22, 1881, 5; "Mrs. Lincoln: Broad Denial," *Chicago Tribune*, Nov. 24, 1881, 3; "Cyrus West Field," in *The Columbia Encyclopedia*, 6th ed., http://www.bartleby.com/65/fi/Field-Cy.html.

60.　Springer was a Democrat from Springfield, Ill. The other three physicians were neurologist Meredith Clymer, ophthalmologist Hermann Knapp, and surgeon William Pancoast. "New York: The Health of Mrs. Abraham Lincoln Not Improving; Examination of Her Condition by Several Distinguished Physicians," *Chicago Tribune*, Jan. 15, 1882, 6; Mary Lincoln to Noyes W. Miner, Jan. 3, 1882, in Turner and Turner, *Mary Todd Lincoln*, 711; "William McKendree Springer," in *Biographical Directory of the United States Congress*, http://bioguide.congress.gov/scripts/biodisplay.pl?index=S000757.

61.　*Congressional Record*, 47th Cong., 1st sess., 1882, 13:402; "New York: The Health of Mrs. Abraham Lincoln," *Chicago Tribune*, Jan. 15, 1882, 6.

62.　Mary Lincoln to Noyes W. Miner, Feb. 5, 1882, in Turner and Turner, *Mary Todd Lincoln*, 712.

63.　*Congressional Record*, 47th Cong., 1st sess., 1882, 13:578, 652, 705–6, 882; "Mrs. Lincoln's Needs: The Relief Bill Passed by the Senate," *New York Times*, Jan. 25, 1882, 3; "Core's Bill," *Chicago Tribune*, Feb. 3, 1882, 2; "Mrs. Lincoln's Pension," *New York Times*, Mar. 17, 1882, 5.

64.　William Herndon to Jesse Weik, Springfield, Jan. 2, 1882, frames 1753–54, reel 9, group 4, H-WC.

65.　Mary Lincoln to Josephine Remann Edwards, Oct. 23, 1881, in Turner and Turner, *Mary Todd Lincoln*, 708–9; "Mrs. Lincoln in Want," *New York Times*, Nov. 22, 1881, 5; "President Lincoln's Widow," *Boston Globe*, Nov. 29, 1881, 1; "Mrs. Lincoln: Another New York Report of Her Meager Means of Subsistence," *Illinois State Journal*, Nov. 30, 1881, 1.

66.　"Mrs. Lincoln Not Blind," *New York Times*, Dec. 19, 1881, 8; "Mrs. Lincoln: Denial of the Report That She Is Blind," *Chicago Tribune*, Dec. 19, 1881, 5.

67.　"President Lincoln's Widow: Under Medical Treatment in New York," *Boston Globe*, Nov. 29, 1881, 1.

68.　"Obituary: Death at Springfield, Illinois, of the Widow of Abraham Lincoln," *Chicago Tribune*, July 17, 1882, 2.

69.　Steven Spearie, "Final Comfort: Mary Todd Lincoln May Have Relied on the Help of Local Nuns in Her Last Days," *Springfield State Journal Register*, July 14, 2006, 6A.

70.　"Mrs. Lincoln's Health," *New York Times*, July 16, 1882, 7.

71.　Affidavit of Decease, Mary Lincoln Estate File, Lincoln Collection, ALPL; "Mary Todd Lincoln: Her Death in This City at 8 O'Clock Sunday Evening," *Illinois State Journal*, July 17, 1882, 6; "Death of Mrs. Lincoln," *New York Times*, July 17, 1882, 1; "Obituary: Death at Springfield, Illinois, of the Widow of Abraham Lincoln," *Chicago Tribune*, July 17, 1882, 2; Thomas W. Dresser to Jesse Weik, Jan. 3, 1889, in Wilson and Davis, *Herndon's Informants*, 671; Evans, *Mrs. Abraham Lincoln*, 344.

72. Evans, *Mrs. Abraham Lincoln*, 342; Hirschhorn and Feldman, "Mary Lincoln's Final Illness," 536.

73. Evans, *Mrs. Abraham Lincoln*, 342.

74. Ibid.

75. William Herndon wrote that Abraham Lincoln contracted syphilis in the late 1830s and then infected Mary. William Herndon to Jesse Weik, Springfield, Dec. 1, 1888, and Jan. 1891, in Hertz, *Hidden Lincoln*, 229, 259. Physicians Norbert Hirschhorn and Robert Feldman concluded in 1999 that Mary could have had syphilis, although they found it difficult to prove and did not diagnose her with it. Hirschhorn and Feldman, "Mary Lincoln's Final Illness," 531, 535, 542. Author Deborah Hayden, in her 2003 study of syphilis, based on the work of Herndon and of Hirschhorn and Feldman, declared that Mary certainly had syphilis and that her later physical symptoms prove it. Deborah Hayden, *Pox: Genius, Madness and the Mysteries of Syphilis* (New York: Basic Books, 2003), 120–32.

76. Extract of letter from Mary L. D. Putnam to her sons St. Clair and Clement Putnam, Jan. 10, 1927, WEBS, vol. 63.

77. "Awaiting the Burial," *Illinois State Journal*, July 18, 1882, 6; Mary Edwards Brown interview, in Kunhardt, *Lincoln: An Illustrated Biography*, 396–97; "Mrs. Lincoln's Funeral," *New York Times*, July 18, 1882, 1.

78. "Dust to Dust: The Body of Mrs. Abraham Lincoln Consigned to the Tomb," *Chicago Tribune*, July 20, 1882, 7; Mary Edwards Brown interview, in Kunhardt, *Lincoln: An Illustrated Biography*, 396–97.

79. "Laid to Rest: The Last Sad Rites Paid to the Remains of Mary Todd Lincoln," *Illinois State Journal*, July 20, 1882, 1; editorial, *Illinois State Journal*, July 20, 1882, 4.

80. James A. Reed eulogy, typescript, frames 297–302, microfilm reel 5, group 5, H-WC; "Laid to Rest," *Illinois State Journal*, July 20, 1882, 1; "Dust to Dust," *Chicago Tribune*, July 20, 1882, 7.

81. "Mrs. Lincoln," *New York Times*, July 18, 1882, 4.

82. "Mrs. Abraham Lincoln," *Chicago Tribune*, July 20, 1882, 4.

83. Jane Grey Swisshelm, "Tribute to the Dead from Mrs. Jane Grey Swisshelm," *Chicago Tribune*, July 20, 1882, 7.

84. Howard Glyndon, "The Truth about Mrs. Lincoln," *Independent* 34, no. 1758 (Aug. 10, 1882): 4.

85. Adam Badeau, "Adam Badeau's Letter: A History of the Insanity of Mrs. President Lincoln," *Chicago Tribune*, Jan. 17, 1887, 10.

86. David Davis to Miss Addie Burr, July 19, 1882, Adeline Ellery (Burr) Davis Green Papers, Duke University Libraries.

87. Robert Lincoln, deposition on personal estate of Mary Lincoln, Sangamon County Court, Sept. 1882, FTC.

88. Mary's estate consisted of $72,000 in bonds, $555 in currency, $5,000 in personal effects, and $6,480 in bond interest. Robert Lincoln, Petition for Letters of Administration, Bond of Administration, Inventory of Real Estate, and Final Report of Administrator, Sangamon County Court, Sept. 1882, FTC, also located in Mary Lincoln Estate File, Lincoln Collection, ALPL; "Mrs. Lincoln's Estate," *Washington Post*, Sept. 29, 1882, 1; "Estate of Mrs. Lincoln," *New York Times*, Sept. 29, 1882, 2.

89. Mary Lincoln, last will and testament, July 23, 1873, FTC.

90. Pritchard, "Dark Days," chap. 7, p. 5, FTC.

91. Mary Lincoln to County Judge, Cook County, July 23, 1873, folder 2, box 1, IF.

92. "Opening of a Letter Written by Mrs. Lincoln," *Chicago Tribune*, July 21, 1882, 8; "A Letter Left by Mrs. Lincoln," *New York Times*, July 23, 1882, 7.

93. Envelope labeled "To be delivered to the County Judge of Cook Co—upon death of Mrs. Abraham Lincoln," folder 35, box 2, IF.

94. Mary Lincoln to James Bradwell, Jan. 17 and 18, Nov. 11, and Dec. 1, 1875, folder 2, box 1, IF.

95. Ninian Edwards to Robert Lincoln, Springfield, Dec. 18, 1875, folder 17, box 2, IF.

96. Pritchard, "Dark Days," chap. 7, p. 4, FTC.

97. Ibid.

98. John S. Goff, *Robert Todd Lincoln: A Man in His Own Right* (Norman: University of Oklahoma Press, 1969), 98.

99. Jason Emerson, "Avoiding the Gilded Prison," *American History Magazine* 39, no. 5 (Dec. 2004): 58–66.

100. "The Feeling for Lincoln," *Chicago Tribune*, Aug. 31, 1887, 1.

101. Friedman, *America's First Woman Lawyer*, 12.

102. Tarbell did not press Bradwell about the letters, however, as her subject was Abraham Lincoln, not Mary. James Bradwell, interview by Ida Tarbell, n.d., Ida M. Tarbell–Lincoln Collection, Allegheny College.

103. "Pioneer Lawyer at Death's Door," *Chicago Tribune*, Nov. 29, 1907, 5.

10. TO BE DESTROYED IMMEDIATELY

1. Hertz, *Hidden Lincoln*, 17–18; Butler, *Across the Busy Years*, 375–76.

2. David C. Mearns thoroughly discredited Butler's story in *The Lincoln Papers: The Story of the Collection with Selections to July 4, 1861* (Garden City, N.Y.: Doubleday, 1948), 1:111–36; Frederic C. Towers, interview by the author, August 2005.

3. Robert Lincoln to Le Grand Van Valkenburgh, May 26, 1913, Robert Lincoln Papers, Lincoln Collection, ALPL.

4. Robert lent some of his father's letters to the 1909 exhibitions of the Chicago Historical Society and a joint exhibit between the City of New York and Columbia University Library, celebrating the one hundredth anniversary of Abraham Lincoln's birth. Robert Lincoln to Darwin C. Pavey, Boston Press Club, Feb. 9, 1909, Robert Lincoln Papers, Lincoln Collection, ALPL.

5. Robert Lincoln deposited his father's personal and presidential papers in the Library of Congress on May 8, 1919, for safekeeping, although he retained ownership and sole control over access. He formally donated the papers, now known as The Robert Todd Lincoln Collection of the Papers of Abraham Lincoln, to the United States of America, "to be deposited in the Library of Congress for the benefit of all the People," on January 23, 1923. "Deed of Gift of Manuscripts and Private Papers of President Lincoln by His Son, Robert Todd Lincoln," Jan. 23, 1923, and St. George L. Sioussat to David C. Mearns, internal Library of Congress memorandum, Apr. 1, 1947, and David C. Mearns to the Librarian of Congress, "Property Rights, Lincoln Manuscripts and the Seward Heirs," July 17, 1951, David C. Mearns Papers, Manuscripts Division, LC. Robert Lincoln deed of gift to LC, Jan. 23, 1923, also in FTC.

6. Mearns, *Lincoln Papers*, 1:111–36.

7. "Mrs. Lincoln Gives Letters to Library," *Washington Evening Star*, Feb. 3, 1927, clipping, and Frederic Towers, writing for Mary Harlan Lincoln, to David Davis, Feb. 15, 1927, box 94, Friends of Hildene, Inc.; receipt for donated materials from Mary Harlan Lincoln to the LC, Oct. 2, 1928, and Frederic Towers to Dr. Herbert Putnam, Librarian of Congress, Oct. 3, 1928, and Mary Harlan Lincoln to Dr. John Franklin Jameson, July 19, 1929, folder 75, FTC.

8. The only people outside his immediate family to whom Robert ever gave access to the papers were David Davis, John Hay, and John Nicolay. Hay and Nicolay were President Lincoln's private secretaries and two of Robert's close friends. From his father's papers, they wrote a ten-volume biography and a two-volume collected works.

9. Frederic Towers to Katherine Helm, Oct. 14, 1927, box 94, Friends of Hildene, Inc.

10. Frederic Towers to Myra Pritchard, Oct. 14, 1927, ibid.

11. Records do not specifically indicate why Mary Harlan Lincoln did not attend the meetings, but a previous letter mentions that the weather was so fine in Manchester, Vt., that she did not want to leave. Frederic Towers to Otis Rockwood, Nov. 22, 1927, FTC.

12. The first books about Mary Lincoln all appeared in 1928: Helm's *True Story of Mary, Wife of Lincoln*; Carlos W. Goltz's, *Incidents in the Life of Mary Todd Lincoln* (Sioux City, Iowa: Deitch & Lamar); and Honore Willsie Morrow's work of historical fiction, *Mary Todd Lincoln: An Appreciation of the Wife of Abraham Lincoln* (New York: William Morrow). The only previous book to mention Mary Lincoln's insanity trial was William E. Barton's, *The Life of Abraham Lincoln*, 2 vols. (Indianapolis: Bobbs-Merrill, 1925), 2: 419.

13. Myra Pritchard used only thirty-one letters in her book, and copies of only sixteen letters were found in the Towers trunk. Pritchard stated in the final installment of her manuscript that she chose not to publish all the letters in her possession. These figures indicate that she had six more letters. However, there also arises a question of semantics, namely, that Pritchard said the thirty-seven letters she owned were "written by Mrs. Abraham Lincoln to my grandparents, Judge and Mrs. Bradwell." Since only twenty-one of the letters quoted in the Pritchard manuscript were written by Mary Lincoln to the Bradwells (with the rest being to and from others involved in the situation), a literal conclusion would be that Pritchard omitted sixteen Mary Todd Lincoln letters. Why Frederic Towers had only sixteen letters is unknown. The former conclusion appears more likely. Myra Helmer Pritchard, "Statement Regarding the Disposal of Mary Lincoln Letters," Mar. 1, 1928, PFP; Pritchard, "Dark Days," chap. 9, p. 14, FTC.

14. Page 1 of Pritchard's manuscript is stamped "EDITORIAL DEPARTMENT PAID MAY 28, 1927," with a handwritten notation stating "OK Pay $5,000."

15. Robert Lincoln to Le Grand Van Valkenburgh, May 26, 1913, Robert Lincoln Papers, Lincoln Collection, ALPL.

16. Myra Helmer Pritchard, "Statement regarding the Disposal of Mary Lincoln Letters," Mar. 1, 1928, PFP.

17. The records do not indicate to which three letters they objected. The letters from Mary Lincoln to Myra Bradwell dated June 18, July 7, and July 14, 1876, seem most plausible not only because of their rancorous content but also the private nature of the property issues involved. Frederic Towers to Otis Rockwood, Dec. 28, 1927, FTC.

18. The case involved Mrs. Woodrow Wilson and Col. Edward M. House. House wanted to publish some of President Wilson's letters to him, but Mrs. Wilson refused. Edward M. House diary, Nov. 22, 1925, entry, Edward M. House Papers, Yale University Library, cited in Godfrey Hodgen, *Woodrow Wilson's Right Hand: The Life of Col. Edward M. House* (New Haven: Yale University Press, 2006), 260–61, 310n.13.

19. Frederic Towers to Otis Rockwood, Dec. 28, 1927.

20. Such a situation occurred for Ida Tarbell, who first wrote a series of biographical articles about Abraham Lincoln for *McClure's* magazine in the late 1890s, containing much new and unpublished information (some of it supplied by Robert T. Lincoln),

and then parlayed those articles into a popular two-volume work in 1900 that sold well. Tarbell then went on to author numerous other Lincoln books.

21. Pritchard, "Dark Days," chap. 2, p. 8, FTC. Horner's Lincoln collection was later donated to the Illinois State Historical Library and was the basis for the current collection at the Abraham Lincoln Presidential Library.

22. Otis Rockwood to Frederic Towers, Dec. 30, 1927, FTC.

23. Otis Rockwood to Frederic Towers, Jan. 6, 1928, FTC.

24. Bert C. Farrar to Frederic Towers, Washington, D.C., Feb. 1, 1928, FTC.

25. Signed agreement between Myra Pritchard, Norman B. Frost, and Frederic N. Towers, Jan. 31, 1928, FTC and PFP.

26. Karl Harriman to Whitney Payne, Mar. 21, 1929, PFP.

27. Agreement between Myra Pritchard and Liberty Weekly, Inc., Jan. 30, 1928, PFP.

28. Pritchard, "Statement regarding the Disposal of Mary Lincoln Letters," Mar. 1, 1928, PFP.

29. This statement was based on the opinion of Eleanor Gridley, a friend of both the Bradwells and Mary Lincoln, who had seen and read the insanity letters. In a sworn affidavit, Mrs. Gridley stated she had knowledge of the letters and their authenticity, and that in her opinion (which is characterized as nearly expert) the letters were worth $50,000 prior to Robert Lincoln's death in 1926. Eleanor Gridley, affidavit, Mar. 8, 1929, PFP.

30. W. R. Dillon, "Memo: re Myra Pritchard Estate Lincoln Collection," Sept. 11, 1947, 4, PFP.

31. Myra Bradwell showed the letters to Eleanor Gridley; Myra Pritchard showed them to Henry Horner, Oliver R. Barrett, and her friend Ella McCaleb. Gridley, "Presentation of Bronze Bust," 6; Dillon, "Memo," 4–5, PFP; Ella McCaleb to Myra Pritchard, Nov. 21, 1928, FTC; Pritchard, "Dark Days," chap. 2, p. 8, FTC.

32. W. A. Evans wanted to see the letters to include in his book, which he was in the midst of writing, *Mrs. Abraham Lincoln: A Study of Her Personality and Her Influence on Abraham Lincoln*. Ella McCaleb was a friend and fellow alumna of Myra Pritchard's from Vassar College who had seen the letters. She mentioned them to William Adams Slade, chief of bibliography at the Library of Congress (who was "married to a Vassar woman"), and he asked whether there was some way the library could acquire them. W. A. Evans, M.D., to Myra Pritchard, Nov. 24, 1928, and Ella McCaleb to Pritchard, Nov. 21, 1928, FTC.

33. Myra Pritchard to Frederic Towers, Nov. 28, 1928, FTC.

34. Frederic Towers to Myra Pritchard, Dec. 4, 1928, FTC.

35. Agreement between Myra Pritchard and the Trustees of the Chicago Historical Society, Oct. 22, 1932, Mrs. Myra (Stuart) Pritchard File, Chicago History Museum. Lincoln's renowned "Definition of Democracy" reads, "As I would not be a *slave*, so I would not be a *master*. This expresses my idea of democracy. Whatever differs from this, to the extent of the difference, is no democracy." It is now on display at the Abraham Lincoln Presidential Library. Abraham Lincoln, "Definition of Democracy," in Basler et al., *Collected Works*, 2:532.

36. Myra Pritchard to the president of the Trustees of the Chicago Historical Society, Battle Creek, Mich., Oct. 22, 1932, and Eleanor Gridley, affidavit, Mar. 8, 1929, PFP.

37. Myra Pritchard to L. H. Shattuck, Oct. 23, 1932, Mrs. Myra (Stuart) Pritchard File, Chicago History Museum.

38. Stefan Lorant, "Where Are the Lincoln Papers?" *Life*, Aug. 25, 1947, 45.

39. Margreta Pritchard, "Affidavit re Destruction of Liberty Magazine Manuscript relative to Mary Lincoln Letters," Sept. 18, 1947, PFP.

40. "Mrs. Lincoln, Widow of President's Son: Married Emancipator's Only Son in Washington in 1868—Dies in Capitol at 90," *New York Times*, Apr. 1, 1937, clipping in Lincoln Family folder, box 15, Ruth Painter Randall Papers, Manuscripts Department, LC.

41. Dillon, "Memo," 5, PFP.

42. Ibid.

43. L. Thorne Arthur to Margreta Pritchard, Sept. 12, and Affidavit re: Destruction of Copies of Mary Lincoln collection, signed by Margreta Pritchard, Mar. 19, 1951, PFP.

44. Henrietta Horner to Ruth Painter Randall, Sept. 26, 1949, container 65, Ruth Painter Randall Papers, LC.

45. Randall, *Mary Lincoln*, 434.

46. I had even already written an article about the insanity period, "'I Have Done My Duty as I Best Know and Providence Must Take Care of the Rest': Reconsidering Mary Todd Lincoln's Insanity Case and Robert Lincoln's Motivations behind It," lecture, Seventh Annual Conference on Illinois History, Springfield, Ill., Oct. 28, 2005.

47. Friedman's book was not noticed or commented on by any Lincoln scholars or Lincoln periodicals at the time of its publication, and, so far as I can tell, remains obscure to Lincoln students. Friedman, *America's First Woman Lawyer*, 71–76; Jane M. Friedman, e-mail to the author, Apr. 7, 2005.

48. Interestingly, Mr. Gordon did not know he had the documents until Friedman found them in his files. Ibid., 12–15.

49. Frederic Towers interview, Sept. 2005.

EPILOGUE

1. Evans, *Mrs. Abraham Lincoln*, 230.

2. Ibid., 312–13.

3. Brussel was a psychiatrist and criminologist who was later dubbed by the media as "the psychiatric Sherlock Holmes." He was chief of neuropsychiatry at Fort Dix during World War II, head of neuropsychiatry for the entire army during the Korean War (including counterintelligence work with the FBI and the CID), and assistant commissioner for the New York State Department of Mental Hygiene in charge of the New York City office. Brussel was one of the earliest criminal profilers and consulted with police on numerous cases. His work led to the capture of the New York City Mad Bomber in the 1950s and the Boston Strangler in the 1960s. "Dr. James A. Brussel, Criminologist, Dead," *New York Times*, Oct. 23, 1982; James A. Brussel, *Casebook of a Crime Psychiatrist* (n.p.: Bernard Geis Associates, 1969).

4. Brussel, "Mary Todd Lincoln," 7.

5. Ibid., 25.

6. Suarez was then with the Department of Psychiatry, Neuropsychiatric Institute, at the University of California Medical Center, Los Angeles.

7. John M. Suarez, "Mary Todd Lincoln: A Case Study," *American Journal of Psychiatry* 122, no. 7 (Jan. 1966): 819. This 1966 description of an illness that was at times psychotic, at times manic, and at times severely depressed is not inconsistent with current concepts of Bipolar Disorder. I am indebted to Dr. James S. Brust for pointing this fact out to me.

8. Ibid., 818.

9. Ibid., 819.

10. Hirschhorn and Feldman, "Mary Lincoln's Final Illness," 512.
11. Ibid., 524–25.
12. Burlingame, *Inner World of Abraham Lincoln*, 297.
13. Hayden, *Pox*, 126.
14. Baker, *Mary Todd Lincoln*, 314.
15. Neely and McMurtry, *Insanity File*, 141.
16. Emphasis in original. Mary Lincoln to Sally Orne, Dec. 12, 1869, in Turner and Turner, *Mary Todd Lincoln*, 534.

APPENDIX 1

1. Bert C. Farrar to Frederic N. Towers, Feb.1, 1928, FTC.
2. Pritchard, "Dark Days," chap. 9, p. 14, FTC.
3. Affidavit re: Destruction of Copies of Mary Lincoln collection, signed by Margreta Pritchard, Mar. 19, 1951, PFP.
4. Turner and Turner, *Mary Todd Lincoln*, 595.
5. Photograph of letter in the Towers Lincoln trunk; also in Pritchard, "Dark Days," chap. 1, p. 15, FTC.
6. Pritchard, "Dark Days," chap. 2, p. 2, FTC.
7. It is unknown who this doctor was; Mary Lincoln had many. In a July 18, 1871, article, the *Chicago Times* names C. G. Smith as her doctor. It could also be Dr. Willis Danforth, who testified about her mental illness at Mary's sanity hearing in May 1875. He stated at trial that he began treating her in November 1873 but could have meant that he began treating her mental illness at that time, not her physical ailments, which may have begun earlier.
8. Jane Grey Swisshelm was an antislvery advocate, newspaper editor, lecturer, crusader, feminist, and Civil War nurse. She met Mary Lincoln at a White House reception in 1863. Jane Grey Swisshelm, *Half a Century* (Chicago: Jansen, McClurg & Co., 1880), 236–37; Randall, *Biography of a Marriage*, 357–61.
9. Pritchard, "Dark Days," chap. 2, pp. 3–4, FTC.
10. Dr. Willis Danforth.
11. Photograph of the first and last pages in the Towers Lincoln trunk; complete letter in Pritchard, "Dark Days," chap. 2, pp. 4–7, FTC.
12. Ellen Fitzgerald, the mother of acclaimed vaudeville actor Eddie Foy, worked as Mary Lincoln's "nurse, guard and companion" from 1872 to 1875. Foy and Harlow, "Clowning through Life," 15–16, 30.
13. The Castillo de San Marcos, which Spain began constructing in October 1672. Upon the American acquisition of Florida in 1821, the name was changed to Fort Marion, in honor of General Francis Marion, the "Swamp Fox" of Revolutionary War fame. It was used mostly as a military prison.
14. Mary refers to Robert, who at that time resided and practiced law in Chicago. He was Mary's only surviving son after the death of Tad in July 1871.
15. Photograph of complete letter in the Towers Lincoln trunk (see fig. pp. 80–81); and in Pritchard, "Dark Days," chap. 3, p. 11, FTC. This is the first letter Mary Lincoln wrote in her attempt to regain her freedom from the sanitarium. Its discovery fills a large gap in the insanity case record. Historians knew that she wrote letters (multiple letters, it was assumed, but this letter proves otherwise) to friends asking them to come visit her; but to whom she wrote and what the letter(s) said could only be supposed from other evidence. See Robert Lincoln to Elizabeth Edwards, Aug. 7, 1875, in LB, 1:133–39, microfilm reel 1.

16. William Sturges (Mary misspelled his name) was a Chicago banker who lived at 723 Michigan Avenue. His wife, Carolina A. Sturges, who died in January 1875, worked with four women's charities in Chicago: the Women's Mission, the Erring Women's Refuge, the Home of the Friendless, and the Half-Orphan Asylum. Also on the board of the Erring Women's Refuge was the Reverend Dr. W. W. Evarts, a Baptist minister and feminist, whom Mary may have mentioned in an undated letter probably written on August 2, 1875 (see note 31). While there is no proof that these are the same people Mary named in her letters, there is good reason to believe they are: they worked for women's charities, and Mary's 1873 will, drawn up by James Bradwell, indicated her intention to establish a fund to create the Lincoln Home for Indigent Women. At some point during her Chicago residence, Mary apparently made the acquaintance of these people and became converted to their social cause. Basler et al., *Collected Works*, 4:394 n.1; "The Late Mrs. Sturges," *Chicago Tribune*, Jan. 14, 1875, 8; "Erring Women," *Chicago Tribune*, Feb. 5, 1875, 3; Mary Lincoln to James Bradwell, Chicago, Oct. 10, 1872, folder 2, box 1, IF.

17. Wilbur F. Storey, editor of the *Chicago Times*.

18. General John Franklin Farnsworth.

19. Pritchard, "Dark Days," chap. 3, p. 12, FTC.

20. John Todd Stuart, Mary Lincoln's cousin and Abraham Lincoln's first law partner. Robert consulted him prior to taking his mother's committal action.

21. Mrs. Ninian W. (Elizabeth) Edwards, Mary's sister. It was to the care of Elizabeth Edwards that Mary went after her release from Bellevue Place Sanitarium in September 1875.

22. Dr. Richard J. Patterson, proprietor of Bellevue Place Sanitarium.

23. Pritchard, "Dark Days," chap. 3, p. 13, FTC.

24. Mary Lincoln's room at Bellevue was *not* protected by grates and bars. As Robert explained to his aunt, "There is nothing about his house to indicate an asylum except that outside of the windows there is a white wire netting such as you may see often to keep children from falling out of the window." Even that wire netting was removed at Robert's request. Mary was separated from the other patients, had a private bath, and kept her own room key. Robert Lincoln to Elizabeth Edwards, Aug. 7, 1875, LB, 1:133–39, microfilm reel 1; Robert Lincoln to Edwards, Jan.17, 1876, in LB, 3:382–83, microfilm reel 4. See also Robert Lincoln to John Hay, June 6, 1875, microfilm reel 8, JMHC; and *New York Tribune*, June 14, 1875, 6.

25. Copy of letter in Myra Bradwell's handwriting, on *Chicago Legal News* stationery, in Towers Lincoln trunk; also in Pritchard, "Dark Days," chap. 3, pp. 14–15, FTC.

26. This is the first historical evidence that Elizabeth Edwards had an operation; no records are known to survive about its cause or nature. This letter proves, however, that when Elizabeth Edwards demurred at the idea of a visit from Mary due to ill health, and, likewise, when Robert Lincoln told Myra Bradwell that Elizabeth was too sick for Mary to visit her, neither of them was lying or obfuscating for some selfish, sinister purpose, as some critics have supposed. See Neely and McMurtry, *Insanity File*, 62–63; Baker, *Mary Todd Lincoln*, 340; and Friedman, *America's First Woman Lawyer*, 58.

27. Pritchard, "Dark Days," chap. 4, pp. 2–4, FTC. This letter was undated, but judging from the placement of it in Myra Pritchard's chronological manuscript and from the mention in the Bellevue Place daily patient progress reports about Mary's receiving a letter from Myra Bradwell on August 1, it is logical to assume it was written August 2. What Mary refers to in the letter that she "had proposed or rather what I had mentioned" remains a mystery.

28. It is not certain who this Robert Anderson was. The Lincolns were friends with the family of Major Robert Anderson, the commanding officer at Fort Sumter at

the beginning of the Civil War. Mary Lincoln also once mentioned "our agreeable friend Mrs. Anderson" in an 1841 letter. See Mary Lincoln to Mercy Ann Levering, June 1841, in Turner and Turner, *Mary Todd Lincoln,* 27.

29. Minerva Grimsley Blow. Henry Taylor Blow was a pro-Union, antislavery advocate before the Civil War. He served as President Lincoln's minister to Venezuela from June 1861 to February 1862 and then as a Republican congressman from St. Louis, from March 1863 to March 1867. How well Mary Lincoln knew Mr. and Mrs. Blow is not known. Mrs. Blow appears to have been one of the many friends Mary Lincoln neglected after the White House years and sought to reconnect with only when she wanted to gather friends about her to fight her Bellevue incarceration. This can be deduced from the fact that Minerva Blow had died in June 1875, two months prior to this letter, and Mary Lincoln obviously was unaware of it.

30. How well Mary knew Mrs. Harriet Farlin, is unknown. The only other discoverable mention of her is in reference to the day of Tad's death in July 1871, when she stayed with Mary to offer support and commiseration. See Robert Lincoln to Mary Harlan Lincoln, July 15, 1871, quoted in Helm, *True Story of Mary,* 294.

31. Possibly the Reverend Dr. W. W. Evarts, pastor of the First Baptist Church in Chicago. Evarts was a feminist who also was connected to the Old Ladies Home and the Erring Women's Refuge in Chicago through his wife, who died in 1866, and thus may have also been acquainted with William Sturges (see note 16). He may also have been acquainted with Professor David Swing, a Presbyterian minister and friend of Mary Lincoln's. "The Empire of Woman: Rev. Dr. W. W. Evarts at Bryan Hall," *Chicago Tribune,* Jan. 13, 1864, 4; "Old Ladies Home," *Chicago Tribune,* Oct. 8, 1863, 4; "Erring Women's Refuge," *Chicago Tribune,* Feb. 9, 1866, 4; "They Took Their Last Look: Thousands Pay Tribute to the Rev. Dr. W. W. Evarts," *Chicago Tribune,* Sept. 29, 1890, 6.

32. Pritchard, "Dark Days," chap. 4, pp. 4–5, FTC. This letter was undated, but judging from the placement of it in Myra Pritchard's chronological manuscript, the mention in the Bellevue Place daily patient progress reports about Mary receiving a letter from Myra Bradwell on August 1, and the fact that its last line about bringing black alpaca refers to the previous letter, it is logical to assume it also was written August 2.

33. Photograph of complete letter in the Towers Lincoln trunk; also in Pritchard, "Dark Days," chap. 4, p. 6, FTC.

34. Photograph of one page of letter and copy of first half of letter, in Myra Bradwell's handwriting, on *Chicago Legal News* stationery, in the Towers Lincoln trunk; complete letter in Pritchard, "Dark Days," chap. 4, pp. 7–8, FTC.

35. The Northern Illinois Hospital and Asylum for the Insane, established in Elgin (Kane Co.), Ill., in 1869.

36. Ann Todd, Mary's younger sister. Ann was the wife of Clark Moulton Smith, a Springfield, Ill., merchant. She and Mary had a cold relationship, as is evident in a letter Mary Lincoln wrote in 1861: "Poor *unfortunate* Ann, inasmuch as she possesses such a miserable disposition & so false a tongue—How far, dear Lizzie, we are removed, from such a person. Even if Smith, succeeds in being a rich man, what advantage will it be to him, who has gained it in *some cases* most unjustly, and with such a woman, whom no one respects, whose tongue for so many years, has been considered 'no slander'—and as a child & young girl, could not be outdone in falsehood—'Truly the Leopard cannot change his spots'—*She* is so seldom in my thoughts I have so much more, that is attractive, both in *bodily* presence, & my mind's eye, to interest me. I grieve for those, who have to come in contact with her malice, yet even *that,* is so well understood, the object of *her wrath,* generally rises, with good people, in proportion to her *vindictiveness.*" The fact that Mary wanted

to visit Ann in August 1875 indicates the depth of her desperation for attention and affection. Mary Lincoln to Elizabeth Todd Grimsley, Sept. 28, 1861, in Turner and Turner, *Mary Todd Lincoln*, 105.

37. Copy of part of letter, in Myra Bradwell's handwriting, on *Chicago Legal News* stationery, in the Towers Lincoln trunk; not in Pritchard manuscript. This letter appears to have been written after the previous letter, as indicated by references to "those two trunks I wrote you about" and the "key of the middle sized trunk." However, since it is undated and not in the Pritchard manuscript, it is not possible to establish a timeline, as was done with the previous undated letters.

38. Pritchard, "Dark Days," chap. 4, pp. 8–9, FTC.

39. Copy of letter, in Myra Bradwell's handwriting, on *Chicago Legal News* stationery, in the Towers Lincoln trunk; also in Pritchard, "Dark Days," chap. 6, p. 2, FTC.

40. Photograph of first four pages of letter (see fig. pp. 116–119) and copy of complete letter in Myra Pritchard's handwriting, labeled "Mrs. Lincoln's Special Letter," in the Towers Lincoln trunk; also in Pritchard, "Dark Days," chap. 8, pp. 2–5, FTC. This letter, due to its incendiary remarks about Robert Lincoln, seems a likely candidate to be one of the three that Mary Harlan Lincoln objected to the publication of in 1928.

41. This probably refers to the division of Tad's estate upon his death in July 1871. By state law, Mary was entitled to two-thirds of his $35,750 estate and Robert to one-third, but she chose to split the amount equally with her oldest son. Robert called this "very generous," as it "makes a difference of about $7,000." Robert Lincoln to David Davis, Sept. 21 and Nov. 9, 1871, folder A-109, box 7, DDFP; Mary Lincoln to Davis, Nov. 9, 1871, in Turner and Turner, *Mary Todd Lincoln*, 597–98.

42. Leonard Swett, a brilliant defense attorney and one of Abraham Lincoln's colleagues on the judicial circuit and closest friends. Swett had long been a sound adviser for Robert Lincoln after his father's death and advised Robert on the insanity case. Robert wrote of Swett, "In the catastrophe, the value of Mr. Swett's earnestness, tact and resources have placed me in debt to him to an extent I can never repay." Robert Lincoln to John Hay, June 6, 1876, JMHC.

43. Franc B. Wilkie, reporter and contributing editor of the *Chicago Times*. His article, "Mrs. Lincoln: Her Physicians Pronounce Her Entirely Sane," published August 24, 1875, declared Mary completely rational and in danger of losing her sanity by being caged in an asylum. As Neely and McMurtry stated, "Mary could not have asked for more had she written the article herself." Neely and McMurtry, *Insanity File*, 64.

44. David L. Phillips, editor, publisher and co-owner of the *Illinois State Journal*, 1862–78.

45. Copy of complete letter, in Myra Pritchard's handwriting, in the Towers Lincoln trunk; also in Pritchard, "Dark Days," chap. 8, pp. 7–8, FTC.

46. Mary bought the house in May 1866 for $18,000 after Congress paid her the remaining $22,000 of President Lincoln's salary. She was forced to leave the house and rent it out in the spring of 1867, due to the high cost of maintaining it. Pratt, *Personal Finances of Abraham Lincoln*, 184.

47. Copy of complete letter, in Myra Pritchard's handwriting, in the Towers Lincoln trunk; also in Pritchard, "Dark Days," chap. 8, pp. 8–10, FTC.

48. Reverend David Swing, a Presbyterian minister in Chicago. While Mary had been friends with Swing and his wife, Elizabeth, since 1866, their relationship grew much closer after Tad's death in 1871, to the point that Mary showered the Swing children with gifts. The vindictive tone of this statement about Swing is in reaction to his August 1875 newspaper editorial defending Robert Lincoln. Schwartz, "'My Stay on Earth,'" 125–36; "Mrs. Abraham Lincoln: What Her Pastor, Prof. Swing, Says about Her Insanity," *Chicago Times*, Aug. 29, 1875, 1.

49. Pritchard, "Dark Days," chap. 8, pp. 10–11, FTC.

50. The identity of Mrs. Ellen Johnson is unknown, but the context of this and other mentions of her make it clear she was a servant, probably a washerwoman, for Mary at some point.

51. Pritchard, "Dark Days," chap. 9, pp. 1–4, FTC.

52. Bessie Bradwell (Helmer), who was an eighteen-year-old student at Northwestern Law School in 1876. She graduated as valedictorian, became a Chicago attorney, and continued publishing the *Chicago Legal News* after Myra Bradwell's death.

53. Chateau de Pau, birthplace of Henry IV of France in 1553.

54. It is not entirely clear who this Baron de Brenneke is, although it could be a misspelling of the name of Le Baron de Bennecker, a government officer in Pau. See Mary Lincoln to Jacob Bunn, Dec. 12, 1876, in Turner and Turner, *Mary Todd Lincoln*, 622.

55. Pritchard, "Dark Days," chap. 9, pp. 4–6, FTC.

56. John A. Logan of Chicago. Logan was a general in the Union army during the Civil War and a U.S. senator in 1877. His presidential hopes were well known. He sought the Republican nomination in 1884 but came in second to James G. Blaine and was made the vice presidential nominee. The ticket lost to Grover Cleveland.

57. Associate Justice David Davis resigned from the U.S. Supreme Court in March 1877 after his election to the U.S. Senate. President Rutherford B. Hayes nominated John Marshall Harlan in October 1877. Harlan served on the Court until his death in 1911.

58. Photograph of first page of letter in the Towers Lincoln trunk (see fig. p. 127); complete letter in Pritchard, "Dark Days," chap. 9, pp. 7–10, FTC. Mary spent two months in Italy in early 1878 visiting Naples, Rome, and Sorrento. Practically nothing is known of that trip. Only three letters from that period have been previously published, all to Mary's banker and mostly about financial matters. This is the first known letter from Sorrento and the first known detailed account of her actions and thoughts in Italy. See Turner and Turner, *Mary Todd Linclon*, 665–67.

59. An ancient Roman resort town buried in lava in 79 A.D. from the eruption of Mt. Vesuvius that also buried Pompeii. It was discovered, in a state of preservation, in the late eighteenth century and excavated.

60. A fourteenth-century castle in Naples, Italy.

61. Harriet Beecher Stowe wrote a romantic novel, *Agnes of Sorrento*, in 1861.

62. Mary had previously stated that Lincoln said he wanted to travel west to California, across Europe, and especially to Palestine to visit Jerusalem. Mary Lincoln to Mary Jane Welles, Oct. 14, 1865, and Mary Lincoln to James Smith, Dec. 17, 1866, in Turner and Turner, *Mary Todd Lincoln*, 276–78, 399–400; Mary Lincoln, interview by William Herndon, Sept. 1866, in Wilson and Davis, *Herndon's Informants*, 357, 359.

63. Pritchard, "Dark Days," chap. 9, pp. 10–12, FTC.

64. A spa and resort town in central France, near Clermont-Ferrand.

65. It is uncertain, but this may be Mrs. George Walker, mentioned in an 1871 letter. She was the daughter of Rhoda (Mrs. James W.) White, who was a friend of Mary's during the White House years. Turner and Turner, *Mary Todd Lincoln*, 136, 590.

66. Mary Lincoln had physical ailments her entire life, which, naturally, became worse as she aged. For the best analysis of her physical condition during her later years, see Hirschhorn and Feldman, "Mary Lincoln's Final Illness."

67. Pritchard, "Dark Days," chap. 9, pp. 12–13, FTC.

68. Ibid., pp. 13–14.

240 · Notes to Pages 177–88

69. Photograph of first and last pages in the Towers Lincoln trunk (see fig. pp. 136–37); summary in Pritchard, "Dark Days," chap. 8, pp. 4–5, FTC. This will, while known to exist from Mary Lincoln's letters to James Bradwell in the Insanity File, has never before been seen or published by those outside the Bradwell family circle. Unfortunately, as stated in the will, there were nine pages to the document, of which only two survive. However, Myra Pritchard does summarize the will (which was in her possession) and its history in part 7 of her 1928 manuscript. According to Pritchard, after her house went to Robert, Mary Lincoln's remaining estate was left to Judge David Davis and her cousin John T. Stuart as trustees to be distributed among Robert's children. There also was a codicil dated January 3, 1874, in which Mary Lincoln made a special bequest of a one-thousand-dollar United States Government Bond to her infant grandson, Abraham Lincoln II, to be paid to him on his twenty-first birthday. She also directed that the interest be paid to him semiannually for pocket money. Pritchard explains no more of the contents of the will, calling those few points its "outstanding features."

70. Robert and Mary Harlan Lincoln had three children, although only two, Mary (born 1869) and Abraham II (born 1873) were alive at the time of Mary Lincoln's will. The Lincolns' third child, Jessie, was born in 1875.

71. Thomas Bradwell, James and Myra's son, also a lawyer.

APPENDIX 3

1. My knowledge of Mary Lincoln's psychiatric illness and all of the primary sources cited in this essay come from Jason Emerson's research as written in this book.

2. American Psychiatric Association, *Diagnostic and Statistical Manual of Mental Disorders*, 3rd ed. (Washington, D.C.: American Psychiatric Association, 1980), 8, 23–32.

3. American Psychiatric Association, *Diagnostic and Statistical Manual of Mental Disorders*, 4th ed., text revision (Washington, D.C.: American Psychiatric Association, 2000), 685–94, 706–17. In recent years, at least one historian has suggested that Mary Lincoln had Borderline Personality Disorder. See Burlingame, *Inner World of Abraham Lincoln*, 297.

4. Austrian physician Sigmund Freud (1856–1939) is familiar to most, and his name and theories have entered the mainstream of popular culture. Swiss-born Adolf Meyer (1866–1950) enjoyed a long and influential career in the United States, culminating in his appointment as professor of psychiatry at Johns Hopkins University, where he served from 1910 to 1941.

5. Elizabeth Edwards to Robert Lincoln, Springfield, Nov. 5, 1875, folder 16, box 2, IF; testimony of Dr. Willis Danforth in "Clouded Reason," *Chicago Tribune*, May 20, 1875, 1; Sayre quoted in "Mrs. Lincoln's Illness," *New York Times*, Oct. 31, 1880, 5.

6. American Psychiatric Association, *Diagnostic and Statistical Manual* (4th ed., text revision), 357–62.

7. Ibid., 362.

8. Robert Lincoln's remark quoted in Elizabeth J. Todd Grimsley Brown to Robert Lincoln, Mar. 16, 1875, folder 10, box 2, IF.

9. Mary Lincoln to Myra Bradwell, Apr. 22, 1878, in Pritchard, "Dark Days," chap. 9, pp. 12–13, FTC.

10. Enclosure labeled "private," in Elizabeth Edwards to Robert Lincoln, Springfield, Sept. 15, 1875, folder 16, box 2, IF.

11. American Psychiatric Association, *Diagnostic and Statistical Manual* (4th ed.), 422–23.

12. Ibid., 297–300, 312–13.

13. For a good review of the history of Manic-Depressive Illness/Bipolar Disorder, see Frederick K. Goodwin and Kay Redfield Jamison, *Manic-Depressive Illness* (New York: Oxford University Press, 1990), 56–61, 70. The terms *manic-depressive* and *bipolar* had not yet come into use during Mary Lincoln's lifetime, and technically they are anachronistic. Likewise, the word *psychiatrist* was not used in that era. However, for ease of understanding, I have chosen to use these modern terms.

Bibliography

ARCHIVAL SOURCES
Abraham Lincoln Presidential Library, Springfield, Illinois
    Orville Hickman Browning Papers
    Conkling Family Papers
    David Davis Family Papers
    Albert S. Edwards Papers
    Ninian W. Edwards Papers
    Anson G. Henry Papers
    Abraham Lincoln Collection
    Robert Todd Lincoln Papers, Lincoln Collection
Allegheny College, Meadville, Pennsylvania
    Ida M. Tarbell–Lincoln Collection
Brown University, Providence, Rhode Island
    John Milton Hay Collection
Chicago History Museum, Chicago
    Myra Pritchard Papers
    Robert Todd Lincoln Papers
Connecticut Historical Society, Hartford
    Gideon Welles Papers
Duke University Libraries, Durham, North Carolina
    Adeline Ellery (Burr) Davis Green Papers
Friends of Hildene, Inc., Manchester, Vermont
    John Goff Papers
    Robert Todd Lincoln Collection
Rutherford B. Hayes Presidential Center, Fremont, Ohio
    Rutherford B. Hayes Papers
Henry E. Huntington Library, San Marino, California
    Ward Hill Lamon Papers
Illinois Regional Archives Depository, University of Illinois at Springfield
Kentucky Historical Society, Frankfort, Kentucky
    Emily Todd Helm Papers
Library of Congress, Washington, D.C.
    Benjamin F. Butler Papers
    Benjamin B. French Family Papers
    Herndon-Weik Collection of Lincolniana

Robert Todd Lincoln Collection of the Papers of Abraham Lincoln
Robert Todd Lincoln Papers
David C. Mearns Papers
John G. Nicolay Papers
[James G. and Ruth Painter] Randall Family Papers
Diary of Horatio Nelson Taft
Frederic N. Towers Collection of Lincoln Papers
Gideon Welles Papers
The Lincoln Museum, Fort Wayne, Indiana
    Mary Todd Lincoln Insanity File
    Mary Todd Lincoln Collection
    Robert Todd Lincoln Collection
National Archives and Records Administration, Washington, D.C.
    Records of the Adjutant General's Office
New-York Historical Society, New York, New York
    Clara Harris correspondence
Pritchard Family Papers, privately owned by James Gordon, Grand Rapids, Michigan
University of Chicago, Joseph Regenstein Library, Chicago
    William E. Barton Collection
    Lincoln Miscellaneous Manuscripts

NEWSPAPERS

Atlanta Constitution
Aurora (Ill.) Beacon-News
Batavia (Ill.) Herald
Boston Globe
Chicago Inter Ocean
Chicago Legal News
Chicago Morning Courier
Chicago Post and Mail
Chicago Times
Chicago Tribune
Christian Register
Illinois State Journal
Illinois State Register
New York Evangelist
New York Herald Tribune
New York Observer and Chronicle
New York Sun
New York Times
State Journal Register (Springfield, Ill.)
Washington Daily National Intelligencer
Washington Evening Star
Washington Post

BOOKS AND ARTICLES

"The Action of Neurotic Medicines in Insanity." *American Journal of Insanity* 28 (July 1871): 114–15.

American Psychiatric Association. *Diagnostic and Statistical Manual of Mental Disorders*, 4th ed. Text Revision. Washington, D.C.: American Psychiatric Association, 2000.

"Analysis of Legal and Medical Considerations in Commitment of the Mentally Ill." *Yale Law Journal* 56, no. 7 (August 1947): 1192–93.

Andrews, J. B. "The Physiological Action and Therapeutic Use of Chloral." *American Journal of Insanity* 28 (July 1871): 35–53.

Arnold, Isaac N. *The Life of Abraham Lincoln.* 1884. Introduction by James A. Rawley. Lincoln: University of Nebraska Press, Bison Book, 1994.

Bach, Jennifer L. "Acts of Remembrance: Mary Todd Lincoln and Her Husband's Memory." *Journal of the Abraham Lincoln Association* 25, no. 2 (Summer 2004): 25–49.

Badeau, Adam. *Grant in Peace from Appomattox to Mount McGregor: A Personal Memoir.* Hartford: S. S. Scranton, 1887.

Baker, Jean H. *Mary Todd Lincoln: A Biography.* New York: W. W. Norton, 1987.

Barton, William E. *The Life of Abraham Lincoln.* 2 vols. Indianapolis: Bobbs-Merrill, 1925.

Basler, Roy P., Dolores Pratt, and Lloyd A. Dunlap, eds. *The Collected Works of Abraham Lincoln.* 9 vols. New Brunswick, N.J.: Rutgers University Press, 1953–55.

Bayne, Julia Taft. *Tad Lincoln's Father.* 1931. Reprint, Lincoln: University of Nebraska Press, 2001.

Bernhardt, Sarah. *The Memoirs of Sarah Bernhardt: Early Childhood through the First American Tour.* Edited by Sandy Lesberg. New York: Peebles, 1977.

Biographical Sketches of the Leading Men of Chicago. Chicago: Wilson & St. Clair, 1868.

Boyden, Anna L. *War Reminiscences; or, Echoes from Hospital and White House.* Boston: D. Lothrop, 1887.

Braude, Ann. *Radical Spirits: Spiritualism and Women's Rights in Nineteenth Century America.* Boston: Beacon, 1989.

Brayman, Mason. *Revised Statutes of the State of Illinois.* Springfield, Ill.: Walters & Weber, 1845.

Brussel, James A. *Casebook of a Crime Psychologist.* N.p.: Bernard Geis Associates, 1969.

———. "Mary Todd Lincoln: A Psychiatric Study." *Psychiatric Quarterly* 15, suppl. 1 (January 1941): 7–26.

Bullard, F. Lauristan. "Mrs. Lincoln's Pension." *Lincoln Herald* 49 (1947): 22–27.

Burlingame, Michael, ed. *At Lincoln's Side: John Hay's Civil War Correspondence and Selected Writings.* Carbondale: Southern Illinois University Press, 2000.

———. *The Inner World of Abraham Lincoln.* Urbana: University of Illinois Press, 1994.

———. *An Oral History of Abraham Lincoln: John G. Nicolay's Interviews and Essays.* Carbondale: Southern Illinois University Press, 1996.

————. *With Lincoln in the White House: Letters, Memoranda, and Other Writings of John G. Nicolay, 1860–1865.* Carbondale: Southern Illinois University Press, 2000.

Butler, Nicholas Murray. *Across the Busy Years: Recollections and Reflections.* 2 vols. New York: Charles Scribner's Sons, 1940.

de Chambrun, Marquis Adolphe. *Impressions of Lincoln and the Civil War: A Foreigner's Account.* Translated by General Aldebert de Chambrun. New York: Random House, 1952.

Dennett, Tyler, ed. *Lincoln and the Civil War in the Diaries and Letters of John Hay.* 1939. Reprint, with new foreword by Henry Steele Commager. New York: Da Capo, 1988.

Deutsch, Albert. *The Mentally Ill in America: A History of Their Care and Treatment from Colonial Times.* New York: Columbia University Press, 1946.

Dewey, Richard. "The Jury Law for Commitment of the Insane in Illinois (1867–1893), and Mrs. E. P. W. Packard, Its Author; also, Later Developments in Lunacy Legislation in Illinois." *American Journal of Insanity* 69 (January 1913): 571–84.

Donald, David Herbert. *"We Are Lincoln Men": Abraham Lincoln and His Friends.* New York: Simon & Schuster, 2003.

Emerson, Jason. "Avoiding the Gilded Prison." *American History* 39, no. 5 (December 2004): 58–66.

————. "'I Have Done My Duty as I Best Know and Providence Must Take Care of the Rest': Reconsidering Mary Todd Lincoln's Insanity Case and Robert Lincoln's Motivations behind It." Lecture, Seventh Annual Conference on Illinois History. Springfield, Illinois, October 28, 2005.

————. "'Of Such Is the Kingdom of Heaven': The Mystery of Little Eddie." *Journal of the Illinois State Historical Society* 92, no. 3 (Autumn 1999): 201–21.

————. "A Very Dreadful Night: Robert Todd Lincoln and His Father's Assassination." *Lincoln Forum Bulletin* 18 (November 2005): 10–11.

Evans, W. A. *Mrs. Abraham Lincoln: A Study of Her Personality and Her Influence on Abraham Lincoln.* New York: Alfred A. Knopf, 1932.

Field, Maunsell B. *Memories of Many Men and Some Women.* New York: Harper & Brothers, 1874.

Fleischner, Jennifer. *Mrs. Lincoln and Mrs. Keckly: The Remarkable Story of the Friendship between a First Lady and a Former Slave.* New York: Broadway Books, 2003.

Foy, Eddie, and Alvin F. Harlow. "Clowning through Life." *Collier's Weekly* 76, no. 26 (December 25, 1926): 15–16, 30.

Friedman, Jane M. *America's First Woman Lawyer: The Biography of Myra Bradwell.* Buffalo, N.Y.: Prometheus, 1993.

Gerry, Margarita Spalding, ed. *Through Five Administrations: Reminiscences of Colonel William H. Crook, Bodyguard to President Lincoln.* New York: Harper & Brothers, 1910.

Gilliam, Nancy T. "A Professional Pioneer: Myra Bradwell's Fight to Practice Law." *Law and History Review* 5, no. 1 (Spring 1987): 105–33.

Goff, John S. *Robert Todd Lincoln: A Man in His Own Right.* Norman: University of Oklahoma Press, 1969.

Goltz, Carlos W. *Incidents in the Life of Mary Todd Lincoln.* Sioux City, Iowa: Deitch & Lamar, 1928.

Good, Timothy S. *We Saw Lincoln Shot: One Hundred Eyewitness Accounts.* Jackson: University Press of Mississippi, 1995.

Good News Bible: The Bible in Today's English Version. New York: American Bible Society, 1976.

Gridley, Eleanor. "Presentation of Bronze Bust of Mrs. Myra Bradwell, First Woman Lawyer of Illinois." Reprinted from the *Transactions of the Illinois State Historical Society* 38, no. 6 (1931).

———. *The Story of Abraham Lincoln; or, The Journey from the Log Cabin to the White House.* New York: Eaton & Mains, 1900.

Hayden, Deborah. *Pox: Genius, Madness and the Mysteries of Syphilis.* New York: Basic Books, 2003.

Helm, Katherine. *The True Story of Mary, Wife of Lincoln.* 1928. Reprint, Manchester, Vt.: Friends of Hildene, 2005.

Hendrickson, Robert. *The Grand Emporiums: The Illustrated History of America's Great Department Stores.* New York: Stein and Day, 1979.

Herndon, William H., and Jesse W. Weik. *Herndon's Life of Lincoln.* Edited by Douglas L. Wilson and Rodney O. Davis. Urbana and Chicago: University of Illinois Press, 2006.

Hertz, Emanuel. *The Hidden Lincoln: From the Letters and Papers of William H. Herndon.* New York: Viking, 1938.

Hickey, James T. *The Collected Writings of James T. Hickey from Publications of the Illinois State Historical Society, 1953–1984.* Springfield: Illinois State Historical Society, 1990.

Hirschhorn, Norbert. "Mary Lincoln's 'Suicide Attempt': A Physician Reconsiders the Evidence." *Lincoln Herald* 104, no. 3 (Fall 2003): 94–98.

Hirschhorn, Norbert, and Robert G. Feldman. "Mary Lincoln's Final Illness: A Medical and Historical Reappraisal." *Journal of the History of Medicine and Allied Sciences* 54, no. 4 (1999): 511–42.

Hodgen, Godfrey. *Woodrow Wilson's Right Hand: The Life of Col. Edward M. House.* New Haven: Yale University Press, 2006.

"Illinois Legislation regarding Hospitals for the Insane." *American Journal of Insanity* 26 (October 1869): 204–29.

"Insanity and Its Treatment." *Scribner's Monthly* 12, no. 5 (September 1876): 643–44.

Kauffman, Michael W. *American Brutus.* New York: Random House, 2004.

Keckley, Elizabeth. *Behind the Scenes; or, 30 Years a Slave and 4 Years in the White House.* 1868. Reprint, New York: Oxford University Press, 1988.

King, Willard L. *Lincoln's Manager: David Davis.* Cambridge, Mass.: Harvard University Press, 1960.

Kluger, Richard. *The Paper: The Life and Death of the New York Herald Tribune.* New York: Alfred A. Knopf, 1986.

Krueger, Lillian. "Mary Todd Lincoln Summers in Wisconsin." *Journal of the Illinois State Historical Society* 34, no. 2 (June 1941): 249–52.

Kunhardt, Philip B., Jr., Philip B. Kunhardt III, and Peter W. Kunhardt. *Lincoln: An Illustrated Biography.* New York: Alfred A. Knopf, 1992.

"Large Dose of Bromide of Potassium." *American Journal of Insanity* 31 (January 1875): 396.

Laws of the State of Illinois, Passed by the Sixteenth General Assembly, the Second Session, Commencing October 22, 1849. Springfield, Ill.: Charles H. Lanphier, 1849.

Lorant, Stefan. "Where Are the Lincoln Papers?" *Life*, August 25, 1947, 45.

"Lunacy Law in Illinois." *American Journal of Insanity* 47 (April 1891): 584–87.

MacDonald, A. E. "The Examination and Commitment of the Insane." *American Journal of Insanity* 32 (April 1876): 502–22.

MacDonald, Charles F. "Hydrate of Chloral." *American Journal of Insanity* 34 (January 1878): 360–67.

Mearns, David C. *The Lincoln Papers: The Story of the Collection with Selections to July 4, 1861.* 2 vols. Garden City, N.Y.: Doubleday, 1948.

"Modern Culture." *Littell's Living Age* 8, no. 1591 (December 5, 1875): 590.

Monaghan, Jay. "Was Abraham Lincoln Really a Spiritualist?" *Journal of the Illinois State Historical Society* 34, no. 2 (June 1941): 209–32.

Morrow, Honore Willsie. *Mary Todd Lincoln: An Appreciation of the Wife of Abraham Lincoln.* New York: William Morrow, 1928.

"Mrs. Lincoln's Wardrobe." *Independent* 19, no. 985 (October 17, 1867): 4.

Neely, Mark E., and R. Gerald McMurtry. *The Insanity File: The Case of Mary Todd Lincoln.* Carbondale: Southern Illinois University Press, 1986.

Nicolay, Helen. *Lincoln's Secretary: The Biography of John G. Nicolay.* New York: Longmans, Green, 1949.

Nuhrah, Arthur G. "A Commission for Robert." *Lincoln Herald* 66, no. 3 (Fall 1964): 143–48.

Packard, Mrs. E. P. W. *Modern Persecution; or, Insane Asylums Unveiled.* 2 vols. Hartford: Lockwood & Brainard, 1874.

Phelps, Mary Merwin. *Kate Chase, Dominant Daughter: The Life Story of a Brilliant Woman and Her Famous Father.* New York: Thomas Y. Crowell, 1935.

Pierce, Edward L. *Memoir and Letters of Charles Sumner.* 4 vols. Boston: Roberts Brothers, 1893.

Plenk, Henry P., ed. *Medicine in the Beehive State, 1940–1990.* Salt Lake City: Utah Medical Association, 1992.

Porter, General Horace. "Campaigning with Grant." *Century Magazine* 54, no. 4 (August 1897): 600, 602.

Pratt, Foster. "Insane Patients and Their Legal Relations." *American Journal of Insanity* 35 (July 1878): 182–85.

Pratt, Harry E. *The Personal Finances of Abraham Lincoln.* Springfield, Ill: Abraham Lincoln Association, 1943.

Pritchard, Myra Helmer. "The Dark Days of Abraham Lincoln's Widow, as Revealed by Her Own Letters." Unpublished manuscript, 1927.

Randall, Ruth Painter. *Lincoln's Sons.* Boston: Little, Brown, 1955.

———. *Mary Lincoln: Biography of a Marriage.* Boston: Little, Brown, 1953.

Ray, I. "American Legislation on Insanity." *American Journal of Insanity* 21 (July 1864): 21–56.

Renton, A. Wood. "Comparative Lunacy Law." *Journal of the Society of Comparative Legislation*, n.s., 1, no. 2 (July 1899): 2

Rhodes, James, and Dean Jauchius. *The Trial of Mary Todd Lincoln.* Indianapolis: Bobbs-Merrill, 1959.

Rice, Allen Thorndike, comp. and ed. *Reminiscences of Abraham Lincoln by Distinguished Men of His Time.* New York: Harper & Brothers, 1909.

Ritter, Gretchen. "Jury Service and Women's Citizenship before and after the Nineteenth Amendment." *Law and History Review* 20, no. 3 (Fall 2002), http://www.historycooperative.org/journals/lhr/20.3/ritter.html.

Roberts, Octavia. *Lincoln in Illinois*. Boston: Houghton Mifflin, 1918.

Ross, Rodney A. "Mary Todd Lincoln: Patient at Bellevue Place, Batavia." *Journal of the Illinois State Historical Society* 63, no. 1 (Spring 1970): 5–34.

Rotundo, E. Anthony. *American Manhood*. New York: Basic Books, 1993.

Sanborn, Alvan F., ed. *Reminiscences of Richard Lathers: Sixty Years of a Busy Life in South Carolina, Massachusetts and New York*. New York: Grafton, 1907.

Sandburg, Carl, and Paul M. Angle. *Mary Lincoln: Wife and Widow*. New York: Harcourt, Brace, 1932.

Schreiner, Samuel A. *The Trials of Mrs. Lincoln*. New York: Donald I. Fine, 1987.

Schwartz, Thomas F. "'My Stay on Earth, Is Growing Very Short': Mary Todd Lincoln's Letters to Willis Danforth and Elizabeth Swing." *Journal of Illinois History* 6 (summer 2003): 125–36.

Schwartz, Thomas F, and Kim M. Bauer. "Unpublished Mary Todd Lincoln." *Journal of the Abraham Lincoln Association* 17, no. 2 (summer 1996), http://www.historycooperative.org/journals/jala/17.2/schwartz.html.

Schwartz, Thomas F., and Anne V. Shaughnessy. "Unpublished Mary Lincoln Letters." *Journal of the Abraham Lincoln Association* 11 (1990): 34–50, http://jala.press.uiuc.edu/11/schwartz.html.

Sellers, John R., ed. *Washington during the Civil War: The Diary of Horatio Nelson Taft, 1861–1865*. 3 vols. Manuscripts Division, Library of Congress, Washington, D.C., http://www.memory.loc.gov/ammem/tafthtml/tafthome.html.

Shenk, Joshua Wolf. *Lincoln's Melancholy: How Depression Challenged a President and Fueled His Greatness*. Boston: Houghton Mifflin, 2005.

Sherman, General William Tecumseh. *Memoirs of William Tecumseh Sherman*. 2 vols. Foreword by B. H. Liddell Hart. Bloomington: Indiana University Press, 1957.

Simon, John Y., ed. *Memoirs of Julia Dent Grant*. New York: G. P. Putnam's Sons, 1975.

Snelders, Stephen, Charles Kaplan, and Toine Pieters. "On Cannabis, Chloral Hydrate, and Career Cycles of Psychotropic Drugs in Medicine." *Bulletin of the History of Medicine* 80, no. 95 (Spring 2006): 95–114.

"Spiritualistic Madness." *American Journal of Insanity* 33 (January 1877): 441–42.

"Spiritual Photography." *Littell's Living Age* 1313 (July 31, 1869): 314.

Stoddard, William O. *Inside the White House in War Times*. Edited by Michael Burlingame. Lincoln: University of Nebraska Press, 2000.

Stronks, Jim. "Mary Todd Lincoln's Sad Summer in Hyde Park." *Hyde Park Historical Society Newsletter* 20, no. 1 (Spring 1998), http://hydeparkhistory.org/mtlincoln.html.

Strozier, Charles B. "The Psychology of Mary Todd Lincoln." *Psychohistory Review* 17, no. 1 (1988): 11–24.

Suarez, John M. "Mary Todd Lincoln: A Case Study." *American Journal of Psychiatry* 122, no. 7 (January 1966): 816–19.

Swisshelm, Jane Grey. *Half a Century*. Chicago: Jansen, McClurg, 1880.

Tarbell, Ida M. *In the Footsteps of the Lincolns*. New York: Harper & Brothers, 1924.

Taylor, Eugene. *Shadow Culture: Psychology and Spirituality in America*. Washington, D.C.: Counterpoint, 1999.

Temple, Wayne C. *Abraham Lincoln: From Skeptic to Prophet*. Mahomet, Ill.: Mayhaven, 1995.

Thayer, William Roscoe. *The Life of John Hay*. 2 vols. Boston: Houghton Mifflin, 1929.

Townsend, Kim. *Manhood at Harvard*. New York: W. W. Norton, 1996.

"Transactions of the Twenty-third Meeting of the Illinois State Medical Society, 1873." *American Journal of Insanity* 31 (July 1874): 120–21.

Turner, Justin G., and Linda Levitt Turner. *Mary Todd Lincoln: Her Life and Letters*. New York: Alfred A. Knopf, 1972.

U.S. Congress. *Congressional Globe*. 39th Cong., 1st sess., 1865–66. Vol. 1. Washington, D.C.

———. *Congressional Globe*. 40th Congress, 3rd sess., 1869. Vol. 2. Washington, D.C.

———. *Congressional Globe*. 41st Cong., 2nd sess., 1870. Vol. 6. Washington, D.C.

———. *Congressional Record*. 47th Cong., 1st sess., 1882. Vol. 13. Washington, D.C.

Van Deusen, Glyndon G. *William Henry Seward*. New York: Oxford University Press, 1967.

Verneuil, Louis. *The Fabulous Life of Sarah Bernhardt*. Translated by Ernest Boyd. New York: Harper & Brothers, 1942.

Villard, Henry. *Lincoln on the Eve of '61*. Edited by Harold G. Villard and Oswald Garrison Villard. New York: Alfred A. Knopf, 1941.

———. *Memoirs of Henry Villard: Journalist and Financier, 1835–1900*. 2 vols. Boston: Houghton Mifflin, 1904.

Warren, Louis A. "Mrs. Lincoln's Mental Collapse." *Lincoln Lore*, no. 1124, October 23, 1950.

Weik, Jesse W. *The Real Lincoln: A Portrait*. Boston: Houghton Mifflin, 1922.

Welles, Gideon. *Diary of Gideon Welles: Secretary of the Navy under Lincoln and Johnson*. 3 vols. Introduction by John T. Morse Jr. Boston: Houghton Mifflin, 1911.

Wendt, Kristine Adams. "Mary Todd Lincoln: 'Great Sorrows' and the Healing Waters of Waukesha." *Wisconsin Academy Review* 38, no. 2 (Spring 1992): 14–189.

"The Widow of Lincoln." *The Round Table: A Saturday Review of Politics, Finance, Literature, Society* 6, no. 142 (October 12, 1867): 240.

Willis, N. P. "The President's Son." *Littell's Living Age* 993 (April 19, 1862): 154.

Wilson, Douglas L. *Honor's Voice: The Transformation of Abraham Lincoln*. New York: Random House, Vintage, 1999.

Wilson, Douglas L., and Rodney O. Davis, eds. *Herndon's Informants: Letters, Interviews, and Statements about Abraham Lincoln*. Urbana: University of Illinois Press, 1998.

Index

Jason Emerson is an independent historian who lives in Fredericksburg, Virginia. He has worked as a U.S. National Park Service historical interpreter at the Lincoln Home National Historic Site, the Gettysburg National Military Park, and the Jefferson National Expansion Memorial and also as a professional journalist and freelance writer. His articles have appeared in *American Heritage, American History, Civil War Times, Journal of the Illinois State Historical Society, Lincoln Herald, Lincoln Forum Bulletin,* and online at the History News Network (hnn.us). He currently is preparing a biography of Robert T. Lincoln.